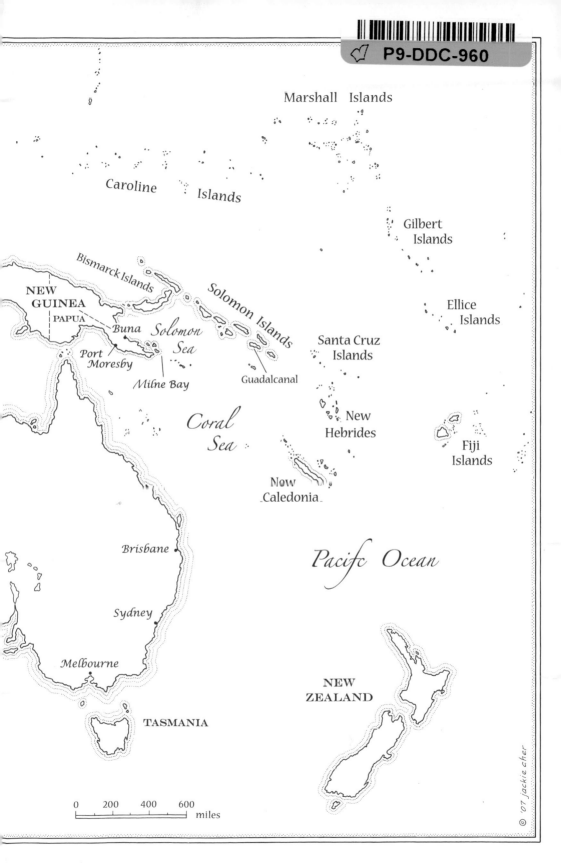

Marshall Islands

Caroline Islands

Gilbert Islands

Bismarck Islands

Solomon Islands

Ellice Islands

NEW GUINEA

PAPUA

Buna

Solomon Sea

Santa Cruz Islands

Port Moresby

Milne Bay

Guadalcanal

Coral Sea

New Hebrides

Fiji Islands

New Caledonia

Pacifc Ocean

Brisbane

Sydney

Melbourne

NEW ZEALAND

TASMANIA

| 0 | 200 | 400 | 600 |
miles

© '07 jackie cher

The Ghost Mountain Boys

The
Ghost Mountain Boys

THEIR EPIC MARCH AND THE
TERRIFYING BATTLE FOR NEW
GUINEA—THE FORGOTTEN WAR
OF THE SOUTH PACIFIC

James Campbell

Crown Publishers   New York

Grateful acknowledgment is made to the following
for permission to reprint previously published material:

Harold Ober Associates: Excerpt from "Sunday: New Guinea" from *Poems of a Jew*
by Karl Shapiro, copyright © 1943 by Karl Shapiro, copyright renewed 1971 by Karl Shapiro.
Reprinted by permission of Harold Ober Associates.

Half title and title page art: U.S. Army Archive

Library of Congress Cataloging-in-Publication Data
Campbell, James.
The Ghost Mountain boys: their epic march and the terrifying battle for New Guinea—the
forgotten war of the South Pacific / James Campbell.—1st ed.
p. cm.
Includes bibliographical references and index.
1. United States. Army. Infantry Regiment, 126th—History.   2. World War, 1939–1945—
Regimental histories—United States.   3. World War, 1939–1945—Campaigns—Papua New
Guinea.   I. Title.
D769.31126th .C36 2007
940.54'2653—dc22   2007013140
ISBN 978-0-307-33596-8
Printed in the United States of America
Interior and endpaper map illustrations by Jackie Aher
Design by Leonard Henderson
10 9 8 7 6 5 4 3 2 1
First Edition

*To Elizabeth, for her patience and grace, and to our
daughters Aidan, Rachel, and Willa*

And to the Red Arrow men of New Guinea and their families

Contents

Contents

A Guide to the Book's Major Characters

U.S. COMMAND STRUCTURE

General Douglas MacArthur: Commander in Chief Southwest Pacific Area

Major General Richard Sutherland: MacArthur's Chief of Staff

Brigadier General Charles Willoughby: MacArthur's Head of Intelligence (G-2)

Major General George Kenney: Commander of Allied Air Forces

Brigadier General Hugh Casey: MacArthur's Engineer Officer

Major General Edwin Forrest Harding: Commanding General 32nd U.S. Infantry Division from February 1942 – December 1, 1942

Lieutenant General Robert Eichelberger: Commander I Corps. Assumed command of all U.S. forces east of the Girua River in early December 1942

AUSTRALIAN COMMAND STRUCTURE

General Sir Thomas Blamey: Commander Allied Land Forces SWPA

Major General Basil Morris: General Officer Commanding New Guinea Force

Lieutenant General Sydney Rowell: Replaced Morris as General Officer Commanding New Guinea Force on August 10, 1942

Lieutenant General Edmund Herring: Replaced General Rowell in late October 1942

Major General Arthur "Tubby" Allen: General Officer Commanding 7th Australian Division

Major General George Vasey: Replaced Tubby Allen as Commanding Officer of the 7th Australian Division on October 27, 1942

32ND U.S. INFANTRY DIVISION

Colonel Lawrence Quinn: Commander 126th Infantry Regiment until November 5

Colonel John Mott: Temporary Commander Urbana Force

Colonel John Grose: Assumed command of Urbana Force on December 4, 1942. Three days later, turned over command of Urbana Force to Colonel Clarence Tomlinson. Then took over command of the 127th Infantry Regiment. Resumed command of Urbana Force on December 20, 1942

Lieutenant Colonel Clarence Tomlinson: Assumed command of the 126th Infantry after Quinn. Took over command of Urbana Force on December 7, 1942. Relieved of duties on December 20 due to exhaustion, but remained Commander of the 126th Infantry

Lieutenant Colonel Herbert Smith: Commander 2nd Battalion 128th Infantry Regiment

Major Herbert "Stutterin'" Smith: Commander 2nd Battalion 126th Infantry Regiment

Captain William "Jim" Boice: Regimental Intelligence Officer (G-2), and leader of the Pathfinder Patrol

URBANA FRONT

Lieutenant Robert Odell: Platoon leader Company F 2nd Battalion 126th Infantry Regiment. Took command of the company in early December 1942

Lieutenant James Hunt: Head of communications section attached to Company E, then F, and eventually Battalion Headquarters 126th Infantry Regiment

Sergeant Herman Bottcher: Platoon commander Company H 2nd Battalion 126th Infantry Regiment. Attached to Company G

COMPANY G 2ND BATTALION 126TH INFANTRY REGIMENT

Lieutenant Cladie "Gus" Bailey: Commanding Officer

Sergeant Don Stout

Sergeant Don Ritter

Corporal Stanley Jastrzembski

Corporal Carl Stenberg

Privates First Class Russell Buys, Samuel DiMaggio, Chester Sokoloski

COMPANY E 2ND BATTALION 126TH INFANTRY REGIMENT

Captain Melvin Schultz: Commanding Officer

1st Sergeant Paul Lutjens

Sergeant John Fredericks

Private First Class Arthur Edson

SANANANDA FRONT

Captain Alfred Medendorp: Leader of the Wairopi Patrol, Commanding Officer of Cannon and K Companies

Captain Roger Keast: Second-in-command Wairopi Patrol, and Commanding Officer Antitank Company

Captain John Shirley: Commanding Officer Company I 3rd Battalion 126th Infantry Regiment

Captain Meredith Huggins: Operations Officer (S-3) 3rd Battalion 126th Infantry Regiment

Lieutenant Peter Dal Ponte: Commanding Officer Service Company 3rd Battalion 126th Infantry Regiment

Lieutenant Hershel Horton: Platoon Commander Company I 3rd Battalion 126th Infantry Regiment

Father Stephen Dzienis: Chaplain 126th Infantry Regiment

Lieutenant Lester Segal: Physician assigned to Wairopi Patrol

Major Simon Warmenhoven: Regimental Surgeon, 126th Infantry Regiment. Served on both Sanananda and Buna Fronts

Author's Note

IN 1884 THE ISLAND of New Guinea was partitioned by three Western powers. The Dutch claimed the western half (it was handed over to Indonesia in November 1969 and is now called the province of Papua, formerly Irian Jaya), and the Germans and British divided the eastern half. The southern section of the eastern half became a British protectorate (British New Guinea Territory) and passed to Australia in 1906 as the Territory of Papua. The northern section formed part of German New Guinea, or Kaiser-Wilhelmsland. During World War I, it was occupied by Australian forces and in 1920 was mandated to Australia by the League of Nations. It became known as the Territory of New Guinea.

Although the Battles of Buna and Sanananda took place in the Territory of Papua, because people generally refer to the island as New Guinea, I do, too, in order to avoid potentially confusing distinctions.

Introduction

NEW GUINEA WAS an unlikely place in which to wage a war for world domination. It was an inhospitable, only cursorily mapped, disease-ridden land. Almost no one—not the elite units of the Japanese forces that invaded New Guinea's north coast in July 1942, not the Australian Imperial Forces or its militia, and maybe least of all the U.S. Army's 32nd "Red Arrow" Division—was prepared for what military historian Eric Bergerud calls "some of the harshest terrain ever faced by land armies in the history of the war."

In New Guinea, exhaustion and disease pushed armies to the breaking point. Losses to malaria alone were crippling. Sixty-seven percent of the 14,500 American troops involved in the battles for Buna and Sanananda contracted the disease. On the Sanananda Front, casualties due to malaria were over 80 percent.

The suffering was enormous on all sides. For the Americans, it could have been alleviated, at least initially, by better planning. But eventually the topography and climate would still have exacted a terrible toll.

By the time the Red Arrow men arrived in New Guinea in September 1942, U.S. Marine troops were already fighting a brutal, well-documented land battle at Guadalcanal in the Solomon Islands. The marines had a superbly oiled publicity machine that kept them in the spotlight. The 32nd Division's soldiers fighting in New Guinea felt forgotten. The American public, in particular, suffered from the misperception that except for Guadalcanal, the South Pacific was a naval war with a few insignificant ground operations thrown in for good measure. By October 1944, they knew that General Douglas MacArthur, who had fled the Philippines, had returned two and a half years later, keeping his promise. But they had little idea of what went on in the interim, which is to say that they had scant knowledge of the land war in New Guinea. Americans' lack of interest revealed a geographical ignorance. The European front—and the exception of Guadalcanal—they could comprehend. The vast blue Pacific with its obscure island nations remained a mystery.

Yet the fighting on the island of New Guinea—especially the early confrontations at Buna and Sanananda—was every bit as fierce as that at Guadalcanal. General Robert Eichelberger, who would assume command of the 32nd, wrote that in New Guinea, "Everything favored the enemy."

Casualties at Buna, in fact, were considerably higher than at Guadalcanal. On Guadalcanal 1,100 troops were killed and 4,350 wounded. The cost of New Guinea's combined Buna-Sanananda-Gona campaign was 3,300 killed and 5,500 wounded. As William Manchester points out in his book *American Caesar,* "If the difference in the size of attacking forces is taken into account, the loss of life on Papua (New Guinea) had been three times as great as Guadalcanal's."

On New Guinea, as at Guadalcanal, topography determined everything. Tanks and artillery, which won the day in Europe, were rendered useless. In the matted jungles, men were forced to fight battles at point-blank range. Soldiers used anything that worked— grenades, fixed bayonets, and, sometimes, their hands. Eric Bergerud described the struggle as "a knife fight out of the Stone Age." George Johnston, an Australian war correspondent, called it one of the "most merciless and most primeval battles."

As fierce as the fighting was, the terrain and climate were just as dangerous. General Hugh Casey, MacArthur's chief engineer, called New Guinea the "ultimate nightmare country." Support units, he said, would face challenges "without precedent in American military history." Before his first inspection of the island, he assumed that nothing could compare with Bataan and Samar. But New Guinea was in a class of its own. War, Casey told MacArthur, would be almost impossible to wage on the island. His warnings proved prescient.

For the troops of the 32nd Division, New Guinea became "the ultimate nightmare country" indeed. Lenord Sill would later say, "All who were alive, were so near death. . . . Our briefing, before we began near Port Moresby, did not prepare us for what we were about to encounter. In the beginning, we were all young, healthy GIs, eager to conquer the world. . . . In a matter of weeks, long before we met the enemy force, all of us had been transformed into ghosts of our former selves."

Bob Hartman of Grand Rapids, Michigan, minces no words. "If I owned New Guinea and I owned hell, I would live in hell and rent out New Guinea." The first time Carl Smestad saw the Sanananda battlefront he was convinced that it would be his graveyard. "God help us," he thought. "We're never going to get out of here alive."

One would think that the 32nd must have been a division of elite fighters, or that it contained units of crack troops. Nothing could have been further from the truth. Although Field Service regulations specified "all troops must be thoroughly acclimated before initiating operations," the men of the 32nd were not ready for the jungle. When it came time to send the division to New Guinea, a commanding general judged it soft and just barely fit for combat.

New to jungle warfare, the division lacked even the basics for survival, prompting one military historian to label the soldiers of the 32nd the "guinea pigs" of the South Pacific. Men were not issued any of the specialized clothing that later became de rigueur for the war in the South Pacific. For camouflage, their combat fatigues were hastily dyed before they left Australia. In the rain and extreme humidity, the dye ran and clogged the cloth, causing men to develop horrible skin ulcers. Soldiers were forced to wade through vines, creepers, brush, dense stands of razor-sharp kunai grass, and elephant grass as high as a basketball rim without the aid of machetes. They did not even have insect repellent—astonishing when one considers that they were fighting in a bug-ridden place. They were not equipped with waterproof containers either. Matches were often unusable. Quinine and vitamin pills, salt and chlorination tablets got wet and crumbled in their pants pockets. Never, perhaps, have American troops been more poorly equipped. Yet, in New Guinea, the 32nd Division was asked to do the extraordinary.

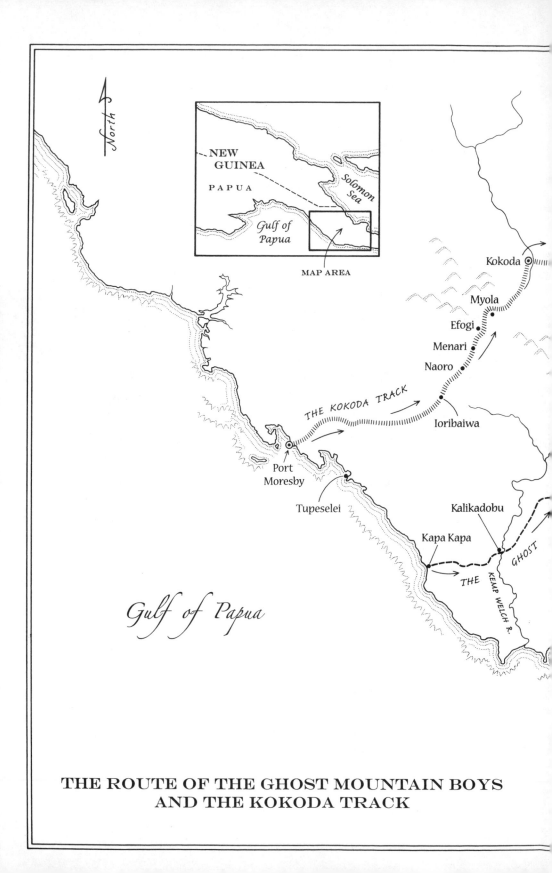

**THE ROUTE OF THE GHOST MOUNTAIN BOYS
AND THE KOKODA TRACK**

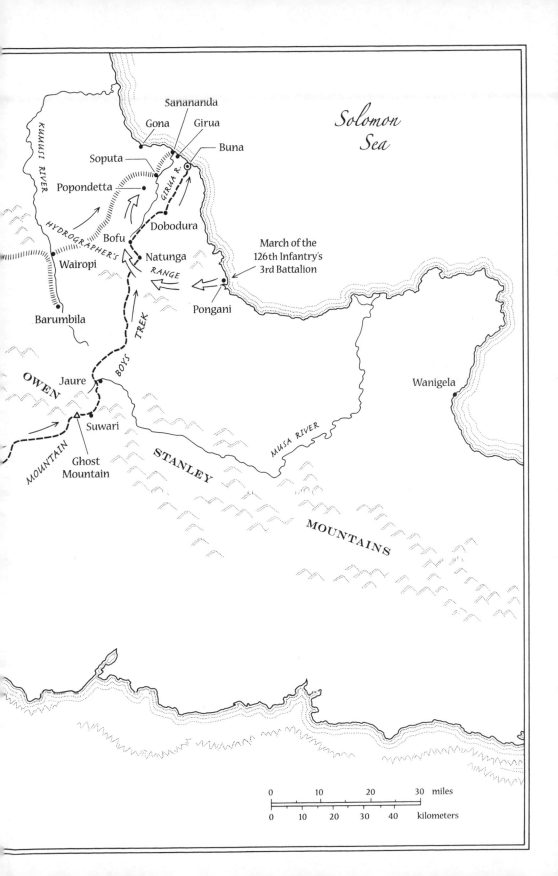

Solomon
Sea

KUMUSI RIVER

Sanananda
Gona
Girua
Buna
Soputa
Popondetta
GIRUA R.
Dobodura
HYDROGRAPHER'S
Bofu
Natunga
Wairopi
RANGE
March of the
126th Infantry's
3rd Battalion
Barumbila
BOYS TREK
Pongani
OWEN
Jaure
Wanigela
Suwari
MUSA RIVER
Ghost
Mountain
STANLEY
MOUNTAIN
MOUNTAINS

| 0 | 10 | 20 | 30 | miles |

| 0 | 10 | 20 | 30 | 40 | kilometers |

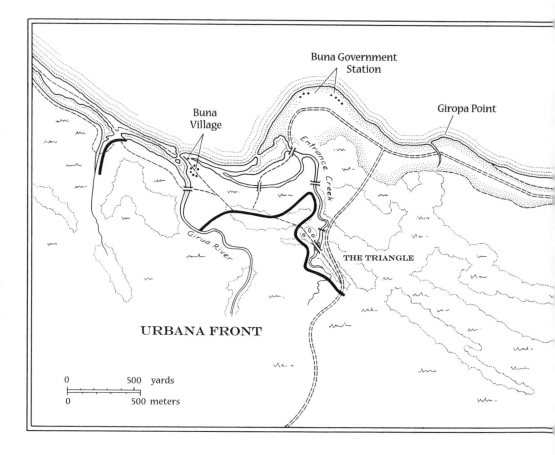

Buna Government
Station

Giropa Point

Buna
Village

Entrance Creek

Girua River

THE TRIANGLE

URBANA FRONT

0   500   yards
0   500 meters

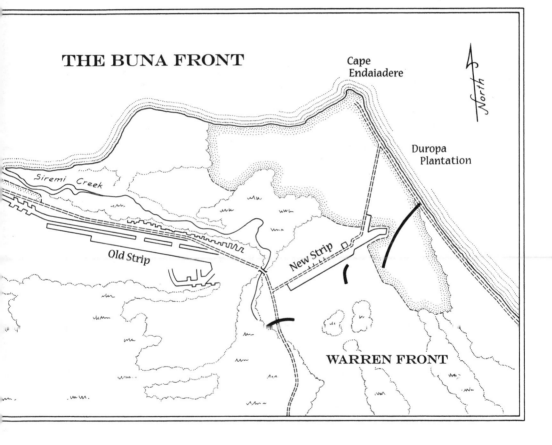

THE BUNA FRONT

Cape
Endaiadere

Duropa
Plantation

North

Siremi Creek

Old Strip

New Strip

WARREN FRONT

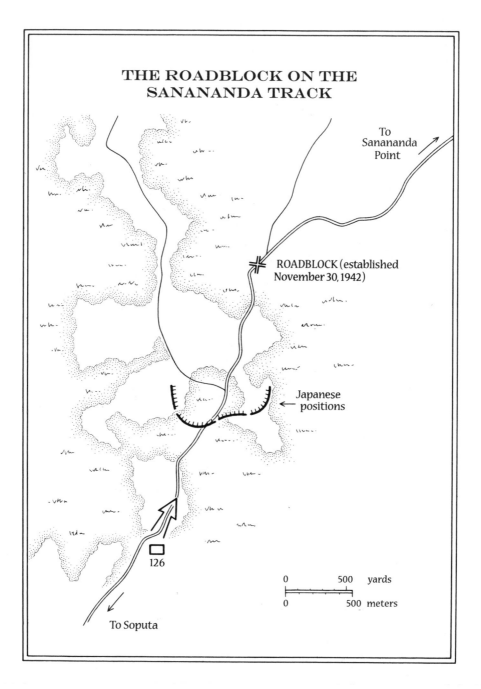

THE ROADBLOCK ON THE
SANANANDA TRACK

To
Sanananda
Point

ROADBLOCK (established
November 30, 1942)

Japanese
positions

126

| 0 | 500 | yards |
| 0 | 500 | meters |

To Soputa

The Ghost Mountain Boys

Dearest Lover:

Is it ever grand out—you know, honey, you've read in stories about the tropical evenings, a warm, sultry night with a slight breeze . . . and a moon peaking thru the clouds. Well, that's the way it was to-night. I stood there for a long time, watching and most of all wishing to have you standing along side of me, and that we could really take advantage of the "Romantic Atmosphere" . . . the stillness of the night—Just two things missing—First and most of all, My Mandy, and then some sweet, faint dance music. Well, we'll just have to postpone it for the present . . . until another night. Give Muriel and Ann my love—I think about you all so often. What a great day it will be when we can be together again.

Goodbye Sweetheart—All my heart's love always—Yours forever, Sam

Thursday Nite 6:00 PM.
July 30, 1942

My Sweetheart:

And how's my Mandy this evening? Let me see, right now it is three oclock in the morning in Grand Rapids, so you should be sound asleep—wish I could tip toe in on you right at this moment honey, and take a peep in at you, I'd carefully put a kiss on your lips, your cheeks, your eyes, and your hair, and then rest my cheek against yours for awhile without awakening you, then take a good long look at you again and tip toe out.

Yours Forever, Sam

Wednesday Nite 7:50 PM.
Sept. 9, 1942

To "My One and Only:"

I'll try my best to get my thoughts on paper, but it's not like being with you darling, sitting across from you, watching the smile on your face, the touch of your legs under the table . . . I miss you love, oh God! How I miss you sometimes . . . All these things I've wanted to tell you, should have told you before I left . . . I hope you don't think I'm sacriligeous but if I were offered my choice between heaven and you, I'd choose you . . . I'm going to say goodbye now . . .
Always your man, Sam

Later that night: Hello darling, here I am again. I hope the censors will let that letter go thru alright. I started out to write this letter, but wrote that one instead. I have hopes they [the censors] won't open the previous letter, certainly no military secrets in there unless it's a military secret . . . that I'm so very, very much in love with you—I'm sure tho that the japs don't care about that.

Wed. Nite 8:00 PM.
Somewhere in New Guinea
October 14, 1942

Dearest Lover:

Oct. 14—this is the eve of two years in the army—Two years ago tomorrow we were inducted . . . Have been under the "weather" a little of late. Been having a little dysentery . . . There are an enormous amount of flies here . . . I suppose you wonder all about New Guinea . . . There are a lot of natives here. Quite a bit of sickness and disease amongst the natives . . . They have a lot of skin diseases and eye infections. Lot of the small children walk about with "pot" bellies due to malnutrition. Pretty near all have rickets—some have large spleens because of malaria. The men folks wear a cloth about the hips . . . The women folks wear a tropical grass skirt . . . The other day I saw a woman nursing a baby on one breast and a small pig on the other—the natives are very much tattooed. They make wonderful boatsmen . . . Night before last crossed a fast streaming river and two of these natives handled a small boat and took us right straight across like nothing . . . The women seem to do much of the work—will see a native carrying a spear coming down a path and behind him comes his wife all loaded down with fruit, coconuts, wood, etc. on her back and head, and perhaps a baby sitting on top of that holding on to her hair . . .

What I'm really looking forward to is the day I step on U.S. soil—what a day that will be . . .

Goodnight, My Mandy, Lovingly Yours, Sam

———————

Monday Nite
New Guinea
Nov. 2, 1942

Dear Muriel:

And how's that big daughter of mine getting along—I've been wondering about you so much now that you are going to

school . . . Mommie tells me you are a big girl now. How nice
you play with Ann. Do you like your baby brother? . . . I sure
miss you Muriel, remember how you and I used to play at
night in the house before you went to bed, that was loads of
fun, wasn't it? Am thinking lots about you.

Love, Your Dad

Late November 1942, Buna Coast, New Guinea:
BEFORE SETTING OUT, they smeared their faces with green paint.
Loaded down with hand grenades, .30 and .45 caliber ammunition,
and two days' rations, the Americans struggled through heavy jungle
and dug in just in front of a battalion of Australians. A second American detachment had its sights set on a spot farther north along the
trail. Navigating through hip-deep swamps, the soldiers clashed with a
Japanese patrol, lost their bearings, and ended up well short of their
destination. Having realized that the main advance was falling apart,
another company left the banana plantation and pushed forward in a
northwesterly direction through nipa and sago palm. Two hundred
yards out it was stopped in its tracks by heavy Japanese cross fire.
Ordered to dig in, the men worked fast. They had just settled into their
trenches when the Japanese attacked. Hundreds of enemy troops bore
down on them. They rushed forward like wild Indians, shouting "Banzai!", crashing through the jungle, their bayonets drawn. The Americans froze. The Japanese soldiers were almost upon them when the
Americans finally fired. The forest filled with the smell of gunpowder.
Called forward, two Australian companies hurried to help, and
together they drove back the Japanese, inflicting heavy losses. At
night, as their foxholes filled with water, the soldiers listened to swamp
rats feeding on corpses.

Three days later, having patrolled the area and drawn up rudimen-
tary maps, the Americans again prepared to attack. They opened up
with artillery and mortars and then moved forward. One detachment
pushed straight north, followed by a platoon of Australians and the

regimental surgeon, Major Simon "Sam" Warmenhoven and a portion of his staff. To avoid the swamp, the soldiers clung to the main trail. A hundred yards out, they slammed into the Japanese and were halted by a torrent of fire. When a mortar landed among the Australians, Major Warmenhoven ran forward, dashing past enemy fire lanes. Five men lay dead; another eight were alive, but the shrapnel had done its work—they were badly torn up. Warmenhoven jumped from one man to the next as mortars exploded around him. He gave each soldier a half-grain of morphine, cut away their clothes, and dusted their wounds with sulfanilamide powder. Then he dressed the wounds as best he could and waited with the moaning soldiers for litter bearers to arrive. Later he would receive the Distinguished Service Cross for his heroism.

BOOK ONE

Thus it was they wrought our woe
At the Tavern long ago.
Tell me, do our masters know,
Loosing blindly as they fly,
Old men love while young men die?

RUDYARD KIPLING

Chapter 1

ESCAPE TO THE SOUTH

ON THE NIGHT OF March 11, 1942, Douglas MacArthur was preparing to flee the island of Corregidor, headquarters of the Allied forces in the Philippines. Only fifteen miles across the North Channel, his army was trapped on the jungle-clothed Philippine peninsula of Bataan.

MacArthur, his wife, his four-year-old son Arthur, Arthur's Cantonese amah, thirteen members of MacArthur's staff, two naval officers, and a technician gathered at the destroyed Corregidor dock. Corregidor rose dramatically from the waters of Manila Bay. What had once been a luxuriant green island was now a devastated, crater-ridden monument to the fury of the battle for the Philippines. Major General Jonathan "Skinny" Wainwright emerged from the shadows.

"Jonathan," MacArthur said, "I want you to understand my position very plainly. I'm leaving for Australia pursuant to repeated orders of the President . . . I want you to make it known throughout all elements of your command that I'm leaving over my repeated protests. If I get through to Australia you know I'll come back as soon as I can with as much as I can. In the meantime, you've got to hold."

Wainwright assured MacArthur that he would do everything in his power to hold Bataan. He wiped the tears from his eyes and MacArthur's jaw quivered. Then MacArthur composed himself and shook Wainwright's hand. "When I get back, if you're still on Bataan, I'll make you a lieutenant general."

Wainwright said simply, "I'll be on Bataan if I'm alive."

MacArthur's long personal crusade to return to the Philippines in victory had begun.

Lieutenant John "Buck" Bulkeley, a naval commander, had already inspected the four escape crafts—mahogany-hulled PT boats, seventy-seven feet from bow to stern, powered by big Packard engines. That said, the PT boats were still risky. After three months of combat, the engines were overused; the boats were fast, but not fast enough to outrun enemy destroyers. To make matters worse, the party would have to travel hundreds of miles over poorly charted waters, using only a compass, crude maps, and dead reckoning. MacArthur, though, could not be dissuaded from his plan. He had already refused to go by submarine—getting a sub to Corregidor would simply take too much time, time MacArthur did not have. Besides, he loved the PT boat, and that was how he wanted to leave the Philippines. The Japanese navy was watching for him, and MacArthur understood the implications. His wife and child were aboard Bulkeley's boat with him. And Tokyo Rose had been broadcasting threats—if captured, MacArthur would be hanged in public in Tokyo's Imperial Plaza. The Japanese, though, would never take him alive. He had two highly polished derringers and two cartridges that he planned to use as a last resort.

It was a moonlit night, and as the boats moved toward Mindoro, south of Corregidor, Lieutenant Bulkeley felt a growing apprehension. They were nearing the Japanese blockade. Pummeled by strong easterly winds, the seas churned, and visibility was poor. MacArthur, Arthur, and Arthur's nurse, lay below, miserably seasick. Arthur was running a fever and MacArthur retched violently. Though also sick, MacArthur's wife Jean tended to both her son and her husband. In the rough seas, the boats became separated, and from that point on, it was every crew for itself.

One of the four PT boats reached the rendezvous point in the Cuyo Islands and waited in the morning mist for the arrival of the others. Suddenly, the commander of the first boat sighted what he thought was a Japanese destroyer speeding toward them. He ordered five hundred gallons of gasoline jettisoned and pushed down on the throttles. Still the other ship gained on them. Realizing he could not get away, the commander reversed course and readied the torpedoes for firing. He was prepared to give the order when he recognized the oncoming ship as Bulkeley's vessel.

After the near mishap, MacArthur and his party waited for the third PT boat (the fourth boat had broken down en route). It was a hot, sultry day, and they bobbed like castaways on the water among the sandy coves and palm-fringed, volcanic islands. Two hours later, the third PT boat limped into the inlet. MacArthur now had an important decision to make. The plan was to meet the submarine *Permit*. At that point, they had to choose—submarine or PT boat. MacArthur was tempted to travel the rest of the way by submarine, but Bulkeley pointed out that Tagauayan, where they were to assemble, was three hours away and that they would never be able to get there in time. MacArthur was getting antsy. Knowing that there would be planes waiting to transport them to Australia, MacArthur decided to make directly for Mindanao in two of the original four PT boats.

Less than an hour after leaving, MacArthur heard the lookout shout, "Looks like an enemy cruiser!" Bulkeley drew in a deep breath when he saw the faster warship's imposing outlines. Then he calmed himself and waited for the inevitable. But the inevitable never came. The seas were rough and the PT boats lay low in the water, surrounded by whitecaps, and skidded by the cruiser without being spotted.

Hours later, in the waning light of the afternoon, they saw the hulking silhouette of a Japanese warship. They cut their engines and hoped they would be mistaken for native fishing vessels. The ruse worked. They had averted disaster—again.

On a clear night, illuminated by the moon, they continued across the Mindanao Sea bound for Cagayan on Mindanao's north coast. When they arrived at the Del Monte cannery in Cagayan in the early morning of March 13, they knew that they had slipped through the Japanese blockade.

But now the group faced another potential disaster. The plan had been to reach Cagayan by water and then to fly directly to Darwin on

Australia's north coast. However, as MacArthur watched one war-weary B-17 land, he grew furious and refused to let anyone board. He had expected four reliable planes, not one dilapidated B-17.

For nearly four days MacArthur and his party risked discovery while his Commander of American Forces in Australia tried to secure navy planes. Everyone was tense, especially Major General Richard Sutherland, MacArthur's chief of staff. Sutherland fumed that they were sitting ducks. A Philippine informant could easily betray them to the Japanese, who were on the south end of the island and regularly patrolled north. On the evening of March 16, two of the navy's best Flying Fortresses landed.

Hours later, as the two bombers crossed the Celebes Sea, enemy fighters appeared out of the darkness. Terror swept through the planes. Had they made it this far only to be gunned down by enemy pilots? They could do only one thing—continue to fly their course. As he watched, the Zeros inexplicably turned back. Then MacArthur knew that they had finally escaped.

When the Flying Fortresses landed forty miles south of Darwin at Batchelor Field, two DC-3s were waiting to transport the group to Melbourne. However, MacArthur refused to fly. His wife had been very sick on the flight, and out of concern for her, he did not want to board another plane. What eventually convinced him not to travel by train was his son's condition. Authur remained very ill; his doctor did not think that he could make the long overland journey. After considerable discussion, MacArthur finally agreed to fly.

When they landed in Alice Springs to refuel, the rest of the crew went by air to South Australia; MacArthur, though, insisted now on traveling by train. But the one that serviced Alice Springs had left the previous day, so arrangements had to be made to bring in a special train.

When it arrived the next day, MacArthur, his wife and son, the amah, and General Sutherland boarded. For three and a half days and over one thousand miles, the slow, narrow-gauge train chugged through the vast, sun-scorched Australian outback to Adelaide. Nearing the city, MacArthur's deputy chief of staff boarded the train and delivered a wrenching blow: The general would not lead a great army against the Japanese. In fact, he would be fighting a shoestring campaign.

Months before, Roosevelt and Churchill had met in Washington, D.C., and together they settled on a "Germany first" policy, determining that the Atlantic-European theater would be the main focus of operations. MacArthur was nearly speechless at the news. "God have mercy on us" was all he could say.

Approaching Adelaide, MacArthur was forced to compose himself. At the station, the gathered reporters were eager to know: He had fled the Philippines; yet his men were still there fighting. Did he have anything to say? MacArthur was tired and still distraught from Sutherland's news, "a lonely, angry man," according to his wife. But he wanted to send a message to his army and the people of the Philippines to let them know that they would not be forgotten. It was then that he delivered his famous words: "The President of the United States ordered me to break through the Japanese lines and proceed for Corregidor to Australia for the purpose, as I understand it, of organizing the American offensive against Japan, a primary object of which is the relief of the Philippines. I came through and I shall return."

On March 18, a day after he arrived in Australia, MacArthur learned the whole truth of America's "Germany first" policy: His U.S. ground troops would be limited to two divisions. He protested to General Marshall "No commander in American history has so failed of support as here."

MacArthur already felt as if Roosevelt had betrayed him in the Philippines. Now he felt betrayed again. His hope for a quick victory against the Japanese in New Guinea evaporated.

●   ●   ●

When MacArthur came to Australia, not only did he not have a great army to lead, but he was being asked to protect a country that was powerless to protect itself. In a show of extreme loyalty, Australia had sent its land, sea, and air forces to join England in its fight against the European Axis in Africa, Greece, and the Middle East.

Australia's national security and twelve thousand miles of its coastline were left to the Australian militia, a group of poorly trained, poorly equipped home guardsmen. Australian officials feared that Japan would invade, and the Australian press shamelessly fueled these fears. Thousands of Sydney residents fled the city for the Blue Mountains fifty miles to the west; people in Darwin, Cairns, and Townsville abandoned their homes.

A month before MacArthur arrived in Australia, the country's growing sense of vulnerability became a reality. Japanese planes bombed Darwin, killing 250 people and destroying nine ships and twenty aircraft.

A feeling of paranoia seized Australia. The Japanese had roared through Hong Kong, Malaya, Guam, Rabaul, Singapore, Java, the Dutch East Indies, and Burma. Eventually, what Japan would call its "Greater East Asia Co-Prosperity Sphere" would cover the entire coastline of Asia, extending from Manchuria to Rangoon, and would include the Pacific in a line running south from the Aleutian Islands. It would occupy one-sixth of the earth's surface. The Australians feared they were next.

On February 3, Japan bombed Port Moresby, New Guinea's largest city, for the first time. By early March, Japanese forces occupied Salamaua and Lae, two cities that were part of Australia's New Guinea mandate. The invasion was staged from Rabaul, a small town on the island of New Britain, four hundred air miles off the New Guinea mainland, which the Japanese had overwhelmed one-and-a-half months earlier despite valiant opposition from the Australian forces garrisoned there. The Japanese transformed Rabaul into their South Sea base. With a magnificent harbor and two airfields, Rabaul held one of the largest collections of troops outside of Japan.

After the Japanese landed in New Guinea, Allied headquarters in Australia did its best to anticipate Japan's next move. Would Premier Hideki Tojo's army invade Australia? Whatever Japan's plans were, there was no denying the reality—Australia, New Guinea, and the Solomon Islands were the last major positions still left to the Allies in the Southwest Pacific.

On February 17, 1942, Army Chief of Staff General George C. Marshall ordered the transfer to Australia of the 41st U.S. Infantry Division. The 41st's mission was to protect Australia's ports and air bases and to provide garrisons for the defense of its eastern and northeastern coastal cities. Despite the imminent arrival of the 41st Division, when MacArthur landed in Australia in mid-March 1942 he began lobbying for more troops and more planes and ships, especially aircraft carriers.

MacArthur combined his obsession with returning to the Philippines with a suspicion that the political powers in the U.S., especially the Joint Chiefs of Staff, and the demands and influence of the navy in the Central Pacific, were depriving him of the resources he needed to wage a war (only 9 percent of U.S. supplies went to the Southwest Pacific). He complained that he was "always the underdog, and was always fighting with destruction just around the corner." To an extent, MacArthur's fears were justified. MacArthur and the navy brass were openly hostile to each other. Both lobbied for a finite supply of resources, for which the navy was often given preference.

Australia's Prime Minister, John Curtin, had been waging his own personal campaign for troops for months, entreating Great Britain for its help before MacArthur ever set foot in Australia. Britain, though, had thrown herself full force against the Germans, and Churchill maintained that he did not have the troops to spare. In desperation Curtin turned to the United States.

The day after Pearl Harbor, Curtin allied Australia with the Americans, declaring that Australia was "at war with Japan." On December 23, 1941, he wrote to Roosevelt and to Churchill: "Our resources here are very limited. It is in your power to meet the situation. Should the government of the United States desire, we would gladly accept an American Commander in the Pacific Area."

At the same time, Curtin demanded three divisions from Australia's

Imperial Forces sent home at once. When Churchill told him that his request was impossible to fulfill, Curtin persisted, and eventually won the return of two out of the three. Churchill argued that to remove the 9th Division from the Middle East would jeopardize the British line. He then suggested to Roosevelt that if the Prime Minister agreed to leave the 9th Division in place, the United States should send to Australia another U.S. Army Infantry division. Marshall chose the 32nd.

A full seven months later, as the Japanese Imperial army ascended a high ridge overlooking Port Moresby, MacArthur dispatched two of the 32nd Division's three regimental combat teams to New Guinea.

•   •   •

Although MacArthur came to Australia in defeat, no one would have known it from his reception. One of the most decorated generals of his time, a man who during World War I was called by America's secretary of war "the finest front line American general of the war," had arrived to defend Australia in her hour of need.

In fact, MacArthur's arrival overshadowed the return of one of Australia's own heroes. Curtin had ordered General Sir Thomas Blamey to return home from the Middle East "as speedily as possible," appointing him Allied Commander, Australian Military Forces.

The March 18 announcement that MacArthur would be the Supreme Commander of the Southwest Pacific Area upstaged Blamey's appointment. Blamey was unhappy about the news, which he got while traveling by train east from Perth. But the Joint Chiefs of Staff had already worked out the organization of the Pacific, dividing the theater into two distinct areas: The Pacific Ocean, which included North, Central, and South, went to the navy, and the Southwest Pacific, including Australia, the Philippines, New Guinea, the Solomons, the Bismarck Archipelago, and a portion of the Dutch East Indies, would go to MacArthur.

Conceding to General George Marshall, who argued that an Australian should command Allied troops, MacArthur reluctantly appointed Blamey as his Commander Allied Land Forces. In an uncharacteristic moment of modesty, MacArthur named himself the

Commander in Chief Southwest Pacific Area (SWPA) rather than Supreme Commander.

Despite MacArthur's choice of Blamey, Australian officers were still unhappy. The staff of MacArthur's General Headquarters was entirely American, composed of trusted advisors who had served on his staff in the Philippines. Not appointing an Australian as a senior member of his staff—which was known as the "Bataan Gang"—was a move by MacArthur that generated bad blood between the Commander in Chief and the Australians, though it was one he defended gruffly. "There was no prospect," he said, "of obtaining qualified senior staff officers from the Australians."

From the beginning, MacArthur regarded Blamey ambivalently: In his words, Blamey was ". . . sensual, slothful and of doubtful moral character . . . [but] a tough commander likely to shine like a power light in an emergency. The best of the local bunch." Blamey's opinion of MacArthur was not much different. "The best and the worst of the things you hear about him are both true," Blamey said.

• • •

On a bright, sunny morning in March, a train pulling MacArthur's private railroad car came to a stop at Spencer Street Station in Melbourne. Six thousand people, including the Prime Minister and other dignitaries, greeted MacArthur with an outburst of adoration. A correspondent for an Australian newspaper said that he had never seen any man receive such acclaim. MacArthur stepped from the car and, though weary, he was an impressive-looking man. He sported a "flourishable cane" and wore his signature gold-embroidered cap dashingly at an angle.

After a brief but dramatic speech in which he took a jab at Roosevelt for consigning him to Australia to command an insufficient army, MacArthur and Sutherland stepped into a limousine and made for the Menzies Hotel. For the next few weeks, MacArthur went into hiding, guarded closely by his devoted chief of staff, General Sutherland, trying to come to terms with the reality of his situation.

• • •

A part of the 32nd Division's fate was sealed when Churchill persuaded Roosevelt to break England's stalemate with Australia by sending Australia another U.S. Army Infantry division. The division's ultimate fate, though, hung in the balance for months after MacArthur arrived Down Under.

The defensive strategy devised by the Australian Chiefs of Staff was to hold the "Brisbane Line," a thousand miles of coastline between Brisbane and Melbourne, the heart of the country's industrial power and its population center. Barbed wire was strung along the beaches in Sydney and Melbourne and a blackout was imposed on the southeast coastal cities.

Initially, MacArthur accepted, or was forced to accept, the Australian strategy. Later, though, he wrote that he never had any intention of abiding by what he considered a defeatist approach. He asserted that from the moment he set foot in Australia, he planned to take the war against Japan's Imperial army to New Guinea.

MacArthur considered New Guinea a backwater theater. His decision to engage the Japanese Imperial army there was a strategic necessity. Japan, on the other hand, coveted New Guinea, one of the last essential pieces in its colossal Asia-Pacific land grab. Once it controlled the island, it could isolate, and perhaps invade, Australia. More important, possession of New Guinea would allow the Japanese to cut off the eight thousand-mile Allied supply line (one of the longest in military history) that ran from the West Coast of the United States to Australia via Hawaii and Fiji, thereby ending Allied influence in the South Pacific.

MacArthur's decision to fight for New Guinea, and Admiral Ernest King's efforts to challenge Japanese expansion in the Solomons by invading Guadalcanal, upset Japanese plans for putting a quick end to the war and suing for a favorable peace that acknowledged its numerous conquests.

But even as MacArthur prepared to send troops to New Guinea, he bitterly resented its necessity, and remained obsessed with the Philippines, vowing to return even if he were "down to one canoe paddled by Douglas MacArthur and supported by one Taylor cub [plane]."

In New Guinea, that pledge would be put to the ultimate test. MacArthur would be up against a Japanese army whose determination to hold the island would initiate one of the South Pacific's most savage campaigns.

Chapter 2

A Train Heading West

THREE WEEKS AFTER MacArthur arrived in Australia, his dream of a speedy return to the Philippines was shattered. Major General Edward King, ignoring MacArthur's orders for a counterattack against the Japanese on Bataan, surrendered to them on April 9, 1942. The capitulation was the largest in U.S. military history.

Three days before the surrender, and ten thousand miles away, the 32nd Infantry Division was loaded onto a train. The decision to move the division puzzled battalion and company commanders who had been led to believe that they were headed for the European Theater of Operations (ETO). The rumor was that the division was now bound for the Southwest Pacific.

Although many of the 32nd Division's men could not have pointed on a world map to the area defined as the Southwest Pacific, they were familiar with Europe's historic battlefields. Called the "Red Arrow," the 32nd Division first distinguished itself in World War I. Because of its exploits, the French gave the 32nd the sobriquet "Les Terribles." Its symbol, which it wore proudly as a shoulder patch, was a red arrow piercing a line. It was said that there was not a line the tenacious 32nd could not penetrate—it was the first division to pierce the German army's Hindenburg Line, for example.

By 1940, though, the 32nd Divison's glory was a distant memory. On October 15 that year, when the Fighting Thirty-Second was "called to colors" in the first peacetime conscription act in American history, it was a largely untrained, loosely organized National Guard unit, comprised mostly of men from Wisconsin and Michigan.

In the lean years at the end of the Depression, many jobless young men saw the National Guard as an alternative to poverty—most felt no special calling or patriotic duty or military ambition. Stanley Jastrzembski of Company G, 2nd Battalion, 126th U.S. Infantry, was one of those men. Born and raised in Muskegon, Michigan, he joined the National Guard to help support his family. Jastrzembski had the longest name in the company—"Jas Trz Emb Ski," the men of Company G used to chant jokingly—and at only sixteen he was its youngest member.

When Germany invaded Poland, Jastrzembski considered going to Poland and enlisting in the Polish army. He stayed home, however, and to help support his family, he joined the National Guard instead. His immigrant parents were dead, and there were six kids living at home. The Jastrzembski children tended a garden and traded vegetables with neighbors for chickens and rabbits. There was no money, though, and the family needed the paycheck the Guard offered.

For Jastrzembski, the Guard offered just enough money to live on. For others, it provided a small beer and entertainment fund. A guy's local Guard unit met one night a week—for that he received a paycheck of $12.00 every three months, enough for him to keep food in the house and to take a gal he was sweet on to the picture show. For weekend maneuvers and three weeks of summer training, the Guard paid extra.

Upon having their service extended beyond one year, many guardsmen threatened to go AWOL. "OHIO" was the code word of their rebellion—"Over the Hill In October." But October 15 came and went. The truth was that life in the army was not half bad. Call-up meant three meals a day, a roof overhead, a chance to shoot guns, and steady pay.

•   •   •

When the 32nd was mobilized in October 1940, it was sent via troop trains to the Deep South, far from its midwestern roots. The send-off was festive. Units marched to train stations, bands played, and thousands of people lining the parade routes shouted their encouragement.

Camp Beauregard, situated at the fringes of Alexandria, Louisiana, was the division's new home. Beauregard, though, was not ready for the 32nd. Built as a National Guard summer camp and equipped to accommodate only one regiment, the camp's infrastructure was overwhelmed by the division's one hundred officers and thirty-two hundred enlisted men, who promptly dubbed Beauregard "Camp Disregard." The tents in which they lived were heated with charcoal, which gave them terrible headaches. And when the cold late-fall rains began, the camp, trampled by the boots of thousands of men and the heavy tires of military vehicles, became a mudhole.

Jastrzembski and the 32nd spent only four months at Camp Disregard, but it was a stay plagued by personnel turnover, equipment shortages, and an inadequate training regimen. One guardsman said bluntly, "We fired our rifles, screamed, and ran at straw dummies. That was the extent of our training." Carl Stenberg, a heavy weapons squad leader in Jastrzembski's Company G, recalls that the training area at Dis-regard lay four miles from camp. Company G marched out in the morning and back to camp at night. He remembers the sound of metal on metal, of rifles clanking against helmets. "Put it this way," Stenberg says, "we did a lot of marching."

On weekends the men would head for New Orleans, Alexandria, or Natchez, Mississippi, attracted by the promise of music, booze, and women. Despite the occasional outbreak of gonorrhea and the lurid films designed to scare the men into abstinence, the buses from Camp Beauregard deposited them every weekend at the front door of a brothel in Alexandria that they called Ma Belle's. One guardsman, who spent his share of time at Ma Belle's, said that the line of eager young men often ran around the block.

In February 1941, the 32nd moved to the newly built Camp Livingston, Louisiana, ten miles northeast of Alexandria. At Livingston, the division began its transformation, losing its old-time Guard officers to "overage" (being declared too old to serve with combat troops) and bringing on board recent Selective Service draftees and junior officers from the Reserve Officer Training Corps (ROTC) and Officer Candidate School (OCS).

With the infusion of troops, Captain Simon Warmenhoven, formerly the senior resident in Surgery at St. Mary's Hospital in Grand Rapids, Michigan, and now one of the doctors in the 126th Infantry Regiment's medical detachment, stayed busy. Warmenhoven was no stranger to hard work. Growing up, he had put in long hours on his father's farm. On summer breaks during college he ran a four-horse grain binder and traveled all over cutting wheat for local farmers. His younger brother Cornelius, who helped him by drumming up business, remembers how Simon would make it back to the house well after dark and practically fall asleep at the supper table. Once he got back to college, he shoveled coal into campus furnaces for spending money.

The new soldiers needed physicals and vaccinations. After days of marching they needed help tending to sore feet. Perhaps what they required most was sound medical advice about the dangers of cavorting with the kind of women who made their living at Ma Belle's. Doc Warmenhoven could only do so much, though. These were young men in the prime of their lives, and he was not given to preaching. Regardless of his warnings, the soldiers sowed their wild oats on Friday and Saturday nights and then, as the saying went, attended church on Sundays "to pray for crop failure."

Warmenhoven, who in his early thirties was practically as old as some of the soldiers' fathers, stayed behind in camp writing letters to his wife Henrietta, whom he called Mandy (she called him Sam). Warmenhoven was a devoted husband and father, and the son of staunchly religious parents. When his parents emigrated to the United States from the Netherlands in 1921 (Simon was eleven years old), they chose the community of Sunnyside, Washington. Sunnyside was founded in 1898 as a Christian cooperative colony by members of the German Baptist Progressive Brethren, who selected the beautiful Yakima Valley as the site for their experiment in Christian living. In every land deed it sold, Sunnyside included a morality code: no drinking, dancing, gambling, or horseracing. By the time Warmenhoven was of high school age, his parents sent him off to Hull Academy, a Christian school in Hull, Iowa, where he boarded with the minister's family. Later, with a student loan from the Christian Reformed

Church, he attended Calvin College in Grand Rapids, Michigan. He was preparing to enter the seminary, fulfilling his parents' dream, when he signed up for dance lessons, and realized that thanks to the church's austere code of conduct, he had been missing out on one of life's great joys. He switched his major to biology, got a Bachelor of Science degree, and later attended medical school at Marquette, a Jesuit university in Milwaukee, Wisconsin.

On Sunday, March 9, 1941, while most of the men were dragging themselves back to camp after boozy weekend jaunts to Alexandria or Natchez or New Orleans, Warmenhoven was listening to the Blue Danube Waltz on the radio and penning a letter to Mandy. Mandy was pregnant with their second child, and as he wrote, Warmenhoven was trying out names. How he hoped to be home for the birth.

●   ●   ●

Livingston was a melting pot of men from all over the Midwest. They came from small towns and farms and industrial cities, from immigrant families, separated by only a generation from Poland, Germany, Holland, Italy, Ireland. At first, the guardsmen and the draftees regarded each other skeptically. The draftees, according to the guardsmen, were not real soldiers. The draftees, on the other hand, considered themselves intellectually superior to the guardsmen. Most of the draftees had graduated from high school; some had even been to college. When they wanted to insult a fellow soldier, they accused him of "acting like a guardsman." But gradually, as they lived and trained together, the barriers broke down.

One of those new draftees was Samuel DiMaggio. DiMaggio was a first-generation American. His father, Giuseppi, came over from Sicily in 1902, using money that someone had agreed to loan him for the voyage. Having worked for two years to pay back his sponsor, Giuseppi traveled back to Sicily to fetch his bride, and after returning began his career as a railroad man in Albion, Michigan, roughly ninety miles west of Detroit. After a few years, he took a job with the largest local employer, Malleable Iron Company, which made parts for automotive manufacturers. Sam Dimaggio was born in 1916 in Albion on a table in a house owned by the company.

Like the Jastrzembskis, the DiMaggios cultivated a large garden in their backyard, growing most of the food they ate. By fourteen, Sam was working at the Malleable Iron Company in order to pay for school supplies and books. On the night shift, he stoked fifty potbellied stoves with coal; it was hard, grimy work. In 1935 he graduated from high schoool, fulfilling a dream. But the dream ended there, and shortly after, he returned to his old job.

In 1941 his life changed forever in the form of a draft notice. He viewed it as the break he had been waiting for. He would put in his year and, in the interim, figure out what he wanted to do with his life. When the gates of the Malleable closed behind him for the last time, DiMaggio glanced back and said, "I'm never coming back here, you son of a bitch!"

On April 11, Good Friday, DiMaggio reported to Fort Custer in Battle Creek, Michigan. A few days after Easter, he was on a southbound train without the vaguest idea where that train was headed. Two days later, he arrived at Camp Livingston, Louisiana. He had never been farther than ten miles from home.

Physically, Camp Livingston was a far cry from Dis-regard. It was a spacious, thoroughly up-to-date camp with gas heaters in all the tents, heated latrines, bathrooms with an unlimited supply of hot water, washing machines, and raised walkways made of crushed stone or oyster shells. Livingston was a veritable military city with over fourteen thousand tents, fifteen hundred buildings, laundries, bakeries, post offices, fire stations, and hospitals.

At Livingston the 32nd's training lacked a sense of urgency. DiMaggio was surprised by how "casual" it was. First Sergeant Paul Lutjens of the 2nd Battalion's E Company admitted, "No matter how much our officers and non-coms talked about combat, we couldn't help but think they were talking about somebody else."

In late summer 1941, the army initiated the Louisiana Maneuvers, the largest peacetime war games in U.S. history. Four hundred thousand men trained in the unrelenting heat and humidity of the hills, valleys, and pine forests of Louisiana and east Texas. The experience was intended to toughen the men, and to develop their skills in the field. With an eye toward the European Theater of Operations rather than the SWPA, the men were trained in modern, mechanized, mobile warfare that emphasized World War I tactics based on big guns preparing the way for infantry.

The maneuvers were considered a great success, though they would have no practical application for the 32nd Division once it arrived in New Guinea, where jeeps, tanks, and trucks were neutralized by a terrain that reduced war to its most primitive. It was not that the opportunities for mimicking New Guinea's conditions did not exist. "The swamps of Louisiana were so available," Major Herbert C. Smith, then the 128th Infantry Regiment's supply officer, wrote with the clarity of hindsight, ". . . but we did not train in them. . . . Had we only known."

•   •   •

During the Depression, fathers earned money any way they could, and Alfred Medendorp was no exception. He had gone to chiropractic school, but after getting his diploma discovered that he did not enjoy practicing. Then he took a sales job with a biological supply company, peddling test tubes and beakers to universities and high schools around the country. Afterward, he opened up his own business and caught and killed stray cats, embalmed them, and sold them to researchers at the University of Chicago. After joining the National Guard in 1931 for the extra money it offered, he had another commitment—and with federalization nine years later, the army became his first responsibility.

In winter 1941, Captain Alfred Medendorp had just arrived home from Camp Livingston on leave to Grand Rapids, Michigan. He had not seen his wife and three sons in nearly a year. On Sunday morning, December 7, he and his boys were traipsing around the hills near the house with bows and arrows, creeping through fields and ducking in and out of woodlots, shooting trees and launching arrows high into the air.

Alfred Jr. crept along with his dad, picking his way over dry leaves and sticks. There was no snow but the ground was frozen. The leaves crumbled like wax paper under their feet.

Dot Medendorp was in the kitchen, tidying up. On the radio The Glenn Miller Band was playing "Don't Sit Under the Apple Tree with Anybody Else But Me," when a newsman's urgent voice interrupted. Dot rushed to the radio to turn up the volume. The Japanese, the newsman reported, had just bombed Pearl Harbor.

Dot hurried to the back door and called out, "Al, Come quick! Something's happened."

Alfred Medendorp rushed toward the house, followed by his sons. Dot was standing at the back door, holding it half-open.

"Japan just bombed," she said, choking on the words.

Medendorp brushed past his wife and sat down at the kitchen table. The voice on the radio repeated: "The Japanese have bombed Pearl Harbor." Medendorp tried to absorb the impact of the news. Then he looked up to see Al Junior standing at the door, holding his little bow.

Later that day Medendorp received a telegram ordering him back to Camp Livingston; the following day he left, but not before Dot took a family photograph. In the photo, Medendorp is standing behind his three sons. The low dun-colored hills that they had wandered the previous morning form the photo's backdrop. His arms encircle the boys. He is in full dress uniform and smiles slightly. The boys, too, are dressed up—hats, Sunday coats. Al Junior wears stockings and tucks his hands into the pockets of his checkered black and red peacoat.

            •   •   •

When Corporal Carl Stenberg heard about Pearl Harbor, he and a bunch of buddies had just come back from Alexandria, Louisiana. It was a weekend ritual for Stenberg. While other soldiers went to Alexandria for the women, the recently married Stenberg made the trip to go to the theater.

When Stenberg and his friends returned on Sunday afternoon, the camp was buzzing with activity.

Trucks waited, their engines idling, and men rushed from building to building. Even before hearing the news, Stenberg knew that something big was up. It was in the mess hall that he learned what had happened.

"The Nips just bombed Pearl Harbor!" exclaimed a cook.

The following day, fearing the Japanese might follow up Pearl Harbor with attacks on other strategic sites, the entire camp mobilized. The division sent soldiers to guard dry docks, factories, shipyards, bridges, chemical refineries, utilities, and sulfur mines across the south, from Mississippi to Louisiana to east Texas. Some officers, including Major Herbert Smith, went to the Infantry School at Fort Benning to learn combat tactics.

Pearl Harbor abruptly ended Stenberg's dream of "putting in a year" and returning home to resume his life. On December 31, 1941, the army informed all one-year soldiers that they were now obligated to serve for the duration of the conflict plus six months. Few soldiers were pleased, but now instead of griping, they spoke of "exacting revenge" on the "yellow bastards" and making "quick work" of the war. "Remember Pearl Harbor" became their battle cry.

Japan's December 7 assault on Pearl Harbor decimated the Pacific Fleet, killed or wounded over 3,500 men, and sent shock waves through America. In Japan, the excited voices of newsmen crackled over radios: "The war with America has begun!" Throughout the day stations across Japan played military songs, including the inspirational "Battleship March." At dawn on the same day, the Imperial army landed at Kota Bharu on the east coast of the Malay Peninsula, beginning its takeover of Southeast Asia.

The day after Pearl Harbor, President Roosevelt asked Congress to declare war on Japan. Winston Churchill, for one, was relieved. He exclaimed that he was "well content" with the news; the U.S. had been forced to enter a war it had long resisted.

America geared up at a furious pace. Across the country, men by the thousands no longer waited to be drafted. Many did not even know where Pearl Harbor was. They knew, though, that the Japanese had just bombed American soil. The Selective Service cracked down on conscientious objectors, and the attorney general rounded up alleged Axis sympathizers. Meanwhile, President Roosevelt issued his infamous Executive Order 9066: By August anyone who was one-sixteenth Japanese, possessing at least one Japanese grandparent, a total of one hundred twenty thousand people, was interned.

By January 1, 1942, the United States would surpass Germany as the world's largest producer of planes. Thousands of defense plants were being built; shipyards were running around the clock. "America Firsters" who, advocating isolationism, had opposed entry into the war no longer had an ideological leg to stand on. The American public supported strict rationing programs, which included limits on paper, shoes, silk, butter, milk, canned goods, meat, and fuel oil. "Use it up, wear it out, make it do, or do without" was a slogan indicative of the kinds of sacrifices that Americans were willing to make. People cultivated "victory gardens," drove at a "victory speed" of 35 miles per hour to conserve gas, and organized scrap drives with slogans like "Slap the Jap with the Scrap!" "Hit Hitler with the Junk!" Bing Crosby sang a song called "Junk Will Win the War." When the War Production Board (WPB) asked for four million tons of scrap metal to be gathered in two months, people responded with five million tons in three weeks. The WPB organized rubber drives and paper drives. The Farm Security Administration began a program called "An Acre for a Soldier." The profit on that acre was used to buy canteens and other essentials for servicemen. Overnight, apathy had turned into fervent patriotism.

•   •   •

By mid-February 1942, concerns about a Japanese follow-up attack had quieted. The men of the 32nd were back at Camp Livingston preparing to go north to Fort Devens, Massachusetts by special troop train. At this point Churchill, Roosevelt, Curtin, and Marshall had not yet struck their deal to send the 32nd to Australia. The plan was to ship the division to Northern Ireland. In fact, its 107th Engineer

Battalion was already on its way. But only six weeks after arriving at Fort Devens, the 32nd was getting ready to move again. Few of the men knew what was in the works. What they did know was that they were no longer headed for Europe.

Katherine Hobson Bailey, wife of Lieutenant Cladie Bailey, had driven to Fort Devens to see her husband off. Bailey, who had been the executive officer of Jastrzembski, Stenberg, and DiMaggio's G Company, was now its commander.

Earning the respect of the men of Company G had not been easy for Bailey when he reported to Camp Livingston in April 1941. The first strike against him was that he was an ROTC officer. National Guard units were insular groups, made up of men whose friendships often dated back to high school, even grade school; national guardsmen were not very accepting of outsiders, especially new officers. The second strike was that Bailey, an Indianan, was an interloper among the tightly knit Muskegon, Michigan, men. But Bailey quickly earned the admiration of the men of Company G with a unique combination of charisma, humor, and toughness. As an ROTC second lieutenant, he had done a two-year stint in the Civilian Conservation Corps, and it was in the CCC that Bailey learned how to motivate men. The key was to be right there with them, struggling under a heavy pack, doing the work that they did. When other officers enjoyed the privilege of riding in jeeps to training areas, Bailey chose to walk with his men. When the occasion called for it, he could be decidedly un-military. One member of G Company recalls, "he ran a light ship, making weekend camp fun . . . no inspections, no reveille, just fun and card games."

It did not take long for everyone to realize that the company's new lieutenant was a natural. And it did not take them long to give Bailey a nickname. The men of G Company simply called their lieutenant "Gus."

Gus Bailey was a man from humble roots who made the most of his considerable abilities. A farm boy, he was no stranger to the kind of backbreaking labor that characterized rural life during the Depression. The house he grew up in had no electricity or indoor plumbing.

His father, Jim Bailey, was a carpenter who built houses and barns all over the county; his mother, Mamie Bailey, sold eggs and cream, and canned with Cladie's help, but mostly the farm provided just enough for the family, including a once-a-week Sunday chicken supper.

A standout athlete by the time he reached high school, Cladie swapped the hardcourt for the baseball diamond and became a star pitcher on the Indiana University baseball team that won the Big Ten Championship in 1934. Bailey was no ordinary jock, though. While at IU, he developed a love of Robert Service's North Woods ballads.

Poetry wasn't something he tried to hide in the army, either. Later, the guys of G Company learned to look forward to his recitations of Service poems, which Bailey performed with flourish. Bailey was a poker player, too. Once he got to G Company, it was Bailey who instigated the all-night games, which invariably meant late nights and tables decorated with empty beer bottles.

It was during the fall of 1940, while Bailey was still teaching and coaching at Heltonville High School, that he and Katherine Hobson began dating. She was a beautiful redhead and recent graduate of Bedford High School, twelve years Bailey's junior. Given that she was the age of the senior girls strolling the halls of Heltonville High, there might have been some who considered the budding romance improper. If so, Bailey would not have cared a whit. He was as taken with Katherine as she was with him.

What had first caught her eye was Cladie Bailey's (Katherine always called him Clade) looks. Bailey was a handsome, square-jawed man with a field of brownish-blond hair. He was a fashionable dresser who wore white starched shirts and pinstriped suits and liked his shoes well polished. But what Katherine had come to love most about him was not his good looks, which he never let go to his head, but his honesty and kindness. "He was the same," she said. "He never varied in his kindness to people."

Once Bailey left for Camp Livingston in April 1941, Katherine and he continued their romance by mail. Two months later, while he was home on extended leave, they were married. It was a small ceremony, just Cladie and Katherine and two witnesses, Sam Bailey (Cladie's cousin) and his wife Mildred, the couple that had set up Cladie and Katherine's first date. The reverend, a Hobson family friend, performed the ceremony in his little parsonage. Afterward, Cladie and Katherine walked out into the steamy night air and watched the Fourth of July fireworks flash across the sky, joking for a moment that the celebration was staged in their honor.

Shortly after the wedding, Cladie and Katherine Bailey set off together for Camp Livingston. In the fall of 1941, Katherine joined Bailey at Fort Benning, Georgia, where he was doing a three-month advanced training stint. Bailey's schedule even allowed the young lovers to take weekend trips. After Fort Benning, Bailey returned to Camp Livingston and Katherine followed. Then in the winter of 1942, she traveled north by car to Massachusetts.

When she arrived on base, she drove out to where Company G was marching. When Bailey saw her car, he halted the men and ran over to welcome his wife. The men waited in the cold as Katherine and Bailey embraced through the open car window—then Bailey double-timed it back to the company.

In Massachusetts, the Baileys rented a small one-room apartment in the town of Ayer near Fort Devens. It was a happy time for Katherine; she was in love, and she was pregnant. In early April, though, the inevitable finally came.

•   •   •

When Zelma Boice came to see her husband off, she presented him with a small black diary. William "Jim" Boice loved literature and was the proud owner of a collection of first-edition novels. It was one of the traits that Zelma admired most about this thoughtful, reflective man. She was his opposite—spirited, quick to act and speak. Their marriage had yielded one child—Billy Jr.—and she and her son made the same trips that Katherine Bailey did from Louisiana to Georgia, back to Louisiana again, and north to Massachusetts.

Zelma's independence and self-reliance had caught Boice's eye. In Swayzee, Indiana, a small town located in the flat farm country north of Indianapolis, he had been dating her sister when Zelma and a beau joined them on a double date. It quickly became apparent to Boice that he was with the wrong woman. Though Boice would never be described as impulsive, it didn't take him long to correct his mistake.

Boice knew, too, that back in Swayzee, Zelma and Billy would be well cared for. Zelma would continue to teach third grade, and on weekends she and Billy would go out to the farm where Zelma's parents still lived.

Billy Boice, just two, stood watching his parents say good-bye, too young to understand the psychological burden his father carried. As a boy who had hardly known his own father—Boice's father was a glass blower who had died young of black lung—Captain Jim Boice was determined to be a loving presence for his own son. The war changed all that.

•   •   •

Major Herbert Smith had been transferred from the 128th to the 126th and was acting as the 2nd Battalion's XO (Executive Officer). He was too busy for teary good-byes; besides, his wife Dorothy and their son Jerry had spent a week at Fort Devens in March. He had discouraged their visit, but Dorothy had a mind of her own, and she and Jerry came by train despite Smith's objections.

For a week, Jerry followed his father wherever he went and was especially happy when his father took him to see the guys in the 128th, Smith's old unit. These were men whom Jerry knew from home in Neillsville, Wisconsin, and Louisiana. When the week came to an end and it was time for Jerry and Dorothy to return to Wisconsin, Jerry, according to his father, was "heartbroken."

Smith himself felt a sense of relief when Jerry and his mother departed. He had to get back to his new regiment. The transition from the 128th to the 126th was not an easy one for him. After having spent his entire military career in the 128th since enlisting in the Wisconsin State Guard in 1919 at the age of sixteen, Smith was faced with having to try to win the loyalty and respect of a bunch of guys he did not know. Truth was, he was lucky to be in the army at all. Smith was a tall (six foot three), raw-boned man with black hair and hollow cheeks. While at Camp Beauregard, he flunked his physical because he did not meet the army's weight requirement. The regimental surgeon granted him a six-month waiver, and Smith was literally told to eat to save his military career.

The 126th, though, was his biggest challenge to date. It was a Michigan outfit, and Smith hailed from Wisconsin, on the other side of Lake Michigan. He was not averse to proving himself. Back home in Neillsville, Wisconsin, the Badger State Telephone and Telegraph was a family-owned business, and Smith was the boss's kid. His father rode him hard, too. The elder Smith expected his son to earn the front office by digging postholes, setting poles, trimming trees, and stringing wire and cable with the line crew.

Now he would have to prove himself again. The junior officers and the grunts were watching closely to see if he was up to the task.

Two things they did know was that Smith was a stutterer, and he had a volatile temper. The guys mocked him behind his back.

"Look out for St-St-St-St-Stutterin' Smith. He'll ch-ch-ch-chew your ass right out."

According to Erwin Veneklase, "when Smith was really mad, the stutter completely disappeared." The guys of the 126th learned to listen for the stutter as a kind of barometer of Smith's mood. Nobody wanted to be dressed down by "Stutterin'" Smith.

•   •   •

On April 7, Colonel Lawrence Quinn, the popular commanding officer of the 126th Infantry, tried to impress upon his men the importance of their mission.

"Our path will not be smooth," he said. "We have much to do in the way of training to attain the goal we have set for ourselves—a rugged, powerful, hard-hitting, fast-maneuvering infantry team . . . But what we lack in perfection we more than make up for in espirit de corps . . . Our destination is secret; and, except for curiosity, is unimportant. What *is* important, however, is the fact that we are on our way to meet the enemy. War is a grim business. It is a killer business . . . Should you experience difficulty developing this desire to kill, you have but to recall what we are fighting for—our homes, our loved ones, our freedom, the right to live as we please."

On April 8 at 5:40 a.m., thirteen freight trains and twenty-five passenger trains departed Fort Devens. The railroad yard, according to one of General Edwin Forrest Harding's staff officers, was a "madhouse." Harding, the 32nd Division's new commander, and most of his staff had left for San Francisco almost two weeks earlier. They would be waiting when the men arrived.

Despite Colonel Quinn's stirring speech, when the train rolled west, few of the men felt the impending doom of battle. The bombing of Pearl Harbor was four months old, and the Japanese had not followed up with other attacks on the American mainland. The men were being shipped off to war—they knew that—but how that war would manifest itself was impossible for them to imagine. As they boarded the train, they shot the bull and joked as if the train ride were just another chance to play cards, pull practical jokes, and see the sights.

Outside of a small cadre of officers, no one knew where the trains were headed. They traveled west via Albany and Buffalo and reached Chicago twenty-four hours later. In Chicago, they stopped so repairs could be made to one of the locomotives. It would be a while before they were moving again, so the men were allowed to disembark to stretch their legs.

They were all curious—just where in the hell were they headed? That's when a sergeant recognized a relative in the train yard. He slipped by the guards at the depot platform who had been posted there to stop the soldiers, for security reasons, from talking to anyone and said, "C'mon, give me the skinny."

As the train headed for Kansas City, the word circulated among the troops.

"Oakland," Jastrzembski heard one of the guys say. "We're headed for goddamn Oakland. I wonder what that means? One thing's for sure, we ain't going to Europe to fight the Krauts."

In Oklahoma, the train stopped and the men took a half-mile run. By noon, it was bound for Clovis in the flat grasslands of eastern New Mexico. En route, Captain Medendorp gave a lecture on Japanese weapons.

Afterward the guys got together in small groups. "That's it. Now it's for sure. It's the Nips; we're going to fight the Nips. Those sons-a-bitches."

If the men were headed to "fight the Nips," no one was in a hurry to get them there. The route to Oakland via the desert Southwest was a puzzling one to say the least. In Winslow and Seligman, Arizona, they disembarked and were ordered to run again. Then there was the train itself; the farther west it got, the slower it traveled. Inexplicably, it was given low-priority status and lost "rail rights" to trains hauling freight.

As far as Simon Warmenhoven was concerned, the train could crawl to the coast. The farther he got from Michigan, the farther he was from Mandy and his daughters. Besides, he loved the West's wild country, the canyons, and the Painted Desert. At one of the Arizona stops, he bought his two daughters each an Indian doll and his wife a Navajo purse. Like some of the other officers, Warmenhoven was lucky enough to be on one of the passenger trains, traveling in style. He ate well, was assigned a sleeping car, and even had stewards to turn down his bed. It sure beat the way he used to get cross-country. In college, he made his way from Sunnyside, Washington, to Grand Rapids, Michigan, on filthy sheep trains. For a free ride, he watered the sheep at stops and herded them back onto the cars.

Gus Bailey also enjoyed the trip. It allowed him and the guys of Company G ample time to do what Bailey loved best—play cards. It also gave him a chance to see the sights. Like many of the Wisconsin, Michigan, and Indiana men of the division, Bailey had never been west. He was awed by the wide-open expanses of the high plains, by the snow-packed mountain passes of New Mexico, and eventually by the ocean. When the train arrived at the Oakland, California, pier on April 13, Bailey took time out from his duties to write Katherine a letter.

"I've made up my mind, " he wrote, "that when I get back we will spend two or three months in this part of the country. You and I and the little one. I hope to God this is over soon so that we may be able to start where we left off, and with a little more to make life happier for us. I am now looking forward to the day when I get off that boat for home and, wherever it is, I want you to be there to meet me."

Chapter 3

Arrival Down Under

WHILE WAITING TO be deployed, a portion of the division stayed at Fort Ord and the Dog Track Pavilion while the rest of the men were put up at a large convention center and rodeo venue called the Cow Palace in San Francisco. According to Stutterin' Smith, the Cow Palace was a miserable, concrete "monolith" as cold and "drafty as the North Pole," and the men hated it. They were forced to sleep draped over stadium chairs and in horse stalls that reeked of manure. But the stopover was essential. Before shipping the division overseas, the army needed to take care of some last-minute business, including issuing extra uniforms, M-1 rifles, new helmets, and modern howitzers to replace the World War I artillery that the division had been using for two decades.

Before shipping out, lots of the men took advantage of San Francisco. The sightseers climbed Telegraph Hill and admired the Golden Gate Bridge. Most, though, just wanted to have a good time. That meant beer and women in Barbary Coast saloons or Chinatown. If they were going off to war, they were going to have one hell of a party first.

Simon Warmenhoven had just been promoted to major, and he was in the mood to celebrate, too. Instead of going with the other men, he sent Mandy a telegram, announcing the promotion, and then wrote her a letter.

Dearest Lover:

I looked at your picture so long last night—Anyway, I had a dream about you . . . I saw you just as plain as if you were standing in front of me, you wore a black dress with white trimming around the collar and your pretty blond hair . . . I didn't even get to kiss you tho . . . Oh, Mandy darling, I miss you so, so much . . . I'd just give anything to to be with you . . . to feel your warm lips on mine. I hate to think how long it is going to be before I'll be able to do that again . . . Before closing—Dearest Lover . . . again let me tell you, I <u>love</u> you so very, very much . . . It'll be like being married again when I see you . . . My love to the girls—and the grandest wife and most thrilling lover.

Lovingly, Yours Always, Sam

       •   •   •

On April 19 the 32nd Division, filled out with over three thousand "selectees," mostly privates fresh from basic training, crammed into seven Matson Line cruise ships, that had been semi-converted to troop carriers. At 5:30 p.m. three days later, the overloaded vessels pulled anchor, escorted by two corvettes and the cruiser *Indianapolis*.

When the 32nd left Fort Mason's wharves, it enjoyed the distinction of being the first American division in World War II to be moved in a single convoy. As the California coastline receded, though, the men had no sense of their place in history.

The ships steamed by Alcatraz, and the men joked that they would gladly trade places with any of its prisoners. When they reached the Presidio they heckled the "soft" garrison soldiers who were staying behind to guard the coast and enjoy the niceties of civilization. With the Golden Gate Bridge in sight, Stanley Jastrzembski grew nostalgic. There was no turning back now. Secretly some of the guys hoped that the transports' smokestacks would not clear the bridge. When they did, Jastrzembski watched the city disappear in the distance. Already he was dreaming of his return home.

No one seemed to have any definite answers about where they were going. Rumors swirled through the ships: Hawaii, some said; others were convinced it was Alaska, or the Far East, New Zealand, India, Fiji, or maybe Australia. Stutterin' Smith, now the 2nd Battalion's executive officer, had slipped a map into his duffel prior to leaving California. Using his compass, he plotted the ship's course—Hawaii first, and then an abrupt turn to the southwest. Smith ventured an educated guess: Australia. Not long after, Division Headquarters confirmed his assumption.

They were at sea for three weeks. By the hundreds, men unaccustomed to the pitch and roll of a ship at sea fell ill and spent much of their time leaning over the ship's rail.

"It's mind over matter, boys," Captain Medendorp asserted as he walked the deck.

It was not the thing to tell a bunch of seasick men. Days later when Medendorp's stomach began to roil and he, too, was standing at the rail retching, many felt that he had received his just reward.

The ships were filled far beyond capacity, and the men had to endure long lines everywhere they went—to the dining room, the showers, the latrines. At night, they bedded down wherever they could. Most slept in "standees," pipe frame bunks piled four or five high in converted staterooms, parlors, party rooms, and the ballroom. According to Carl Stenberg, the ballroom was dubbed "Stinking Sock Alley." Those who had it worst, though, slept on sheets of plywood in the bowels of the ship. As the convoy approached the equator, men vied for space on the deck to avoid the stifling heat.

The officers, though, enjoyed a bit of pampering. They slept two men to a stateroom, dined at tables set with fine china and silverware, and were treated to sumptuous meals because the ship's food locker was still full of fare that would normally be reserved for its paying civilians.

Although officers held mandatory orientation courses emphasizing Australia's people and customs and staged battalion conferences, the men still had lots of time to fill. They spent their days doing calisthenics, walking around the ship's crowded deck, writing letters home, singing, and watching the sea. The novelty of flying fish, ocean-wandering albatross, gliding hundreds of miles from land, and moon-lit nights did not last, however. The "Abandon Ship" drills and fire drills and the "Order of Neptune" ceremony, performed when the division crossed the equator, provided some excitement. But it was the poker games—instigated in some cases by Gus Bailey—and the craps games that did the most for the men's spirits.

For General Edwin Forrest Harding's staff, it was get-acquainted time, and they liked what they saw. The division's new commander had an agile mind. He could quote T. S. Eliot or Tennyson or Kipling, or discuss astronomy and history like an Ivy League professor. But he did not put on airs. He had sparkling eyes and a midwesterner's common touch. And there was no one who understood the modern military better than he.

Harding had written the book on it. When George C. Marshall went to Fort Benning to become the school's assistant commandant entrusted with updating the army, he brought his friend Forrest Harding with him as an instructor and put Harding in charge of Benning's influential Infantry School publications. In 1934, Harding edited *Infantry in Battle*, which disseminated across the world the school's new ideas on modern military strategies. The triangular division was one of those ideas, and no one understood its simple genius better than Harding did. Unlike the square division of World War I, which was designed for attrition warfare, the smaller triangular division, consisting of three regimental combat teams and a simplified command structure, emphasized agility, adaptability, and a lower casualty rate.

On May 7, the convoy crossed the International Date Line, and eight days later the ships docked at Port Adelaide in South Australia in the early afternoon. The 32nd Division had traveled 8,500 miles in twenty-one days.

Throngs of Australians turned out to greet the division. As the men walked down the gangplank, they received a hero's welcome that rivaled MacArthur's. Some of the men expected "to be met at a primitive wharf by aborigine porters on kangaroos." What they got instead were young Australian women who swooned at the handsome American GIs.

"I could get used to this awful quick," Willie La Venture said, winking to his best buddy Stan Jastrzembski. La Venture and Jastrzembski had been through a lot together, but they had never seen anything like this reception. They had not even fired a shot in defense of Australia, and already they were being celebrated as heroes. According to Jastrzembski, "Young women were throwing flowers, blowing kisses, waving handkerchiefs, and crying."

The adoration was short-lived. Officers herded the men onto trains as swiftly as they could, and shortly after six that evening the division was bound for one of two camps outside of Adelaide—the 126th went to Camp Sandy Creek, and the 127th and 128th went to Camp Woodside, thirty miles from Sandy Creek. Two hours after leaving Adelaide, the battalions arrived at the appointed camps in the dark of the night without lights to guide them. Both Sandy Creek and Woodside were under strict blackout orders.

"Damn, it's cold," Jastrzembski said, stepping off the train. "It's like winter. I thought Australia was supposed to be warm."

"Where are the beaches and the girls?" someone asked.

"They're here, all right," another guy said. "The army's gonna surprise us."

The following morning they were not joking around. Camp, they discovered, was a bunch of tin warehouses and huts with canvas roofs and no insulation. Their beds were nothing more than burlap bags filled with straw.

The various units spent the next week getting settled. They worked fast because company commanders were eager to get them on their feet again. After three weeks at sea, the men had grown soft, and because of the seasickness, many had also lost weight.

By late May, the division began its "toughening up" anew in South Australia's gently rolling farm country. "Toughening up," at least initially, meant basic, no-frills road marches. Eventually, as the men regained their strength, they performed scouting, field, and patrolling exercises, and put in lots of hours at the rifle range.

Like many of the men of the 32nd, Stanley Jastrzembski was dumbfounded to find himself in Australia. Jastrzembski was twelve years old before he ever even left Michigan. He was a small kid but wiry and athletic and did the high jump and broad jump for the Polish Falcons of the National Polish Alliance. When the Falcons were invited to LaPorte, Indiana, for a regional track meet, Jastrzembski accompanied the team. Although he won two medals in LaPorte, he will always remember that trip for another reason: The Muskegon team stayed in a hotel. There, Jastrzembski took a bath in a real bathtub for the first time in his life.

Although the division was being prepared for battle, the men felt more like wide-eyed sightseers on a tour of "Down Under." Adelaide had a powerful draw on them. A city of roughly a million people, it offered abundant entertainment. According to Stutterin' Smith, who was no puritan, soldiers quickly learned to indulge in the "Aussie penchant for having a good time." The men learned to "Give 'er a go" Australian style, whether they were drinking flat Aussie beer or chasing Aussie women. The Americans were well paid—they would be awarded 30 percent raises when they went overseas—especially in comparison to their Australian counterparts, and they "spent with abandon on food, drink, and girls."

Prostitution was legal in Australia, and in May 1942, venereal disease became a serious problem for the 32nd Division. These were pre-penicillin days. Warmenhoven had to hospitalize soldiers for thirty days even for cases of gonorrhea. With the help of local public health officials and the police, however, division medical officers set up prophylactic stations across the cities and towns frequented by the troops.

Warmenhoven clearly had his hands full, but he still found time to write Mandy.

Tuesday Nite 8:00 PM.
June 2, 1942

Dearest Lover:

Before I forget to mention it, from now on, send all your letters air mail . . . seems that if you send it air mail, it is then taken across the ocean by these bomber planes . . . I'd sure feel so much better after hearing from you . . . that old heart starts aching for news from the loved ones way back in the States . . . I keep wondering about you all. I suppose Ann is quite a walker by now, isn't she? I remember so distinctly when Muriel first began to walk, how after she got into it, how she used to run all the time up and down the rooms, then every once in awhile she'd take a nice spill on the slippery floor in the kitchen . . . I suppose pretty soon you'll be going to the cottage. Sure would love to spend a weekend with you out there, lover—so many sweet and fond memories are contained in the cottage . . . I suppose that you've read all about the big air raid over Germany by 1000 bombers . . . Well, those Germans certainly have it coming to them. Don't feel sorry for them at all . . . isn't it awful the way they are murdering those poor Czech families because of the attempted murder on that 'butcher' Heydrich . . . if the Russians can keep up their present tempo, and a few more such air raids over Germany, I then think that Germany won't last long anymore. Then they can all concentrate on Japan and that phase of it will be simple enough. Sure hope I don't have to stay out here too long.

    Yours Forever, Sam

———————————

Six days later, he wrote again:

Monday 4:30 PM.
June 8, 1942

To My "One and Only"

    My first letter from home . . . to-day. I've read it over and over and almost know it by heart. This certainly was quite a letter, honey. And so my Mandy is going to have another little "Warmy" . . . I sure was thrilled to read about it sweetheart,

altho I must honestly say, not surprised. Remember the last
time I examined you, I think that was around March 20 . . . I
hoped then that you would be pregnant—I didn't like to say
anything about it then because I just had a premonition that
after I would leave you there, I wouldn't be seeing you again
for a long time . . . Well Darling . . . I'd sure be tickled to have
a son . . . The thing that makes me feel bad is not being home
with you to watch them grow up . . . I'll bet when I get home
he'll say, "Momma, who's that man?"

There's a lot of things I could write about . . . if I were sure
that you were the only one reading them; So many places
you'll have to read between the lines . . . so much I'd like to tell
you . . . whatever may happen to either one of us, always
know this my darling, I've always most sincerely and most
deeply loved you . . . I'll be so anxious to hear from you all the
time now, darling—I'll be praying for you. Give Muriel and
Ann a hug and a kiss for me—and Mandy, darling—all your
Warmy's heart's true love . . .

Forever yours, Sam

The soldiers that Warmenhoven treated could hardly be blamed for
their casual attitude about their training. They were doing what came
naturally to young men: They were living day-to-day, making the best
of a situation over which they had no control. War might be just
around the corner, but they would deal with that when the time came.

Had they been privy to the intelligence that showed that Japan
coveted the island of New Guinea, they might have reacted differently.
As early as May 19, as the regiments were settling into Camps Sandy
Creek and Woodside, ULTRA, the name for the Allied code-breaking
system that had cracked Japanese and German wireless codes,
revealed that the Japanese army planned to attack Port Moresby via a
mountain route from the north coast.

On June 9, when Allied Intelligence again notified MacArthur that
the Japanese were contemplating an invasion of New Guinea's Papuan
Peninsula, he alerted General Blamey, his Commander of Allied Land

Forces. "There is increasing evidence," he wrote, "that the Japanese are displaying interest in the development of a route from Buna on the north coast of southern New Guinea through Kokoda to Port Moresby. From studies made in this headquarters it appears that minor forces may attempt to utilize this route . . ."

Blamey directed MacArthur's inquiry to Major General Basil Morris, who at the time was commander of New Guinea Force and also head of ANGAU (Australia New Guinea Administrative Unit), the military government that ran New Guinea after Japanese planes bombed Port Moresby. Morris replied that there were ANGAU officers, native constables, two Papuan Infantry Battalions (a unit made up of natives), and a company from the Australian Infantry Battalion patrolling the area around Kokoda.

Blamey followed up with another message instructing Morris "to take all necessary steps to prevent a Japanese surprise landing along the coast, north and south of Buna, to deny the enemy the grasslands in that area for an airdrome, and to assure that we command the pass at Kokoda."

Morris replied, "Re the Japs, I don't think you need to worry about them. It is not likely they will want to commit suicide just yet."

Despite Morris' assurances, MacArthur was concerned. The Allies had just finalized their own plans for seizing New Guinea. Operation Cartwheel called for a powerful two-pronged attack by MacArthur's ground forces and the U.S. Pacific Fleet. MacArthur's troops would sweep through New Guinea by land while the navy moved up through the Solomon Islands by sea. Operation Providence stipulated that Australian troops and American engineers would march over the Kokoda track to Buna and prepare the area for the arrival of a main Allied landing force, which was to make the trip from Port Moresby. That force would travel around the tail of the Papuan Peninsula and then north up the coast in a series of small coastal steamers. The main body was to arrive in mid-August and prepare Buna for antiaircraft defense and begin construction of a large airbase at Dobodura, fifteen miles inland.

The resounding booms to the north on the evening of July 21 puzzled Captain Sam Templeton. A thunderstorm? How could it be? The sky was a cloudless blue.

Templeton had no time to investigate. After receiving a directive from Allied Headquarters in Brisbane, General Morris had ordered him and a company of Australian militiamen to cross the mountains via the Kokoda track and defend the Kokoda airfield from a possible Japanese invasion. On July 21, they picked up twenty tons of supplies at Buna, including machine guns, and with the help of native carriers were transporting those supplies back to Kokoda.

As Templeton and his party made their way toward Kokoda, one of his sergeants was urgently trying to relay a message: "A Japanese warship," he said, "is shelling Buna . . . to cover a landing at Gona or Sanananda. Acknowledge, Moresby. Over . . ."

Despite sending out repeated warnings, the sergeant received no reply. In the meantime, three coastwatchers forty miles northwest of Buna picked up the message and relayed it to Port Moresby.

The following day, Templeton learned what had happened from native constables who had witnessed the shelling and had traveled all night to Awala, where the track begins its climb to Kokoda.

The Japanese landing terrified the natives. Arthur Duna, a Buna villager, described the scene:

As if you had a dreamlike spirit chasing you and you want to run; [but] you cannot run and the spirit catches you. It was just like that. There was a great panic. That afternoon you have to run away from where you were at the time of Japan landing. There was not time to go to your village to gather your family or collect your valuable belongings. Wife ran naked without her husband and children. Husband ran naked without wife and children. A child ran without his parents and even if he was with his small ones, he deserted them. All ran in different directions into the bush. All ran like rats and bandicoots in the kunai grass. The night fell and each individual slept either in the grass or under trees. The soil was your bed and the rotten logs your pillow. You go to sleep wherever you happened to run into.

The Japanese invasion force made camp east of Basabua at 3:30 a.m. on July 22. By 6:00 a.m. on July 23, the men were moving again, eager to reach what they thought was a road running from Buna to Kokoda. After taking a wrong turn, the force did not arrive at Buna until fifteen hours later.

Led by Colonel Yosuke Yokoyama, the invasion force was made up of elite soldiers who had fought in Shanghai in 1937, Guam in December 1941, and Rabaul in early 1942, and nine hundred men of the Tsukamoto Battalion, under the command of Lieutenant Colonel Hatsuo Tsukamoto, part of the superbly trained 144th Infantry Regiment.

The 144th was assembled in Kochi City, a country town situated in the verdant hills at the mouth of the Niyodo River on the island of Shikoku. Its members were hardened, enthusiastic volunteers, the sons of farmers and tradesmen.

Rounding out the force were soldiers from the 15th Independent Engineers Regiment, who doubled as combat infantry; mountain and antiaircraft artillery units; a force of highly skilled naval shock troops; one hundred Formosan troops, praised for their fearlessness and endurance; fifty-two horses; and twelve hundred native conscripts from Rabaul.

Yokoyama's orders came directly from Japan's South Seas headquarters in Rabaul. Initially his mission was to reconnoiter the presumed "road" running from Buna to Kokoda and Kokoda south to Port Moresby, and to put the first portion in a condition to handle vehicles, packhorses, and bicycles. However, by the time he departed Rabaul on July 19, that mission had changed. Yokoyama's men were now considered an invasion force.

Leading the advance guard of the invasion force was Colonel Tsukamoto, a "thundering old man" with a great affection for sake. On the afternoon of July 24, he was at the head of a long line of men bound for the government station of Kokoda. Kokoda was an outpost with huts, native gardens, a school, and a small hospital, situated on a plateau in the northern foothills of the Owen Stanley Mountains. Kokoda also possessed a strategically important airfield.

Seizo Okada, a war correspondent assigned to the invasion, described the march inland. "The unit continued to walk with single-mindedness . . . Each man is required to carry provisions for thirteen days in his backpack, comprising 18 litres of rice, a pistol, ammunition, hand grenades, a spoon, first aid kit . . ."

A patrol of scouts from the Tsukamoto Battalion traveled lightly and even faster than the rest of the battalion. Its objective was "to push on night and day" to Port Moresby.

While the Japanese soldiers marched on Kokoda, engineers remained behind to solidify Japan's hold on the north coast. They built an airfield and fortified the beachhead with antiaircraft guns and a system of reinforced and interlinked bunkers. Some of the engineers also constructed a palm log road from Buna to the inland village of Soputa; the Japanese plan was to build a vehicle base and radio station there. Clearly, they were still under the illusion that the Kokoda track was navigable.

Yokoyama's engineers toiled tirelessly in torrential rains. When trucks stalled in channels of thigh-deep mud, soldiers were turned into pack mules. They worked around the clock carrying supplies from the coast. Sleep was a luxury, and when they did rest, they did so in riverbeds, where they risked being swept away during flash floods. "Our duty to reach the front line," one Japanese engineer wrote, "would not let us rest for one moment."

They completed the Buna-Soputa passage in just three days. It was an incredible achievement, though it received little recognition. The Japanese soldier was expected to endure misery, fatigue, hunger, and disease.

•   •   •

The Japanese had beaten MacArthur to the punch, but even as they stormed ashore, MacArthur and his advisors dismissed the invasion as a minor threat. Brigadier General Charles Willoughby, MacArthur's head of intelligence, clung to the notion that the Japanese would penetrate inland only as far as they needed to build airfields. The airfields, Willoughby argued, would allow Japanese pilots to attack Port Moresby and the Cape York Peninsula of Australia, and could support a possible seaborne invasion of Port Moresby and Milne Bay. But a major land assault on Port Moresby was inconceivable.

Ten days after Yokoyama landed at Basabua, General Marshall contacted MacArthur. Keeping Port Moresby in Allied hands and re-establishing Allied control over Papua's north coast, he insisted, was of paramount importance. MacArthur reassured Marshall that he was doing everything in his power to secure New Guinea.

MacArthur had just ordered two Australian Infantry Division (AIF) brigades to Port Moresby. Comprised of seasoned soldiers, the brigades had returned from the Middle East in late March 1942. Upon arriving in Australia, however, most of the soldiers were sent to Queensland to perform menial labor, finishing airfields and fortifying the coastline, thus forfeiting valuable training time, so when they arrived in Port Moresby in mid-August, they lacked the skills for jungle fighting. They had the wrong equipment, too. For example, instead of jungle green, they wore bright khaki-colored battle gear; instead of pants to keep away the mosquitoes, leeches, and chiggers, they had knee-length shorts similar to the ones they wore in the deserts of North Africa. And in a land where every additional pound was a burden, they carried too much weight in their fieldpacks.

MacArthur was not ready to send in the 32nd yet. As Colonels Yokoyama and Tsukamoto marched inland, the American division was thousands of miles from New Guinea, traveling by train from South Australia to a tent encampment called Camp Tamborine. Situated in semi-tropical country thirty miles south of Brisbane, Camp Tamborine was fifteen hundred miles north of Adelaide. Rather than launching into jungle training exercises the moment they arrived at Tamborine, the troops had to build the camp from scratch. Soldiers who should have been learning to patrol and to maneuver at night were forced to cut down and clear trees and dig latrines.

It was weeks before the division was able to drill again. Watching the Red Arrow men, Harding remembered that General Marshall had counseled him against taking over the division. The 32nd, Marshall said, was poorly trained and rife with Midwestern small-town politics, enmities, and allegiances. At the time, Harding thanked his old friend for the advice and accepted the division anyway. The chance at his first field command was too attractive to resist.

As soon as he was able, Harding implemented a live-fire infiltration course called the Sergeant York and set up commando, sniper, and tommy gun schools. One of his most capable instructors was a man named Herman Bottcher.

Bottcher was not new to Australia. Though German-born, Bottcher left his native country at the age of 20, bound for Sydney, Australia, in May 1929. As he roamed the city looking for employment, he studied a German-English dictionary. Eventually he found a job as a carpenter on a sheep station in New South Wales. While there he saved his money and nursed a dream of coming to America. In November 1931, when he landed in San Francisco, that dream became a reality.

With sixty dollars in his pocket, he took a room at a hotel on Third Street and searched for work. Jobs were few, so he traveled south to San Diego. Nine months later he had saved enough money to get back to San Francisco, where he took a job in San Francisco's Crystal Palace markets and attended classes at night at San Francisco State College. Four years later, he was off again, lured to Spain by the Civil War, where he enlisted with the International Brigade. He spent two years fighting with the Loyalists, rose to the rank of captain, and was twice wounded. Attempting to re-enter the United States, he was detained by Immigration officials at Ellis Island. After questioning him about his political affiliations, Immigration eventually let him go. Bottcher returned to San Francisco, where he worked as a cabinetmaker. The day after the Japanese struck Pearl Harbor, Bottcher enlisted, and less than a month later he reported to Camp Roberts, California.

• • •

No one would have known from watching the 32nd that MacArthur was preparing to transport it to New Guinea. The majority of the division's training consisted of twenty-five-mile marches through the modest terrain of the Mount Tamborine area; field exercises, where men lived in tents and ate from mess kits; compass and first aid courses; and pulling sentry duty along the coastal beaches. The kinds of small-unit activities that worked in the jungle were not stressed. Harding understood their importance, but how could he teach sudden attacks and withdrawals, infiltrations of the perimeter, and night assaults when the division was lacking in basic field skills and conditioning?

Although the 32nd had earned high marks in the Louisiana Maneuvers, since then it had been on the move—Louisiana to Fort Devens to San Francisco to South Australia and now Camp Tamborine. In twenty months it had participated in only a few night training exercises. The men knew little of stream, swamp, or river crossings. They understood nothing about living and fighting in the jungle, or the effects of extreme humidity on the maintenance of weapons. And they had almost no practice with live fire. Nevertheless, many of the soldiers were under the illusion that they were "tough as nails" and ready to do battle with the Japanese.

In contrast, the Japanese trained for war in what military historian Geoffrey Perret calls "tropical dystopias." During the 1930s, the Japanese Imperial army sent recruits to the rugged island of Formosa. The training there was intense, rigorous, and designed to inure soldiers to suffering. In the process, the Japanese army learned some very basic lessons: Do not overburden soldiers; provide them with light weapons and light loads; give every soldier a headband to absorb sweat that would otherwise pour into his eyes; do not confine troops' movements to trails; and use the jungle and the element of surprise to outwit and outmaneuver the enemy.

The Imperial army also simulated island landings. Crammed into the holds of ships, soldiers were deprived of water and forced to endure unbearable heat. Then they were dumped onto beaches under combat conditions. Meanwhile, Japanese engineers developed barges with innovative bow ramps that could carry and quickly discharge men and even light tanks. By late in the war, the barges were already obsolete; but early on, the innovation afforded the Japanese forces a technological advantage over the U.S. Army.

. . .

The thirty men whom Templeton had sent back to investigate the Japanese landing first sighted Tsukamoto's scouts a few miles from Awala, well inland from where the Japanese had disembarked—they were clearly moving fast. The bayonet blades of their long-barreled .25 caliber Arisaka rifles and Type 38 bolt-action rifles gleamed brightly in the glare of the tropical sun.

Templeton's platoon fell back to the village of Wairopi on the Kumusi River. At 9:00 a.m. the following morning, the platoon received a message from Templeton instructing it to retreat to Oivi. Ten of the men remained at Wairopi. They cut the cables of the wire-rope bridge that spanned the river, sending it tumbling into the current. Then they lay in wait for Tsukamoto's scouts.

The Kumusi roared through a deep gorge en route to the coast, but Tsukamoto's scouts were superbly conditioned men. Upon encountering the sixty-foot-wide river and the remnants of the bridge, they plunged into the current and fell into the Australian ambush. Templeton's men killed fifteen Japanese. The scouts kept coming, though, and eventually the small Australian force fled.

Back in Port Moresby, General Morris, despite his earlier insouciance, was scrambling to get enough troops to Kokoda to stop the Japanese short of the village and its airstrip. Four of his companies, however, were still south of the mountains. Even if they had been able to walk round the clock, it would have taken them days to make Kokoda. Aware that he could not get the battalion there in time, Morris chose instead to fly in the battalion's capable commander, Lieutenant Colonel William T. Owen. Owen assessed the situation and made a rash decision: He would torch Kokoda, leaving little for the Japanese.

The following day, Owen recognized his mistake: He was handing Kokoda and its vital airfield to the Japanese without a fight. Owen returned to Kokoda with a scanty force and waited among the burned remnants of what had once been a flourishing village. Smoke rose from the charred buildings, creating a ghostly impression in the misty morning light.

At 2:00 a.m. on July 29, with wispy clouds veiling a fat moon, four hundred of Tsukamoto's men plunged into the jungle void. Screaming like wild animals, they scaled a nearly vertical hill and stormed the Australian stronghold.

In the chaos of the battle, Owen was shot. The battalion medical officer and a number of stretcher bearers rushed to his side, but a bullet had lodged in Owen's head and brain tissue oozed out of the wound. Owen had survived the bloody January 1942 Japanese invasion of the island of Rabaul only to fall dead to a sniper's bullet in the first large-scale battle on the New Guinea mainland.

When the generals at GHQ in Brisbane learned of the loss of the Kokoda airfield, they insisted that the airstrip be recaptured. On August 8, Australian forces attacked, catching Tsukamoto's surprised troops off guard. By afternoon, Kokoda was back in Australian hands.

For two and a half days, Tsukamoto's men threw themselves at the Australians. Second Lieutenant Hirano, a platoon leader in Tsukamoto's battalion, was unnerved by the fierceness of the Australian defense. "Every day I am losing men," he lamented. "I could not repress tears of bitterness."

On the evening of August 10, as a heavy fog fell over the yawning Mambare River, Tsukamoto's forces sprang out of their trenches and rushed the Australians. "The stirring and dauntless charge," wrote Hirano in his diary, "is the tradition of our Army and no enemy can withstand such an attack." He was right: The Japanese soldiers overwhelmed the Australians.

The following day, what should have been a celebration turned into a dour ritual. Though the Japanese were again in possession of Kokoda, they were forced to gather up their dead. Lieutenant Hirano found time to make an entry in his diary. "The bloody fighting in the rain during the last few days seems like a nightmare," he wrote. Then regaining his defiance, he added, "I swore to the souls of the warriors who died that I would carry on their aspirations." The next morning, he wrote in a more sentimental vein, "The day was beautiful, and the birds sang gaily. It was like spring."

Six days later, on August 18, 1942, with Colonel Tsukamoto in possession of Kokoda, the main body of Japan's famous Nankai Shitai (South Seas Detachment), including its commander, Major General Tomitaro Horii, landed at Basabua, right under the nose of unsuspecting Allied air units.

Chapter 4

SONS OF HEAVEN

MAJOR GENERAL TOMITARO HORII was a tiny, bold man with a flair for the dramatic—he liked to ride into battle on a white steed with a sword hanging from his side. But his instructions in New Guinea were straightforward: to march on Port Moresby as swiftly as possible, employing battle-tested Japanese field tactics of surprise, encirclement, and night attacks. Horii had already proved himself during the invasion of Rabaul, which he had commanded. Though he had misgivings about the mission on New Guinea's mainland, as a Japanese officer he was prepared to obey his orders absolutely.

Although the Japanese succeeded in landing the main body of the Nankai Shitai, two battalions of the 144th Infantry, two artillery companies, crack naval landing troops, and a huge support force, they were not yet finished sending troops to New Guinea. A day after Horii's men arrived at Basabua, another regiment left Rabaul bound for the Buna coast. Like the Nankai Shitai, the 15th Independent Engineers and the Tsukamoto Battalion that preceded it, the Yazawa Detachment, under the command of Colonel Kiyomi Yazawa, was a veteran fighting force.

Again, the Japanese navy's luck held. The convoy that carried the Yazawa Detachment reached Basabua under cloud cover on August 21, bringing Japan's troop count to a total of eight thousand army troops, three thousand naval construction troops, and 450 troops from the Sasebo 5th Special Naval Landing Force.

These were not the "minor forces" Allied intelligence had predicted. Still, Willoughby persisted in his stubborn appraisal of Japanese plans. When Allied air reconnaissance discovered that the Japanese were lengthening a landing strip at Buna, Willoughby seized on the report as evidence that he had been right all along—the Japanese would penetrate inland only as far as they needed to build airfields.

In dismissing the threat of a land-based assault on Port Moresby, Willoughby, MacArthur and his advisors, and the Australians were forgetting the lesson of Malaya. There, British forces had relied on a vast jungle to the north to defend Singapore from a Japanese incursion. The Japanese overcame that jungle through sheer force of will, once again proving themselves capable of enormous daring, and forced the surrender of eighty thousand British troops.

The "ghost" in the modern Japanese army that allowed military strategists to forgo caution and field officers to push their troops beyond what was considered humanly possible was the samurai spirit. Around the ninth century, as feudalism evolved in Japan, samurai, or "those who serve," were a small, elite warrior class within the feudal system. The samurai emphasized the twin virtues of loyalty and self-sacrifice and evolved an ethic known as *bushido*, the "way of the warrior." In the first half of the twentieth century, the Japanese military resurrected bushido, and distorted it as a way to transform Japan's entire male population into willing warriors. In fact, at the time, the whole of Japanese society was being systematically indoctrinated and militarized. Slogans were omnipresent: *"Ichoku isshin"* (One hundred million [people], one mind) *"Hoshigarimasen katsu made wa"* (Abolish desire until victory). Dissent was aggressively suppressed. Unwavering dedication to the emperor, to Japan, to a culture that considered itself morally superior to the degenerate West became the norm. In fact, by World War II, the average Japanese citizen had been instilled with a master race mentality that was every bit as dangerous as the German conception of the Aryan race.

Many Japanese soldiers who came ashore at Basabua in July and August carried with them a copy of the famous Imperial Rescript to

Soldiers and Sailors. The Imperial Rescript, which was promulgated by Emperor Meiji in 1882, articulated a series of virtues similar to the traditional samurai code of bushido. Bravery and loyalty were seen as the ultimate manifestations of a soldier's commitment. He was encouraged to relinquish all personal initiative. Consequently, Japanese soldiers carried out orders unquestioningly. To become an officer, a cadet had to pass through the military academy at Ichigaya, where absolute obedience was inculcated during every waking hour, originality and individuality were stifled, and death was glorified as a transcendent act that brought honor to oneself and one's family. A good soldier was said to die with the "Emperor's name on [his] lips." And death, even a grisly one, was preferable to surrender. Surrender was the consummate disgrace, a humiliation that would forever haunt not only the soldier, but the soldier's family, too. Mothers, bidding farewell to their sons, were said to encourage them to commit suicide instead of being taken prisoner.

•   •   •

On August 19, as the morning burned into midday and the tropical sun bore down on them, General Horii and his men marched with all the confidence of invaders certain of victory. Soldiers led the way. Then came more troops lugging mortars, machine guns, and field pieces, followed by Rabaul natives carrying ammunition.

Horii believed that his campaign was a sacred one: "To extend the light of the Imperial power" over the "Greater East Asian Co-prosperity Sphere" and to eliminate the "White Race from Asia." A popular regimental song reflected similar sentiments: "Of Heavenly Japan / The Emperor's power is clear / We must build a new World Order . . . / While we have this weighty Mission / Even if in the waters, grass-grown corpses soak / Let us go, Comrades, with hearts united."

By the time Horii, whom a lieutenant described as an "unsympathetic man," reached the village of Soputa ten miles inland and set up camp in a coffee plantation, he was already frustrated with his troops' progress. He feared a protracted struggle and worried over the reliability of his supply line, which extended by ship from Rabaul to Buna and, eventually, as he advanced, by carrier into the mountains. He had hoped that they might be able to navigate the trail on horseback, but by the time he got to Soputa, he realized that the terrain was far too rugged for horses, and that he had seriously underestimated the difficulty of the advance.

As little as Allied Headquarters in Brisbane knew about New Guinea, the Japanese may have known even less. Yokoyama and Horii had no maps or geographic surveys and no conception of the topographical hurdles and medical problems their troops would encounter. Horii's faith in the inevitability of Japanese victory was illustrative of a broader Japanese conceit—"victory disease." Encouraged by Japan's stunning successes in Southeast Asia, "victory disease" caused its military leaders to ignore warning signs.

The impetuousness of the Japanese plan was in keeping with the Japanese Imperial army's modus operandi. "Fighting spirit" was valued at the expense of strategy and planning. Patience and prudence were antithetical to the most revered of all of Japan's martial virtues: action. Supply considerations were given little attention; troops were forced to make do with inferior weapons. In many cases, infantrymen carried a Type 38 bolt-action rifle that shot only five rounds. Grenades were left over from the Russo-Japanese War of 1904–05, and were highly unreliable. The Japanese did have two exceptional weapons, a wheel mounted artillery gun (carried in pieces), and the Juki heavy machine gun. For the most part, though, the Imperial army relied on speed, surprise, and courage. Never concerned with heavy casualty rates, the Japanese regularly employed suicide squads and night attacks to strike terror into the hearts of its enemies.

On August 26, as the first rays of dawn cut through the enveloping night fog, General Horii began his advance from Kokoda down the track. His orders to his enthusiastic troops reiterated basic Japanese battlefield tactics. "Lay in wait," Horii advised them, "and then go around the flank . . . Harass them and exhaust them by ceaseless activity. Finally, when they are completely exhausted, open the offensive . . . The enemy must never be allowed to escape."

Lieutenant Hirano's company commander had issued his enigmatic message days before. "In death there is life," he said. "In life, there is no life." Hirano, however, required no encouragement. "I will die at the foot of the Emperor," he wrote in his diary. "I will not fear death! Long live the Emperor! Advance with this burning feeling and even the demons will flee!"

Before Horii could march on Port Moresby, however, his Nankai Shitai would need to conquer a whole succession of villages, beginning with Isurava, roughly six miles south of Kokoda. Anticipating only feeble resistance from the Australian 39th Battalion, and certain of his troops' superior skills, Horii held Yazawa Force in reserve at Kokoda and dedicated only three of his battalions to the attack.

At Isurava, Lieutenant Colonel Ralph Honner and his men were under orders to "stand and fight." If any man could hold, it was Honner. He was widely regarded as the best company commander in the Australian army and his unit, the 39th, was the top unit in the Australian militia.

Honner's men watched the approach of Horii's troops. Adorned with leaves and branches they marched "as purposefully as soldier ants." As the Japanese neared Isurava, they divided: One group scrambled up Naro Ridge, which overlooked Isurava; another moved to the east in the vicinity of the Abuari waterfall; the third, advancing from Deniki, stuck to the track.

At 7:00 a.m. on August 26, the battle for Isurava commenced with the crack of rifles, the insistent pounding of Juki heavy machine guns, and mortar and mountain-gun fire.

Despite the dramatic beginning to the battle, General Horii was actually biding his time, waiting for nightfall. Twelve hours later, when darkness descended over the mountains, Horii's troops began to move out. Once in position, they began to rhythmically chant, beginning in the rear and rising to the front lines like a crashing wave. Then, the cries of the Nankai Shitai soldiers tore through the jungle: "Banzai! Long live the Emperor!" Suddenly "all hell broke loose," wrote

Honner. Horii's troops were "shooting, stabbing, hacking, in a . . . surge of blind and blazing fury."

It was a suicidal assault, and the ensuing battle was a blur. Men screamed, bayonets flashed, bullets ripped through flesh. Separated by only a few yards of jungle, they lunged for each other's vital areas like wide-mouthed animals. Honner's men had never encountered such rage. They fired haphazardly into the tangle of onrushing soldiers. Japanese fell by the dozens, but still they came.

If not for the timely arrival of elite AIF soldiers, Isurava might have fallen that evening. But together Honner's men and the fresh AIF forces beat back the Japanese. According to Honner, the reinforcements were a "providential blessing." Honner's men were "gaunt spectres with gaping boots and rotting tatters of uniform hanging around them like scarecrows. . . . Their faces had no expression, their eyes sunk back into their sockets. They were drained by [disease], but they were still in the firing line . . ." One AIF soldier wrote that he "could have cried when [he] saw them."

The morning of August 27 dawned quietly, and the Australians began to search the jungle for what Honner grimly called the "jetsam of death." Lacking litters, medics draped bloodstained men over their shoulders and floundered back to camp.

On the Australians' eastern flank, the scene was just as grim. Unable to stop the oncoming Japanese, Australian soldiers lunged into the overgrown jungle, leaving behind ammunition, food, clothing, and weapons. Soon, according to Honner, "Mortar bombs and mountain gun shells burst among the tree tops or slashed through to the quaking earth. . . . Heavy machine guns . . . chopped through the trees, cleaving their own lanes of fire to tear at the defences . . . bombs and bullets crashed and rattled in unceasing clamour."

Day and night the Japanese kept up the bombardment, while patrols tested the Australian perimeters, sneaking in to bayonet soldiers distracted by the mortars. At the Naro Ridge Front, Horii's troops dispensed with stealth. Honner wrote: "Through the widening breach poured another flood of attackers . . . met with Bren gun and tommy gun, with bayonet and grenade; but still they came, to close with the buffet of fist and boot and rifle-butt, the steel of crashing helmets and of straining, strangling fingers." Corpses, according to Honner, "soon cluttered that stretch of open ground."

August 28 came and went, but on the evening of August 29, Horii assembled his troops for what he hoped would be the coup de grâce, an attack so ferocious it would "shatter the Australian resistance beyond hope of recovery."

That night, after again being beaten back by the Australians, Lieutenant Hirano wrote that one of the company commanders, a friend of his, had been killed. "Only this morning," wrote Hirano, "he and I . . . were gaily conversing over a cup of 'sake' from his canteen. Now it is only a memory. How cruel and miserable this life is!" Despite their personal sadnesses, the Japanese army did not relent. Facing a torrent of fire from the Australian Bren and tommy guns, Horii's troops kept coming, preferring death to the dishonor of staying back.

At noon, the Japanese threw caution to the wind. Scaling a steep hill, they ascended straight into the throat of the Australian defense, breaking through. The Australian troops withdrew down the track. Isurava was now General Horii's.

The four-day battle for Isurava was a bloodbath. The Australians lost 250 men. Hundreds more were wounded. One battalion was reduced to half its initial size. For the Japanese, the victory was Pyrrhic at best. Horii lost over 550 men, and had more than a thousand wounded.

After Isurava, Horii's army continued to chew up ground. With each new conquest, Horii would symbolically raise the Japanese flag. For Damien Parer, an Australian war photographer, it was a terrible sight.

Parer and the Australians could not know, though, the price Horii was paying to fly the white Japanese flag with its dazzlingly red sun. In each village it seized, Horii's men were forced to build great, pyramid-shaped funeral pyres to cremate their dead. "Our casualties are great," a Japanese officer wrote in his diary. "The outcome of the battle is very difficult to foresee." Lieutenant Sakamoto, a machine gunner with Horii's advance force, wrote somberly of corpses "piled high."

As General Horii's desire to take Port Moresby took on a quality of stubborn fanaticism, his preoccupation with his supply line grew. Thanks to relentless bombing by U.S. Fifth Air Force and Royal Australian Air Force units, the line was hanging by a thread. "It is humiliating," wrote Sakamoto, "to see enemy planes strafing us, and not a single plane of ours to assist us."

As the Nankai Shitai approached Eora Creek, Horii demanded that his commanders "exercise the most painstaking control . . . so that every bullet fells an enemy and every grain of rice furthers the task of the Shitai." He then cut the daily ration of rice to one and one-half pints per man. According to Sakamoto, men were already slashing through the jungle to search for "taroes and yams to satisfy our hunger."

Still, by early September, the Japanese attack on Port Moresby had acquired an air of inexorability. Horii's men had fought their way over the divide. They had climbed "breath-taking cliffs" and waded through "muddy swamps," and seized the vital Australian dropping grounds at Myola on the southern slopes of the Owen Stanleys. Now, in addition to trying to stop the Japanese, the Australians had to contend with their own supply problems. With Myola in Japanese hands, carriers had to lug huge loads on their backs all the way from Port Moresby. To make matters worse, frightened native carriers, sensing that the Australian army's defeat was imminent, dropped their supplies and fled into the jungle.

While Horii's army was routing the Australians on the Kokoda, other Japanese soldiers were attempting to capture Milne Bay.

At the extreme southeastern tip of New Guinea, Milne Bay is strikingly beautiful. On both sides of the bay, four-thousand-foot jungle-clad mountains rise precipitously out of the blue-green tropical waters. Between the mountains and the bay lies a thin coastal strip of swamp, sand, and dense, dripping rain forest.

The Japanese had never even expected to be at Milne Bay. Their initial plan was to seize the island of Samarai, southeast of Milne Bay, and launch a seaborne invasion of Port Moresby from there. However, when Japanese planners discovered that the Allies were constructing a garrison and an airfield at Milne Bay, they switched gears, choosing at the last minute to invade.

The Allied base was located at the head of the bay, on the only dry ground in the area. Though one airfield was in use, engineers were constructing two more. They were also building corduroy roads and improving the existing wharf.

Milne Bay was a vital piece of real estate. In Allied hands, it would allow them to guard the Coral Sea and Port Moresby against seaborne attacks from the east. It would also enable Allied pilots to hit Japanese bases in New Guinea and the Solomon Islands without having to fly over the Owen Stanley Mountains.

Although Japan's strategists in Rabaul chose an elite naval landing force to lead the invasion of Milne Bay, and followed up with reinforcements, by the end of August it was obvious that Milne Bay was a losing effort. On the nights of September 4 and 5, Japanese troops were evacuated.

·   ·   ·

Having secured Milne Bay, MacArthur could now turn all his attention to the Kokoda. What he saw there in mid-September 1942 alarmed him. Surely he had ordered enough fighting men to the front. Why then could the Australians not hold back Horii's army? Chafing at MacArthur's insinuation that the Australians were not fighting, Lieutenant General Sydney Rowell, head of New Guinea Force, a position that put him in command of all Australian and American troops, tried to set the record straight. His men were exhausted, sick with dysentery and fever and, despite the reinforcements, outnumbered.

The Japanese were hardly better off. One of Horii's section leaders kept a diary of the campaign. On September 9, he wrote, "We are in the jungle area. . . . The jungle was beyond description. Thirsty for water, stomach empty. The pack on the back is heavy. . . . My neck and back hurt when I wipe them with a cloth . . . the sweat still pours out and falls down like crystals . . . the sun of the southern country has no mercy. . . . The soldiers grit their teeth and continue advancing quiet as mummies. . . . 'Water, water,' all the soldiers are muttering to themselves. . . . We reach for the canteens on our hip from force of habit, but there isn't a drop of water in them. Even yet, the men still believe in miracles. . . . The men sleep while they walk and sometimes bump into trees . . . planes fly above the jungle and repeatedly attack."

When later in the day the Japanese troops spot a stream tumbling through a valley, the section leader writes again. "Water! Water! The soldiers forgot their fatigue and ran. The water we were longing for was now flowing in front of us . . . Indeed there is a blessing from above! They bent down and put their mouths to the stream. . . . That water was not just plain water. It was the water of life and the source of energy. It was a gift from heaven for soldiers."

Seemingly indifferent to the suffering of his men, General Horii initiated a series of savage attacks over the course of the next few days and on September 17, his troops ascended Ioribaiwa Ridge and celebrated with loud, triumphant shouts of "Banzai!" and tears of joy. Three weeks after landing at Basabua, Port Moresby was within their grasp. The Japanese had done exactly what Allied General Headquarters had said they would not, could not, do.

Chapter 5

Cannibal Island

Before the Nankai Shitai clambered up Ioribaiwa Ridge, General MacArthur was confident that the reinforced Australians would be capable of halting Horii's progress on the Kokoda track, and made plans for an offensive on "three axes."

On the first axis, the Australians would engage Horii's army in a "frontal action" on the Kokoda. The third consisted of "large-scale infiltrations from Milne Bay along the north coast of Papua." But it was the second axis that was so bewildering. This one called for an American flanking movement that would penetrate and cross the Owen Stanley Mountains. In other words, MacArthur proposed to send a large group of American soldiers over the very mountains that a month earlier he believed would prevent the Japanese from reaching Port Moresby. The basic blueprint was for American troops to duck in behind the Japanese line on the Kokoda track, catching the enemy army by surprise. Then the combined American and Australian force would converge on the Buna coast with the third axis.

On September 11, MacArthur informed General Blamey, Commander of Allied Land Forces, of his intentions, and a day later dispatched a plane to Port Moresby. The plane carried Brigadier General Hanford MacNider and a very small group of intelligence and supply men, including Captains Jim Boice and Alfred Medendorp. The group's task was to make arrangements for the arrival of the first American infantry unit to set foot in New Guinea.

MacArthur made the decision to send the 32nd to New Guinea despite General Harding's objections that it was not yet ready. In a letter that foreshadowed the eventual clash between MacArthur and Harding, Harding wrote his wife Eleanor, "I prefer to get a crack at them [the Japanese] when the time comes. . . . When I go, I hope it will be with plenty of power—air, land, and sea—enough to make sure that none of those I am taking along with me will be sacrificed needlessly." Not long after, he wrote his mother, "I want to bring back as many of the Red Arrow lads with me as I can. That ambition won't be furthered if we move before we are good and ready to go."

Harding was not surprised by MacArthur's decision. In late August 1942, while the Japanese advanced down the Kokoda track, MacArthur showed up at Camp Tamborine (re-named Camp Cable by Harding for the first casualty of war in the South Pacific) with all of his colorful ribbons and medals, "decorated like a peacock," according to a member of the 32nd Division who was on hand to see him. It was not an impromptu appearance.

At Camp Cable, MacArthur delivered what Stutterin' Smith called a "gung-ho and inspired talk" full of the kind of grandiose language for which he had become famous. From MacArthur's speech it was apparent that he, too, may have understood that the 32nd was far from battle ready. So instead of emphasizing the soldiers' training, which was clearly lacking, he appealed to what the Japanese would have called their "seishin," their will to fight.

"The Jap," MacArthur told the men, "is no easy enemy. He is a hard fighter. . . . He gives no quarter. He asks for no quarter. . . . All I ask of you men when you go into action is that each of you shall kill one Japanese. If you do, we will win. But if, when you are hard pressed, you begin to look for a position in the rear, or begin to think it beyond human endurance to continue to fight, you will not only be destroyed physically, but you will lose your reputation in the eyes of your friends and your country . . . if a man has the fighting courage, even if he has poor equipment, poor training, and if he has the fighting spirit, he will win. Always, the fellow wins who fights to the end, whose nerves don't go back on him, who never thinks of anything but the will to victory. That's what I want of you men—and that's what I expect."

MacArthur finished his speech by invoking the image of a benevolent God watching over the men. "It won't be very long now, probably, before you are in action," he intoned. "It is possible that I won't see a great many of you again; but I want you to know wherever you go, it will be my hope and prayer that Almighty God will be with you to the end."

•   •   •

Despite their proximity, the island of New Guinea (the world's second largest) and the continent of Australia have little in common. Created by the explosive tectonic forces of the Pacific Ring of Fire, New Guinea is geologically a much younger, more dramatic land. A series of immature volcanic mountain ranges run down the middle of the island like a bulging spine, spilling out toward the coast in a series of lesser but still imposing peaks. Rugged interior ridgelines rise to fifteen thousand feet and then fall off almost perpendicularly, only to rise again.

As the Americans would discover, New Guinea is also a land of staggering topographical contrasts. Savannas and vast malarial swamps of mangrove, sago and nipa palm, cane, and spear grass dominate the coastal region. Farther inland, savanna and swamp give way to grassland openings, mountain-fed rivers, and a lowland hill forest of garamut, nutmeg and fig trees, magnificent Araucarias, rosewoods, mahoganies, walnuts, and Pandanus pines adorned with vines and creepers. Between eight thousand and ten thousand feet lies an eerie forest of oak, beech, bamboo, red cedar, and pine, covered in mosses, lichens, and luminous fungi, surrounded by swirling clouds of ice and rain. Higher yet, the trees disappear and are replaced by fields of alpine flowers, shrubs, and staghorn ferns.

Shaped like a large prehistoric bird, New Guinea sits perched atop Australia with its head jutting to the northwest into the Maluku Sea and almost touching the equator near the Indonesian island of Halmahera. The attenuated tail dangles in a southeasterly direction into the

Coral Sea just above Australia. One of the wettest places on earth, New Guinea is affected for half the year by unstable air masses, moving down from the north on the monsoon. For the other half, it is subjected to the stray airflows of the southeast trade winds. The monsoon and trade winds bring constant rain—in some areas over two hundred inches a year—carving a tangle of trackless ravines into the great volcanic ridges.

The rain also brings abundance. New Guinea is home to an unparalleled diversity of butterflies, birds, plants, strange marsupials, crocodiles, ninety species of snakes—including the taipan, death adder, Papuan black, and python—and over three thousand varieties of orchids. Although botanists have discovered around 1.5 million species on the planet, some speculate that there may be three times that many "undiscovered" plants on the island of New Guinea alone. The island also contains over eight hundred of the world's languages, esoteric tongues of largely unknown origins, which evolved among people living in isolated universes of ravine and swamp and mountaintop.

.   .   .

The first European to encounter New Guinea was Jorge de Meneses, a Portuguese governor from the Spice Islands, whose ship was caught in a monsoon on a voyage from the Malay Peninsula. In 1526 he landed on the island of New Guinea and christened it "Ilhas dos Papuas" from the Malay term "orang papuwah," meaning "fuzzy-haired man." In 1545, Ynigo Ortiz de Retes, returning from the Moluccas to Mexico, sailed by the island and named it Nueva Guinea either because he thought its natives resembled those of African Guinea, or because the island was exactly opposite Guinea. Centuries later, New Guinea still remained largely untouched by outsiders.

The obstacles of terrain, climate, and disease successfully repelled the world's colonial powers and their appointed adventurers. Those undaunted by the endless swamps, by the island's impenetrable mountains and cloud forests, by the threat of malaria, scrub and murine typhus, filariasis, and leishmaniasis, were deterred by something else—New Guinea's reputation for being inhabited by cannibals who ate the bodies of their dead parents as a gesture of love and head-hunters who punctured their enemies' skulls and sucked out the brains.

Headhunting and cannibalism were vital customs in New Guinea. Although the Australian territorial government outlawed the practice of headhunting as early as 1920, it was impossible to enforce. Canni-balism was also discouraged, though with little success. Along the Fly River, for instance, west of Port Moresby and the Gulf of Papua, if an enemy was killed in battle, warriors would often cut up the dead body and pack the flesh into bamboo logs for easy transport. Back at the vil-lage, the flesh would be cooked with sago. Some speculate that the people ate human flesh out of necessity because of the paucity of pro-tein, a lack that was particularly acute in the Highlands. Among cer-tain tribes, human flesh was eaten in the belief that the strength of the deceased would be transmitted to the living. Headhunting also served a variety of purposes. Heads taken in battle were often preserved as a means of communicating with the spirit world, for initiation rituals, and as trophies, which warriors displayed to enhance their standing in the villages. Even among tribes that did not take heads, the belief that the skulls and bones of dead relatives possessed magical properties was common. In the Sepik River region of New Guinea, a widow was obliged to stay in a hut with the body of her dead husband until the flesh had rotted from his skull and bones.

Although cannibalism and headhunting were not practiced by all of the tribes, much of New Guinea was populated by an intensely ter-ritorial and martial people, who were mistrustful of outsiders. Even tribes living along the same river system engaged in near-constant pay-back skirmishes, fueled by a simple principle: an eye for an eye. If one tribe stole a pig from another tribe, the offended tribe would be honor-bound to stage a raid and take a pig. If in the process, the raiding tribe killed a man, they could expect that the death would be avenged.

Because of the warlike reputation of its people, New Guinea became a place where for centuries imagination and invention substi-tuted for hard facts. However, by the mid-1800s, whalers and sealers were plying the plentiful waters of the "cannibal islands"; traders, searching for pearls, tortoise shells, sandalwood, ebony, wild rubber, copra, and bêche-de-mer, explored the mainland; and ruthless "black-birders" rounded up young men as slave laborers for Peruvian mines and South Pacific sugar plantations. Given the burgeoning interest in the island, the world's powers could no longer ignore New Guinea. Emissaries from Britain, Germany, and the Netherlands ventured there, and many of the expeditions ended very badly.

One of the first recorded disasters occurred in 1782. The captain of the *Northumberland,* a Dutch ship that was cruising off the coast of New Guinea, sent ten men ashore, not for the purpose of exploration, but for water and vegetables. "They came down on us like unto a half moon, men, women, and children, such as could take a bow and arrow into their hands," wrote the only survivor. "They came down into the water then fired their arrows as thick and as fast that we could not see for the darkness of their arrows. . . . They carried one of our boys out of the boat and cut him through the middle and throwed his bowels into the air. I perceived them broiling the remains of poor Mr. Sayce."

A century later, bona fide explorers fared no better. At age thirty-two, Otto von Ehlers joined the German East Africa Company and climbed Mt. Kilimanjaro. Following his service in the company, he began a series of journeys to Zanzibar, Bombay, Kashmir, Nepal, Burma, Ceylon, Hong Kong, Canton, Peking, and Korea, and wrote of these adventures in flashy, self-aggrandizing travel books. When he came to New Guinea in 1895, it was said that he stood proudly "on the pinnacle of his success." If anyone could conquer New Guinea, Von Ehlers surely could.

On August 14, von Ehlers set off with forty-one native porters and W. Piering, a German police master stationed in northern New Guinea. Von Ehlers immediately noted the terrain, which was unforgiving—a cruel, endless succession of ridges and valleys. Up and down, down and up, his team struggled for days hacking their way through the thick jungle. Rattan thorns ripped at their clothes and exposed skin, and leeches either fell from the overhanging trees or slithered upward from the ground, attaching themselves and later dropping off, leaving small exposed wounds, which were soon infested with red maggots. Von Ehlers' face and body were covered with infected sores, and Piering could walk only with the help of two carriers. Nearly forty days into the trip, the team's food ran out. Von Ehlers finally agreed to let Piering kill his beloved mastiff, though von Ehlers refused to eat any of it. The team then subsisted on grass shoots and young leaves. Already weakened by hunger, both men came down with dysentery. When the porters became too weak to carry their loads, the team abandoned much of its luggage. Days later, they arrived at a large river. Von Ehlers ordered two of the porters to construct a raft, having decided that he and Piering and the two porters would abandon the others and float to the coast, leaving the rest of the porters to do whatever they could to survive. Von Ehlers' cowardice was aptly rewarded, however, when the two porters killed him and Piering and continued on, though they, too, later got their comeuppance, when they were beheaded by the Gaib people.

By the early twentieth century much of the work of exploration was being done by prospectors and missionaries, many of the latter of whom were fueled both by an explorer's sense of adventure and a desire to spread God's message. Initially, however, most of the missionaries confined their proselytizing to the coast. Those who dared to set foot in New Guinea's interior never made it out.

The terrifying stories did not discourage the Reverends James Chamlers and Oliver Tomkins of the London Missionary Society, two ardent men of God. Although they knew the reputation of the Fly River people—who they had been told were practicing cannibals and did not greet outsiders kindly—they set off in 1901 from Daru to bring God's word to the benighted people. Only two weeks into their trip, they were captured by a river tribe and beheaded. They were then cut into pieces, and cooked with sago and yams.

Thirty-four years later, over half a century after much of the Amazon basin had been mapped, Australian gold prospectors stumbled across a previously undiscovered society numbering seven hundred fifty thousand people in what was thought to be an uninhabited area of the island (today's Western Highlands Province of Papua New Guinea). Using stone tools, these people had been practicing a sophisticated form of agriculture for almost ten thousand years, making theirs one of the oldest agrarian societies in the world.

In 1942, when the 32nd Division arrived in New Guinea, the island was still terra incognita. Its interior was largely unmapped, its coastline a puzzle of coral reefs, its swamps and grasslands a breeding ground for disease, its climate as pernicious as any ever encountered by an army. In New Guinea, MacArthur neglected warfare's most important lesson: The island was his enemy, yet he remained only vaguely aware of the hardships his troops would confront there.

BOOK TWO

And over the hill the guns bang like a door
And planes repeat their mission in the heights.
The jungle outmaneuvers creeping war
And crawls within the circle of our sacred rites.

I long for our disheveled Sundays home,
Breakfast, the comics, news of latest crimes,
Talk without reference, and palindromes,
Sleep and the Philharmonic and the ponderous Times.

I long for lounging in the afternoons
Of clean intelligent warmth, my brother's mind,
Books and thin plates and flowers and shining spoons,
And your love's presence, snowy, beautiful, and kind.

KARL SHAPIRO,
"SUNDAY: NEW GUINEA"

Chapter 6

FORLORN HOPE

ON SEPTEMBER 15, two days before the Japanese climbed onto Ioribaiwa Ridge, Company E, 2nd Battalion, 126th U.S. Infantry broke camp at 4:00 a.m. and assembled at Brisbane's Amberley Airfield. The men were issued ammunition. The men's newly dyed fatigues, sporting a mottled green jungle design, clung damply to their skin. Green burlap hung from their steel helmets.

Even at that early hour, the men were edgy with anticipation. Sergeant Paul Lutjens had written that "it was quite a shock walking up that gangplank" when the division loaded onto the ships leaving California. But now the adrenaline really pumped through their young bodies. This was it, what they had come ten thousand miles for. No one uttered a word until somebody with a timely sense of humor—it might have been Sergeant John Fredericks, another Big Rapids man—started whistling an old cavalry bugle call, and the men were still chuckling when Captain Melvin Schultz appeared. Schultz would not say much about where they were going, not that Lutjens or any of the others expected him to, but it did not take a genius to figure out that they were being airlifted to New Guinea. For many of them, the flight to New Guinea would be the first of their lives.

Though Melvin Schultz was Company E's commander, he was raised in Muskegon, Michigan, and was regarded as something of an outsider. It was First Sergeant Paul Lutjens of Big Rapids, Michigan, who often ran the show. Lutjens was an affable but physically imposing man. He was also devoted to Company E. Twice during training in Louisiana he refused a commission because he did not want to leave his friends.

Like Lutjens, nearly 50 percent of Company E's men were from the Big Rapids National Guard unit. In fact, many of the guys had joined together, continuing ties of friendship that went back to childhood. Mostly it was a reason to drink and play poker and avoid the realities of life at the tail end of the Depression. Lutjens was one of the few who was employed, but work in a factory was not exactly the kind of thing a guy dreamed of doing. In other words, few of the men seemed destined for greatness. If someone had asked the people of Big Rapids if Lutjens and his crowd were going to amount to anything, they might have shaken their heads—"They're not bad boys, really, but no more than a few of them will do anything with their lives."

For the men of Big Rapids, mostly beer-swilling party boys by their own admission, joining the National Guard during peacetime was just something you did. Lutjens simply liked the look of the uniform. "When I got my first uniform . . ." he said, "I was just in my second year at high school and I thought I was pretty big stuff. I wore out the mirror in the hall downstairs admiring myself . . ." According to Lutjens, Big Rapids had a "swell" armory, too, and large dances were frequently held there. Lutjens confessed, ". . . We used to worry a lot more about the dances than the drill."

A lot of the new guardsmen, like Lutjens, were underage. Rules said that inductees had to be at least eighteen. The National Guard, though, did not care who you were, or how old you were, "as long as you had a pulse," joked one former guardsman. "Its philosophy was, 'If the body is warm, we'll take it.'" Anybody could be a weekend warrior—postmasters, bankers, teachers, mechanics, cooks, factory workers, the unemployed.

•   •   •

On the afternoon of September 15, the men of Company E, a platoon of engineers, a medical officer, and four aid men, divided into groups, a dozen to a plane.

"We were pretty tense and mighty afraid," Lutjens remembered. "Some of the men sort of sat in their seats and just gulped like Li'l Abner. But most of them got into a colossal crap game, right on the floor of the plane."

The men of Company E imagined that they were going straight into combat, jumping off the plane and storming the Japanese amidst a barrage of bullets. It would be dramatic stuff, something to make the folks back home in Big Rapids proud. After an uneventful flight across the Coral Sea, the Douglas and Lockheed transport planes neared Port Moresby, and Lutjens took a moment to look out the window. "There were big fresh-looking craters on the landing strip down on the edge of the jungle. Over on one side were the smoking ruins of two planes that had evidently just been hit by Japanese bombers," he wrote. But when the planes reached Seven Mile Drome outside of Port Moresby, the men disembarked with their bayonets sheathed. There were no Japanese to be found.

A blast of hot air nearly brought Lutjens to his knees. In the back of the transport truck, he was already writing in his diary. "September 15, 1942, 5:30 P.M. Temperature 115 degrees. Japs twenty miles away. New Guinea weather is hotter than the lower story of hell." Even Fredericks, a former farmer accustomed to toiling in the hot sun, was barely able to stand the heat.

Fredericks, like the others, must have wondered how he had ended up in New Guinea. He and his buddies did not know anything about the jungle. What he knew was that it was full of things that could kill a man: Japs; blood-sucking bats; rats as large as collies; wild boars; snakes; crocodiles; moniter lizards over six feet long; diseases that could make a man's scrotum swell up to the size of a pumpkin; and hungry cannibals who enjoyed the practice of eating living meat. They would tie a live captive to a tree and cut off chunks of flesh, as they needed it. And the heat, God, the heat—would they ever get used to it?

For a moment, Lutjens and the others were able to forget about the temperature. When their truck passed a group of Australian soldiers and a small group of American pilots, they were cheered heartily.

Lutjens and the boys from Big Rapids were enjoying their new role. Back home, nobody had expected much of them, and now they were being treated like avenging heroes.

The following day, Captain Schultz woke the men at 5:30 a.m. and ordered Lutjens and Staff Sergeant Henry Brissette to assemble the troops. Lutjens smelled the sea and felt the sticky salt air on his skin. Even in the morning, the heat hung over the land like a blight. To the north, the Owen Stanleys rose menacingly out of bulky, dark gray rain clouds. Their steep, forested slopes were visible for a moment. Then they were gone, obscured by fog.

The entire company was loaded onto trucks. The men were probably looking to Lutjens for an explanation, as if to say, "Hey, what's up now, Lootch? Are we finally gonna get into it?" If Private Swede Nelson was anything like people described him, it would not have mattered to him where they were going as long as there was a fight in the offing.

The trucks took the men southeast along the coast until a few miles later the dusty road dead-ended at a patch of gum trees with drooping leaves. Captain Schultz bellowed at the men to get out on the double. Schultz looked up and down the road, making a mental picture of the land. Then he cleared his throat and spoke. The men listened, hanging on his every word, still trying to picture their first brush with combat. What Schultz had to say, though, was a huge disappointment. Company E's mission was to build a jeep road from Tupeselei, a few miles southeast of Port Moresby, to Gabagaba on the southeast coast. After Schultz delivered the news, the men groaned and complained. This was bullshit! Anything but beating the Japs into submission would have been an anticlimax. But building a road? They were fighting men, not engineers.

Real engineers of the 91st U.S. Engineers, an all-black unit that had been formed at Camp Shelby in Mississippi, joined the men of Company E that day. Although the 91st was a legitimate engineering unit, it was no better equipped than the men of Company E. Using picks, shovels, axes, saws, machetes, and their hands to hack a road for forty miles along the coast, the engineers and Lutjens' men worked shirtless in mosquito-infested coastal jungles, sago swamps, and broad, sun-soaked savannas.

It was the job of Lieutenant James Hunt to drive a truck rigged with a winch and to locate usable sections of the trail. Hunt was a communications specialist who had flown over with Company E. Upon arriving in Port Moresby, however, Captain Schultz informed him that his services would not be needed. He was to act as a rifle platoon leader, which meant for the time being that he was nothing more than a road builder.

While the rest of the men of Company E worked on the road—largely an upgrade of a native trail, known as the "Tavai track" that linked the southeast coastal communities to Port Moresby—Lutjens and Privates Barney Baxter and Arthur Edson reconnoitered the territory between Tupeselei and Gabagaba. Undoubtedly, some of the guys griped that Lutjens, Baxter, and Edson had received the plum assignment, but the truth was that few of them would have traded places with Lutjens or the others. New Guinea was a dangerous country, and no one knew whether the reconnaissance patrol would encounter Japanese, or headhunters, or man-eating crocodiles. Although the three patrolmen were probably relieved that they would not have to build a road, it is equally certain that none of them felt particularly lucky about the assignment. Writing in his diary, Lutjens admitted to being scared.

Baxter, like Lutjens, was from Big Rapids, Michigan, a typical Midwest town in the middle of Michigan's Lower Peninsula, surrounded by farms and woodlots. Edson was the woodsman of the bunch. He had left Saranac, Michigan, at the age of fourteen to work as a lumberjack in Michigan's wild Upper Peninsula, and later settled down in the U.P. to run a 120-acre beef farm. All three of the men were acquainted with the outdoors; none of them, though, had spent a single day in the jungle.

"Started through the jungle today," Lutjens wrote. "It is ten times worse than you can imagine. . . . Wearing green head-nets to keep off mosq. . . . They damn near smother you."

That night Lutjens, Edson, and Baxter camped somewhere along a coastal trail, perhaps outside of a small fishing village called Barakau.

Their first tropical sunset must have struck them as spectacular—the blazing sun falling swiftly below the horizon, searing the blue sky with streaks of orange and red.

Later that night they were awakened by the sound of a dog's frantic barking. Were Japanese soldiers creeping through the dark sago swamp that bordered the beach? It was what every soldier would come to dread most—the night maneuvers of the Japanese soldiers. Lutjens might have clutched his hunting knife. The army did not issue decent knives, so Lutjens had brought his all the way from Big Rapids. If a Jap was going to jump him, he would be in for the fight of his life. If Lutjens could, he would cut him from his lower abdomen right up to his throat. He would cut him like a big buck, snapping his sternum with a swift stroke.

When the Japanese troops did not rush them, Lutjens, Edson, and Baxter grabbed their M-1s, pressed their bodies into the soft sand, and searched the dark, ready to send a burst of bullets into the night. While they scanned the jungle, they heard something: It sounded like the snapping and crushing of bones. A yelp followed, and then silence. That now familiar adrenaline was slamming through their veins.

Lutjens woke with a start the following morning and searched for a sign that a Japanese patrol had been in the area that night. Just ten feet from where Baxter and Edson were lying, Lutjens saw something that chilled him—the tracks of a very large crocodile. Then Lutjens and the others pieced together the details of the previous night. The crocodile had caught a dog and had chosen to eat it not far from where they were sleeping. Better to take a Jap bullet than die a slow death in the jaws of a crocodile.

●   ●   ●

As Lutjens reconnoitered the coast, the news that General Horii had captured Ioribaiwa Ridge shook General Headquarters in Brisbane like the impact of an artillery shell. The Japanese army was now only thirty miles from Port Moresby.

MacArthur immediately called Prime Minister Curtin. The Australians, he said, did not have enough fight in them. They had forfeited every major position along the Kokoda track and had forced the Allies "into such a defensive concentration as would duplicate the conditions of Malaya." MacArthur did not mention Bataan, but the implications were clear—Bataan had fallen and now he was in danger of losing New Guinea, too. Only six months before in Bataan, MacArthur's army had been pushed up against the South China Sea. Now the Australian army's back was up against the Gulf of Papua. With the specter of Bataan still haunting him, and his career hanging in the balance, MacArthur informed Curtin that he would send American troops by air and sea to prevent New Guinea from being "stitched into the Japanese pattern of quick conquest." By the end of September he hoped to have forty thousand men in New Guinea. "If they fought," MacArthur continued, "they should have no trouble in meeting the situation. If they would not fight, 100,000 would be no good." MacArthur then requested that General Blamey be sent to New Guinea to take command and "energize the situation." Curtin was in full agreement.

MacArthur ended the conversation on a note of self-pity—a quality that he had revealed on other occasions, and one that was as much a part of his enigmatic emotional make-up as his extravagant self-confidence. "Must I always lead a forlorn hope?" he asked the Australian prime minister.

On September 18, only hours after speaking with Curtin, MacArthur mobilized two of the 32nd's three regimental combat teams—the 126th and 128th U.S. Infantries. The plan was to send the 126th minus its artillery team by ship to New Guinea. The 128th would leave Australia via the airfield at Townsville in what would be the first mass movement of troops by air in Would War II. Originally, MacArthur was opposed to the idea, but General George Kenney, MacArthur's Commander of Allied Air Forces in the Southwest Pacific, convinced him that in the time it would take to move the men by ship, the Australians might already "be behind barbed wire at Port Moresby."

•   •   •

While his buddies were building the coastal road, Lutjens arrived in Gabagaba. It had taken him, Edson, and Baxter five days to cover the thirty-five miles from Tupeselei. When they reached Gabagaba (which the soldiers mispronounced as Kapa Kapa), a beautiful village of hibiscus- and bougainvillea-lined walkways, tall, graceful coconuts, and thatched huts built on stilts over the shallow water of a small protected bay, they set up temporary headquarters near the village's wooden wharf.

Although Gabagaba was a small coastal village, the people were familiar with the war. Less than forty miles from Port Moresby, the villagers heard the frequent Japanese bombing raids on the town, and had been buzzed by Zeros. Just weeks before Lutjens arrived, a village elder and his wife were working in their garden southeast of the village when they saw a plane drop into the sea. The old man and woman left the garden and paddled out to the wreckage in an outrigger. There they discovered an American pilot hanging on to a piece of the plane, trying to stay afloat. The old man dove in, grabbed him, swam to the dugout where he and his wife managed to lay him in the narrow boat, and then they paddled back to the village. After a week of convalescing in the village, the pilot made his way to Port Moresby on foot and by boat, and two weeks later flew over the village and airdropped food as a thank-you.

The war also had a much more tangible effect on the village. ANGAU officers who were organizing carrier teams for the Americans were already in Gabagaba preparing for the possible American march over the Owen Stanleys. Hundreds of native carriers would be needed, and the officers would eventually recruit all able-bodied men from Gabagaba and area villages. They considered any male with hair under his arms—the ANGAU officers literally lifted the arms of a boy to see if he qualified—old enough to work. Those who balked at the prospect of carrying for the Americans were conscripted at gunpoint. Often, the only people left in the villages were old men, women, and young children.

Gabagaba was not as primitive as Lutjens had expected. An Australian expatriate ran a bakery out of the village, and had Lutjens and his men wanted to, they could have enjoyed fresh-baked bread every morning. Far from being the murderous headhunters that Lutjens must have expected, the villagers of Gabagaba—a Motu word meaning "small drum"—were shy, gentle, and kind-hearted.

Though Lutjens does not mention it in his diary, while he and Privates Edson and Baxter waited for the road builders to reach them, they probably had time to enjoy village life. Gabagaba was part of a world they had never even imagined. When the tide was in, children paddled around the bay in little outriggers, chattering and singing, or used the wooden ladders to their houses as diving boards. The Motuan women, unashamedly bare-breasted, wore grass skirts and bore striking face and arm tattoos. When they were not nursing their babies, young mothers carried them in colorful, beautifully woven string bags, which they fastened to their heads with tumplines. The bags hung to their hips, so that when they walked the babies swung gently back and forth. When not tending to their children or working in the garden, the women spent much of the day cooking over fires on open-air porches.

Until they were pressed into duty as carriers, the men went off each morning on fishing excursions. When they were not fishing, they accompanied the women to the jungle, where they tended small garden plots with long wooden sticks. As fascinated as Lutjens would have been by the people of Gabagaba, the villagers, especially the children, were surely drawn to the Americans. Frank Gabi was four or five at the time the first Americans came and remembers them passing out biscuits and lollipops in return for papaya, sugar cane, and coconuts. In the short time the American's were there, the villagers grew accustomed to them and began to call them their *tura*—friends.

Lieutenant James Hunt, who, along with a platoon of men, went ahead of the roadbuilders to guard the growing supply depot, describes the scene at Gabagaba:

Although the plan was to build the road suitable for truck traffic, supplies were already being moved to Kapa Kapa by small coastal boats which could not come close to shore but were unloaded some distance at sea onto native outrigger canoes, which transported their load to shore. Some items, such as oil drums, were merely dumped into the water and pushed to shore by the natives. A large group of natives were assembled for this purpose and made their camp near the beach. The village consisted of native huts built on pilings or stilts in the ocean, all connected by narrow walkways.

During our stay in Kapa Kapa, the natives discovered that a slap on an empty oil drum made a drum sound very pleasing to them. They assembled one evening at the beach and put on quite a show using several oil drums with some impromptu dancing and merry making which we enjoyed very much.

When the men of Company E and the 91st U.S. Engineers arrived in Gabagaba, they were exhausted from their road-building exertions, and took a day to recuperate before Captain Schultz gave them their new orders: MacArthur wanted the road extended from Kapa Kapa to a rubber plantation four miles inland at the village of Gobaregari on the Kemp Welch River.

After Company E and the 91st U.S. Engineers set up camp in the village of Gabagaba, it did not take long for trucks and jeeps carrying supplies to rumble in from Port Moresby. The Americans had suddenly transformed a quiet village of four hundred into a major operations base. The people of Gabagaba were frightened at first by the big trucks and the roaring noise. Soon, though, emboldened by their relationship with Lutjens, Baxter, and Edson, the villagers mingled with the new arrivals, doing their wash for them, gathering food, and teaching them a few basic Motu phrases like "Good morning"—*Dada namona*— and "Good night"—*Hanuaboi namona*. In return, the Americans good-naturedly gave away their remaining Australian shillings, reasoning that where they were going the money was worthless to them anyway.

As interested as the villagers of Gabagaba were in the men of Company E, they were fascinated by the black men of the 91st Engineers. The people of Gabagaba had been living under the imposition of the Australian colonial administration for over three decades, an era known still as "*taim bilong masta*." Although the Australians governed less harshly than other colonial administrations, the divisions between white and black were clearly defined—natives were laborers and white men were their bosses. The natives were expected to work when told to. When they saw the men of Company E and the black engineers working side by side, they imagined that in America black men and white men lived in a kind of harmonious equality. What they did not know, of course, was that the U.S. Army units were racially segregated and racial tension ran high, much as in American society in general. While black men were allowed to serve as engineers, they were not allowed in the infantry.

While the rest of his company and the engineers took a much-needed break from their road building efforts, Lutjens and Sergeants Henry Brissette and Hubert Schulte made a reconnaissance upriver. Word was that MacArthur wanted a road to Gobaregari in order to convert what was a rubber station into an advance base for the overland invasion. It was Lutjens' job to figure out if it could be done.

After scouting the area, Lutjens, Brissette, and Schulte were eager to get back to Kapa Kapa to deliver their report. The notion struck all of them at the same time—why walk two days to the coast when they could use the river? If they could build a raft and float down the Kemp Welch, they might be able to make Kapa Kapa before nightfall.

The raft was not a thing of beauty, but the question was, Would it float? When they shoved it into the water, the river was flat and calm, and once Lutjens got over his astonishment that the raft had not sunk, he found himself admiring the scenery. That is when he felt a jerk. His muscles tensed and his pulse raced. The raft rounded a bend, and the current quickened. Up ahead, the course was studded with boulders.

The three men frantically tried to pole their way to the riverbank, but the raft spun round and round, out of control. Lutjens grabbed for a log, and then they heard it—Crack! They had hit a large rock. The collision shot the raft into the air, and hurtled the men into the river.

Schulte surfaced first and swam to safety. Brissette grasped a floating log and was kicking for the riverbank when he saw Lutjens caught between two rocks in the middle of a powerful whirlpool. Laying his chest on the log, Brissette straddled it, and pushed himself back into the current. When he passed the whirlpool, he caught Lutjens by his helmet. Gripping Lutjens' helmet as tightly as he could with one hand, he used his other arm to paddle. When he reached the bank, he pulled Lutjens out of the water and they both collapsed in the mud at the river's edge.

It was night by the time the men regained their strength. Now they had to confront the reality of their situation: They were weak, wet, and growing cold, and their only choice was to walk. Plunging into the jungle, they used the sound of the river as their guide. They had not been walking for long when they spotted the light of a campfire tended by a lone native hunter. The Americans approached him carefully, and Lutjens, who had the most experience with natives, mimed their experience, the building of the raft, turning over, swimming to safety. Then Lutjens asked the most important question—could the man guide them to the coast? Somehow Lutjens was able to get his point across. He offered to give the man his pocketknife if he would be willing to lead them back to Kapa Kapa. The native hunter agreed.

In the dark of the jungle, the native man led the way, expertly navigating through a maze of knee-deep swamps, fallen trees, and a tangle of limbs and vines. Lutjens was amazed by the man's ability to find his way. Without his guidance, setting off through the jungle might have been a deadly decision. Lutjens and his party, holding hands and single file, made six river crossings that night, and each time the native hunter unerringly found sandbars on which they could walk, avoiding the river's deep holes and the fast current. When one of the men stumbled, the native man, hardly half the size of Lutjens, would tighten his grip and hold him up. Lutjens later remembered that the man's hand was "like steel." In the early hours of the morning, the hunter led Lutjens and others to the army encampment. Lutjens thanked the man for his service and gave him his pocketknife, and the man trudged off into the jungle.

Lutjens, Brissette, and Schulte were exhausted, and their legs were covered with cuts, scrapes, and bruises. Later that morning, Lutjens consulted with Captain Schultz, informing him of the difficulties a road building crew would encounter upriver. Schultz radioed Colonel Quinn, who had just arrived in Port Moresby. Quinn did not deliberate long. Company E and the 91st U.S. Engineers would have to hack another road through the jungle.

Chapter 7

THE BLOODY TRACK

FROM WHERE THEY STOOD on top of Ioribaiwa Ridge, General Horii's soldiers could smell the salt air. They were "wild with joy," wrote Seizo Okada, the war correspondent attached to the Yokoyama Advance Force. From the summit, the men looked down on the dusty town of Port Moresby, situated in the rain shadow of the Owen Stanleys, with its treeless, camel-backed hills and native gardens. They knew their long journey was almost over. The "endless waves of mountains," which Seizo Okada wrote had become a "living animal," had finally "vanished." Soon the dying would be over. Horii's army had marched "with only one objective in view, asleep or awake—Port Moresby," and now the Allied base was within its grasp.

Seizo Okada effused:

We gazed over the Gulf of Papua from the peak of the last main ridge we had fought to ascend. "I can see the ocean! The sea of Port Moresby!" The officers and men who had endured such bloody conflict embraced on the top of a stony ridge, crying and pointing. There were no longer any deep mountain ranges in front to block their progress. An undulating ocean of verdant green forest fell away before us. In the gaps between the trees, half obscured by the mountain mist, something was glittering. It was undoubtedly the sea. The Gulf of Papua. . . .

Later that evening, we stood on the peak and saw the lights of Port Moresby. We could just make out the searchlights shining over the airfield at Seven Mile to the north of the city.

Captain Nakahashi of the 55th Mountain Artillery was moved to write in his diary: "Over there was Port Moresby, the object of our invasion, which had become an obsession. Officers and men alike embraced one another overcome by emotion. . . . The line of captured positions more than atones for their blood."

It had been a hard-won victory for General Horii and the men of the Nankai Shitai. Of the six thousand combat troops that Horii had committed to the invasion of Port Moresby, only fifteen hundred remained, and at least half of these men were wounded, sick, or severely weakened by hunger and disease.

"The only thing that kept up the morale was the thought of Port Moresby," wrote Seizo Okada. For a moment Horii's men could forget the loss of so many friends and the hunger that gnawed at their bellies. Their jubilation, though, would not last.

·   ·   ·

As the Japanese contemplated victory in New Guinea, Guadalcanal thrust itself onto the main stage. Despite the diversion of resources and troops to the Solomon Islands, the Japanese were in trouble there. When U.S. Marines virtually destroyed an entire Japanese detachment in the Battle of Bloody Ridge in mid-September, Japanese General Headquarters in Rabaul once again was forced to amend its plans for taking Port Moresby. Their strategic situation was complicated by another disturbing development—Japanese war planners learned of MacArthur's intention to attack Buna.

Though news of Japan's defeat at Guadalcanal filtered forward along the Japanese supply line to Ioribaiwa Ridge, General Horii refused to accept its implications. He and his troops had come too far and suffered too much to turn their backs on Port Moresby. Privately, Horii brooded. But publicly, he proceeded as if the news from

Guadalcanal had no consequences for him or his troops. Horii designated September 20 as the day on which his army would resume its attack on Port Moresby, and sent out patrols over the Goldie River, which separated Ioribaiwa from Imita Ridge, to identify enemy positions and to assess the terrain that lay ahead.

Horii's soldiers were too busy foraging in the jungle and among the scattered native gardens to contemplate the aftermath of Japan's defeat at Bloody Ridge. Despair, though, filled their diaries. On September 11, hoping to conserve his food supply, Horii had cut the daily rice ration to less than a pint per man. Yet by September 17, the rice was nearly gone.

Horii's supply situation was desperate. Allied pilots pounded Rabaul with 1,760-pound bombs and attacked transport ships bound for Buna. Those supplies that made it to the north coast and were marked for the front line rarely made it that far forward—starving soldiers and carriers pilfered them along the way.

On Ioribaiwa Ridge, sick and wounded men were left to die because there was not enough food to nurse them back to health. When malnourished native carriers crumbled under their loads, Japanese soldiers beat them. The celebrated Japanese "seishin" was being tested as never before. Back in Kokoda, at the Japanese field hospital, the sick and the wounded languished. They were "packed in like sardines." Those without beds lay on leaves. Soldiers screamed out in pain, but doctors had no morphine to help them. They performed operations and amputations without anaesthetic. A newly dug graveyard sat just outside the hospital's entrance, so that the dead would not have to be dragged too far.

Horii's candid section leader, who earlier wrote of the soldiers' quest for water, wrote in his diary on September 18 of the shortage of food. "How long is this state of affairs going to last . . . ? My eyes have sunk in. Who would take me for a man of this world. . . . No one has any strength to work and if you lie on your side you stay that way. You cannot help feeling weak on 5 SHAKU of rice a day. . . . We are taught in the training manual to overcome any hardship or obstacle, but are there any battles as difficult as this? I'm keeping my diary, but even holding a pen tires me. How I'd love to eat something! Anything to fill my stomach!"

Lieutenant Sakamoto despaired: "Dreamed all night of lost subordinates. . . . Hurried on with the construction of positions. Detailed men from remaining TAI [unit] to dig for yams and taros. . . . How will we live in our present position without food? In another few days, we will have to eat roots or tree bark."

On September 19, Sakamoto laments the scarcity of food and medicine. Then he comes as close to disloyalty as a Japanese soldier dared. "Wonder what General HQ are doing? Patients will die and we will soon starve. How can we fight against this?"

On September 20, as the dark clouds emptied themselves of rain, he continued, "Not a single grain of rice left. Taros sufficient for only another day. From tomorrow, we will have to chew grass or bark." Then Sakamoto, as if recognizing his near-mutiny, rallies and regains his soldierly composure: "The battle we are fighting now is an important one," he writes. "The eyes of the world are upon us."

That same day, September 20, Horii had hoped to resume the attack on Port Moresby. His army, though, stayed put. Recognizing the need to boost his soldiers' morale, Horii assembled his troops and read to them a message he had prepared:

More than a month has elapsed since the Shitai departed from Rabaul. Following in the footsteps of the gallant Yokoyama Advance Tai, we have crushed strong positions at Isurava, the Gap, Eora, Efogi, etc; advanced swiftly, and after a fierce battle, destroyed the enemy's final resistance at Ioribaiwa. We now hold securely this high hill, the most important point for an advance towards Moresby.

Each Tai has tramped over mountains and through dark valleys . . . and pursued the enemy for over 20 days. We have waded through knee-deep mud, climbed breath-taking cliffs, uncomplainingly carried heavy weights of guns and ammunition, overcome the shortage of provisions, and thus accomplished a break-through of the so-called impregnable Stanley Range.

Words cannot describe the hardship. . . . The enemy at Tulagi and Guadalcanal have not yet been annihilated. . . .

Then Horii continued his deception. "The reason we have halted," he lied, "is to regain our fighting strength, in order to strike a crushing blow at the enemy's positions at Moresby. . . . Realize the value and importance of your mission. Bolster your morale and make your preparations complete, so that we can throw in the full fighting strength of the butai. . . ."

Four days later, as the sun evaporated below Imita Ridge, Tomitaro Horii sat "solemnly upright on his heels, his face emaciated, his grey hair reflecting the dim light of a candle, that stood on the inner lid of a ration can." Lieutenant Colonel Tanaka sat across from him. To Seizo Okada, they looked like "two lonely shadows."

Horii and Tanaka were pondering a series of wireless messages sent earlier in the day by the commanding general of the Southern Army in Rabaul. For Horii, who harbored the illusion that he and his army might still deliver a "crushing blow" to the Australians, the contents of the messages were troubling. "Stop attacking Port Moresby, and wait for further instructions," the first one said. Then came a second, less ambiguous message. "Withdraw from present position to some point in the Owen Stanley Range which you consider best for strategic purposes."

Horii refused. "I'm not going back, not a step," he raged. "I cannot give such an order." Horii, according to Seizo Okada, then, "grasped his samurai sword," and held it near Tanaka's neck and vowed not to "retreat an inch."

Darkness settled over Ioribaiwa Ridge, and Horii was determined to push on to Port Moresby. How could he retreat, he asked, "after all the blood the soldiers have shed and the hardships they have endured?" Besides, the Japanese army had never retreated before. Horii could not bear the disgrace. Then came a third message, bearing orders from Rabaul, instructing Horii "to withdraw completely from the Owen Stanleys and concentrate on the coast at Buna."

If Horii was resolved to disobey the order to withdraw, the next message left him no option. It came directly from Imperial Headquarters in Tokyo. "The Emperor himself" had authorized it, according to Seizo Okada.

When the order to retreat was circulated, Horii's troops were in disbelief. Imanishi Sadaharu, who had fought in China for three years and had landed with the Yokoyama Advance Force in July, wrote that Japanese soldiers "didn't know how to retreat." Besides, how could they withdraw when Port Moresby was within their grasp? According to Seizo Okada, "Hot-blooded commanders advocated a desperate single-handed thrust into Port Moresby."

When Takita Kenji, a naval officer, heard the news, he wrote of a "terrible grief" that "cut deep into our hearts."

"Like a bolt from the blue," wrote Lieutenant Hirano, who just a week before had walked back to Isurava to bring forward supplies for the assault on Port Moresby, "we received an order to withdraw. It left us momentarily in a daze." Earlier Hirano had sworn to the souls of his dead friends that he would continue their "aspirations." Now he wrote of his regret over the futility of their deaths.

In the late morning on September 25, the Australians began an artillery bombardment of Ioribaiwa Ridge. With each roar of the cannon, the Australian soldiers whooped and howled. They had winched, lugged, wrestled, and pushed a cannon thousands of feet up to Imita Ridge and now they were celebrating its thunderous blasts.

Lieutenant Sakamoto described the shelling. "Ten shells landed directly in front of the Okazaki Tai. Spent all day in the trenches . . . 2nd Battalion area pounded with mortars all night." The following day, September 26, he chronicled the start of the Japanese withdrawal. "Butai to leave present position at 1700 . . . No. 6 Coy [company] acting as rear guard." That evening, before abandoning Ioribaiwa Ridge "through the woods under the moonlight," Sakamoto took a moment to record a few lines in his diary. "It is truly regrettable," he mourned, "having to leave this hard-won area and the bodies of comrades behind. Sleep peacefully, my friends. We will meet again in heaven."

The following day, he scribbled a few more sentences: "Tired and dizzy. Marched almost unconsciously . . . Men are searching in the moonlight for food. Sickness increased. Everyone is pale and weak."

According to Seizo Okada, as the Japanese soldiers retreated, they dug up native gardens "inch by inch." If at first the natives, who were paid in worthless Japanese invasion currency, were uncertain about which side they would support, the sight of plundered gardens and abused bearers, stumbling with exhaustion, their wounds "crawling with maggots,"convinced them to align themselves with the Allies. Deprived of the prize of Port Moresby, once proud and disciplined Imperial Army troops sank into madness, turning to mindless acts of rage and destruction.

Seizo Okada witnessed the disintegration of the mighty Japanese fighting spirit. "They fled for dear life," reported Seizo Okada. "None of them had ever thought that a Japanese soldier would turn his back on the enemy. . . . As soon as they realized the truth, they were seized with an instinctive desire to live. . . . Discipline was completely forgotten. Each tried for his life to flee faster than his comrades."

The wounded and the sick, who had clung to life despite being deprived of food and medical attention, were carried out on stretchers by soldiers determined to save them. Soon, though, it became apparent to the company commanders that it was an impossible task. Then the order was given. They shot the wounded lying in their stretchers.

Still General Horii hoped. At some point, he knew that he would halt the retreat and dig in. Then even his sickest soldiers would fight till the end. If they could hold off the Australians long enough, buying time for Japanese forces to retake Guadalcanal, Rabaul would divert troops to New Guinea. A portion of them would seize Milne Bay and then Rabaul would resurrect the original two-pronged invasion plan: A large collection of troops would attack Port Moresby by sea, while the rest would join Horii's army, resuming the overland assault on the city.

Back up the trail, the Australians made plans for their counterattack. Three battalions began the advance on September 26. They came down off Imita Ridge, forded the Goldie River, and took up positions near Ioribaiwa Ridge, holding tightly to its plunging slopes. The following night, September 27, they shelled the Japanese position.

Early the next morning, the Australians started their advance. An air of uncertainty hung over the army. Company commanders were mystified by the absence of Japanese resistance. As they moved forward, the men felt a combination of excitement and dread. What kind of trap had the Japanese army laid?

A few hours later, unsure of what awaited them, two Australian companies scrambled up Ioribaiwa Ridge. The Japanese were gone. Tomitaro Horii's army was in full retreat, bound for the Buna-Sanananda beachhead. Fleeing soldiers struggled to reach the scanty food reserves farther back along the supply line. In blinding downpours, they stumbled along, tripping and falling over Australian corpses. Strafed throughout the day by Allied planes, they made no pretense of fighting back.

The Australian counteroffensive began in earnest on October 3 with a visit from General MacArthur. With war correspondents close by, MacArthur sat in his jeep above the Goldie River Valley, looking proud and undaunted. As the men of the 16th Brigade marched by, he took the brigade's commander aside:

"Lloyd," he said, calling the officer by his first name, "by some act of God your brigade has been chosen for this job. The eyes of the Western world are upon you. I have every confidence in you and your men. Good luck and don't stop." Then MacArthur's driver turned the jeep around. The following day, MacArthur was on his way back to Brisbane. His first visit to New Guinea had lasted hardly more than a day, his first visit to the troops barely an hour.

Chapter 8

MARCHING INTO THE CLOUDS

OCTOBER 6, 1942. As Captain Jim Boice was lying low in the mountain village of Jaure on the north side of the Owen Stanley divide, he scribbled a note in his diary: "Lonesome for back home. Rain and rest."

If Boice was enjoying a rare moment of self-congratulation, the situation warranted it. He had just led a reconnaissance team for seventeen days across the mountains via an obscure trail that the Americans came to call the Kapa Kapa, which no one other than native hunters and a 1917 government patrol had ever walked.

The Australians had counseled MacArthur against using Boice's route, and the Australians knew what they were talking about. They had been locked in a death grip with the Japanese on the Kokoda since late July, a campaign made fiercer by the terrain. But the Kokoda was what the Australians called a "track." A difficult, but established trail, it served as a government mail route, stretching from outside Port Moresby north across the Owen Stanley Mountains.

Since inheriting Papua from the British in 1906, the Australians had explored portions of the Papuan Peninsula, imposing a kind of Pax Australiana over the territory. According to its twenty-five-year-old colonial patrol report, the terrain over which MacArthur proposed to send a battalion, and possibly an entire regiment, though only thirty miles east of the Kokoda track, traversed much rougher country. The trail was too rugged, they said, the rivers too fast, and the mountain passes too high.

If anyone had the guts to scout a trail across the Papuan Peninsula, it was Jim Boice.

Boice did not look the part of a pioneer. He was a nearly bald, plain-looking man, and at thirty-eight, he was hardly young. He was also one of General Harding's favorites: intelligent, confident but unpretentious, undersized but tough, as Harding himself was. In fact, Boice was so small that he had been afraid that the army would reject him. One week before his physical he stuffed himself with food and water to make the Army's minimum weight requirement.

Boice liked the look of Jaure. With its large meadow, he knew it would be ideal for airdrops. The jungle had been a dense mesh of trees, leaves, vines, and fronds, but here, for the first time in weeks, the forest opened up and he could see in every direction. Flocks of white parrots, mountain pigeons, and green lorikeets flashed across the sky. Hawks and swiftlets cruised on updrafts.

Two days earlier, after sending a runner with his trail notes back toward Gabagaba, Boice radioed the divisional command post. The route across the mountains, roughly eighty miles from the coast, as the crow flies, was "taxing," he said, "but practicable."

Although Jim Boice may have been a reflective man, neither his message nor his diary offers many clues about how tough the trek really was. The reality was that by the time his small patrol reached the Owen Stanleys, the trail lost six hundred feet for every thousand feet it gained, climbing steeply up mountainsides, then plunging at sixty-degree angles into surrounding valleys. Some days, hiking from dawn till dusk, Boice and his men covered no more than two miles, though progress was difficult to measure because Boice's map included only approximate distances. It was so cold in the mountains that they would have to worry about hypothermia. The airdrops that they depended on were days late and inaccurate, and much food that the crews pushed out of the planes was lost to the jungle.

By the time they reached Jaure, Boice's feet were swollen and sore, and it was impossible for him to get his boots off. For two and a half weeks he had hiked in them, crossed rivers in them, and slept in them. Now the leather seemed glued to his feet. If he yanked at the heel, his skin felt as if it would tear. Finally, out of frustration, he may have taken his knife and cut slits in the leather to relieve the pressure. It did not matter; the boots were worthless anyway. They were rotting off his feet. Until the next airdrop, he was better off going barefoot like the carriers.

On the evening of October 6, a cold mountain fog settled in, and the rain came down in icy, gray sheets. Boice huddled under his shelter half. He had been lucky. He had made it to Jaure through tangled rain forest and clouds of mosquitoes and sweat bees, across gushing rivers, and over the Owen Stanley spine, without a serious mishap. Considering that he knew nothing of the route before he set out, it was an amazing accomplishment. Now the mountains lay behind him surrounded by clouds.

As was his habit, Boice removed two photos from a tin rations box. One of the photos was of Billy sitting in a Scout Flyer wagon. The other was of Zelma, Billy, and the family dog standing in the front yard of their Swayzee home. Boice held the photos in his hands until his fingers grew cold, then put them back in the rations box and took his diary out of his pack. Boice stored the diary in a large sheet of tinfoil. It was a small black pocketbook version that his wife Zelma had given him at Fort Devens. Boice set it on his lap and pulled out his prized fountain pen, the pen he had used to mark his high school students' papers back in Swayzee, Indiana. Swayzee: Even the name sounded breezy, slow-paced, and peaceful.

No matter how miserable he was, no matter how short the entry, Boice was dutiful about writing. He liked the feeling of the diary in his hands. Just to hold it seemed to fill him with Zelma's love. And the act of writing allowed him to conjure walking with Zelma through the quiet neighborhood while Billy slept in his arms and friends sat on their front porches sipping lemonade in the still, hot summer air. It enabled Boice to live, if only for a moment, in his former life.

•   •   •

With Boice's message that the Kapa Kapa trail was "taxing, but practicable," MacArthur's plan for an overland advance on Buna was ready to be put into motion. The crux of the plan was this: The 250-man Wairopi Patrol, under Captain Alfred Medendorp's command, would set out first. It would be followed by troops from the 126th Infantry Regiment, with the regiment's 2nd Battalion leading the way. From the Australians' experiences on the Kokoda track, the U.S. Army knew that a large group of soldiers could not rely on carriers alone. They got sick, they deserted, they needed food. Medendorp's job, therefore, was to establish drop sites along the route that pilots could easily identify. He and his men would also be counted on to clear the trail of Japanese interference. The 2nd Battalion did not need to be fighting its way north across the mountains.

MacArthur originally wanted the 126th to penetrate and cross the Owen Stanleys, cut west, and sneak in at the rear of the Japanese on the Kokoda track, where it would ambush Horii's army, cut off his supply line, or at the very least, hasten the Japanese army's retreat to the north coast. Because of Boice's report, however, MacArthur knew that he could never get a large number of troops over the mountains fast enough, so he amended his strategy. The 126th's new mission was to reach Jaure and secure the Kumusi River valley west to Wairopi on the Buna Kokoda track, a maneuver designed to cover the right flank of the advancing Australians. In time, the 126th would push north to the villages of Buna and Sanananda, where the Japanese army had established its coastal stronghold.

•　　　•　　　•

The blast-furnace heat was crippling. At Nepeana, Captain Alfred Medendorp stood in the shade of a coconut palm, trying to escape the sun, waiting for General Harding's jeep to arrive.

Working from dawn till dusk, Company E and the 91st Engineers had slashed a road not just to Gobaregari, but another ten miles upriver to the village of Nepeana. Although the road, which Company E dubbed "Michigan Avenue," was nothing more than a "peep trail," a bone-jarring path that quarter-ton vehicles could negotiate, it allowed the Americans to transport supplies farther inland. The advance base was located just south of Gobaregari at Kalikodobu, which the Michigan boys, following a theme, called "Kalamazoo." The name also brought to mind a favorite 1940s song—"I've Got a Gal in Kalamazoo."

Like Boice, Medendorp might have been trying to conjure images of home. Autumn in lower Michigan: the yellow-orange hickories shining in an electric blue sky; ducks in the sloughs; field corn ready to be picked; crisp nights and a big, shining harvest moon. He might have tucked in his shirt and massaged his hair into place. How absurd, to care about his looks in a place like New Guinea.

Growing up in his hometown of Grand Rapids, Michigan, Medendorp had been regarded as a handsome ladies' man. Unlike many other young men his age, his popularity with the opposite sex did not stem from his ability as an athlete. In fact his father, a Dutch immigrant, had never liked the brutality of football, and refused to let his son play on the high school team. Instead, Medendorp focused on music. He had a talent for it. Just out of high school he started a jazz band in which he played the saxophone and clarinet. At five foot eleven and 190 pounds, he was strong and built like an athlete, and he was proud of that. Dorothy Schutt was one of his many admirers. After meeting at a dance where Medendorp's band played, they dated and a year later married.

Now, Medendorp and his men were preparing for the day's march. In the blue-green haze, they yawned and stretched, and shaded their eyes from the glare of the tropical morning. A few were shaving. Who knew when they would get the chance again? Native carriers with vines tied around their ankles for traction shinnied up long, bare trunks to the tops of coconut trees, where they cut off coconuts and threw them down to waiting GIs.

Some of the other carriers, using fiber ropes, were tying bags of food to poles fashioned out of saplings, which they would carry on their shoulders, two men to a pole, one in front and one in back. An Australian sergeant barked at the carriers and told anyone willing to listen, "You gotta treat them with a firm hand, or they'll run all over you."

Medendorp had not had much experience with natives, but he had watched other Australians manage natives, and he knew that he did not like this sergeant's style. Besides, he understood that the patrol, as he would later write, "depended on them utterly," and they were to be treated as kindly as possible.

An old native man collected stray cigarette butts, taking a few remaining puffs. Other natives sat on their haunches passing a bamboo pipe in which they smoked a pungent trade tobacco. They were all fabulously decorated and tattooed, and the soldiers looked on as if they were watching an exotic movie; their eyes, according to Medendorp, "popped out at the sight." The native men wore laplaps—colorful skirts with a waistband and a small codpiece—shell earrings and strings of shells around their necks and woven bracelets of dyed fiber high on their muscular arms. Their teeth were stained a deep red from chewing betel nut. Their bare feet were broad and calloused. Pigs, the natives' prized possessions, snorted and trotted around casually, as if they were used to having the run of the place. When the bony hunting dogs ventured too close, the men kicked at them and shooed them away. The native women and children remained out of sight.

The men of the Wairopi Patrol oiled their weapons and sorted through their fieldpacks. They moved in slow motion, already listless from the heat. Sergeant Ralph Schmidt watched them. Schmidt was a bear of a man who had grown up on a farm in Coopersville, Michigan. Baling hay, he could outwork any man in the county. If Medendorp needed to rely on someone to keep the men on their toes, it was him.

When General Harding arrived in Nepeana by jeep over Michigan Avenue, he, like everyone who tried to negotiate the road, was splattered with mud and dripping sweat. No matter; he was eager to hear of the patrol's ten-mile march from Kalikodobu to Nepeana. Medendorp did not intend to paint a pretty picture; he knew that Harding would want the unvarnished truth.

Medendorp told General Harding that for many of his men the

trail had been a nightmare. The men of the Wairopi Patrol carried eighty pounds from "the skin out": the clothes on their backs, their backpacks, ten-pound M-1 rifles, two bandoliers of ammunition, and pineapple grenades. It was too much weight. Under a battering tropical sun, through jungle and rolling savanna country with mosquitoes teeming in the long grass, they walked sluggishly. Nothing in their training—no twenty-five-mile hike through the tablelands of Australia, no Louisiana Maneuvers—could have prepared them for the strain of it.

Medendorp's assessment of that first day must have left Harding uneasy. Harding could see General MacArthur's grand plan for an overland assault collapsing before his eyes. He instructed Medendorp to assemble his men, and did his best to rally them, reminding them of their crucial task. Only thirty miles to the west, on the Kokoda track, the Australian army was battling against the Japanese. The Australians were some of the world's best soldiers, but they could not lick the Japanese alone.

Harding then ordered the men to lighten their loads. They could cut down on their ammunition—twenty rounds per riflemen, eighty rounds for automatic weapons—and leave their "brain buckets" (steel helmets) behind.

As he watched the patrol move out, Harding, who had taught history as an assistant professor at West Point, must have wondered if New Guinea was to be Medendorp's Gedrosian desert. In 326 B.C. Alexander the Great led his army through the Gedrosian desert in what is now Iran. According to Plutarch, during the sixty-day crossing, Alexander lost three-quarters of his men to exhaustion and starvation.

•   •   •

Strinumu.

It had been only three days and roughly twenty miles into the Wairopi Patrol's crossing of New Guinea's Papuan Peninsula, but Captain Medendorp could not shake the feeling that he was on a fool's errand.

New Guinea was nature gone mad. The trail, what there was of it, was no wider than a garden row of beets, hemmed in by jungle "so dense," according to Medendorp, "as to afford almost constant shade." In backbreaking bursts, Medendorp's men scrambled up and down over a series of forested, hogbacked hills. Their rifles kept slipping off their shoulders. They frothed at the mouth and grunted like pack animals in the choking humidity.

Captain Boice had called the trail "practicable," but Medendorp knew Boice; Boice did not know the word quit. When Boice boarded the native lugger outside Port Moresby on September 17 for the twenty-four-hour trip to the trailhead, Medendorp was on hand to see him off. If Jim Boice had called the trail "taxing," Medendorp might have guessed that it would be sheer hell.

Only three days out and already the terrain and climate made a mockery of military order. Seeing the condition of his men, Medendorp must have realized that drastic measures were needed. A devoted officer, it is easy to imagine him walking up and down the line, shouting words of encouragement, coaxing the patrol along. Fortunately, he had one man with him he would not have to coax, and that was Roger Keast.

·   ·   ·

Keast was head officer of the Antitank Company and Medendorp's second-in-command. According to Medendorp, Keast was "loved and admired" by everyone who knew him. He was also the perfect complement to Medendorp. Medendorp was a cautious rule maker and follower. Keast was more impulsive. He had great physical strength and charisma and regarded all things military with a healthy dose of skepticism.

At Lansing Central High in Michigan, Keast had been movie-idol handsome and a star athlete—a football, basketball, and track man—famous for returning a fumble for the game's only touchdown against rival Lansing Eastern. After graduating from Central, he went on to a stellar career in football, basketball, and track at Michigan State. As the fifth fastest quarter-miler in the country, Keast made All-American in

1932. After setting the mile and two-mile relay records, Keast's team was invited to take part in the 1932 Olympic Games in Los Angeles. Because of illness, though, the team had to withdraw.

After graduating, Keast worked as a teacher and coach. He was a natural-born motivator, and in 1940 his basketball team at Graveraet High School in Marquette, Michigan, won Michigan's Upper Peninsula Class B championship. Keast was already a lieutenant in the Army Reserves when in the spring of 1941 he was called up and reported for duty at Camp Beauregard, Louisiana.

• • •

North of Strinumu, where the cold, mountain-born Mimani and Lala Rivers feed into the Kemp Welch, Medendorp and Keast stopped for a rest. At any other time of year the soldiers would have been able to fill their canteens, but now the rivers were swollen from recent rains. The water was undrinkable, so men resorted to licking the salt off the palms of their hands and sucking the sweat off their arms, or lapping at the raindrops that dripped from their faces.

Farther down the trail the lead platoon again caught sight of water—according to their simple map, the Arokoro River. The men rushed the river and cupped their hands and drank, as if the water had been sent from heaven. Many of them were resolved never to walk again, yet when the patrol moved out, they did too, driven on by the fear of being left behind.

Each and every American soldier had heard the stories: The Japanese were jungle supermen who liked to attack in the night. They would slither through the forest and disembowel a man or slit his throat and then crawl back to their units without being noticed.

After drinking at the stream, the men slowed to a snail's pace, their bellies full of water. Medendorp, Keast, and Schmidt did their best to keep them moving. It must have been unnerving, though—already the Wairopi Patrol was being undone by the jungle.

The first steep ascent nearly killed them. Boice had reported that soldiers would need hobnail boots. Rubber heels, he said, "were of no value." It did not take long for the Wairopi Patrol to discover just how right Boice was. Men slipped, stumbled, and fell, and got up, only to slip and stumble and fall again. Some leaned on wooden sticks slashed from trees. Others used creepers and vines and ferns, which cut and tore their hands, to pull themselves up the steep inclines. Parrots screeched as if heckling them.

According to Medendorp, the trail "told a tale of exhaustion and misery." Strong young men in their late teens and early twenties, men hardened by the Depression and manual labor, high school and college athletes, lay at the side of the trail in a stream of ochre-colored mud, cursing their fate. Their legs had given out, their chests heaved and they gasped for air. Some retched, coughing up volumes of water.

Later Medendorp would write: "We had to go slowly. We struggled through thick tangles of brush, over steep hills, over slippery stream bottoms. The column was like a long snake. Our sick were in the rear, staggering along with the help of the faithful aid men."

Many of the men opened their packs and discarded what they could: Some things, leather toilet seats, for instance, were ridiculous, a testament to just how little the U.S. Army knew about outfitting its soldiers for jungle warfare. But they threw out essentials, too—soap, towels, extra socks, shelter halves, mosquito netting, blankets, under-wear, and raincoats. Later, many of the men would come to regret it. How could they have known that in the mountains a World War I-era raincoat would be worth the two or three extra pounds?

Near dusk a native runner reported that Captain Keast had lo-cated a bivouac site two miles up the trail. In different terrain, two miles would have been a cinch. But two miles in New Guinea was like walking fifteen or twenty through the hills of Australia. However, that evening, Medendorp and the main body of the patrol finally limped in. Dusk had fallen and the jungle came alive with shrieking birds, the incessant yodeling of millions of frogs and whistling crick-ets, cracking branches, and the rustling of leaves. The men's imagina-tions were in overdrive. The rain on the forest canopy sounded like footsteps.

Long after the men had curled up like wet dogs under their shelter halves, which were nothing more than two sheets of canvas fastened together at the ridge line, Lieutenant Lester Segal, one of the medical officers assigned to the patrol, walked in with what Medendorp called a "flock of cripples." The stragglers were soaked, dazed, and weary.

In the few days on the trail, Lieutenant Segal had already proved himself equal to just about any task. He not only carried his pack like the others, but had to lug a heavy load of medical supplies, too. It was a pleasant surprise for Medendorp, who had been nursing a grudge against Segal, and was none too pleased that the lieutenant had been assigned to the patrol. Months before at Fort Devens, Massachusetts, Segal had raked Medendorp's Service Company sergeant over the coals for keeping a dirty kitchen, and had written a request that the sergeant be busted to private. Medendorp was incensed. The company had been at Fort Devens for only a few days and was working day and night to tidy up the kitchen.

Watching Segal in action, though, Medendorp forgave him. There was no denying it; Segal was good. He was strong and imperturbable, part medic, coach, and tough-as-nails drill sergeant.

Segal led his men through the maze of shelter halves and reported to Medendorp. Medendorp expressed concern about the condition of the men. They needed food and water, their sores bandaged, and antibacterial lotion to treat their jungle rot.

This, the patrol's third night on the trail, was "miserable," according to Medendorp. The men were unable to build fires and the rain forest canopy choked out what little light the stars might have offered. Frightened men searched in vain for a glimpse of a buddy. Only the carriers slept comfortably. Medendorp wrote that they "constructed frail huts to keep off the rain, built a fire by rubbing sticks and slept naked around the fire like a tangle of snakes."

•   •   •

A day later, Medendorp and his men reached Arapara, thirty miles inland. The patrol had been making slightly more than seven miles a day, two-thirds of a mile an hour, but Arapara was the gateway to the high mountains, and Medendorp knew that the next fifty miles would be much harder on his men.

Private Boyd Swem felt the chill of the approaching night. After accepting Captain Medendorp's invitation to join the patrol, Swem acted as Medendorp's "faithful orderly and friend." Medendorp recalled that Swem looked like the "most woebegone soldier in the column," and that "everything seemed to hang loosely on his frame." Still, each and every night, Swem found the energy to build a fire for Medendorp.

At Arapara, Swem crouched over a small pile of damp wood shavings and struck a match. The shavings caught, but only for a moment. Swem leaned toward a flickering spark and blew, trying to coax a fire. He was an irrepressible, happy-go-lucky character who kept the men entertained along the trail with his constant banter and off-key tenor. But as the fire fizzled, Swem was as irritable as the rest of the men. All around him, men were cursing: There was not a goddamned dry piece of wood in the entire jungle.

Ten minutes later, Swem and the entire patrol stared slack-jawed at what confronted them. All at once flashlights were aimed at a group of soldiers in shredded uniforms. At first, the men of the Wairopi Patrol thought they were seeing ghosts. But they were real enough: thirty-five Australians who had been fighting the Japanese on the Kokoda track thirty miles to the west. Segal opened his aid station. As he tended to the men, their story circulated among the Americans.

The Japanese had cut off the men from the main body of their battalion at Isurava on the Kokoda track. The group's leader, Captain Ben Buckler, sent a platoon commander to seek help, while he and his men hid out in the hills above Eora Creek. For six days the group lay low, fearing that they would be captured and tortured. They lived off sugar cane and sweet potatoes, not daring to move during daylight. Eventually they set off to the northeast through the jungle in the direction of the coast. Almost three weeks later, Buckler's group stumbled into the village of Sangai, where the village men carried twelve-foot pig spears. Buckler and his men expected to be killed, and possibly eaten, but instead they were given shelter and food. Buckler left behind his wounded and walked with the rest of his troops back inland.

At Wairopi, he and his men headed up the Kumusi River valley, past Kovio and the Owalama Divide, bound for Jaure. At Jaure, they turned south and headed over the wilderness of the Owen Stanleys, the same terrain that the Wairopi Patrol proposed to navigate. After more than a month of walking, they were already broken men when they entered the mountains, but the peaks north of Arapara nearly killed them.

The sight of Captain Buckler and his troops haunted the men of the Wairopi Patrol. What kind of place was this New Guinea? In a matter of a day, Medendorp's men had gone from the heat of the hill country to the frigid mountains.

Nothing about Captain Buckler's story, though, unsettled them as much as the possibility of torture at the hands of the Japanese. The barbarism of the Japanese army was legendary. A Japanese soldier would put a gun to his head, or hold a live grenade in his hand, or perform *seppuku*, gutting himself before he allowed himself to be captured. If captured, he expected to be tortured because that is what he would do in turn. Though they had signed the Geneva Convention of 1929, which articulated a policy for the humane treatment of POWs, the Japanese never ratified it. At the onset of the war, Prime Minister Tojo boasted that "In Japan, we have our own ideology concerning prisoners of war . . ."

In late January 1942, Japan's famed South Seas Detachment—the Nankai Shitai—ran their barges ashore and captured almost a thousand Australians at the Rabaul garrison. The Japanese soldiers tied 160 Australian prisoners to coconut palms at Tol Plantation. While the remaining Aussies looked on, Japanese trainees used the men for bayonet practice. Bayoneting was officially sanctioned by the Japanese military. It was said to "eradicate a sense of fear in raw soldiers." The plantation was filled with the cries of dying men and the grunts of Japanese recruits digging their bayonets into the bellies of their Australian captives. Privately, some of the Japanese soldiers expressed their revulsion, but publicly they kept quiet for fear of being perceived as cowards.

●   ●   ●

Arapara to Imiduru.

Mendendorp was upset about the lack of trail discipline. It was not only unmilitary, it was dangerous. From Arapara on, Medendorp insisted that platoons and companies stick together. With each day, the column was getting closer to the possibility of a Japanese ambush.

The men hardly heard him. The Wairopi Patrol was not made up of superbly conditioned soldiers specially trained in jungle and mountain survival. Prior to the march, many had never even climbed a hill higher than a thousand feet.

The soldiers who made up the patrol were not even infantrymen. They were heavy weapons guys of the Cannon and Antitank Companies, new units formed in Australia as part the division's streamlining. But with no antitank weapons or tanks to shoot at, they became foot soldiers, pressed into duty because the 126th Infantry Regiment's commanding officer, Colonel Quinn, did not want to disrupt his own battalions by providing the patrol with riflemen.

Lieutenant Segal must have been completely perplexed by the assignment, too. He was a doctor, after all. He had not been trained to walk a mile, much less be part of a grueling hike across the Papuan Peninsula. Even Medendorp—especially Medendorp—was no infantryman. He was a supply specialist. He had been an assistant Service Company commander. Supply often attracted talented rascals, jokers, and iconoclasts who enjoyed "wheeling and dealing" and the challenge of breaking army rules and getting away with it. But it also appealed to meticulous, can-do soldiers who followed army regulations to a T. Medendorp was the latter. He liked a good pair of socks, a knife with a blade sharp enough to cut paper, and clean silverware. When the general in charge of supply for the entire Southwest Pacific area was looking for a conscientious supply professional to identify airdrop sites at four-day intervals along Boice's route, he chose Medendorp. It was a daunting task under the best of circumstances. Nine hundred men of the 2nd Battalion were scheduled to follow Medendorp's patrol. Although it would use hundreds of native carriers, it would still need to resupply along the trail.

What Medendorp did not know was that some of the men from his former company were happy to see him go. He was an able officer, but he could also be a vain, demanding man. "He was always talking about separating the men from the boys," says a former Service Company soldier. "He rode the guys hard, but he was a physical man, and could back it up."

After scaling Turner's Bluff outside Arapara, the men knew they were in the mountains for real. A series of imposing, razorback ridges stretched as far as they could see. "Sometimes," Medendorp wrote, "the patrol was marching above the clouds."

Even Keast, the former star athlete, found the trail grueling. In a letter to his brother Bob in Lansing, Michigan, he wrote, "We are . . . in the clouds about 20 hours out of 24. You can guess from that that it's pretty wet most of the time. The sun is really hot when it's clear. The country here is supposed to be the most geologically disturbed (25 cent word) in the world. Most mountainous country is continuous ranges but this is many short ranges and cross ranges. There is absolutely no flat ground. . . . Mountains all around with deep valleys in between. There are no roads . . . just a narrow 'goat' trail that winds over the mountains or along the streams with steaming jungle growth on all sides."

The march to Imiduru, the patrol's fifth day on the trail, gave Medendorp reason to hope. The patrol climbed three thousand feet in four hours of hiking, and platoons stayed together.

But that evening Medendorp's hopes were dashed. The men's feet were shot, and their backs ached. Medendorp knew he could not afford to lose any of them, so he instructed Sergeant Schmidt to let the men who were worst off use the abandoned native huts instead of their leaky shelter halves (later in the Pacific war, soldiers would use jungle hammocks with a rainproof cover and mosquito netting). At first, the men were relieved to get out of the rain. But once they turned off their flashlights, rats nibbled at their toes and cockroaches as big as mice crawled over them. Even so, the men hardly moved a muscle—rats and cockroaches were a price they were willing to pay to have a roof over their heads.

The next morning, Medendorp had to contend with more bad news. The native huts had been teeming with fleas, and the men who had slept there were now infested. To make matters worse, all but twenty of the patrol's carriers "went bush," fleeing in the middle of the night and hiding with other villagers in secluded jungle caves. Their pay—a shilling a day, plus rations, a stick of tobacco, and maybe some salt—was not enough for them to overcome their fear of the mountains. They hailed from societies governed by an intricate web of magic, myth, and sorcery, and the sight of Buckler's emaciated men trudging out of the darkness confirmed their superstitions; the mountains were a place of bad spirits—*masalai*—and ghosts. The carriers warned that anyone who ventured into the high country would go blind, that his nose and ears would rot away, and his teeth would get so cold they would shatter in his mouth.

As Medendorp later noted, the carriers were also concerned about the patrol's supply of food. They had no concept of an airdrop. According to them the patrol was marching "straight into starvation."

After losing the bulk of his carrier force, Medendorp was livid. Who was going to lug the food through the mountains? How was he going to feed his men? Could he ask them to carry more? Could he hope for an airdrop at Laruni?

Medendorp made the only decision available to him. He instructed his men to shoulder as much extra weight as they felt they could. Then he told the remaining carriers that anyone caught trying to desert would be shot on sight.

•   •   •

Two days outside of Arapara, and fifty miles from the south coast, the Wairopi Patrol stopped near the village of Laruni on the banks of the Mimani River, which, fed by daylong rains, now barreled out of the mountains. No one could have been more surprised that Medendorp had made it that far than General Harding's intelligence officer, who had just taken part in an aerial reconnaissance of the trail. On October 9, he wrote in his diary, "never saw such mountains . . . all jumbled together in no arrangement of ranges—just a tangled mass with ridges and spurs running in all directions, a creek in every draw and the whole thing covered with jungle so dense that the ground was no- where visible."

Standing at the banks of the river, one of the carriers pointed to the clouds. Medendorp looked up. "Laruni?" he asked, and the carrier nodded.

Medendorp knew that his men would never be able to make the climb. Loaded down with extra weight, they were exhausted. Med- endorp instructed them to make camp; he would hike up to the village along with the patrol's radio crew. From there he would radio regi- mental headquarters and request a special airdrop.

Keast set down his pack and leaned against the trunk of a tree. Earlier in the day, he had wrenched his knee. It was sore and swollen. To take his mind off the pain, he took out of his fieldpack the only two photos he had brought with him to New Guinea. In one, his pretty wife Ruth was sitting on the running board of the family car, holding their baby son. In the other, his oldest boy Harry was standing in front of the car, smiling at the world.

Keast had not seen his family since the summer of 1941. Unlike Zelma Boice and Katherine Bailey, Ruth Keast never made it to Fort Devens. That would have required traveling by train or car from Michigan with young Harry, who was six at the time, and with Roger Jr., who was very young. Keast did not mind Ruth not being there. He felt more comfortable knowing that she was at her parents' farm with the boys. Besides, she had already said good-bye when she and Harry left Georgia.

While Keast was at Fort Benning during the summer of 1941, Ruth and young Harry rented a shack the size of a one-car garage out- side town. Farther back off the road, a creek coursed through the woods and alligators lounged along its muddy banks. Occasionally, feral pigs emerged from the thickets, raiding and spilling the garbage cans and rooting among their contents. Ruth could tolerate the alligators and the pigs; what she could not stand was the humidity. Though she had grown up on a farm outside of Dimondale, Michigan, and was no stranger to the outdoors, she wilted in Georgia's sticky summer heat.

Back in New Guinea, Medendorp needed a cigarette and a break before climbing into the clouds, and sat down next to Keast. Wiping his dirty hands on his sleeves, Medendorp asked his friend for a look at the pictures. He had seen them before, but that did not diminish his interest. He enjoyed Keast's photos almost as much as he enjoyed his own. Medendorp smiled—it was good for a guy to remember that he had family back home.

After looking at the photos, he and Keast studied their crude map of the trail. Even with the map, both knew that navigating the terrain ahead would require a good amount of guesswork—accurate depictions of the Papuan Peninsula extended only fifteen miles inland. Daunting river crossings also awaited them. If a guy lost his balance and fell, the Mimani's current would wash him away before his buddies had time to drag him out of the water.

Medendorp was certain of another thing—the march to Jaure would be a "daily hell." The route took a roller-coaster ride through the mountains, falling abruptly from cloud-covered peaks into deep, dripping valleys. Medendorp and Keast were discussing what lay ahead when someone interrupted them.

It might have been Sergeant Schmidt.

"We lost eight more, Captain," the sergeant said.

"What do you mean, Sergeant?"

"Carriers, sir. Eight more ran out on us."

The warnings had clearly had little effect.

Medendorp kicked the ground in disgust, and leaving Keast in charge of the camp, he assembled the radio crew and climbed to the village. He knew from Boice's report that the patrol would need to resupply before it entered the high mountains. Despite the assumption that Laruni was a poor choice for an airdrop, Medendorp inspected the area and realized it would be ideal. The village was located on a broad ridge among bare grasslands. From the ridge, Medendorp radioed regimental headquarters. Maybe the weather would clear long enough to allow the planes in.

Medendorp wanted "50 raincoats, 75 shelter halves, 50 native blankets, leggings, sweaters, denim coats, pants, handkerchiefs, flashlights, batteries, matches, and mail." The men had not received any mail in over a month, and Medendorp hoped that a letter from home would serve as a spirit booster. Leaving behind a radioman to wait for an answer, Medendorp slid back down to the bivouac site.

At dusk, the communications team descended the mountain in the fading light and rushed to the makeshift hut the carriers had erected for Medendorp to report that they had received a message from Boice: Boice and his pathfinder patrol were still in Jaure and had sighted a group of Japanese. They did not have an accurate count, but the Japanese looked to be marching to meet Medendorp and his men.

That night Medendorp posted sentries. If he thought that this precaution would ensure his men a night of rest, he was mistaken—no one could possibly sleep with a Japanese patrol in the area.

The next two nights passed uneventfully, and then on the morning of the patrol's third day in Laruni, three C-47s with fighter escort rumbled out of the clouds. The men were jubilant at the sight of the planes. They grabbed each other and danced and jumped in celebration. The U.S. Army had not forgotten about them.

Their elation was short-lived, though; the drop was a disappointment. The regimental band members who assisted with the drops kicked the food out of the side of the planes. Much of it, though, fell into the surrounding valleys, and lay scattered in the rain forest. The men knew that it would be their job to retrieve it, and the prospect filled them with dread. Finding small bundles of food in the jungle was like searching for needles in a haystack.

That afternoon Medendorp and the Wairopi Patrol set out for Jaure already tired from the morning's food hunt. Medendorp left Laruni with a heavy heart. Because of the injury to his knee, Keast was unable to walk and Medendorp ordered him to remain behind. He hated to leave behind the man he described as "an intimate personal friend," and knew that he would miss Keast's spirit and physical strength. "Keast," he wrote, "had more endurance than anybody else. Each morning he went ahead and selected a bivouac area for the night, and took care of the tired troops as they came in."

But Medendorp had spent the last two nights listening to Keast "crying out with pain." Although he was concerned about his friend's health, he was even more concerned about the patrol. They needed to make good time, and they needed to be mobile, especially if Japanese soldiers were marching to meet them. With Keast, Medendorp left behind Sergeant Ludwig and fifty-two men who Medendorp decided were unfit to cross the mountains.

It was a mixed bag for the men who stayed behind. They were grateful for the much-needed rest, but being left behind frightened them. Keast and Ludwig were accomplished soldiers, but fifty-two tired men would be no match for a sizable Japanese patrol.

Before setting off for Jaure, Medendorp radioed regimental head-quarters. Using the code words that the regiment had established for the villages along the route, which the men had named after cities in Michigan, Medendorp informed Colonel Quinn that Keast would remain in Laruni.

"Starting for Holland," Medendorp said, referring to Jaure by its code name. "Keast has bad knee. He is staying at Coldwater (Laruni) with fifty men. Received supplies."

•   •   •

Only a mile out of Laruni, it looked like the end of the line for the Wairopi Patrol. A dense fog crawled up the mountains, and the trail disappeared. The native carriers were almost a liability now. In the jungle they had often helped Medendorp to locate the trail; to find cold, pure water, filtered by stones; to distinguish between harmless and killer snakes; and to forage for food to supplement the soldiers' rations. But in the mountains, they were lost and terrified, and had to be alternately encouraged and berated to continue.

Everything that Medendorp had feared about the march to Jaure was coming true. "Words," he wrote later, "cannot describe the hardships of that march over the mountains." The rain that fell the previous evening turned the trail into a pit of shin-high mud that sucked at the men's boots. The patrol made excruciatingly slow progress over tier after tier of sharp mountain peaks, and dangerous descents on slippery trails. Sometimes men lost their balance and tumbled into the jungle. When they struggled to their feet, they were covered in half-inch-long leeches. Getting them off after they had attached themselves was not only a chore, but the leeches left small, stinging red wounds that, if not treated, invited infection. The men also discovered that the forest teemed with something like stinging nettles. The natives called it "salat," and rubbed the leaf on tired muscles to relieve soreness. They had to choose carefully, though—just a touch from the wrong salat leaf left behind a painful red rash.

Massive trees with trunks the size of army jeeps, adorned with lianas and wrapped in a swarm of vines resembling large pythons, flanked the trail. At first the men marveled at them, but less than an hour into the hike, they were incapable of admiration. The faint hunting trail rose nearly straight up, and soon they were on all fours, slopping through the mud, grabbing at roots, trees, ferns, bushes, sharp-edged leaves, anything they could grasp to keep from falling backward down the slippery mountain. Everything they reached for came equipped with spurs or thorns or tiny but sharp bristles, and often swarms of angry red ants.

Medendorp had to keep his troops moving. "We were marching," he wrote, "again with only the rations we could carry. . . . If we couldn't get to the next dropping ground . . . we would be stuck in the jungle without supplies."

Two days out of Laruni, after a series of false summits, surrounded by frigid, swirling mists, the Wairopi Patrol confronted the highest point on the trail, the 9,500-foot Mount Suwemalla, which sat in the midst of the cloud forest, a strange, icy, god-forsaken place where the sun never shone. Glowing moss and phosphorescent fungus covered every tree, and subterranean rivers roared beneath the men's feet. They were convinced that the peak was haunted and promptly dubbed it Ghost Mountain.

Ghost Mountain—the men could not wait to leave it behind. Soaked in sweat and trembling from the cold and rain, which "fell without ceasing," Medendorp's patrol began its descent. "At one place," Medendorp wrote later, "we right-stepped over the face of a stone cliff with our bellies pressed against the stone and our arms outstretched like a Moses in prayer. . . . It is still a miracle to me that all of our men got over that point safely." As darkness fell, the patrol made it to level ground. Medendorp continued, "Finally, we reached the bottom and made camp beside a clear running stream, and in a constant rain." Too exhausted to prepare camp or to build fires, they ate their rations cold and shivered in the chilly night air. As much as they had hated the heat of Nepeana, the men longed to be warm again.

By noon of the next day, the patrol reached Suwari. Medendorp wrote that the village's "wild" natives fled in terror. Despite the probability of fleas, the native huts looked too warm and dry to pass up, so Medendorp halted the patrol. They would spend the rest of the day and the night in the village. Then Medendorp issued a warning: "No souvenirs." Nothing was to be touched. The soldiers were to leave tobacco behind as a thank-you. Medendorp wanted the people to know they could trust the American soldiers.

Medendorp's precaution was a smart one. The patrol had reached the north side of the mountains, and that meant the possibility of Japanese. The last thing the patrol needed was angry natives who could report its presence to the Japanese and spoil the entire plan—or worse yet, get a lot of people killed.

In the middle of October 1942, many New Guinea natives had still not allied themselves with either the Japanese or the Americans and the Australians. They were waiting for the outcome of the early battles and watching to see who treated them best. It was an unsentimental calculus on their part. They wanted, simply, to side with the winning army in order to minimize the war's impact on their people.

That night, the eight remaining natives—four more carriers had fled before the patrol began its ascent of Ghost Mountain—sang and danced in their hut until morning. Whether they were singing out of gratitude for their safe passage over Ghost Mountain, or fear, no one knew. Medendorp allowed them to celebrate, though. Anything to keep them happy.

Before setting out for Jaure the following morning, Medendorp left behind a platoon under a lieutenant to guard the village. If the Japanese sneaked into the village, they could ambush the 2nd Battalion, which Medendorp knew from periodic radio reports was slowly making its way north.

•   •   •

Two days out of Suwari, and fourteen days after setting out on the trail, Medendorp and the Wairopi Patrol walked into Jaure, at the headwaters of the Kumusi and Musa Rivers. It had taken the patrol nearly a week to travel the last sixteen miles. At Jaure, they discovered Boice's pathfinder patrol, from which they had not heard anything since Laruni. Everyone, it seemed, was okay—after sighting the Japanese patrol, Boice decided that it was safer not to try to make radio contact.

Boice, who had been out scouting, returned to the village. What he saw stunned him: Medendorp and his men were a pitiful sight. For a moment Boice may have experienced a twinge of doubt. Had his report on the feasibility of the route across the mountains consigned hundreds of men to misery? For him and his small patrol, the trail had been extraordinarily tough, but it was "practicable." But what would become of an entire battalion? What would happen when the monsoons arrived? Would the trail be "practicable" then?

Boice did not express any of these reservations to his friend.

"Well Al, you old son of a gun," he said, shaking Medendorp's hand.

Hoping to achieve a bit of humor, Medendorp paraphrased Stanley encountering Livingston.

"Jungle Jim, I presume."

The following day, Medendorp dispatched a fifty-man detachment into the Kumusi River valley. When Sergeant Jimmy Dannenberg's group left Jaure, everyone was outfitted with new boots that had been dropped days before. Few had a pair that fit well, but no one cared. New boots, ill fitting or not, were something to be grateful for.

Medendorp stayed behind to radio Colonel Quinn. Then, because every porter with whom he had begun the hike had deserted, he spent the day rounding up seventy-five native carriers.

Medendorp described the new carriers as "wild" looking. To be sure, the natives of Jaure were some of the most isolated people on the Papuan Peninsula. Except for infrequent contact with Australian colonial patrols and perhaps the odd prospector, they had no exposure to the outside world. They were tattooed men, who wore bone necklaces, ear and nose ornaments, loincloths of beaten bark, and fur hats; they smeared their bodies with pig fat to protect against the cold. They believed in sorcerers, supernatural forces, the dream world, and spirits that had to be propitiated through elaborate rituals.

Lieutenant Segal examined the natives. Many were covered in bug bites, and because of a vitamin B deficiency, they also had skin diseases, festering sores, peeling skin, and grayish scales. In truth, Segal was only able to give them basic care. He had sent numerous radio messages requesting surgical instruments, and though food and ammunition came, the instruments never did. It was a constant frustration for Segal. How was he to care for an entire patrol and its carriers with only one scalpel and a few hemostats?

Using that one scalpel and his knife, Segal first took care of the soldiers' boils and ulcers. Some of the men had skin ulcers where their fatigues had rubbed and the straps of their backpacks had pressed against their shoulders. Some had malaria, with temperatures hovering at 103 degrees. They complained of tender bellies, aching joints, confusion, impaired vision, and nightmares. For them there was nothing Segal could do. He was almost out of quinine.

Late that night, Medendorp limped over to Segal. He had an ulcer on his leg that had been causing him pain since Ghost Mountain. He had ignored the advice of Boice's patrol to treat "small wounds," because they "fester rapidly." Segal sterilized his knife over the fire and sliced into the ulcer. Medendorp tightened his jaw and clenched his fists. The ulcer oozed a putrid, yellowish-brown pus.

Three days later, Medendorp and his men dragged themselves into Barumbila, a village down the Kumusi River in the shadow of Mount

Lamington, about ten miles southeast of Wairopi. Medendorp was "weak from almost constant dysentery and . . . a fever." At Barumbila, which was an ideal site for a dropping ground, he spent the day recruiting a large force of natives to collect and carry supplies for the approaching 2nd Battalion. Soon after, he learned that General Kenney and his Fifth Air Force had airlifted the entire 128th U.S. Infantry Regiment to a village called Wanigela on the Papuan Peninsula's north coast, where pilots put down on a crude airstrip carved out of the kunai grass by missionaries and area villagers. MacArthur had discovered a better way to get troops across the mountains.

Chapter 9

ONE GREEN HELL

ALFRED MEDENDORP WAS AT THE VILLAGE of Laruni when the 2nd Battalion got the go-ahead. Though Major Simon Warmenhoven worried about the myriad medical needs of nine hundred men marching across New Guinea, there was little he could do now. A team of medics and a platoon of engineers would accompany the battalion. Warmenhoven could only hope for the best.

Company E led the way for the 2nd Battalion with the battalion's other companies—F, G, H, and Headquarters—following at one-day intervals.

It was fitting for Company E to be out front. When General Harding came to Amberley Airfield to see the company off on September 15, he told the men that they had been selected to go first because they "were the best in the outfit." He called them the "spearhead of the spearhead of the spearhead." Lutjens and his men liked the sound of it and began referring to themselves as "The Three Spearheads." It was a distinction the company could be proud of: The 32nd was the first combat division of the U.S. Army to embark on an offensive mission against the Japanese. That meant that Company E was leading the way for the whole division.

Private Art Edson, who had scouted the coastal route to Gabagaba with Lutjens, took a moment to write his sweetheart.

123

Dearest Lois,

I take the chance to drop you a line as I may not have the chance again for a long time, as we are now some where in New Guinea. . . . This island is the Hell Hole of the world. I never expected to see natives used for pack horses or dressed like you see in shows, grass skirts and that is all. . . . Have seen quite a few crocodiles and have shot a couple. We shot a snake today, nine feet long. Will write more as soon as possible.

Love Forever, Art

On October 13, the day before Company E set out, Lutjens made a brief entry in his diary: "Been three weeks in New Guinea . . . I'm afraid it will become much worse than this. We are now starting into the foothills of the Owen Stanley Range. . . . We are going to carry six days' rations—one pound of rice, one handful of green tea, a little sugar and two cans of bully beef. Plus our field equipment."

What Lutjens described was a situation in which each man was carrying an almost impossible amount of weight. Provisions and field equipment, ammunition, plus a weapon—a ten-pound M-1, or a nine-pound model 1903 Springfield rifle, or a twelve-pound Thompson .45 caliber submachine gun, or a twenty-pound Browning Automatic Rifle (BAR)—meant that the average man in Company E carried nearly as much as Medendorp's men—sixty to eighty pounds. In other words, no one had learned from Medendorp's experience.

The machine gunners had it the worst. A .30 caliber machine gun alone weighed thirty pounds, not counting the tripod and ammunition. Together the gun, tripod, and ammunition were so heavy they were divided among three men. Still, the machine gunners struggled under loads that would have broken lesser men trekking across the flat fields of Kansas.

The men lugged 60 mm mortars over the mountains, too. One carried the fourteen-pound baseplate, another carried the long, eighteen-pound tube or cannon, another the legs, which weighed just over fifteen pounds, and three men lugged the mortars—three four-pound rounds per man.

Company E's trek began, ironically, with a party. At Nepeana, the natives danced and sang and lavished them with rice, yams, and pawpaws. The day after, reality set in with pelting monsoonal downpours that drenched the soldiers to the bone and turned the trail into a river of mud and clay.

Lutjens described what would become an ordinary day:

We'd start at six in the morning by cooking rice, or trying to. Two guys would work together. If they could start a fire, which was hard because the wood was wet even when you cut deep into the center of a log, they'd mix a little bully beef (canned mutton) in a canteen cup with rice, to get the starchy taste out of it. Sometimes we'd take turns blowing on sparks, trying to start a fire, and keep it up for two hours without success. I could hardly describe the country. It would take five or six hours to go a mile, edging along cliff walls, hanging on to vines, up and down, up and down. The men got weaker; guys began to lag back. It would rain from three in the afternoon on, soaking through everything. The rivers we crossed were so swift that if you slipped it was just too bad. It was every man for himself. No one waited for anyone else, unless he was hurt. An officer stayed at the end of the column to keep driving the stragglers. There wasn't any way of evacuating to the rear. Men with sprained ankles hobbled along. . . . If they hadn't made it, they'd have died.

The engineers did their best to remove roots, deadfall, and large rocks from the trail. At river crossings, they toppled trees that could reach the far bank. At steep ascents and descents and along treacherous cliffs, they sometimes erected handrails.

On the way to Strinimu, the men of Company E, like Medendorp's men, began to jettison equipment they considered extraneous. After all, what need would they have for a gas mask or a razor or a mess kit? The guys got together in groups of three; one kept a spoon, another a knife, another a fork. Later, they would share the utensils. One guy would dip into a can of beans, take the biggest bite he could, and pass on the spoon.

As they approached the mountains, Lutjens watched as men discarded equipment regardless of its utility. They threw out blankets, raincoats, mosquito nets, and extra underwear. They cut their pants off just below the knees and their shirts at the shoulders. They sliced off the extra leather at the top of their boots. Some ripped the buttons from their shirts. They kept their toothbrushes, though; they needed something to clean their rifles.

The waste delighted the native carriers, many of whom brought along nothing more than tobacco, a machete, and a string bag. The practice of platoon leaders like Lutjens was to stop every hour for a ten-minute rest. While the men rested, the carriers set down their loads and backtracked, scavenging everything they could fit in their bags.

When Company E finally reached Laruni, the rain came down in waves. Lutjens was huddled under a shelter half with his best friend, Staff Sergeant Peeper, and Sergeant John Fredericks. All were wet and caked with mud. Their bodies ached, but they were too hungry and exhausted to sleep. What they did was to talk about food. Back home on the farm in Michigan, Fredericks had been a great eater, so Lutjens and Peeper deferred to him.

Fredericks did not disappoint them. He talked about sprawling farm breakfasts and heaping suppers, and about canning apples. When Lutjens and Peeper joined in they discussed Christmas dinners and swore that if they made it out of New Guinea and back home alive that they would devote their lives to the joyous pursuit of food and eating. In other shelter halves, men were discussing the same thing. The subject of women never came up, at least not in a sexual way. When they talked about women, they fondly remembered the smells of their mothers' kitchens, the comforting odor of cookies and apple pies baking in the oven.

What they might have craved more than anything else was salt. Lutjens later wrote, "The sweat in that drippy, oozy place took all the salt out of our bodies." He dreamed of "good salty bacon or a dill pickle."

Up until Laruni, food consisted of Australian bully beef and half a canteen cup of rice, which the soldiers stored in a sock that they knotted at the top. Even the hungriest of men considered the bully beef too vile to eat. Some, like Lutjens, could stomach it only when mixed with rice in what Lutjens called a "hobo's stew." If Lutjens ate it plain, he got "sick as a dog." But at Laruni, Company E got lucky. One morning, a pilot making a drop dove dangerously low, skimming over the tops of the trees. Men rushed to recover the boxes, dreaming of the possibility of finding a chocolate bar. According to Lutjens, a guy "would sell" his "soul for a chocolate bar." They thought they were fantasizing, when instead of chocolate, they found another treat—hard candy! Lutjens wrote that the candy dropped "from the jungle vines overhead like a hail storm," and was scattered across the rain forest from "hell to breakfast."

The soldiers' joy at discovering the candy was short-lived. Beyond Laruni, wrote Lutjens, the march became "one green hell." Still, Company E kept moving, motivated by a curious sense of pride. "No one," according to Lutjens, "wanted to get passed by another unit."

*   *   *

As bad as Company E had it, the men of Companies F, G, and H had it worse. The boots of nearly two hundred soldiers—those of Company E—had turned every square foot of trail into something resembling a pig wallow.

It was man against jungle, and it was obvious to Don Stout, a platoon sergeant from Muskegon, Michigan, that the jungle was winning. Stout had joined the Michigan National Guard in 1939 at the age of fifteen. He had never liked school anyway and if the recruiter sensed that Stout was too young, he chose to ignore the Guard's eighteen-year-old requirement. Stout was proud of his new uniform, though he had to contend with people who called him a freeloader living off the federal government.

When Stout joined the Guard, he never envisioned himself slogging through the jungles of New Guinea.

"You should have seen 'em," Stout says. "Guys were straggled out so far along the trail. When they were too sick or tired to move, they would set up a pup tent—if they hadn't tossed it already—and pray that they would get better before the last company came past."

At twenty-five, Don Ritter, a staff sergeant also from Muskegon, was something of an old-timer, especially compared to Stout. But he certainly did not lack for strength. "One hundred and seventy-five pounds and not an ounce of fat," he says. "That's how much I weighed when I started." When the malarial fevers hit, though, they laid waste to his body. The first full-blown attack struck one day out of Nepeana. Ritter could not understand it. The jungle was a humid 100 degrees, but his body shook as if he were back in Muskegon walking shirtless on a chilly October morning. By the time the medic was able to check him out two days later, Ritter's chill had turned into a 103-degree fever. On the trail he walked like a zombie. His buddy Russell Buys helped him out, but Buys was himself exhausted. Ritter's legs were buckling on him, and his teeth rattled like a train going over the tracks. He drifted in and out of delirium. Thousands of parasites were reproducing at will inside his liver and exploding into his bloodstream.

"I don't know if I can make it," Ritter told Buys. "I'm sicker than a dog. Just leave me here."

Buys, though, insisted that his friend keep moving. "And somehow," Ritter says, "I did. I didn't have a choice. It was walk or die. They couldn't get you out. Evacuation just wasn't a possibility."

Stanley Jastrzembski says, "Everybody had malaria, and everybody was throwing stuff out of their packs. The guys with quinine pills were popping them like gumballs. Things got really bad when guys started getting dysentery, too. Then we all damn near died. I had 'jungle guts' so bad, I could scrape the crap off my legs with a tin ration can. Some guys had to go thirty times a day and all that came out was blood."

The food and water did not help the situation. If there was not a nearby stream or river, men drank from muddy jungle puddles. And often when they reached camp, they were so tired they did not bother to cook their rice. "We just soaked it in water to soften it and then ground it up in our mouths like animals. It was hell on our bellies," says Jastrzembski.

A stench followed Company G through the jungle. Jastrzembski's body soured with the smell of encrusted sweat, excrement, and oozing sores. The worst dysentery cases dropped their pants and voided their bowels where they stood, or, like toddlers, fouled themselves as they walked, too tired to take down their pants. Some resorted to cutting the backs out of their pants and relieved themselves whenever nature "called."

.   .   .

DISEASE HAS ALWAYS been the enemy of armies. MacArthur witnessed this firsthand in the Philippines and, before that, as a divisional commander in World War I, when trenchfoot and the flu ravaged battalions. In the Philippines, dysentery, ringworm, hookworm, dhobi itch, and especially malaria disabled countless men. By March 1942, the combat efficiency of MacArthur's troops had fallen by more than 75 percent due to disease and malnutrition. But MacArthur had never encountered anyplace like New Guinea. It was the perfect incubator for a host of debilitating tropical diseases. The bodies of the men—of Stout, Ritter, Jastrzembski, and countless others—who made the march across the Papuan Peninsula coursed with pathogens. Although the dysentery outbreaks might have been avoided through better hygiene, the men were largely defenseless against insect-borne diseases like malaria.

The 32nd Division suffered several types of malaria, especially *vivax* and *falciparum*. Vivax debilitated its victims, making them susceptible to potentially lethal secondary infections. Falciparum, vivax's wicked cousin, sometimes caused men to go mad, and occasionally, if left untreated, caused death. Despite the prevalence of malaria, however, army physicians knew very little about treatment of the disease.

Traditionally, soldiers fighting in malarial regions of the world relied on quinine as a malaria suppressant. An alkaloid extracted from the bark of the cinchona tree, quinine was discovered by Spanish missionaries in the seventeenth century in Peru and Bolivia. Though quinine masks the effects of malaria, it does nothing to cure it, as some of the men of the 2nd Battalion discovered. Quinine was unreliable in more than one way. It had become a sole-source commodity, grown only on the island of Java, which fell to the Japanese in January 1942. Quinine shortages proved disastrous in New Guinea. Eventually, soldiers fighting there would have an alternative—atabrine (quinacrine hydrochloride), which, ironically, had been developed as a synthetic substitute for quinine by the Germans in the early 1930s. In 1939, realizing atabrine's potential, the United States began a crash program to become independent of foreign sources. But atabrine had its drawbacks. It was so new that medical officers, experimenting with dosage, feared its toxicity and worried about potential "atabrine psychosis." More basically, soldiers loathed the taste of it. Company commanders trying to enforce a daily regimen were also up against a rumor that atabrine caused impotency and sterility. When their skin took on the yellow hue of an "atabrine tan," soldiers did not need any more convincing. They were young men who hoped to return to wives and girlfriends. They would take their chances with malaria.

But in October 1942, all that was available to soldiers like Ritter and Jastrzembski was quinine. Without the aid of waterproof containers, though, the quinine was almost impossible to preserve. In the heat and humidity, the pills dissolved in their pockets before they could use them. Some men did not care. The quinine made their ears ring so badly they refused to take it. If a guy could not trust his ears, he was as good as dead.

In addition to malaria, New Guinea served as a breeding ground for a variety of other nasty diseases: dengue or breakbone fever, which was carried by the aedes mosquito (the same breed that causes yellow fever) and was accompanied by terrific headaches and throbbing body pains; and the dreaded scrub typhus, which brought on high fevers, hallucinations, and severe, sometimes fatal hemorrhaging. The culprit, in the case of scrub typhus, was not the mosquito, but a tiny chigger. Just as dangerous for the men of the 2nd Battalion were jungle rot and leishmaniasis (caused by the bite of sandflies), both of which were characterized by open sores. Because they could lead to serious complications, and because most soliders tended to ignore the sores, jungle rot and leishmaniasis scared the hell out of the medics. Then there was beriberi, directly linked to the soldiers' diet of polished white rice. Caused by a thiamine deficiency, beriberi presented a whole assortment of debilitating symptoms, including vomiting, confusion, loss of sensation in the hands and feet, edema, and rapid heart rate.

The U.S. Army in New Guinea forfeited huge numbers of men to disease. This raises the question: How could MacArthur have failed to give sufficient consideration to the effects of fatigue, climate, landscape, and the ravages of jungle-borne pathogens on a physically depleted army? In September 1942 he told the head surgeon in the G-4 Section at his General Headquarters that malaria had played such an important part in his defeat in the Philippines that he wanted to keep it under control in New Guinea. Despite this, General Headquarters never implemented a determined plan to deal with disease in New Guinea. This omission would prove to be ruinous for the entire 32nd Division.

●　　●　　●

The medics of the 19th Portable Hospital, who accompanied the 2nd Battalion across the mountains, bore the brunt of this oversight. After the dysentery epidemic struck, they divided into four teams, established way stations along the trail, and treated the men as best they could given their limited resources. All the while they were cursing General Headquarters because even when medical supplies did make it to Australia, they often did not make it north to New Guinea.

Although the medics were seemingly working miracles, they could do nothing for Lieutenant Colonel Henry Geerds, the 2nd Battalion's commander, who suffered a heart attack outside of Strinimu. Geerds was an "old-timer," a veteran of World War I. The march across the Papuan Peninsula was simply too much for him.

Stutterin' Smith, who was running a radio detail at the trailhead at the time, received the news of the battalion commander's heart attack that evening. Using the landline, Smith notified regimental headquarters. The following day, Colonel Quinn ordered him to catch up with

and take command of the battalion. Smith had not been pleased about
being left behind at the trailhead in some rear echelon job while the
men that he had helped to train trudged off to fight the Japanese. But
now he must have wondered: Could he lead a battalion across New
Guinea?

Smith may have experienced a moment of doubt, but Colonel
Quinn had no such reservations. Smith had no airs about him. He was
a rough, likable straight shooter, an "enlisted man's officer."

Late on the second day, Smith and his small team, which included
Captain John Boet, an accomplished doctor whom Warmenhoven had
instructed to accompany Smith, reached Strinimu. Smith and Boet were
"lame and tired," and if initially Smith underestimated the difficulty of
the hike, he did not anymore. The following morning, he recruited a
local guide. Romee was a slender, athletic-looking native man, who soon
rendered himself indispensable to Smith. Romee could speak and read
and write English, and became the group's chief cook, translator, and
fire builder, too. Romee's greatest gift, though, was as a trader. At villages along the trail, Romee often used the small group's supply of salt
tablets and safety matches to barter for precious fruits and vegetables.

⬤   ⬤   ⬤

As Smith and his party of men hustled to overtake the rest of
the battalion, Lutjens and Company E entered the high mountains
north of Laruni. According to Captain Schultz, the trail became so
narrow, with sheer cliffs on either side, that "even a jack rabbit
couldn't leave it." The men kept plodding forward, oblivious to
almost everything but the trail itself.

"One day, I swear, I saw gold nuggets in the bottom of a stream,"
Lutjens would later recount. "There's gold nuggets, but what the hell's
gold, you can't eat it. It must have been a beautiful country, but all you
could see was mud and the guy's feet ahead of you. . . . The only time
anybody really commented on anything would be when he fell down,
and then he would cuss because it was so hard to drag yourself
back up."

In all likelihood, Lutjens was not imagining it when he thought he spotted gold. Adventurous prospectors had discovered gold in the mountains of the Papuan Peninsula in the early 1900s. Wau-Bulolo, northwest of the Kapa Kapa (in what is today Papua New Guinea's Eastern Highlands Province), was the scene of a two-decade gold rush that began to taper off by the start of World War II. The gold rush drew young men from all over the world, including Errol Flynn, who arrived in New Guinea in 1928. In addition to working as a patrol officer, a tobacco farmer, and a slave trader, Flynn managed a small claim in the mountains before landing in Hollywood and embarking on his movie career.

By late afternoon on October 23, Company E confronted Ghost Mountain. It was a day they had dreaded, and one that they would never forget. The native carriers, who had been such a great help on the jungle trail, now balked. Lutjens understood their fear. Ghost Mountain, he recalled, "was the eeriest place" he had ever seen.

The trees were covered with green moss half a foot thick. We would walk along a hog's back, straddling the trail, with a sheer drop of thousands of feet two feet on either side of us. We kept hearing water running somewhere, but we couldn't find any. We could thrust a stick six feet down through the spongy stuff . . . without hitting anything real solid. It was ungodly cold. There wasn't a sign of life. Not a bird. Not a fly. Not a sound. It was the strangest feeling I ever had. If we stopped, we froze. If we moved, we sweated.

You can hardly realize how wild and ghostlike this mountain country is. Almost perpetual rain and steam. . . . We have been traveling over an almost impassable trail. Our strength is gone. Most of us have dysentery. Boys are falling out and dropping back with fever. Continuous downpour of rain. It's hard to cook our rice and tea. Bully beef makes us sick. We seem to climb straight up for hours, then down again. God, will it never end?

When Company E finally dragged itself into Jaure late in the day on October 25, Lutjens regarded it as a small miracle. For the previous two days, they had not been able to march for more than fifteen minutes at a stretch without lying down to catch their breath. Their hearts felt like they would burst from the exertion. It took them seven hours to ascend Ghost Mountain's final two thousand feet. Men were crawling on their hands and knees. According to Lutjens, by the time Company E reached Jaure, "We were down to a shadow. Our eyes were sunk deep in our heads. We were gaunt as wolves and just as hungry."

By the time Company E reached Jaure, Company G was already in Laruni. At the dropping ground operated by the Wairopi Patrol's Captain Roger Keast, whose knee was still mending, Company G picked up sweaters and replenished its rations. "God, what a gift the sweaters were" says Stanley Jastrzembski. "The jungle got so cold at night."

The rations—soup, biscuits, and even chocolate D-bars—were a godsend, too. "We were hungrier than we'd ever been in our lives, but still we couldn't eat the bully beef," says Russell Buys. "Guys tried to choke it down, but they couldn't; they'd just retch." Worse yet, the beef was often contaminated. It came in four- or five-pound tins. After opening the tins, the beef spoiled quickly, especially in the hot jungle.

Laruni revived the men, but they had no time to linger; they needed to be back on the trail, moving as fast as they could in the direction of Jaure.

A day out of Laruni, Sam DiMaggio was disconcerted by the change of weather. In the lowland jungles he had been as hot as he was when he stoked the stoves at the Malleable Iron Company. Now, he was hiking in his sweater to cut the cold.

Two days out, somber gray clouds slid down from the mountains, and it began to rain—a cold, lashing rain that must have reminded Corporal Carl Stenberg of an early spring day on Lake Michigan.

Stenberg had worked on and off with his cousins on the big lake as a commercial fisherman. It was a tough, cold, dangerous way to make a living, especially in early spring and late fall, twenty miles out, with a set of thirty nets. But it was the Depression, too, and people did what they could to get by. If a storm blew in, especially out of the north where the fetch had over a hundred miles to build, they would have to make a run for dry land. Stenberg had seen his share of storms, more times than he cared to count. Still, he never got used to them.

Stenberg had joined the Guard to escape a hard, uncertain life on Lake Michigan and because he did not want to be drafted. He feared he would be one of the first guys chosen and the Selective Service Act contained a sentence about serving six months after the end of the conflict. Stenberg did not like that clause. "When it's over it's over," he thought.

The day after he and his buddy O'Donnell O'Brien joined the Guard, they were inducted into federal service. The toughest part about the whole thing was telling his girlfriend Frances. They had been going steady since 1939, and he had not mentioned anything to her about joining up. A week later, Stenberg was forced to say good-bye to Frances, and he and O'Brien were on a train bound for Louisiana. Had he gone with his gut, he would have joined the navy. He had always loved the water. And in the navy he would have had a bunk to sleep in and decent food.

Now, here he was, carrying a Thompson submachine gun, 250 rounds of ammunition, and a field pack to boot. Stenberg had it better than some of his buddies, though. He still had not come down with malaria.

Even Herman Bottcher, a hardened veteran of the Spanish Civil War, suffered. "We were never dry," Bottcher said. "Sometimes in twelve hours' marching we would make three miles—some days only a mile." Fortunately, according to Bottcher, the native carriers showed the soldiers how to find dry wood by "sounding trees." Like lumberjacks, the carriers would use their machetes to strike the trunk of a tree, listening for the vibrations. A hollow sound meant the wood was damp and decaying and would be no good for building a fire.

The natives who accompanied Company G proved to be invaluable. Lieutenant James Hunt, who had helped Company E build the coastal road, writes of one terrible climb. Exhausted, he lay down and closed his eyes. "When I opened them," he writes,

I was surrounded by a small group of native men, who were silently watching me. When I started to move, they helped me to my feet, took my pack and assisted me on the way. I had stopped within a few hundred yards of the top of a hill, and when we reached it one of the men climbed a coconut tree and got a fresh coconut, which their leader opened so I could drink the milk, which was cool and refreshing. They then went with me down to the bottom of the hill to our camp site. . . . I thanked them and gave each one a cigarette, which pleased them greatly. I then lay down on a canvas litter. . . . The afternoon rain started . . . but I was so exhausted I just lay there in the rain.

At midday, Gus Bailey called for a brief rest. Bailey had never seen anything like what confronted him on the trail. Here he was, a lieutenant in the role of a captain, and his company was falling apart. Bailey wrote his wife Katherine that the men were so weakened by dysentery that sometimes he had to carry his own pack as well as the packs of two other men. Katherine would later write him back, telling him to take it easy, to avoid being a hero. According to Katherine, his response was always the same: "I won't ask my men to do anything I will not do myself."

One of Bailey's second lieutenants remembers that despite the circumstances, Lieutenant Bailey never appeared discouraged. Jungle rot had left the skin on his ankles and feet as brittle as onionskin. The skin peeled off as he walked and blood seeped through his socks.

When, late in the day, Bailey called for the men to stop and set up camp, Stenberg was relieved. His muscles were shot. He breathed shallowly in the rarified air and chewed on a piece of foot-long sugarcane he had cut from one of the native gardens. The sugarcane hung like an amulet from a sock stretched and fastened to either end and worn around his neck.

Around him, men staggered; some fell to the ground and lay there as if dead. Men who could still walk searched for flat ground on which to set up their shelter halves. Some did not see any point in trying.

After regaining some of their strength, a number of men tried to build fires, but the wood was soaked.

When all the men were situated, Bailey finally sat down. He removed his boots for the first time in days. Jastrzembski could see that his feet were raw, but Bailey never even grimaced. In fact, he told a few jokes, and the men listened and laughed.

A few even remember Bailey singing, which was odd because he was not a singer. Home was the theme: "Home on the Range"; "Show Me the Way to Go Home." The mood was lighter, and when Jastrzembski discovered a large vine, he called some of the guys over.

"Watch this," he said, grabbing the vine and swinging. "I'm Tarzan." Then he let out a deep woods yodel. The others joined in, each man trying to swing higher and farther than the rest.

That night, after taking care of his feet, Bailey treated his men to a recitation of his favorite poem—Robert Service's "The Cremation of Sam McGee." "There are strange things done in the midnight sun / By the men who moil for gold / The Arctic trails have their secret tales / That would make your blood run cold; / The Northern Lights have seen queer sights, / But the queerest they ever did see / Was that night on the marge of Lake Lebarge / I cremated Sam McGee."

For Bailey it felt good to say the words. The poem reminded him of Katherine. In Indiana when they went out for a drive, Bailey would recite it for her.

But New Guinea was not the back roads of Indiana. Later that evening, it began to rain again, and it grew cold in the mountains. They were lucky, according to Jastrzembski, if they managed to doze for ten or fifteen minutes. Most stayed awake talking, trying to comfort themselves with fond memories of Australia.

Had Carl Stenberg overheard the talk, he would have reminded the men that Australia had not been all roses. Australian Imperial Force troops, who had fought overseas, had begun to return while the 32nd was still in Australia. They were national heroes, and they were worshipped. Australia is a huge country, but it was not big enough to accommodate both the 32nd and the returning AIF fighters. Russell Buys explains the problem. "These men came back to find their wives pregnant and their daughters knocked up. They knew that the American army was there, and they weren't a bit happy about it." Inevitably, brawls erupted in the streets and in the pubs of Brisbane and Melbourne. An Australian general described the confrontations as "a most despicable thing between allies." Carl Stenberg recalled that when an outmanned group of American soldiers was jumped by a larger group of Australian soldiers, the Australians' battle cry had been, "Put the bloody boots to 'em!" Things were so bad that General Harding assembled his officers and told them that he wanted them to make certain their men were avoiding "altercations with Australian soldiers . . . particularly when there is . . . liquor involved."

The Japanese were smart enough to exploit the situation. One wartime cartoon depicted an American soldier having sex with a young Australian woman. "Take your sweet time at the front, Aussie," it read. "I got my hands full right now with your sweet tootsie at home."

While the single men dreamed of their Australian girlfriends, Gus Bailey conjured images of what it would be like when he saw Katherine again. Together, they would tour the landscapes of the West that he had admired on the train ride from Massachusetts to California. No longer, though, would it be just the two of them. Cladie Alyn Bailey, a boy, had been born only one-and-a-half months before Company G had begun its march. On the day Katherine returned from the hospital, the postman arrived at her door with a present. The postman waited as she opened the package. When Katherine pulled out an opal ring that Bailey had sent from Australia, the postman was beaming, too. A picture arrived sometime after Katherine received the present. The picture showed a proud Gus Bailey reading to his men the telegram that announced the birth of his son.

•   •   •

When G Company reached Ghost Mountain and the bizarre realm of the cloud forest, they were as spooked as Medendorp's men and Company E had been. In the heavy fog, the trees—huge, moss-draped oaks and beeches—looked like apparitions. Ghost Mountain was a world all its own, where time seemed suspended in perpetual twilight. The soldiers tiptoed along a series of limestone ridges. Occasionally, a man would slip and he would hear rocks tumble into the abyss.

Two days later, Company G crossed the divide, where Major Stutterin' Smith's party overtook it. Though Smith was cheered by the reunion, he was appalled by the condition of Gus Bailey's men. They looked "haggard, tired and tattered." He wondered how he looked to them—a tall, gaunt bag of bones. How had any of them made it through the jungle and over the mountains?

General Harding had been under no illusions about the preparedness of his men, but neither he nor Smith could have anticipated the trek's toll on them. Harding would later write, "I have no quarrel with the general thesis that the 32nd was by no means adequately trained for combat—particularly jungle combat. . . . Unfortunately we had no opportunity to work through a systematic program for correcting deficiencies. From February when I took over until November when we went into battle we were always getting ready to move, on the move, or getting settled after a move. No sooner would we get a systematic training program started than orders for a move came along to interrupt it . . ."

On October 28, Smith's small party and Companies G and H arrived in Jaure. According to Smith, it was a day of "mud, washes and wading." His boots were rotting off his feet. The trail from what Smith called Umi Creek to Jaure was especially grueling. Though not given to expressions of self-pity, Smith called it "torture."

En route to Jaure was Lieutenant Robert Odell, who would later command a platoon in Company F. Only three months before, he had been the assistant military attaché in Wellington, New Zealand. Now, he was in charge of a small group of men bringing up the rear of the battalion. His team had departed the trailhead camp at Kalikodobu after Major Smith's crew, and it was hustling now to catch up with the rest of the battalion. Odell and his men made good time, but what they saw along the trail to Jaure filled them with dismay. Piles of discarded government-issue equipment told a tale of the battalion's ordeal.

Though Bailey was hoping to rest his troops once they reached Jaure, Boice, who was still in Jaure keeping a handle on things, informed him that Company G was to join him and Company F on the march to Natunga early the following morning. Lutjens and Company E had left for Natunga the previous day.

Prior to leaving Jaure for Natunga, Boice received a message from Colonel Quinn.

Your Msg Signed Six Forty Five Morning Two Seven Referring To Batting Average And Confidence Just Received Stop Sorry If I Have Said Anything To Raise Such Questions Stop Same Farthest From Thoughts Stop Have Utmost Confidence [in] Your Ability And Loyalty Stop Have Tried to Show It By Turning Whole Show Over To You Stop You Are Not Only Leading The League In Batting But Have Been Unanimously Selected Most Valuable Player Stop I Am Personally Interested In You And Every Man Out There And Wish I Could Be With You Stop Its Tough Being So Far Away Stop I Know You Will Win Repeat I Know You Will Win Stop Keep Your Chin Up Jim Back Here We Are All Pulling For You Hundred Per Cent

What precipitated the exchange between Quinn and Boice has been lost to history. Perhaps as the one who gave the go-ahead for the march across the peninsula, Boice was burdened by a sense of uncertainty about whether he had done the right thing. Had the trek indeed been too much for the men? They had made Jaure, but each and every one of them had suffered mightily. Had Quinn sensed Boice's ambivalence and sent the message to bolster his sagging spirits? Or perhaps it was the colonel who initially voiced his worries about the men's condition. Maybe Boice interpreted his inquiry as a vote of no confidence. Whatever the reason for the exchange of messages, the one irrefutable fact is that the trek from New Guinea's south coast to Jaure brought each man face-to-face with the limits of his physical and emotional endurance.

As Boice and Companies F and G were preparing to proceed to

Natunga, Smith assumed his new role as battalion commander. His first responsibility was an unusual one: Romee asked if the carriers could hold a celebratory dance.

Though the prospect of sixty dancing natives did not thrill Smith, he told Romee that he would, at least, consider the idea. Smith then called a meeting of his company commanders.

"What do you think, boys?" Smith asked. "I think it's imperative to keep the porters happy. We can post guards just in case they get carried away."

The setting for the celebration could not have been more perfect. The natives found a natural amphitheater at the base of a "gently rising slope." As the sun slid behind the Owen Stanleys, the men began a slow dance to the accompaniment of reed and bamboo panpipes and small drums with heads made of dried reptile skins. As darkness advanced, the tempo increased, and Romee joined Smith on the hill overlooking the celebration grounds. Romee explained that the dancers were reenacting historic battles between the mountain tribes and the coastal natives, which often centered on the precious commodity of salt. The mountain people would come to the sea to evaporate seawater and obtain salt. When they did this, they were trespassing on the tribal lands of the coastal people. Romee assured Smith, though, that the dancers had no intention of becoming warlike.

Herman Bottcher describes the mood at Jaure that had seized everyone, soldiers and carriers alike. It was electric.

The Owen Stanleys were behind us and far in the distance we could see the beautiful green lowlands of the Buna Peninsula. We were overjoyed—particularly the faithful native porters. . . . We made our first comfortable camp, and the natives gathered coconuts, green bananas, squash, taro roots, sugar cane, paws-paws, limes. . . . We had an orgy of eating and they stayed up all night, dancing and beating on the tom-toms. . . . We had accomplished the . . . march with only about twenty casualties . . . one man died.

Early the next morning, Companies F and G hit the trail for Natunga, two days' march northeast of Jaure. Once they reached the village, the bulk of their journey would be behind them. Situated in the steep foothills of the Owen Stanley Mountains, Natunga was roughly thirty miles south of the Buna coast.

Smith and Company H stayed in Jaure until 9:30 a.m. while a message from Colonel Quinn containing new orders was received and decoded: The entire battalion was to lay over in the village of Natunga. Forward scouts had indicated that the village was an ideal location for an airdrop; it sat on a prominent hilltop with fifteen acres of open grasslands. Colonel Quinn complimented Smith and the rest of the battalion on its determination. He also passed along some uplifting news: The Japanese were in full retreat on the Kokoda track. Then he added, "Hug and kiss Jim Boice for all of us."

Chapter 10

TO SWALLOW ONE'S TEARS

(namida o nomu)

IN LATE OCTOBER 1942, the Australians pressed their counter-attack on the Kokoda track. By the time Horii reached the village of Myola, his men were manifesting symptoms of beriberi, typhus, dysentery, colitis, and malaria, for which many didn't even have quinine. Others were slowed to a virtual crawl by jungle rot.

Lieutenant Sakamoto wrote angrily, "It is damp and dark here in the thick woods. We have no more than a handful of rice left. If we are to remain until the end, we will all die from beriberi. What is the Army doing?"

As they grew sicker, soldiers watched, with a growing bitterness, their officers "endeavoring to evade hardships." Some rode horses and hoarded food while ordinary soldiers walked and starved, eating grass, roots, leaves, a few grains of rice they found in the dirt and mud, the flesh of dead horses, and anything else they could scrounge along the way.

Days later, Sakamoto was diagnosed with beriberi and feared that he would not be able to go on. "Cruel nature," he wrote, "God take us to Paradise. Each day, we are nearing our death."

By the time Horii's troops reached Templeton's Crossing, they were doing anything they could to stay alive. Lieutenant Sakamoto's dispassionate diary entry of October 19 read, "Because of the food shortage, some companies have been eating human flesh (Australian soldiers)."

After weeks of consuming grass and roots and putrid horseflesh, Sakamoto added, "The taste was said to be good."

Advancing Australian soldiers discovered evidence of cannibalism. The Japanese had tied Australian soldiers to trees, cut strips of flesh from the bodies, and wrapped the strips in large leaves in order to preserve the meat. Now the Australians, despite suffering from malaria, dysentery, and fatigue, pushed forward, bent on revenge.

Watching from afar, MacArthur grew frustrated with what he considered the Australians' cautious advance. When Arthur "Tubby" Allen, the Australians' commanding general, reached Myola on October 17, a message awaited him. In it, MacArthur made it clear that he was unhappy with the pace of the counterattack. The casualties, he said, were "extremely light." Allen refused to let his men rush blindly into an ambush. What he knew, and MacArthur did not, was that at some strategic point, the Japanese would turn and fight.

That place was Eora Creek. Once they reached the ridge that towered over the gorge, they stopped running and dug in. They erected log bunkers in which they placed their machine gunners. While the healthy and semi-healthy were ordered to stand and fight, carriers behind the lines lugged the diseased and wounded back to the field hospital in Kokoda, and in some cases, all the way back to the north coast, a ten-day journey.

When the oncoming Australians reached the Eora Creek gorge on October 22, Brigadier Lloyd smelled a trap and divided his brigade. He wanted a portion of his men to attack head-on while the others took to higher ground, outflanking the enemy army. But the units charged with sneaking in above and behind the Japanese lost their way in the dense forest, and a mere platoon made it to a spur above the Japanese position. Hoping to catch Horii's army off guard, it attacked. But the Japanese, old pros at encirclement, cut off the platoon's escape route, and the killing commenced. Thirteen of the platoon's seventeen men were lost.

The other group was met by Japanese machine gunners who, swinging the barrels of their guns, strafed the oncoming Australians as they fought to cross the rushing creek. Eventually, though, a group of a hundred men bored straight ahead and stopped to grub out trenches within shouting distance of the Japanese position.

Concealed behind log bunkers, Horii and his officers celebrated with cups of sake. "How tasteful it was!" wrote Lieutenant Sakamoto, the faithful diarist. They had seized the high ground and stopped the advancing Australian army in its tracks.

By October 26, the Australians had been bogged down at Eora Creek for four days, and MacArthur's temper boiled over. Again, he had a message sent to the front: "In spite of your superior strength enemy appears able to delay advance at will. Essential that forward commanders should control situation and NOT allow situation to control them. Delay in seizing KOKODA may cost us unique opportunity of driving enemy out of NEW GUINEA."

A day later, acting as MacArthur's personal henchman, General Blamey relieved Allen of his duties. Then, mounting a furious attack from a nearby ridge, the Australians descended on Horii's troops. Those enemy soldiers who fled into the jungle survived; those who fought died. The Japanese lost hundreds of men at Eora Creek, but the Australians, too, paid a dear price for victory. Nearly three hundred Australian soldiers were killed or wounded.

.   .   .

By late October, Major-General George Vasey was leading the Australian counteroffensive. Vasey was a man of courage, driven to succeed. On November 1, as the Australians bore down on Kokoda, he told his officers, in words reminiscent of General Horii's, "The enemy is beaten. Give him no rest and we will annihilate him."

As Vasey spoke of defeating Horii's army, the Japanese general, having been told that Rabaul would provide him with 20,000 reinforcements, resurrected his dream of capturing Port Moresby.

The following day, Horii and his army abandoned Kokoda. He chose the west side of the Kumusi River, near the villages of Oivi and Gorari, to make his stand.

"We will hold the position until reinforcements arrive," wrote an exuberant Lieutenant Sakamoto. "The tide is turning in our favor."

A mile separated the villages of Oivi and Gorari. Though Horii had three thousand soldiers at his disposal, many were so weak they could barely shoulder their weapons. Desperate for protein, they killed horses, and then again resorted to cannibalism. This time, though, the Japanese soldiers were not eating Australians. "We ran short of rations," Sakamoto wrote on November 4. "We devoured our own kind to stave off starvation."

Five days later, according to Sakamoto, the "enemy began its offensive. They have encircled us, while throughout the morning their planes bombed and machine-gunned us."

Cutting off all their possible escape routes, Vasey had laid a death trap for the Japanese. On the dark and rainy night of November 11, four thousand Australian troops, wrote Dudley McCarthy, the official army historian of the Kokoda campaign, "were gathering themselves for the kill." When they attacked, they came at the Japanese from all sides, nursing a hatred of the Imperial army so intense that only slaughter could satisfy it. Lieutenant Sakamoto died in the fighting.

General Horii, however, escaped. Hoping to reach the coast and reassemble his army with the addition of reinforcements, he fled to the Kumusi River. Swelled by recent rains, the Kumusi surged at its banks. The bridge was gone, bombed into rubble by Allied pilots. Realizing that the river was too deep to ford, Horii fled on a raft with a small group of officers, leaving Colonel Yazawa at the river's edge to tend to nearly three thousand men.

Yazawa had to act quickly. Soon, Vasey would be in hot pursuit. Yazawa ordered the men to construct basic rafts. Shoving them into the slashing current, they prayed that their rafts would hold up. Some did, but others fell apart, sending the soldiers tumbling into the river. Men drowned by the dozens as the river pulled them into its muddy depths and swept them downstream. Trucks waited to transport those who had made it across. With room enough only for the seriously wounded, most were forced to walk.

Seizo Okada, the war correspondent who had landed in New Guinea with the Yokoyama Advance Force in late July, vividly described the scene. "Their [the Japanese soldiers'] uniforms were soiled with blood and mud and sweat, and torn to pieces. There were infantrymen without rifles, men walking on bare feet, men wearing blankets or straw rice bags instead of uniforms, men reduced to skin and bones plodding along with the help of a stick, men gasping and crawling on the ground . . . some of them lying there for a while and struggling to their feet again, while others stirred no more."

A mile and a half downriver, Horii's raft ran aground, and he and his party scrambled up the bank, followed the river toward the coast, and discovered a native canoe. The canoe, though, was too small to accommodate the entire party. The decision was an easy one. While the rest of the party stumbled its way toward Awala, Horii, his staff officer, and his personal orderly floated down the river toward the coast, his mad hope of reinforcements shattered. The troops Rabaul had promised were being diverted to the Solomons.

No one would ever see the general again. Accounts of his death differ. Some say that the canoe overturned and Horii drowned. Others suggest that he paddled out to sea where the canoe, hit by fierce winds, capsized. Horii's staff officer drowned and the general and his orderly attempted to swim to shore. Miles out, Horii tired. With enough energy for a final dramatic gesture, legend has it he raised his hands over his head, and in a resounding voice, shouted, "Tennoheika Banzai!" ("Long Live the Emperor!")

Back at Gorari, the Australians celebrated. Vasey was heralded as a hero. From Port Moresby Blamey effused, "The greatest factor in pressing the continuous advance has been General Vasey's drive and personality."

Vasey, though, was hardly satisfied with half a victory. The Japanese were still firmly entrenched on New Guinea's north coast, and Vasey was envisioning a final, decisive battle.

It's "Buna or bust," he told his men, "And we will not bust."

*   *   *

In the mountains things were not going well for Stutterin' Smith's Ghost Mountain boys. Short of food, they marched from Jaure to Natunga, raiding gardens, shooting domesticated pigs, and scrounging whatever they could find along the way, especially bananas and papayas to guard against scurvy. Out of desperation they disobeyed one rule that Medendorp insisted was unbreakable—never touch the natives' property.

By the time the battalion reached Natunga, many of the men flopped down in the mud at the village's edge and lay there without moving, more dead than alive. "Malnutrition, malaria, dysentery," Lutjens wrote. "Shoes and clothes are all shot to hell."

Back at regimental headquarters on the south coast, Colonel Quinn had grown increasingly concerned about the condition of his troops. When Smith alerted him that the men needed food and medical supplies to continue, Quinn took matters into his own hands. He would personally oversee the airdrop.

Natunga looked to Smith like the perfect spot for a drop. In the distance, Mount Lamington loomed blue and ominous, its peak obscured by clouds. Heavy jungle stretched from Natunga to the mountain's steep slopes and north along the rain-swollen Girua River, but Natunga itself sat in a large meadow on a hilltop. Smith realized that it might be the battalion's last chance to resupply before going into battle.

Natunga also had a ready supply of healthy, well-fed natives to carry provisions. They were stout and strong men, who sported full body tattoos that they had acquired during elaborate initiation ceremonies. They wore their hair in long plaits interwoven with cloth made from the tapa tree, and plucked their beards and their body hair.

For days, the sky hung low over the village. Smith was beginning to despair when on November 5, the weather broke. Smith sent Quinn an urgent message: "Weather clear. Drop. Drop."

When Quinn left Seven-Mile Drome outside Port Moresby, the jagged peaks of the Owen Stanleys pressed up against a cloudless sky. Perhaps, at last, Lady Luck would be on the 2nd Battalion's side. Looking down from the plane, Colonel Quinn would have been able to see the terrain that Smith's men had covered. It must have made him shudder. Solid jungle sprawled in every direction.

As the plane neared Natunga, Quinn spotted the clearing. The pilot made a pass and Quinn, who was at the door, prepared to kick out the wrapped and bound packages to which they had attached parachutes to improve the recovery ratio.

Below, everyone—the soldiers, the native carriers, and the villagers of Natunga—watched in horror as one of the parachutes opened sooner than it should have. It billowed out of the cargo door and became entangled in the plane's tail assembly. The plane wavered and then plunged nose-first into a nearby hill. Not everyone saw the crash, but they all heard the explosion. Hoping that maybe someone had survived the crash, Smith sent out a salvage team.

While the salvage team was out, Smith learned from regimental headquarters that Colonel Quinn had been aboard the plane that had crashed. Privates, corporals, and officers alike wept when they learned that Quinn was one of the casualties. Medendorp, upon learning of the colonel's death, captured the mood of the entire regiment. "To our sorrow," he wrote, "our magnificent Colonel was killed."

When Sam DiMaggio heard the news, he trembled. Back at Camp Livingston, Colonel Quinn had asked him to be his personal runner, and DiMaggio had seriously considered the offer. All the men knew that Quinn was a "stand-up guy." He was a regimental commander who really cared about his soldiers. There was another attraction, though. As Quinn's personal runner, it was likely that if a war broke out, DiMaggio would be spared front-line duty. In other words, he would have a better chance of making it home alive. Joining Quinn, however, would have meant leaving his buddies in Company G. As a draftee, it had taken a long time for him to gain the acceptance of the Muskegon boys from G Company, but they had become his family. So when Quinn presented the idea, DiMaggio respectfully declined. There were times when he kicked himself for passing on the offer. On November 5 in Natunga, DiMaggio realized that had he accepted the invitation, he probably would have been aboard Quinn's plane.

Jim Boice must have been devastated by Quinn's death. Initially, they had both been outsiders in the 126th—Boice was an Indianan; Quinn was an Oklahoman, ten years his senior, who had fought in World War I and had been awarded the Silver Star and a Purple Heart. Both were family men. Boice had one son and Quinn had a daughter,

June. Perhaps because of a similarity of circumstance, they developed a friendship, which is reflected in the messages they traded as Boice was making his way toward Buna.

On October 23, Quinn sent Boice a message that had a paternalistic quality: "You have done a grand job and we are all proud as hell of you."

Two days later, on October 25, Quinn sent Boice another one: "My Birthday ninth November. Would like very much have tea with you in Buna that day. Good luck." It was vintage Quinn—funny, encouraging.

Later that day, Boice responded, "Please have faith in us. We will lick [the] hell out of them."

A few days later Boice received another message from Quinn, which Quinn asked him to read to the troops. The colonel wrote:

A few weeks ago this force was assigned a mission described by many as "impossible." You have advanced with your arms and equipment over the "impossible" Owen Stanley range. You have overcome almost unsurmountable obstacles. You have proven yourselves to be rough and rugged field soldiers of the highest order. Today I am especially proud of you.

Now comes the second phase of this "impossible" operation, the advance to contact, the attack and the destruction of the enemy. I know you are tired . . . but I also know that your morale is high and that your spirit of never say die is stronger than ever . . . I know you will advance boldly, destroy the enemy wherever you meet him and once again accomplish the "impossible."

Yet despite the sense of loss Boice must have experienced when he learned of Quinn's death, he mentions it only briefly in his diary: "Col. Quinn killed." The entry says less perhaps about Boice and his relationship to Quinn than it does the nature of war. In the face of death, resignation is the only defense.

After the initial shock, Smith, too, reacted soberly to Quinn's death. There was little time to mourn. He radioed Captain Keast at Laruni and ordered Father Stephen Dzienis sent forward to perform the burial ceremony.

Lutjens had just returned from the village of Pongani, where he and Art Edson had been directed to make contact with the 128th in order to get its radio frequency so that Smith could stay in touch with General Hanford MacNider and his coastal force. Upon arriving in Natunga, Lutjens noted that the salvage team pulled out "mashed bodies" with one hand and enjoyed undamaged fruitcake it had found among the wreckage with the other. For the minute or two it took the men to devour the cake, hunger trumped grief.

Affected perhaps by Quinn's death, Art Edson felt the need to write his sweetheart, though he could not have known if the letter would even make it out of New Guinea.

Dearest Lois,

Just a few lines to let you know that I'm still alive and kicking. We are still in New Guinea.
Forever, Love Art

On the other side of the mountains, General Harding knew that the 32nd had just lost a good man and his "best regimental commander, and that by a wide margin."

On November 8, the 126th held a memorial for Colonel Quinn in Port Moresby. The regimental chaplain presided over the service. "He is not present to lead the regiment," the chaplain said, "but Larry Quinn marches on and will lead this regiment. What he put in you will not be lost in this war or after. But when you go, and you will go soon and you will go far, I am sure as I stand here that the spirit of Larry Quinn will go forward with you and join with you in making the name of 'Les Terribles' death in the eyes of our enemy."

Chapter 11

FEVER RIDGE

ON NOVEMBER 6, 1942, the day after Colonel Quinn died in the plane crash, MacArthur moved his headquarters from Brisbane to Port Moresby, leaving behind his wife and son. Upon arriving in New Guinea, MacArthur settled into the comfortable Government House, which had been the residence of the colonial governor for the last fifty years. The house had been refurbished for his arrival. It was probably the only building on the entire island of New Guinea with modern plumbing. It was appointed with fine tropical furniture, hardwood floors, and even a library. MacArthur enjoyed a menu of fresh eggs, milk, salad, and meat. He also had a staff of nine native boys, who wore serving gloves and pressed white lap-laps decorated with blue stars and red stripes.

The house, which the soldiers referred to as the "Ivory Tower," was situated in a grove of stately coconut palms on a grassy hill overlooking the port area. From its spacious veranda, adorned with bougainvillea, hibiscus, and pink frangipani, MacArthur could lounge in his silk dressing gown with a black dragon emblazoned on the back, enjoy the breeze, and admire his handiwork. He had ordered his chief engineer officer to transform the port into a first-rate base, and the officer had done just that.

Four days before leaving Australia, MacArthur established a tentative date for the Allied attack on the Buna coast, postponing it by two weeks from the original plan. The 128th Infantry Regiment, which had been waiting for orders to move out since arriving at Wanigela by plane, greeted the announcement with anger and frustration.

After arriving at Wanigela during the third week of October, the 128th had begun marching in the direction of Pongani. En route there, however, the regiment got mired in the vast swamps of the Musa River delta, which slowed its movement to a crawl. When it became obvious that the regiment could not continue its journey on foot, the men hiked back to Wanigela, where they were picked up and transported north to the village by a small flotilla of shallow-draft luggers, the only vessels MacArthur had at his disposal.

Pongani, roughly thirty miles southeast of Buna, was a sweltering, sun-beaten hellhole infested with sand fleas, flies, and mosquitoes. After setting up camp, the men waited for orders to move on Buna.

Conditions at Pongani, which the men christened "Fever Ridge," were dreadful. According to Lieutenant Colonel Stanley Hollenback, commander of the portable surgical hospital there, the hospital was filled way beyond capacity with malaria and dengue fever cases, and quinine was in short supply. Dysentery, which the men came down with shortly after arriving in Port Moresby in late September, raged through the camp. Everyone, it seemed, had a case of jungle rot. Boots that had gotten wet on the aborted walk from Wanigela to Pongani never dried out. Trenchfoot became a problem. Men's feet swelled and numbed and turned bluish-white. It felt as if they were walking on wood blocks. As the trenchfoot grew worse, their feet blistered. When the blisters burst, men were in such pain that they could barely stand up. To make matters worse, the soldiers began to suffer from malnutrition, too. Their daily intake amounted to "one-third of a C-ration and a couple of spoonfuls of rice a day," hardly more than a thousand calories.

The weather added to their misery. The camp felt like a sauna. Soldiers withered from lack of fresh water. When it rained they collected it in their helmets; when it was not raining, the tropical sun burned their backs red. Many of the men were so sunburned that it hurt to move.

After two weeks a general malaise set in. Men stopped washing; they did not bother about the bugs; they did not see the point in sterilizing their mess kits; they grew absentminded and forgot to drop an iodine tablet in their water; those who had quinine discarded it because it made them sick.

According to a ground forces observer at Pongani, "the lid really blew off" when they heard the news of MacArthur's decision. He wrote:

> The reason for the order was, of course, to gain time to stockpile supplies for the impending advance, but the division, restive and eager to be "up and at 'em" did not see it that way. Opinions were freely expressed by officers of all ranks . . . that the only reason for the order was a political one. GHQ was afraid to turn the Americans loose and let them capture Buna because it would be a blow to the prestige of the Australians who had fought the long hard battle all through the Owen Stanley Mountains, and who therefore should be the ones to capture Buna.

MacArthur also postponed the attack because he was reluctant to concentrate large numbers of Allied troops on the Buna coast until the situation on Guadalcanal clarified itself. Recalling the tragedy of Bataan, what he feared most was that if the Japanese took Guadalcanal they could commit the full might of their forces to an invasion of New Guinea. The Americans would then be trapped on the north coast.

MacArthur insisted on a plan for the swift withdrawal of Allied troops, and General Blamey assured him that he had one. Blamey had already endorsed General Harding's plan to fly the remaining portions of the 126th Infantry Regiment into Pongani, where a usable airfield had been discovered and improved. Aware of MacArthur's reservations, Blamey added his own wrinkle: After landing, they would hike inland and temporarily join Major Smith's 2nd Battalion at the village of Bofu, north of Natunga, and wait for orders to attack. The entire route, Blamey assured MacArthur, would be protected by the Hydrographer's Range, a sprawling series of mountains that butted up against the coastal plain. At worst, if the Japanese invaded en masse, the

128th Infantry Regiment could use the same route to evacuate the coast. On the other hand, if all went well and the Japanese were preoccupied with Guadalcanal, the Allies could launch a three-pronged advance on Buna, beginning sometime in mid- to late-November after the Australians had crossed the Kumusi River.

MacArthur was satisfied with Blamey's blueprint, and the transfer by air of regimental headquarters, and the 1st and 3rd Battalions of the 126th Infantry Regiment began on November 8, two days after MacArthur arrived in Port Moresby.

Major Simon Warmenhoven, preparing to be airlifted to New Guinea's north coast, wrote his wife a hurried letter:

> Somewhere in New Guinea
> Sunday Nite 10:45 PM.
> November 8, 1942
>
> My Lover:
>
> Hello Mandy darling. I'm going to sit down here and dash off a letter . . . Things are moving fast right now and am taking time out to let you know that my thoughts are with you, the grandest and most wonderful person in my life . . . Don't be surprised hun if there'll be a little lull in my letters.
> I'm ever so much in love with you . . . Until next time . . .
> Lovingly Always, Sam

.   .   .

As the Allies were assembling their forces, MacArthur received news from Guadalcanal: Admiral Halsey's fleet had destroyed an eleven-ship Japanese convoy carrying most of Japan's reserve troops. It was now safe for Marine Corps troops, reinforced by the army, to begin their raid on the Japanese-held garrison. Admiral Halsey's victory was a turning point in the war, one to which MacArthur, weighing the impact of the report from his secluded veranda, must have responded ambivalently. Though he no longer had to worry about a massive Japanese assault on

New Guinea, he desperately wanted to beat the Marines to the punch and claim for himself the first American land victory in the South Pacific.

A few days later, General Harding issued the divisional plan of attack. The bulk of the 128th Infantry Regiment would advance on Buna from the east and southeast. One battalion would approach Cape Endaiadere, two and a half miles east of Buna Government Station (which the American army incorrectly called Buna Mission) via a coastal route. A second battalion would advance on Buna by way of *Siremi* (mistakenly called *Simemi* in military history accounts of the battle), a village located about three miles inland of Cape Endaiadere, while the 128th's 2nd battalion would be held in reserve.

Though Major Smith's Ghost Mountain boys were still a ways out, the plan was for them to advance on Buna by way of Bofu, at the headwaters of the Girua River, roughly twenty miles from the coast. West of the Girua River, the Australians would begin to move toward the coast.

Although they would soon be entering battle, none of the men were physically ready. The men of Major Smith's Ghost Mountain Battalion were in Natunga, trying to recover their strength. The 128th did not have to endure the march over the mountains, but they were no better off. Then there were the Australians, who had pursued the Japanese from Ioribaiwa Ridge across the Owen Stanleys to the Kumusi River crossing. They were in no shape to fight either.

The men of regimental headquarters, the 126th's 3rd Battalion and elements of its 1st Battalion, halfway through a twelve-day march from Pongani to Bofu, were suffering, too. William Hirashima, the regiment's only second-generation Japanese-American (Nisei) soldier, remembers how rugged the trail was. Hirashima had been assigned to regimental headquarters as an S-2, specializing in intelligence work— captured documents and prisoner interrogation. "We were very disorganized," he says.

> Each of us started out with a minimum full pack, but by the time we got half-way there . . . our arms were down to a minimum. We had thrown our steel helmets away and spare

ammunition. . . . By the time I was on the trail for three or four days most of my original equipment was gone. I had thrown it away. I kept a quarter of a pup tent, one blanket. My mess kit was down to just the pan. . . . I just had one big spoon. . . . It wasn't just me; everybody was doing it. . . . Some of the people had thrown away most of their ammunition, down to perhaps two clips. So we were not really a battle prepared unit. . . . I was carrying a rifle, an M1. Then I was given a carbine because I had these weighty dictionaries to carry, too.

William Hirashima was born and raised in Santa Barbara County, California. His father emigrated to the United States during Japan's rice crisis of the 1890s. Reaching Hawaii, he had worked as a cutter in the pineapple orchards. Later he left Hawaii and moved to the Santa Barbara area to work on the railroad. It was backbreaking labor even for a man accustomed to toiling in farm fields from sunup to sundown. After getting a job as a janitor at the Seaside Oil Company, he felt he was finally settled, and sent back to Japan for a bride. His son William was born in March 1920, the second of three brothers.

Hirashima grew up like any other kid in America. In fact, he was treated better than the Oklahomans who flooded California during the Depression. The Hirashimas tried their hardest to be a typical American family. Like many Japanese-Americans, they eschewed any association with Japan and Japanese culture. They attended July 4 parades and on Memorial Day went down to the town flagpole and set out flowers to commemorate the service of World War I veterans. In school, William recited the Pledge of Allegiance with conviction; America was his country. By the time he was a teenager, he was playing football and baseball, earning varsity letters in both sports.

It was not until he attended the University of California at Berkeley that he experienced any sort of racism. There, Japanese-Americans lived in segregated boarding houses and he and his friends were shunned by their "hakujin" (Caucasian) classmates.

Hirashima studied chemistry at Berkeley, but became disillusioned with the program when he realized there were few job opportunities for a Japanese-American. He was resigned to spending his life in the farm fields like the Issei—first generation Japanese-Americans—and Nisei he knew, and after dropping out, he started at the Salinas Vegetable Exchange as a lowly lettuce trimmer. He probably would have ended up working there for much of his life if not for the draft. In February 1941, much to his surprise, he received his notice. The general population of Japanese-Americans were considered 4-C, enemy aliens, and were not usually eligible for the draft.

A few weeks later he was on his way to Fort Lewis, Washington, where he was placed in the army, 15th Infantry, 3rd Division. Just over six months later he was sent to the Language School at the Presidio in San Francisco. The army needed translators. Though Hirashima's knowledge of Japanese was basic at best, he was chosen to attend. At the Presidio, Nisei students drilled in Japanese night and day.

In the spring of 1942, Hirashima boarded a Liberty ship with eight other Nisei and a Marine unit. Like the soldiers of the 32nd Division, he did not even know where he was going.

The ship stopped in Auckland, New Zealand, and then continued on to Melbourne. By August, 1942, while the 32nd Division was training at Camp Tamborine, Hirashima was at Camp Indooroopilly, a short train ride from Brisbane, where he was refining his translation and prisoner interrogation skills.

Back in the United States, though, the tolerance that Hirashima had grown up with was a thing of the past. Thanks to President Roosevelt's Executive Order 9066, Hirashima's parents and older brother were living in a horse stable in an internment camp (Tulare) between Sacramento and Fresno.

The country that his parents had come to love and worship had betrayed them. Japanese-Americans had their homes, farms, and businesses seized. They were herded up and forced to live like animals.

Although Hirashima felt a great resentment, that experience did not turn him against the country he loved. It made him more determined than ever to prove his patriotism.

•   •   •

As the Americans negotiated the treacherous trail, Hirashima prayed they would not run into the Japanese. The men could barely walk, much less fight. For Hirashima, the thought of being killed in battle was frightening, but being taken prisoner would be the worst possible fate. For a Japanese-American soldier, the Japanese would reserve a special brand of cruelty.

They did not encounter any Japanese on the march, which was a good thing because they were in no condition for battle. When they finally arrived in Bofu, they were tired, hungry, and nursing a variety of ailments.

Simon Warmenhoven was grateful to have made it over the mountains. When on November 8 he wrote his wife Mandy to express his love and alert her that there would be a lull in his letters, he had no idea what was in store for him. He had walked over the mountains shouldering his own pack, a smaller bag of medical supplies, and occasionally the pack of another doctor. Once they reached Bofu, the men collapsed, but Warmenhoven's work had just begun. He had managed to keep the men of the 126th healthy while they were training in Australia. He treated venereal diseases, and on a small scale, malaria, dengue fever, and an assortment of skin ailments. That was comparatively easy. Now, it seemed, everyone had some kind of ailment. Soldiers were burning up with fevers, and some had dysentery so bad he worried about dehydration. Everyone had feet torn up with blisters, sore knees and shoulders, and backs scorched by the sun, and he had not even gotten around to visiting Stutterin' Smith's Ghost Mountain boys. What would happen once the fighting started? How could he treat all the sick and wounded? How would the newly created portable hospital units (forerunners to MASH, mobile army surgical hospitals) function? Knowing how long it would take to evacuate soldiers to a field hospital and knowing the dangers of infection in a climate like New Guinea's, the idea behind the portable hospital was to treat the wounded as far forward as possible, and to be mobile. Units would include twenty-five beds, moving as the battle shifted. On paper, the concept seemed workable, even brilliant. But Warmenhoven needed qualified medical personnel to man the hospitals. And like the other regimental surgeons, he was up against a shortage of doctors and corpsmen.

For Warmenhoven, battle was not a hypothetical. Back in Port Moresby, Japanese Zeros, intent on taking out the airfield, came at dusk one evening, dropping bombs across the area. Portions of the 126th were camped near the end of the runway. Men dove into fox-holes or dashed into the jungle. One unlucky soldier was hit by shrapnel while lying in his cot. He was sobbing when his friend, Sergeant Jack Hill of the 126th's 3rd Battalion, ran to him. Turning on his flashlight, Hill realized that the hot metal had torn off his buddy's kneecap, and the smell of burning flesh made him retch. Hill yelled for a medic, and Warmenhoven appeared, instructing him to shine the flashlight on the wound with one hand and with the other to press a tourniquet to his friend's leg. Then Warmenhoven calmly amputated the leg while bombs exploded nearby. At one point a soldier shouted, "Put that goddamned light out or I'll shoot it out!" Warmenhoven looked at Hill. "Keep the light steady," he said. "Keep it steady."

As the division prepared for battle, Harding was also worried about the condition of his men, especially since he had no reserve troops. As a keen student of history, he knew what disease had done to General George Washington's colonial forces, especially at the Battle of Quebec, where Washington's army, under the command of Colonel Benedict Arnold, was crippled by smallpox.

Despite the poor health of his troops, and the fact that MacArthur had consistently denied him the 127th Infantry Regiment, which was still back at Camp Tamborine, Harding was upbeat about his army's chances. Both ground and air reconnaissance indicated that the Japanese strongholds each held only two hundred to three hundred Japanese. His intelligence officers speculated further that the Japanese had already decided to relinquish Buna.

These reports had clearly made their way to the officers. Quinn's message to Jim Boice about having tea in Buna on his birthday testifies to the prevailing belief that the Japanese invasion force had been reduced to a ragtag bunch of tired and sick soldiers. One Ground Forces observer ventured "Buna could be had by walking in and taking over."

It was General Willoughby who challenged these optimistic appraisals of Japanese troop levels. On November 10, he estimated that about four thousand troops were holding the beachhead. He also thought it unlikely that the Japanese would abandon their position on the north coast. But four days later, after assessing Japanese losses on the Kokoda track, Willoughby revised his estimate downward and ventured a guess that the Japanese were capable only of fighting a delaying action at Buna. "The seizure of the Buna area," he said, "is practically assured."

BOOK THREE

Train the arm and school the eye.
Steel the heart to ice-lipped death.
They are God's who learn to die
Having learned life's shibboleth.

C.T. "BUCK" LANHAM, "INTERIM"

Umi yukaba, mizuku kabane,
Yama yukaba, kusamusu kabane,
Okimi no he ni koso shiname.
Kaerimi wa seji.

(Across the sea, corpses soaking in the water,
Across the mountains, corpses heaped upon the grass,
We shall die by the side of the Lord.
We shall never look back.)

OTOMO YAKAMOCHI, "UMI YUKABA"

Chapter 12

THE KILL ZONE

ON NOVEMBER 16, the Australians had just completed their crossing of the Kumusi River at Wairopi and began marching on Gona and Sanananda, northwest of Buna village via the Buna-Kokoda track. On the coast, the 128th moved out, too, in the hazy light of a tropical morning. The men lined their dog tags with rubber tubing so the clang of metal on metal would not give them away in battle. In addition to their packs, they carried canteens, knives, first aid kits hooked to their belts, cigarettes, Zippo lighters, two extra bandoliers of ammo per man, and hand grenades.

After weeks of idleness, they were happy to be on the move at last. One officer remembered the mood as "like the eve of a celebration to come. We were to go in to 'raise the flag' and there was to be a great victory for the American forces with very little effort on our part."

For the first time since landing on the north coast the men appreciated the island's luxuriant beauty—the picturesque coastline with its regal coconut palms, waves lapping at the sandy beach, a blue sky stripped of clouds, the first bands of sunshine filtering through the trees.

It was a puzzling thing to see—soldiers moving into battle without a touch of gravity, hardly conscious of their own mortality. Gangly young men, soaked to the bone, chuckled and gibed with each other and told jokes, the raunchier the better, raising their voices not to overcome rampaging fear, but to deliver punch lines. Though they were tired from having walked twenty miles through knotted jungle with bad feet, fevers, and oozing sores, and though they were hungry after the previous night's meager dinner of rice and boiled, under-ripe papayas, they believed what they had been told: The beachhead was lightly defended, they would mop up, they would kill a few starving, near-sighted Japs, take a few scalps maybe, knock out some gold fillings, and push on up the island's north coast toward bigger battles and then get back to civilization as quickly as they could. Once home, they would drink, race fast cars, date every pretty gal they could, take baths every day, eat until they could not stand, and sit on their front porches and wave to passersby.

Despite their initial cockiness, by the afternoon the men were beat, and they, too, rid themselves of everything they considered nonessential. But even after lightening their loads, they struggled in the 100-degree heat. By nightfall it was all they could do to wade a waist-deep creek. After crossing, they made camp at the creek's mouth, near the village of Boreo, just north of coastal headquarters at Hariko.

Just behind the encampment, soldiers were assembling two Australian 3.7-inch mountain howitzers, which would provide long-range artillery for the attack. Using a captured Japanese barge, General Albert Waldron, Harding's artillery officer, had brought in Australian mountain guns and two hundred rounds of ammunition early that morning. It was a daring move. He and his crew put ashore in an area that had not yet been scouted by Allied troops, unloaded, and then headed back down the coast to Oro Bay to pick up General Harding and his party, the members of a portable hospital unit, two 25-pounder field pieces, 81 mm long-range mortars, .50 caliber machine guns, rations, radio supplies, and ammunition. Harding and Waldron and his party were expected to arrive later that night.

By the time Waldron made Oro Bay, the supplies had been divided among three ships: the *Alacrity*, the *Minnemura*, and the *Bonwin*. Waldron's barge was loaded and then all four ships departed for the front. The cruise north was a pleasant one. It had been over a month since a Japanese plane had been sighted along the north coast, and the crews of the various ships were relaxing for perhaps the last time before going into battle.

Just off Cape Sudest, General Harding, who was aboard the *Minnemura,* was enjoying dinner with the captain and its crew. It was nearly dusk, and the sky throbbed with the rich shades of a tropical sunset. A slender native boy stood at the bow of the ship, throwing out a plumb line and shouting out the depths. Angelfish gathered around the line, and the sea was radiant with color. Off the starboard bow, the black fin of a shark broke the surface of the water. In the distance, the *Alacrity,* the largest ship in the convoy, was already dropping anchor off Hariko. The *Alacrity* towed a barge and carried most of the ordnance, forty native carriers, and the twenty-nine-man hospital team.

Harding was sipping a cup of coffee when suddenly he heard the far-off sound of airplane engines. As the drone of the engines grew louder, everyone thought the same thing—Are they ours? The *Minnemura*'s captain stood and searched the rose-colored horizon with his binoculars. When he saw the blunt noses, he knew—Zeros! The *Minnemura*'s skipper swung the ship toward shore. The captain grabbed an ammunition belt and lunged for the machine gun mounted on the port deck. The native boy no longer shouted out depths. He had slipped silently over the side of the boat. Moments later, eighteen Zeros with red balls on the underside of their silver wings appeared out of the evening sky.

The Zeros buzzed overhead and kept on going as if on a bombing mission in some far-off place. Everyone on the boats held his breath, wondering if the planes would return. Without Allied aircraft escorts, which had already left for Port Moresby in hopes of making it over the Owen Stanley "hump" before darkness, the ships were sitting ducks.

Minutes later, the Zeros materialized out of the southern sky. They came in fast and low, bent on destruction, strafing the *Bonwin,* the third ship in the convoy. Aboard the *Bonwin,* men were hugging the decks inside the main cabin. Incendiary bullets ricocheted off barrels and wood planks. Though they were unaware of it, a fire fueled by burning gasoline was making its way to the main cabin, which was soon engulfed in flames. The ship was going down.

Three Zeros then attacked the plodding barge. The pilots were making one run after the next, "spewing tracer bullets," according to

Lieutenant Colonel Stanley Hollenback, who from the beach watched the attack unfold. When the bullets tore into gasoline drums, a surge of black smoke shot into the sky and surrounded the barge. It did not take the men long to realize that they were goners if they stayed aboard. Anyone who was able to swim, including General Waldron, dove as far from the barge as they could with bullets smacking around them.

Aboard the *Alacrity*, crewmen were firing back with .50 and .30 caliber machine guns and rifles. It was a futile fight. In less than a minute, the *Alacrity* was ablaze. Men hurled themselves into the water. A bomb fell among the natives, who had abandoned ship at the same time, and killed all but twelve of them. A chaplain stayed aboard long enough to toss over hatch covers and oil drums that the men could use to stay afloat. A lieutenant remained aboard ship, too, trying to subdue the fire and save what he could. Then he dove overboard and he and a number of men struggled to pull the boat to shore as bullets broke the water.

Lastly, the Zeros fell upon the *Minnemura*, which had run aground on a reef. Harding had grabbed an M-1 and was hiding behind boxes of C-rations. The pilots were making one pass after another, firing tracers and dropping bombs, and Harding was shooting back. The boat's captain, though hit in the leg, filled the sky with bullets. He fired until his machine gun jammed. When the stern of the ship and a fuel tank were hit and fire swallowed the lugger, Harding and the captain dove overboard.

The water was filled with screaming men and blood from the wounded, which pooled and then dissipated like the rings of a rising fish. To escape the strafing, those who could swim dove under the water, ripping their legs, chests, and bellies on the coral. Those who could not swim flailed their arms and struggled to stay afloat or grabbed and clung to pieces of wreckage. Phosphorescence swirled around them.

Risking their lives, some men on shore pushed a life raft into the surf and paddled out to the boats. They picked up General Harding, but when Harding realized that there were nonswimmers who were likely to drown without the aid of the dinghy, he tore off his clothes, plunged into the water, and swam for shore. Whenever the Zeros fired he dove under and held his breath for as long as he could. The guys aboard the raft hauled in several wounded men, pulling them over the lip of the dinghy. Then they went to search for more. When the dinghy was full, they turned the boat toward the beach. Exhausted men, for whom there was no room in the dinghy, threw their arms over the side gunwales and were tugged to shore, where officers mobilized rescue parties, sending out small boats to search among the burning wreckage for survivors.

That night General Harding was able to assess the scope of the damage. Fifty-two men, including twenty-eight native carriers and Colonel Laurence McKenny, the division quartermaster, were killed in the attack. McKenny had been aboard the *Bonwin* when it ignited, and either drowned or burned to death. In addition, one hundred men were wounded. According to Lieutenant Colonel Hollenback, doctors "operated all night long on the men, mostly with abdominal wounds, sewing up the bullet holes in their intestines."

The following morning, Harding realized the full extent of the catastrophe. In addition to the human toll, he had lost tons of supplies, including rations, artillery shells, the two 25-pounders, and the 128th's heavy weapons. Now he would be entering battle with no mortars or artillery.

Under normal circumstances, a division would have dozens of 105 mm howitzers plus another twelve 155 mm howitzers. Harding had made numerous appeals for bringing in the big guns. Each time, however, Headquarters rebuffed him. The division, GHQ argued, did not have the means to transport them, or to keep them supplied once they had been delivered. The argument carried General Kenney's imprint. Kenney was working behind the scenes, and he was determined that Buna would be an Army Air show. It was a classic turf war, and Kenney triumphed. "The artillery in this theater flies," he said.

Later that morning, Zeros disabled two of the three remaining Oro Bay luggers that were hauling supplies to the front. Harding, though eager to carry out the attack, had to concede that his battle plan had been dealt a terrible blow.

•   •   •

Despite the disaster, and after much deliberation, Harding delayed the advance by only two days, scheduling it for 0700 on November 19. If intelligence estimates of Japanese troop strength were accurate, it was better to attack before Rabaul was able to send in more men.

At 0700 on November 19, 1942, the Australian mountain guns roared, signaling the start of the attack. Then two columns of troops moved out into the wet and blurry morning, trudging forward from Boreo along a muddy, tree-covered coastal trail, staying off the beach to avoid detection by Japanese reconnaissance planes. As the men of the 128th marched into battle, rain slashed diagonally through the forest canopy.

Two squads led the charge, grenades hooked by their spoons over their belts, safeties off, fingers on the thin metal of their triggers, ready to snap off shots at the slightest movement, the slightest sound, their eyes flaming like wildfire. The same question kept tracking through every man's head: How will I do once the shooting starts? They all prayed that they would live to see another day. But they also prayed that they would not disgrace themselves.

The Japanese knew that they were coming, and because of the delay had two extra days to prepare their defenses. The night before, the Japanese had whetted and sharpened their bayonets, oiled their weapons, inspected their machine gun belts to make sure they would not jam in the heat of the battle, and checked their firing lanes.

Since landing in mid-July, engineers had been busily fortifying the area. The Japanese had established a series of masterful positions along a narrow eleven-mile front, extending from Gona on the west to Cape Endaiadere on the east.

The Japanese defense of the beachhead was built around three main positions. One was at Gona, the other along the Sanananda track, and the third was in the Buna area from the Girua River east to Cape Endaiadere, a promontory just west of Cape Sudest and the American's coastal headquarters at Hariko.

Girua, located just up the coastal trail from Buna Village, was the main Japanese base with a supply dump and hospital. It was defended by a variety of positions and packed with bunkers, blockhouses, and trenches. Farther south, for miles along the Sanananda track, the Japanese established a main position and a handful of forward outposts. All the positions were situated on dry ground, surrounded by tangled, stinking, crocodile-infested sago, nipa, and mangrove swamp.

Beginning east of the mouth of the Girua River and continuing southeastward, the Japanese line of defense cut through a coconut grove and then turned southward to the trail junction where a track forked to Buna Village on one hand and to Buna Government Station on the other. The area between the forks became known as the Triangle. An offshoot of the Girua River called Entrance Creek bisected it. Sweeping north, the Japanese line enclosed the Triangle and then turned eastward to the grassy area known as Government Gardens. From the gardens, it led south and then east through the main grassy area to Siremi Creek, near an old airstrip. Continuing southward, it enclosed the bridge over Siremi Creek between the old strip and a new airstrip. Then, making a right-angled turn to the new strip, it followed the edge of the strip to within a few hundred yards of the sea. Cutting sharply northeast, it emerged on the sea at a point about 750 yards below Cape Endaiadere in an area of coconut palms known as the Duropa Plantation.

In the Siremi Creek area the only dry ground was occupied by the two strategically important airfields, one called Old Strip, which was bombed relentlessly by Kenney's pilots; and the other called New Strip. Although the airfields were primitive, MacArthur coveted them. In Allied hands, they would serve to check any further Japanese threat to Port Moresby. They would also aid an Allied advance along New Guinea's north coast and make bombing raids on Rabaul far more practical.

Access to Buna and the airstrips, however, was almost impossible. By water, Buna was protected by a maze of shallow coral reefs. By land, it was surrounded by a swamp, only three feet above sea level, reaching far inland. The natives used the few dry areas for gardens of taro, yams, sugarcane, bananas, and breadfruit. The drier areas outside the perimeter of the swamp were barely more accessible. They were covered with coconut palm plantations and broad fields of golden kunai and elephant grass. The elephant grass grew to heights of ten feet, and both grasses were razor sharp.

In the area east of the Girua River, the Japanese had erected hundreds of impregnable coconut log bunkers between eight and thirty feet long. In designing them, the Japanese engineers had attended to the smallest of details. The bunkers were reinforced with coconut logs, I-beams, sheet iron, and forty-gallon steel oil drums filled with sand, and camouflaged with earth, grass, rocks, and more logs. Because of the high water table, engineers constructed them seven or eight feet above ground and carved out firing slits in them. The entrances were positioned so they could be covered by troops in adjacent bunkers, and they were angled to protect soldiers from hand grenades. The bunkers opened directly onto fire trenches, or were connected to them by shallow crawl tunnels.

Bunker and trench systems protected all of the inland approaches to Buna Village and Buna Government Station. The approaches, in turn, were honeycombed with enemy emplacements.

Colonel Yokoyama, the commanding officer of the 15th Independent Engineers, took charge of all the Japanese forces west of the Girua River. Captain Yasuda, the senior naval officer, took command east of the river.

The Japanese line at Buna left the 32nd Division no room to maneuver, and forced the Americans into swamps, putrid with decay, or onto paths where the Japanese could concentrate their firepower. The situation clearly called for an amphibious assault using shallow-draft landing craft, but all available Higgins boats had been diverted to Guadalcanal.

•   •   •

As the men of the 128th closed in on the Japanese positions, the jungle, according to Robert Doyle, a *Milwaukee Journal* reporter assigned to the 128th, "was as quiet as a church."

Another hundred yards down the trail, the 128th met a hailstorm of fire. Men were scythed by Japanese machine gunners, by snipers who used a smokeless powder and were tied into the tops of trees with enough water and food to last them days, and by riflemen hiding in their bunkers. The Japanese shells made a small flash, so the Americans could not tell where the shots were coming from. If a tribe of headhunters wielding spears had attacked, the Americans could not have been more shocked. They had stumbled directly into the enemy's kill zone.

One scout took a bullet to the head. His killer was only four feet away, invisible in his camouflaged bunker. When the men saw the scout go down, they scattered. They dove from the trail and fired wildly. Bullets ripped through the jungle. Men cursed, "I can't see the bastards!" It did not take long before wounded soldiers were sobbing, "I'm hit, I'm hit!" Then came the awful "Stretcher bearer!" It was the first time any of the men had ever heard the call. Those who survived the war would always remember it.

A medic was jumping from one man to another, opening his pouch to get at first aid supplies, and dusting gaping wounds with sulfa powder to fight infection. The jungle was full of injured soldiers, blood-spattered vines and ferns, shards of shattered bone, and strings of bloody intestines hanging from gaping holes in men's bellies. The Japanese snipers were especially fond of the gut shot. A gut-shot soldier would act like a decoy—he would cry out for help, drawing in more soldiers.

Japanese troops continued to rain down lead on the bewildered Americans, who clutched trees, hid underneath sprawling mangrove roots, and dug down into the muck. But every movement, every muscle twitch drew more fire from the Japanese. Some men were on their bellies, heads down, crawling forward blindly, bumping into dead bodies strewn along the trail. In no time the bodies would swell in the tropical heat, and then the flies and the maggots would find them.

A soldier sprinted forward. When he finally stopped, he realized that he was standing on the roof of a Japanese bunker. Before he could mutter "Goddammit," a bullet ripped into his arm. Instinctively, he hit the ground and rolled off the bunker and kept rolling. It must have seemed like a miracle. When he came to a stop, he was alive and there was a medic at his side.

An engineer observer watched it all.

The first opposition from the enemy was a surprise and a shock to our green troops. The enemy positions were amazingly well camouflaged, and seemed to have excellent fields of fire even in the close quarters of the jungle. . . . Snipers were everywhere. . . . The enemy habitually allowed our troops to advance to very close range—sometimes four or five feet from a machine gun post—before opening fire; often they allowed troops to bypass them completely, opening fire then on our rear elements, and on our front elements from the rear.

Our troops were pinned down everywhere. . . . It was impossible to see where the enemy fire was coming from; consequently our own rifle and machine gun [fire] was ineffective. . . . Grenades and mortars . . . were difficult to use because, first, it was difficult to pick out a nest position to advance upon with grenades, second, the thick jungle growth, and high grass, made throwing and firing difficult, and, third, because it was nearly impossible to observe our fire.

It was "the longest [day] of my life," said one of the American soldiers. "We were surrounded by the terrible din and confusion of battle—the clatter and clang of rifles and machine guns.

"The parade of injured GIs was heartbreaking to watch. . . . The walking wounded struggled past us. . . . A few were being carried on litters, and some were left where they died, until the next day when they could be taken care of by special burial squads."

Eventually, the chaos ended. The sun was dropping fast. Unaccountably, the Japanese did not launch a massive attack. If they had, they would have caught the Americans back on their heels, disorganized and dispirited.

As it was, the Americans had a chance to lick their wounds, recover some of the dead bodies, and assess their losses. The Japanese had stopped them in their tracks, mauled them, and the Americans had little to show for it—nothing more than thirty feet of lousy jungle.

The Americans did not take any chances with the few Japanese soldiers who had tried to slip around behind the advancing army and were killed. They bayoneted them or shot them again. Native carriers sent out to collect the enemy dead were instructed to slit their throats before moving them. The Japanese were known for their tricks. Wounded soldiers would lie among the corpses, feigning death, "playing possum," and would open up on a squad or platoon after it had passed.

Most of the Americans could not resist the chance to view the dead Japanese. They were stunned by what they saw. What they were looking at were not the gaunt corpses of men who had fought and starved in the mountains. These were strong, well-armed physical specimens, and the Americans went from thinking they were fighting "a few sick Japs" to believing they were in combat against "jungle supermen." Sergeant Roy Gormanson of Company A said, "I always thought that the Japanese were small people, but then I saw my first dead Jap. He was six feet one or better."

The reality was that despite a formidable Allied air presence, the Japanese had succeeded in landing nine hundred fresh troops at Basabua on November 17. These were probably the soldiers that Gormanson had come upon. Many of them were from the 144th Infantry and the 3rd Battalion's 229th Infantry, a unit whose two sister battalions were fighting on Guadalcanal. The 229th was made up of experienced jungle troops who had fought in China, Hong Kong, and Java. All nine hundred men were deployed east of the Girua River in the Cape Endaiadere-Duropa Plantation area, under colonel Yokoyama, who formerly was in charge of the Sanananda-Girua area, west of the river.

As curious as the Americans were to see the bodies of Japanese soldiers, they were unnerved and frightened at the sight of their own dead. Some of the men avoided the corpses. The shock that they had experienced in their first battle had turned into a kind of despair—to look upon a dead friend might mark them for death in the next battle.

Others came to pay their last respects before the bodies were covered up. Many cried. A handful turned bitter and made silent promises to themselves that they would pretend to fight, but when the bullets were spraying across the jungle, they would crawl behind a tree. They had no intention of dying in some godforsaken place.

Others vowed revenge. In future battles, they would kill like machines and afterward take souvenirs. It was a barbaric ritual, but one that became commonplace. These men rifled through the pockets of the Japanese dead, scrounged through their packs taking whatever they could: photos, flags, insignias, sabers, pistols, hara-kiri knives, money, diaries, even boots and the split-toed tabi shoes that many of the Japanese soldiers wore. Some would cut open the mouths of the dead from ear to ear. Then, with the butts of their rifles they would smash a dead man's teeth and take his gold crowns. Some cut off fingers and kept them for good luck. One guy cut the ears off a Japanese soldier and kept them.

•   •   •

That evening, after rounding up the corpses, the soldiers of the 128th dug in. The medics, who had been shot at all day, removed their red crosses and arm brassards and began dyeing their white battle dressings green. Japanese snipers loved to zero in on the white bandages.

None of the men slept. It was raining, and they wrapped themselves in leaky raincoats or shelter halves. Their foxholes were filled with water. And their minds played tricks on them, too—vines became gun barrels, trees skulking Japanese soldiers. Dead buddies came back to life. Cicadas and crickets shouted obscenities.

The Japanese were on the move, too. Ray Bailey, a platoon sergeant with Company B, remembers stringing up triplines that night. He and two of his buddies—they called themselves the "Three Musketeers"—used C ration cans and grenades. They pulled the pins on grenades and then crammed the grenades into the cans, knowing they had only five seconds—One Mississippi, Two Mississippi—before the grenades splattered their guts all over the jungle. Once in the can, the grenade handles would not budge. If a Japanese creeping through the jungle hit the string they had tied to the handles, the grenade would come tumbling out of the can and trigger the detonator.

Bailey and his buddies thought that they would sleep easier after setting the triplines, but the Japanese had other ideas. "They had one of our guys," Bailey says. "He was hollering. They were torturing him so we could hear and there was nothing we could do about it." The day before, the Americans had brought in a Japanese prisoner. "We never felt any hate against him," Bailey recalled. "But after that, everyone vowed they would never bring in another Jap prisoner."

Back at his headquarters at Embogo, Harding was stunned by the 128th's defeat. Allied Intelligence had seriously underestimated the number of enemy soldiers at the beachhead, maintaining that the Japanese army had only fifteen hundred "effectives," when in actuality its troop strength numbered nearly 6,500 fighting men. To make matters worse, Harding was still reeling from the news he had received that afternoon: He would have to forfeit his 126th Infantry Regiment to General Vasey, who wanted it west of the Girua River on the Sanananda track, a move that had MacArthur's blessing. While the 128th attacked from the east, up the coast, Harding had hoped to use the 126th as his left-flank force in a head-on advance on Buna Village and Buna Government Station. It was a classic double envelopment, intended to squeeze the Japanese out of their bunkers through overwhelming force. Now, only a day into the assault, he had lost a whole regiment to the Australians, and was forced to commit his reserve, the 128th Infantry's 2nd Battalion. Still he would be short of men.

Colonel Clarence Tomlinson, the new commander of the 126th, was equally puzzled by the news that his regiment would be fighting with the Australians. He tried to reach Harding, but failed to make radio contact. Unwilling to move without confirmation, he radioed Port Moresby instead. Port Moresby informed him that the order was legitimate, and early on November 20 Tomlinson set out for Popondetta, accompanied by Captain Boice. Late that afternoon, Tomlinson and Boice reported to General Vasey. Vasey, in turn, sent Tomlinson and Boice and the entire 126th on to Soputa.

Late in the afternoon on November 20, after slopping through thick mud for more than half a day, the 126th arrived at Soputa and received their orders. They would have a day of rest and on November 22 they would be committed to battle. Though wet and hungry, they were still feeling cocky—they would show the Australians how to fight! The exhausted Australians, whom they had been sent in to relieve, could have been offended by their brazenness; instead, they merely smiled knowingly. Dudley McCarthy, an Australian historian who witnessed the arrival of the Americans, wrote that, ". . . the Australians were content to sit back for a while and watch the Americans. There was a very real interest in their observation and a certain sardonic but concealed amusement. The Americans had told some of them that they 'could go home now' as they (the Americans) 'were here to clean things up.'"

The following day Tomlinson and Captain Boice scouted the front, and that evening met with the 126th's battalion commanders to discuss plans for the next morning's attack. Their only map was a vague, sub-par, one-inch-to-one-mile sheet, which did not contain descriptions of the terrain ahead, so the advance was going to require a good amount of guesswork. Tomlinson and Boice were certain of one thing, though: The fighting was not going to be easy. Heavy jungle and swamp lay at the junction of the Soputa-Buna and Soputa-Sanananda tracks west of the Girua River, and the Japanese were dug in and waiting.

Chapter 13

A POOR MAN'S WAR

WITH NO SHORTAGE OF bad news coming from the front, MacArthur's publicity team in Port Moresby was busy creating a message that had almost no basis in reality. The same day the 126th arrived at Soputa, MacArthur's communiqué read, "Our ground forces have rapidly closed in now and pinned the enemy down on the narrow coastal strip from Buna to Gona. We are fighting on the outskirts of both places."

As if convinced by his own PR, MacArthur issued orders calling for a full-scale advance on the Buna-Sanananda-Gona Front early the following morning. "All columns," he said, were to be "driven through to objectives regardless of losses." The message that General Harding received from MacArthur read: "Take Buna Today At All Costs. MacArthur."

Harding could not believe his eyes. His 128th was up against thousands of Japanese troops, blistering fire, log bunkers, and a huge swamp that limited his army's mobility. His 126th had been stolen from him. He had no artillery and he was dealing with a supply crisis. His luggers and trawlers had been sunk off Hariko, and the Dobodura airstrip was not yet fully functional. He was operating on what he called a "hand-to-mouth, catch-as-catch-can basis." It was not the way to run a war, much less win it.

As if the terrain was not tough enough, equipment failures made his problems worse. Radios used by mortar platoons to coordinate firing did not work. Because of their short fuses, the few 81 mm mortars that made it to the front had almost no effect on the Japanese bunkers because they blew up on impact. Harding was also to have received a number of tanks, but Murphy's Law prevailed—when the tanks were loaded onto barges at Oro Bay, the barges sank. Harding had no options but to take the bunkers out "by hand."

Harding was also deeply concerned about casualties. In just three days of fighting, he had lost sixty-three men, and in one day of fighting alone, a single battalion suffered forty-one killed and wounded. Now MacArthur wanted him to take Buna regardless of the costs. Harding knew that if he followed orders he would be sentencing hundreds of Red Arrow soldiers to a certain death. "I know as well as anybody that you can't win battles without getting a lot of people hurt," Harding wrote in his diary. "But I also know . . . that infantry can't break through an automatic weapons defense without first knocking out the automatic weapons. Anyone who knows his World War stuff knows that." What Harding did next was to tell his officers that they were to push the offensive only as long as the progress they made justified the losses. Progress in the jungle, though, was tough to calculate. Was it a hundred feet, two hundred? Harding let his officers be the judges. He would accept the responsibility for defying MacArthur's orders.

After three days of disappointment, General Harding needed good news, and it came with a pick-me-up late in the day on November 21. After the loss of his 126th Regiment, Harding had been troubled about the state of his left flank, and practically begged Lieutenant General Edmund Herring to return a portion of his men. Having taken over for General Rowell, who had been dismissed by Blamey in late September, Herring was now commander of all Australian and American forces in New Guinea. Herring agreed to Harding's request and instructed General Vasey to pick a battalion to turn over to Harding for action east of the Girua River. For Vasey it was an easy choice: He selected Major Smith's 2nd Battalion, the Ghost Mountain boys, who everyone seemed to agree had been done in by their 130-mile march across the Papuan Peninsula.

Smith's men were weary and filthy, and their dirty uniforms hung loosely on their gaunt frames. They looked more like haggard Depression-era hobos than fighting men. But at least Harding had another battalion with which to work.

Early on the morning of November 22, Colonel Tomlinson pulled Smith aside.

"Good luck, Herbie," Tomlinson said, "and get the hell out of here before the bastards change their mind."

Smith took Tomlinson's warning to heart and he and his men double-timed it for the Girua River crossing.

By late morning the 2nd Battalion was at the riverbank. It had only been a few days since they last forded it, but during that interval, fed by recent rains, the river had risen dangerously. Someone volunteered to swim the hundred yards and run a cable across the river, but moving the battalion across the river even with the use of the cable was a risky proposition. If surprised by a Japanese patrol while attempting to cross, they would be defenseless.

The battalion's luck held, however, and by evening Smith's men crossed the Girua without a single mishap. But if any of them had convinced themselves that their fortunes had changed, they soon discovered otherwise. Smith's orders were to join the 2nd Battalion of the 128th Infantry Regiment at the Triangle. Of all the Japanese strongholds, the Triangle may have been the most impenetrable. For a group of men that had already undergone a seeming lifetime of misery, this was the worst possible assignment.

Along with naval pioneer troops, Captain Yasuda had over eighteen hundred men defending the Triangle. Yasuda had a series of superbly hidden machine gun positions south and north of the Triangle on the Dobodura-Buna track, the only man-made route to the Buna coast. In the Triangle itself, Japanese engineers had built an elaborate system of bunkers. In the Coconut Grove and Government Gardens just to the north and northeast of the Triangle, the engineers had designed more bunkers. Everything else was covered in swamp.

Smith and his Ghost Mountain Battalion reached the Triangle on the morning of November 23, and learned that the two battalions would come under the heading of Urbana Force (named after I Corps commander General Robert Eichelberger's Ohio hometown) to be commanded by another Smith—Colonel Herbert A. Smith.

Thirty-nine days after leaving Nepeana on the other side of the mountains, Stutterin' Smith's Ghost Mountain boys were about to be blooded.

•   •   •

West of the Girua River on the Sanananda Front, Colonel Tomlinson was being asked to lead an attack despite the fact that he had just lost Stutterin' Smith and the 2nd Battalion. He was now in command of only fourteen hundred troops, which included only one full battalion— the 3rd Battalion of the 126th Infantry Regiment.

Tomlinson's troops spent the last week in November trying to get in position to establish a roadblock behind the main enemy position on the Sanananda track. His troops, their faces smeared with green camouflage paint, took to the swamps to the west and east of the track, but with little training in patrolling, inaccurate maps, and no lateral trails, they often lost their bearings. Colonel Tsukamoto and hundreds of fresh 144th Infantry replacements, relying on savage night-time raids, caught Tomlinson's tired, disoriented troops off guard. Casualties were heavy.

While Tomlinson's troops tried to work in behind the Japanese, William Hirashima strove to make himself useful. He went out on patrols where he risked being shot by soldiers from both sides. Japanese snipers wanted to shoot him because he wore an American uniform and Americans would shoot him because he looked Japanese. Hirashima also negotiated with a wounded Japanese machine gunner who was stranded in a field. To do that, he had to walk out ahead of the frontline troops. He was completely exposed and only sixty yards separated him from the Japanese soldier. He could have been gunned down before he had a chance to utter his first word.

Hirashima shouted to the soldier. Was he willing to surrender? Just then a shot rang from the jungle. A Japanese sniper had spotted him. Hirashima dove into a nearby trench. He waited for a few minutes before crawling out. It had been a close call, but Colonel Tomlinson still wanted him to try to talk with the machine gunner. To take a prisoner so early in the battle would be a real stroke of luck; who knew what they might learn?

Hirashima agreed to try again. Seeing ahead of him a little rise, he decided to make for it. It would be dangerous, but the soldier needed to be able to hear him. Half expecting to hear a crack from the jungle and to feel a bullet tear into his belly, he stood on top of the rise and tried to coax the machine gunner out of hiding, saying he would be treated kindly. The soldier, though, was reluctant. Surrender was the ultimate disgrace.

Just then another shot ripped through the trees. Hirashima threw himself to the ground. He had been lucky; the sniper had missed again. No more pushing it though—the third bullet was bound to find its mark.

That day Hirashima thought he had proved his loyalty, but he still wondered if his fellow soldiers trusted him. Guys muttered under their breath: Whose side was he on? They better watch their backs. He looked like a goddamn Jap.

.   .   .

Captain Medendorp's Cannon and Antitank Companies, which were considered to be part of Tomlinson's fourteen hundred men, were in the vicinity of Wairopi. Since crossing the mountains, they had spent the last month in the Kumusi River valley on what Medendorp called "hell raising" patrols, essentially guerilla activity that, according to Medendorp, consisted of "playing hide and seek with the Japs." Medendorp was still suffering from a badly ulcerated leg and in the past few weeks he had been racked by malarial fevers. His men were no better off. The "sick," he wrote, "were struggling along with their arms thrown over the shoulders of friends walking on each side of them." There was no time for them to recuperate, though. Tomlinson was in need of men.

Before Medendorp began marching toward the Sanananda Front, he and Captain Keast paid off the native carriers and scouts who had so ably assisted them on their patrols. Medendorp wrote later, "The parting was very sad."

Medendorp's consolation was that he and Keast had been reunited. Medendorp later wrote, "It was a greater pleasure than I can tell you to see Roger again when I climbed up that last hill into the village. He was smiling from behind his beard." Waiting for his knee to mend, Keast had been tending the dropsite at Laruni while Medendorp scouted the Kumusi River valley.

On November 25, Medendorp, Keast, and the Wairopi Patrol began marching, but as they neared the front, Medendorp was slowed by the ulcer on his leg, so Keast went ahead to establish contact with Tomlinson. Moving in the opposite direction, however, away from the battlefield, were groups of natives "carrying stretcher after stretcher" of wounded Americans. It was an unnerving sight for Medendorp's troops. Among the wounded they recognized friends. The natives, straining and sweating under their loads, treated the casualties with great compassion. Medendorp would later write, "There was no jostling. It was a symphony of movement. If the wounded man was too far gone to hold a banana leaf to shade his eyes from the sun . . . then a native walked behind a stretcher holding a broad leaf over the man's eyes. . . . Their [the natives'] shoulders were sore and bandaged, and fatigue showed on their blank faces, still they trudged on like a stream of ants."

Soon, the Wairopi Patrol heard rifle and machine gun fire, the explosions of mortars and "high overhead the soft sigh of . . . shells on their way to blast the enemy." It was "sweet music" to Medendorp. But the Japanese were returning fire, too. When that noise "developed a lower pitch and became harsh and severe, like a buzz saw going through a knot," Medendorp knew it was time to dive for cover.

Medendorp finally reached Tomlinson's command post. Keast informed him that after a series of setbacks—just two days before they had lost more than a hundred men killed or wounded—Colonel Tomlinson, a hard-nosed West Pointer, had scheduled his largest attack yet for the morning of November 30. Medendorp was relieved by the news of the delay. He and his men badly needed a day of rest.

The day before the attack, Colonel Tomlinson pulled aside Medendorp and Keast to discuss plans for the following day's attack. Tomlinson's shirt was streaked with sweat and salt. He had large rings under his armpits and a skunk-like band that ran from his neck to the small of his back.

"There's only about half a dozen Japs out there," Tomlinson roared. "Three of those have dysentery and the other three fever! They move one machine gun from place to place. Our men are green, and they think that every bullet has their name on it. We must teach them to keep on advancing as long as they are not exactly being fired at. After hitting the ground they must learn to get up and get along. Now get in there and do your part in cleaning them out, or I'll just have to tell the Australian general in command on this front that our regiment cannot accomplish its mission."

Neither Medendorp nor Keast knew what to make of Tomlinson or his speech. They had had almost no contact with the new colonel. Quinn had been their regimental commander, the leader they loved, but Quinn was now buried in a grave in the misty mountains. Who was Tomlinson kidding, trying to convince them that they were up against only a skeleton force? They had seen the wounded Allies being carried from the front.

"It won't be any pushover tomorrow," Keast said, when he and Medendorp left Tomlinson.

Medendorp's account of Tomlinson's speech was infused with sarcasm: "Properly impressed with the necessity of giving the enemy a killing, we started out on the half-day march to get into position."

As the men were assembling, Father Stephen Dzienis paid the soldiers a visit. By now Dzienis had proved himself. He had earned Medendorp's respect on the long, cold journey from Camp Livingston, Louisiana, to Fort Devens, Massachusetts, when instead of going by troop train he went with Medendorp in an unheated army-issue truck with a canvas top and side curtains. More recently, he had volunteered to march across the mountains with the 2nd Battalion. Never again would he be thought of as a pampered chaplain.

Dzienis had a great field of a beard. As always, he was filled with spirit and good cheer, though his legs, Medendorp noticed, were a "mass of running sores." At one point, Dzienis pulled Medendorp aside. "Be sure," he winked, "to use plenty of hand grenades, Skipper. They're buried up to their eyebrows."

Medendorp carried Tomlinson's orders for the attack in his pocket. When he and Keast got to the front, Medendorp turned them over to the battalion's executive officer, who scratched out a diagram of the plan in the soft, black jungle humus. The orders called for Medendorp and Keast to attack eastward from the left flank on November 30. Another group of men would attack head on, and one would advance from the right. The goal of the attack was to establish a roadblock north of the main Japanese position on the Soputa-Sanananda track.

"We'll get those bastards," Captain John D. Shirley assured the battalion XO after the meeting. "Tomorrow, we'll get those bastards."

Captain John D. Shirley was from Grand Rapids, Michigan, and he and Medendorp had been inducted together as second lieutenants in the National Guard. Shirley pointed to a position just down the track where a platoon commanded by Lieutenant Hershel Horton was set up, and volunteered to escort his old friend and Keast there. Medendorp gladly accepted.

"Shirley was a bundle of energy," Medendorp would later write. "Every move he made was on the double. I couldn't keep up with him, for I had already been in the jungle for two months. I could get where it was necessary to go, but couldn't put out any spurts of energy. The trail to Horton's position led through kunai grass. Shirley bent forward and ran along like a pheasant."

It was not the first time Medendorp realized just how hard he had pushed himself in the last two months. But he and his men were in the same boat—they were all weary, even the youngest of the soldiers. Now, trying to keep up with a relatively fresh soldier, it was obvious that he was not up to it. Just what had the last two months done to him? Medendorp knew that he had lost weight, maybe forty pounds, since entering the jungle in early October; he could feel his ribs and his hipbones and the sharp corners of his shoulders. Now only 150 pounds, he tired easily. On the short hike to Lieutenant Horton's position, he had to stop a number of times to catch his breath. Then there was the ulcer that looked like it might never heal.

Shirley dropped off Medendorp and Keast with Lieutenant Horton. Keast flashed Horton a smile. They had known and competed against each other since their college days when Horton was a track man at Notre Dame.

"Hello Horton. Glad to see you again," Medendorp said.

"Quiet," Horton snapped. "And get down."

Medendorp, Keast, and Horton lay on their bellies like snakes in the sharp three-foot kunai grass. The hot sun beat down on them and the air was thick and wet. Except for the occasional shot, the front was largely silent. Even the birds grew quiet.

Horton, Keast, and Medendorp went over the plans for the following morning.

"This is how it's gonna happen, boys," Horton told them. "I'll fire two shots with my pistol and that will be the signal to begin the attack."

Keast said, nodding in agreement, "Two shots."

That night Keast, like the other men, drifted in and out of sleep. He would doze off and then wake with a start, his heart pounding, his head cobwebbed with images. His son Harry moved in and out of his dreams as if he were real. Sometimes, it was as if Keast could reach out and hug him; he would pull Harry in close and hold him in his arms. Awake, his head cleared and his eyes adjusted. All he could see was darkness and the phantom shape of trees. Then the dank smell of the jungle would fill his nostrils, and he would remember where he was.

On the morning of November 30, the men were stretched tighter than piano wires, and smeared in mud with sweat dripping off their foreheads. The combination of salt and dirt clouded and stung their eyes—how in the hell were they supposed to kill Japs when they could hardly see?

In tense whispers, they passed the word down the line.

"Two shots. Listen for 'em. And then we go."

As they waited, touching their triggers and trying not to

hyperventilate, they imagined the various ways they might die. "Keep a tight asshole," someone said. "Now is not the time to be shittin' your pants!"

Squinting and adjusting his gaze, Keast tried to make sense of the shapeless jungle. Where was the enemy? All he could see was the morning haze cut by a dim sun, shimmering trees, and in some areas where the 3rd Battalion and the Australians had already clashed with the Japanese, bare patches where trees had been stripped of their leaves.

Lying in the kunai grass waiting for Horton to give the signal, Keast recalled the details of his photographs: Ruth sitting on the running board of the family car holding their baby son; Harry with his perfect doll face, smiling at the world. Where were they now? What were they doing? For a moment he might have dreamed of the future: chasing his sons in the back yard; watching them swing their arms in that exaggerated way kids did when they ran; throwing the football with Harry; seeing Roger Jr. heave a basketball up to a rim, all coiled up, launching the too-big ball with all his might.

Keast's feet were burning and a dull ache had settled into his knee. The rest in Laruni had helped, but the knee was still weak.

Then, two shots. Gunfire exploded from the line. To pull the trigger after waiting for so long gave the men a giddy sense of release. Soldiers shot in the general direction of the enemy and hoped that their bullets struck flesh. Japanese troops returned fire. The volley was loud, theatrical, but brief. Medendorp heard the sound of empty clips popping out of rifles. He turned to Keast.

"Sure," he said, "Only half a dozen sick Japs!"

After ten minutes of artillery, with Medendorp assisting Lieutenant Daniels, the Australian Artillery forward observer, in registering the shots, the telephone operator got on the phone. "Guns off," he said.

Medendorp and Daniels stepped in front of the lines to assess the damage. Company I, under Captain Shirley, was ready now. Company I and the Antitank Company under Captain Keast moved forward supported by fusillade from Medendorp's men.

"Follow the sun," Shirley shouted. "Follow the sun."

Medendorp watched as the "advancing men crawled over wounded and dead." He was startled by the fury of the Japanese response. They "gave back every bit they received." The .25 caliber Japanese Arisaka rifles had a peculiar, high-pitched sound—like the "crack of a bull whip." Each of those cracks was answered by the coarse bark of American .30 caliber M-1 rifles.

While bullets ripped through the jungle and dense kunai grass, Medendorp leaned against a large, rotten tree stump, consulting his compass and trying to get bearings on the Japanese locations. Enemy bullets hit the tree stump, splattering wood chips all around him. Somewhere in the jungle a Japanese Juki machine gunner opened up. Medendorp could tell it was a Juki by its slow, heavy thud.

Just behind the front line, Lieutenant Segal worked, according to Medendorp, "as calmly as in a hospital at home." His aid station was nothing more than a thatched hut with a mud floor and assistants with flashlights.

On the battlefield soldiers improvised stretchers of balsa wood or split bamboo, wrapped them with telephone wire or denim jackets, and went out to recover the wounded. They had to act fast; it did not take long for open wounds to become infected, even gangrenous. Once off the line, they carried their comrades into slit trenches to protect them from rifle fire and mortar fragments. There, the wounded lay wrapped in dirty, blood-soaked battle dressings until Segal could attend to them. Though Segal was sick himself over the past two months, Medendorp had watched him grow thinner and paler—he worked mightily to stabilize the wounded before they were carried back to the regimental station. There were times, though, when even a talented medical doctor like Segal was powerless. That is when Father Dzienis took over. Dzienis had buried his first man—Colonel Quinn—at Natunga, surrounded by the mountains and the green solitude of the jungle. Here, he walked along the slit trench, holding his rosary, administering last rites to the dying while the battle raged around him.

Back at the front, Shirley and Keast's assault was stalled after four hundred yards by withering enemy fire. Notified that the advance had bogged down, the battalion executive officer rushed to the front to rally his troops and led the way across a large kunai field. When the attack slammed up against a wide stretch of swamp through which the Japanese had cut lanes of fire, the jungle vibrated with the sound of machine guns, and the executive officer was killed. Realizing that the only way across the swamp was through the machine gun nests, one of Shirley's sergeants assembled a patrol—ten men with two automatic rifles, a tommy gun, and a bunch of grenades between them.

As they crept and slithered through the swamp, bullets ripped through the trees and over their heads. The men knew that the Japanese were firing indiscriminately. If the machine gunners actually spotted them, however, it would be like a carnival shoot. The Japanese could wipe them out in a matter of seconds.

When the patrol got within thirty feet of the machine gun nests, the men decided not to push their luck. They rose and tossed their grenades. The barrage stopped.

Seeing their opening, Keast and Shirley drove their men through the Japanese line. When the Japanese retreated, the two captains agreed to rest the troops. They had gained another six hundred yards. In the jungle, where success was measured in double-digit increments, it was a tremendous accomplishment.

Late in the afternoon, as a gray mist settled over the jungle and fruit bats gathered in the darkening sky, Shirley's scouts located an enemy bivouac off the main Soputa-Sanananda track. Shirley and Keast realized that if they hoped to make a move on the enemy stronghold, they would have to do it before nightfall.

"Fix your bayonets and let's cut the guts out of them," Shirley said.

If his men, who had been locked in battle for almost the entire day, were surprised by the order, they should not have been. Shirley's ferocity was well known. Do or die, he was determined to get the bastards.

Shirley and Keast divided their companies into three platoons and then they led the charge through the jungle.

"Keep moving," someone yelled out. Giant ferns and vines ripped at their legs. Branches gashed their faces. They did not know where the

Japs were until they saw the muzzle flashes, then they hit a solid mass of enemy soldiers. Men fired at each other at point-blank range and slashed and lunged with their bayonets. Blood splattered everywhere. Shirley had hold of a man's neck, and he could feel the Japanese soldier thrashing under his hands.

When the Japanese defenders scattered, Shirley and Keast wasted no time securing the track. They dug in and placed rifle squads in all directions around the new position. The men were wet with sweat and covered in muck. Their hands were sticky with blood. But they had succeeded, beating the Japanese at their own game. They had established a perimeter three hundred yards to the rear of the Japanese position on the track, and had isolated the enemy's forward units. But as dusk fell, they realized the precariousness of their own position. Surrounded by Japanese snipers and machine gunners, they were cut off from the main body of the Americans by more than a mile of thick jungle.

Shirley knew he had to get word back to battalion headquarters. "Where the hell is the phone?" he wanted to know. When one of the signalmen confessed that he had left it a hundred yards back in a kunai patch, Shirley ordered him to get it.

News of Shirley's and Keast's attack electrified battalion headquarters. But the victory had come at a price. On the way back to the command post, Mcdendorp saw the graves of the men lost that day. "There were more," he wrote, "but they were out there between the lines where they could not be gotten." He heard wounded men crying out and saw corpses already bloated by the heat. That night, a breeze came in off the coast, cooling the jungle. Then, Medendorp said of the unrecovered bodies, "We could smell them."

.   .   .

East of the Girua River, as Colonel Smith began moving on the Triangle, he was heartened by the arrival of Major Stutterin' Smith's 2nd Battalion.

Smith, too, was happy to be back among familiar faces. The 128th had been his home for more than twenty years. One of the first people he saw was Lieutenant Mack Fradette, an old friend. Fradette was stunned by the condition of Smith and his men. Smith, who had always had problems keeping weight on, was as thin as a cornstalk. He had also just recovered from a bout of malaria. His men all wore long beards and in Fradette's opinion looked like "walking skeletons."

As the battalion got settled, Colonel Smith gave Stutterin' Smith a quick tour of the area. However, the major would have very little time to familiarize himself with the lay of the land; the attack was scheduled for the following day. He must have hesitated for a moment when he saw the battlefield. "Buna," Smith wrote, "was a nightmare . . . of jungle . . . kunai grass higher than a man's head . . . and swamps . . . that rose and fell with the tides. . . . The Japs had built bunkers" with "excellent fields of fire covering approaches from inland routes. . . . These bunkers" were "practically invisible."

That night, Stutterin' Smith put Lieutenant Odell in charge of a platoon in Company F. Odell was forty pounds lighter than when he had come to New Guinea. Still, he realized that the "hardships thus far encountered were nothing compared with the hell that was to come."

Just short of midnight on November 23, Colonel Smith and Stutterin' Smith held a council of war at the colonel's command post, which was situated along the Soputa-Buna track three-quarters of a mile short of the Triangle. They had already resolved the confusion that might arise from two battalions fighting side by side, each one commanded by a Herbert Smith. Stutterin' Smith became Red Smith and Colonel Smith was White Smith. They also laid out the plans for the following day's attack. It would come from three directions and would begin at 0800 with bombing and strafing by American pilots. Before the troops moved out, four 25-pounders, new to the front, would open up on the Triangle.

Despite the plans, both Smiths knew that they would be flying by the seat of their pants. They had no topographical maps of the area and their aerial photographs proved worthless; a large cloud covered the zone in which the attack was supposed to take place.

Dawn came in with a rush and at 0800 the planes appeared. Twelve P-40s strafed the Triangle, but for some reason the bombers never showed. Worse yet, the P-40 pilots completely missed their target. Both Smiths hesitated. They could not possibly send their men into the Triangle now; it would be a suicide mission. They called for more planes, which arrived five hours later—but only four of the twelve they had requested. Rather than firing on the Triangle, though, the four P-40s, unable to identify their targets in the thick foliage, turned their guns on Colonel Smith's command post.

It was chaos. Men screamed at the top of their lungs and dove into the jungle. "We're Americans, you stupid bastards! We're goddamn Americans!"

The strafing stopped as quickly as it had begun. When Major Smith assessed the damage, he was relieved to discover that it had not been as disastrous as he feared. Only one man had been wounded. The Triangle, though, had been untouched.

But there was no turning back. Though fully conscious of the dangers of sending men into the maw of the Triangle, the decision had been made—the attack would go as planned. Both Smiths felt the pressure to push the offensive. According to headquarters in Port Moresby, they were to have taken Buna half a week earlier.

Before the men pushed off, 60 mm mortars fired on the Triangle. From Ango, the 25-pounders with ranges of nearly eight miles boomed. At 2:28 that afternoon the troops jumped off.

On the left, Captain Melvin Schultz and Sergeant Lutjens and the men of Company E swung wide around the Triangle. The night before, after the company received its orders, Lutjens had taken a moment to scribble a few lines in his diary. "God only knows what we are about to face," he wrote. "If I said I am not afraid I would be a liar. Reread an old letter trying to place myself back in the states. To find something to fight for . . . I'm afraid of dying as much as anybody else. Maybe life wasn't so pleasant for me, but God it seems good now. If I don't come through this it will be God's will."

The plan called for Company E to cross Entrance Creek and sneak in behind the Japanese stronghold. Although the 128th's Company F had made some progress on the left three days before, it took Company E eight hours to advance eight hundred yards across the dense

swamp. The men could not see more than ten feet in any direction and
they were under strict instructions to hold their fire even if fired at.
Their mission was reconnaissance.

Men swore under their breath about how easy it would be for a
bunch of Japs to ambush them in the swamp—they were goddamn sitting ducks. A Juki machine gun could wipe them out before they knew
what had hit them.

When the first shot rang through the swamp, "everybody,"
according to Lutjens, "flopped down and sank his face into the mud. I
don't know exactly how the rest of the guys felt, but it scared the hell
out of me. Somebody whispered, 'That's a Jap.'"

One guy, who was out on the post, was trying to figure out where
the shot had come from. When he reported that it had originated from
behind a tree, Lutjens must have shaken his head. Talk about stating
the obvious; the swamp was full of trees.

Though neither Lutjens nor Schultz knew it, Company E had
stumbled smack into a Japanese outpost. The Japanese were guarding
the bridge that spanned Entrance Creek, northwest of the Triangle.
Lutjens' men were scared, but they were not content to stay put. They
crept forward. "We all wanted a peek at them [the Japanese]," Lutjens
admitted. "After coming all that way, we wanted to see what they
looked like."

Despite their curiosity, Schultz and Lutjens eventually did the pru-
dent thing—they halted the company. Men stood as still as man-
nequins. As dusk neared, a fog settled over the swamp. The men grew
cold and uncomfortable. A few guys decided to light cigarettes to calm
their nerves. It was a soldier's prerogative—if he was going to be miserable, he might as well have a smoke. The Americans might have been
short of 81 mm mortar ammunition, but they sure were not short of
cigarettes.

According to Lutjens,

The Japs had automatic fire emplaced in coconut trees, and as
soon as they saw the matches flare up, they let us have it—not
from just in front, but from all sides. We'd walked right into

the middle of them. We started to dig in, and I mean quick. Three of us dug a hole in five minutes flat, with our hands. We thought it was all over with. We couldn't see a thing. The Japs were shooting all around us. They stopped for a while, and by the next morning we were all dug in. They couldn't spot us too well through the jungle, but every time a man moved, they'd open up. One guy had the tip of his bayonet shot off. He didn't move a muscle. Nobody fired. I sometimes think it took more guts not to than it would have to shoot back. Then it began to rain. It was a cold, cold rain. We had left our packs behind when we started, and all we had with us was a few rations in our pockets. Then the tide began to come up through our foxholes.

At this, soldiers left their foxholes and leaned against trees while the black water lapped at their waists. The lucky ones found high ground on the outstretched roots of mangroves, which spread over the area like giant spiderwebs. The Japanese, they knew, were fond of fighting at night, but in the belly of the swamp, it hardly mattered, day or night. The sun could not penetrate the ceiling of twisted branches.

Some of the men managed to nod off. Others, like Lutjens, waited hyper-alert, listening for the sucking sound of Japanese scouts slogging through the muck, watching the water for animals—giant long-haired rats, deadly snakes, crocodiles, and rabid, bloodthirsty bats—which they feared almost as much as the Japanese.

·　　·　　·

While Company E was stranded in the swamp to the left, Company F, led by Captain Erwin Nummer, and Company H, White Smith's heavy weapons company, attacked up the middle. It was a scary proposition. Some of the men had fathers who had fought in World War I. From them they had heard grisly stories about attacking a trench system and the carnage that followed. A head-on assault on the Triangle, they feared, would be no different.

They were right. Captain Yasuda was waiting, eager to unleash the full fury of his firepower on anyone who blundered down the trail. Yasuda was supremely confident. He knew that whatever his men could not accomplish, the surrounding swamps would.

After only three hundred yards, the Americans encountered barriers of barbed wire that the Japanese had laid across the track. As they walked up to it to assess their options, the Japanese opened fire. Some of the men were so close, they could taste the gunpowder. Lieutenant Odell hit the ground and rolled off the track into the swamp that flanked it. He and the others had just two options: to dig in or to retreat. Captain Nummer called for a retreat. If they had any hope at all of advancing, they would need engineers with explosives to clear the trail.

In the swamp to the right, White Smith's men, like Lutjens and company, were trying to work their way behind the Triangle when a large enemy force attacked them. It was a classic Japanese attack— near dusk, the Japanese riflemen unleashed savage yells and bore down on the Americans. Though the Japanese could not have known just how raw and unseasoned the American soldiers were, the reality was that they were up against men who had never before experienced battle. Furthermore, they had caught them off guard. The Americans scrambled to defend themselves, only to have their weapons fail. According to the official report, "[M]ortars fell short because increments [the propelling charges in the mortar ammunition] were wet. Machine guns jammed because web belts were wet and dirty and had shrunk. Tommy guns and BARs were full of muck and dirt, and even the Mls fired well only for the first clip, and then jammed because clips taken from the belts were wet and full of muck from the swamp."

When their weapons failed, the Americans panicked and fled into the swamp. The following day, White Smith's company commanders met with him at his command post. Red Smith was on hand for the meeting, too. Outraged that American soldiers would so easily relinquish a position, he wrote later that "Smith should have kicked their fannies right back into the forward positions."

White Smith, however, saw the situation differently—his men were hungry and exhausted. Besides, he had little faith in the possibility of success on the right. His decision, he wrote, was "to abandon for the time being any action on the right and concentrate on the left . . . " When he made General Harding aware of his decision, Harding agreed—"the left hand road to Buna" was best. That put the burden of the attack squarely on the shoulders of Stutterin' Smith's Ghost Mountain boys.

Chapter 14

If They Don't Stink, Stick 'Em

From the safety of Port Moresby, MacArthur watched in impotent fury. Offensives on both the Warren and Urbana Fronts had yielded nothing but bad news. Making matters worse, the Japanese landed more troops on the night of November 24.

The next day, Generals Blamey and Herring paid MacArthur an unexpected visit at Government House. In the course of their conversation, both generals lobbied for bringing in reinforcements. MacArthur proposed calling in the 41st Division, which had been training in Australia for over six months. The Australian generals wasted no time being polite—they were unimpressed with the 32nd Division, they said. They preferred to use Australian troops. For Blamey and Herring, who remembered MacArthur's remarks about the efforts of their troops on the Kokoda track two months before, it was sweet revenge.

According to General Kenney, who was staying at Government House at the time of the Australian generals' visit, the accusation that the Americans wouldn't fight was "a bitter pill for MacArthur to swallow." Kenney did not bother to defend the 32nd either; in fact, he was openly critical of the division's commanders, who, he said, were unable to inspire their inexperienced troops. MacArthur was all ears. As a career army officer he did not have much faith in National Guard officers. In fact, the only one he trusted was General Hanford

MacNider, and MacNider was recuperating in Port Moresby after being wounded by a Japanese rifle grenade while observing the fighting on the Warren Front.

The day after the generals' visit, MacArthur sent two operations staff officers to the front with strict orders to observe what they could and to report back to him.

One of them arrived at the Warren Front, east of Buna Government Station, the day after Thanksgiving. Everyone knew by looking at his purposeful way of walking and his pressed uniform right off the quartermaster's shelf that he was from HQ, "a typical, theoretical staff officer" devoid of "practical knowledge" of combat operations. The men did not bother to put on a show for him either. They were sick and tired, and their morale was low. According to E. J. Kahn, a member of Harding's staff and a former staff writer for *The New Yorker*, they were "gaunt and thin, with deep black circles under their sunken eyes. They were covered with tropical sores and their jackets and pants . . . tattered and stained. Few wore socks or underwear. Often their soles had been sucked off their shoes by the tenacious, stinking mud." To make matters worse, after a full week of fighting, they had nothing to show for their efforts.

After consulting with War Department observers, the HQ man was convinced that there was not only a lack of leadership on the Warren Front, but that the men had no fight left in them. The observers told him of soldiers who refused to advance, relying instead on aircraft, mortars, and artillery. He heard stories about men who in the heat of battle abandoned their weapons and fled into the jungle. Two days after arriving at the Warren Front, he was back at Government House, where MacArthur was awaiting his report.

The officer's assessment was damning, and exactly what General Headquarters wanted to hear. GHQ wanted to make changes and now it had the evidence it needed to justify them.

What the observer had omitted from his report was that without more troops, heavy artillery (especially 105 mm howitzers, which were ideal for destroying pillboxes and bunkers), tanks, flamethrowers (which marines at Guadalcanal were using with great success), grenade launchers, and bangalore torpedoes, the Japanese bunker system was virtually unassailable.

General Harding's head was on the chopping block, and he knew it. He had already dispatched Colonel John W. Mott, his chief of staff, to the Urbana Front. Mott's orders were clear: Do what he needed to do to invigorate the attack. Mott wasted no time asserting his authority, or according to some, his ego. He relieved two of the 128th's company commanders.

Mott also held a conference with the two Smiths. Earlier Colonel White Smith had convinced General Harding that redirecting the efforts of the two battalions toward Buna Government Station instead of Buna Village might energize the stalled advance and drive a wedge between the Japanese positions. However, when Mott asked Colonel Smith if he had a plan for doing just that, Smith confessed that he had not.

Mott then turned to Stutterin' Smith. Did Major Smith have a plan? Smith said he had been thinking about it since Colonel Smith had proposed the idea. Though there was nothing ingenious about it, in his opinion throwing troops at the Triangle was a recipe for disaster. Japanese defenses were too strong. The key was to move troops into position on the far west side of the Triangle and stage an attack from there, behind the main Japanese position, while simultaneously striking at the head of the Triangle. They might catch the Japs by surprise. Mott was impressed enough to adopt the plan, and he and Smith hashed out the details. He also told Smith that he would soon get a chance to put it into action: General Harding had scheduled an attack on both fronts for the last night of the month, November 29–30.

Meanwhile, Harding was in the process of moving his headquarters and staff from Embogo on the coast to the inland Allied airfield at Dobodura. Fifteen miles from the coast, with a trail running on the left to the Urbana Front and on the right to the Warren Front, Dobodura was the logical choice for the new headquarters.

Dobodura was an area of broad grasslands that a tribe of coastal natives had inhabited to avoid the attacks of a neighboring coastal tribe. "Dobo-duru," the native name, mispronounced by the Americans, literally meant "under the shade of the dobo tree." Hoping to alleviate supply problems at the fronts and to free the Allied effort from its dependence on a depleted, vulnerable, and inefficient fleet of luggers, the Allies were converting Dobodura into a huge airstrip.

By the time Harding and his party left Embogo at 9:00 a.m. on November 29, the tropical sun had already burned off the morning mist and was beating down on the coast. It was a hot, tiring walk, and Harding and his sixty-man crew stopped often. Agile native climbers gathered coconuts in the tops of trees, and Harding and his men replenished their energy with the sweet juice. Late in the afternoon, they took a swim in the Samboga River. At dusk, they finally arrived at Dobodura.

General Herring's senior liaison officer was there to greet them. Herring had just opened up an advanced headquarters behind the Sanananda Front, and had sent out his liaison officer to make contact with the Americans. That evening Harding learned that General Sutherland, MacArthur's chief of staff, would also be paying him a visit.

It didn't take Harding long to grasp what was going on: MacArthur's triumphant script, which he had written from the comfort of his breezy veranda, was in jeopardy of being undone. And MacArthur, the stage manager, was not at all happy.

•   •   •

The attack that General Harding had scheduled for the last day in November was for all the marbles. All the men realized it, especially Smith's Ghost Mountain boys, whose return Harding had fought so hard for.

Looking at them, Colonel Mott must have wondered why. Stanley Jastrzembski, the wet-behind-the-ears Polish kid from Muskegon, Michigan, was riding out another fever. The rumbling in his ears sounded like a train roaring through a valley. He had a temperature of 103 degrees and no quinine. He fumbled with his field pack, searching for the sweater he had picked up weeks before in Laruni. Soon the chills would come. Then his teeth would rattle so wildly they would feel as if they were going to fall out of his mouth.

Between the anticipation, the malaria, and the dysentery that had been with him since the 2nd Battalion's march across the mountains, he could no longer control his bowels. He had not bathed in a month and could barely stand the smell of himself. He stank like rotten meat. "Dear Lord," he prayed, "give me the strength and courage to continue."

Even as Jastrzembski uttered these words, he knew that there were hundreds, perhaps thousands, of other American soldiers spread across the front, weakened by fatigue and dysentery, and burning up with fever. Prayer was their only recourse. With almost no quinine to soften the effects of malaria or bismuth to treat stomach ailments, Doc Warmenhoven and his staff could do little for the soldiers. If a man came back to a portable hospital with a high fever, a medic might allow him to lie down on a litter for a few hours, but unless he was at death's door, he was expected to fight.

The men of the 2nd Battalion understood the importance of this attack. Some of them were going to die. Their tongues swelled, their skin felt too tight, their eyes were bloodshot. Tense and plagued by spasms of diarrhea, guys ran back and forth into the bushes to relieve themselves. Those who could eat, ate perfunctorily. Fires were forbidden, so they spooned out cold tinned baked beans and ham and eggs. Jastrzembski emptied a K ration box into his mouth. He gagged, but then worked up enough spit to swallow the crackers. A trickle of rain fell. He turned his helmet upside down to catch what he could.

Then there were the men who did not bother with water or food at all. A handful walked back and forth as if in a daze, wearing a blank look that soldiers would instantly recognize as the "Buna stare." These were the "psychotics," men broken by hunger, disease, exhaustion, and the grind of combat. Some had willed themselves to forget everything they loved—the taste of cold beer and Sunday suppers, what it was like to be with a woman, the rumbling engine of a fast car, the slap of a ball hitting a catcher's mitt, the smell of fresh-cut alfalfa.

General Douglas MacArthur
(National Archives)

General Edwin Harding
(National Archives)

General Robert Eichelberger
(National Archives)

32nd Division Insignia
(32nd Division Veterans Association)

Simon Warmenhoven *(family photo)*

Stanley Jastrzembski, then
(family photo)

Stanley Jastrzembski, now
(family photo)

Herman Bottcher, Stanley Jastrzembski, and Eleanor Roosevelt
(family photo)

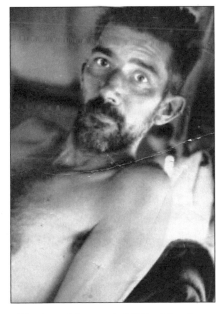

Herbert "Stutterin' " Smith, then
(family photo)

Herbert "Stutterin' " Smith; photo
taken just before his death in 2005
(family photo)

Carl Stenberg, then
(family photo)

Carl Stenberg, now
(family photo)

William "Jim" Boice
(family photo)

Alfred Medendorp
(family photo)

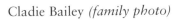

Cladie Bailey *(family photo)*

Samuel DiMaggio, then
(family photo)

Samuel DiMaggio, now
(family photo)

Roger Keast
(family photo)

Opposite:

Top: Ghost Mountain
(Philipp Engelhorn)

Inset: The 32nd Division
advance on Buna
*(Wisconsin Veterans
Museum)*

Below: Maggot Beach
*(Wisconsin Veterans
Museum)*

Paul Lutjens
(family photo)

Native carriers for the 32nd Division
(Wisconsin Veterans Museum)

Timothy Ungaia Doroda, former
carrier, Buna village *(author photo)*

Dancer in Suwari village
(Philipp Engelhorn)

Others obsessed on the smallest of details—keeping their mess kits sparkling clean, their boots tied as tightly a possible, figuring out the numerical combinations of their serial numbers. Anywhere but New Guinea, company commanders would weed out these men as fast as they could. Bizarre behavior was a sure-fire ticket off the front line, so much so that men affected or exaggerated their symptoms. At Buna, though, what company commanders needed more than anything else was warm bodies to throw at the Japanese bunkers.

Looking around at his men, some who were only half his age, Stutterin' Smith must have wondered how many of them would survive the attack. Smith was not a man given to outpourings of emotion, but goddamn, he loved these boys. And that Gus Bailey might have been the best of the bunch. Bailey never lost that twinkle in his eyes.

A haze of cigarette smoke hung over the 2nd Battalion's camp. Men fieldstripped their rifles, oiled them and wiped off the excess oil, sharpened their bayonets, and chain-smoked cigarettes down to stubs to dull their anxiety and temper their hunger pangs. The 2nd Battalion might have been short on food, but there was no shortage of "coffin nails." The smokes were enclosed in their field rations and each GI was given a liberal supply. "Just like the fuckin' army," someone said. "No goddamn food, but all the cigarettes you want."

They were new enough to war that they had not developed any superstitions or rituals that experienced troops rely on to keep them safe. Soldiers were writing letters back home just in case, or reading letters from home. Mail drops were made at Laruni, Jaure, and Natunga and some guys had a stack of letters that they read and re-read until they had memorized them. As Lutjens said in his diary after receiving two letters from home, "No one will ever know what they mean to me."

From the folks back home the soldiers learned that things were tough there, too. People could not buy tires, so everyone was forced to learn how to recap and retread. To save on gas, they coasted down hills and never let their cars idle. Nobody went for Sunday drives anymore. Paper, especially toilet paper, was hard to come by. The

Andrews Sisters and Glenn Miller were doing their best to make the deprivation bearable. Still, Uncle Joe was forced to do without his morning cup of coffee and the butter he loved so much. Women could not find silk stockings and were wearing the hemlines of their skirts higher in a kind of brazen "patriotic chic" to conserve on material. Canning companies were working around the clock to produce enough canned peas and sweet corn for the soldiers. Farmers collected urine from their horses, which was being used to make penicillin. People were saving and collecting everything they could—scrap iron, newspaper, rags, grease, tin cans—to be salvaged and sent to factories for military use. Children were harvesting milkweed seedpods, which, because they floated, were used in life jackets. Wives and girlfriends, sisters and mothers were rolling bandages to meet their Red Cross quotas. Everyone with a son or daughter serving overseas flew a blue star flag. A gold star meant that they had had a son or daughter killed in action.

Some of the guys were writing letters to their wives or sweethearts, encouraging them to get on with their lives. They could barely make their hands shape the words: "I love you, Darling. Please know that I love you. But I ain't coming home. I got this feeling I'm never coming home."

As Gus Bailey waited for orders to move out, he must have wondered how he would ever tell Katherine about the hatred he felt. If it were not for Japan, he would be lying in her arms or holding Cladie Alyn, the son he referred to as the "little one" in his letters home.

Jastrzembski was fighting off demons, too. Woozy with fever, he laid his head back and studied the incandescent Southern Cross that was partially obscured by ragged clouds. Like all soldiers, he would come to hate the hours before battle. He was glad of two things, though. First, he was out of the mountains. Under no circumstances would he ever make that march again. He wouldn't do it, couldn't do it.

Second, he was grateful that he was not out on guard. The guys on the posts had it the worst. They were in a no-man's land, close enough to heave a stone and hit an enemy sniper. Jastrzembski knew that they were dug in like rodents, watching the jungle, hugging the inside of their foxholes. Though they had been issued watches with glow-in-the-dark dials, they made sure to cover them. They could not even smoke. A sudden light would draw fire from both sides—enemy and friendly. At night in the jungle, even the fireflies were not safe.

In the swamp northwest of the Triangle, Lutjens and his men had been pinned down for a week. They were tired, hungry, and antsy, especially Sergeant Halbert Davidson, the boxer, who resented the fact that he had been sent out on a fact-finding mission and confined to a wet foxhole for seven days. One day he left his foxhole and slipped over to the company's flank, crept up on two Japs, and killed them with two short bursts from his rifle. Captain Schultz could hardly punish him. The Japanese already knew they were there, so it was not as if Davidson had given away Company E's position. Besides, according to Lutjens, Davidson "was that kind of guy. He couldn't bear not to shoot at them. He wanted to win the war."

On the night of November 29, a messenger from battalion headquarters navigated his way through the thick swamp to deliver Company E the news—the attack would kick off at midnight. Schultz assembled Lutjens and his other platoon leaders. They huddled close together, lighting their maps by scraping phosphorous from a log.

After the meeting Lutjens retreated to his diary. There was a woman: Frances "Lorraine" Phillips. They had gone to high school together back home in Big Rapids. Lutjens believed that she was "out of his league," but he loved her still. Now, on the night before the battalion's first big push, Lutjens wrote her (although the letter is dated "Nov of 1942," from the text it's safe to assume that he wrote it on November 29). It was a letter he would probably never have the chance to send.

> To a girl I love.
> Dearest,
>
> You will never know what you have meant to me since I have known you. I guess I've loved you since the first day I saw you 10 years ago. Many times I have tried to drive you out of my thoughts knowing how hopeless it was. Just to know that

one day you smiled on me gives me courage to face most anything . . . You probably don't even know I'm alive. Many a
night, lying in the mud and hell of this country you have been
my consolation and friend my courage and my life. The only
time I would ever think of saying this is now when my life
means nothing. Forgive me for taking this unforgivable privilege and please don't laugh . . . If I do come through this everything will go back as it was. Never would I dare to mention
this. Only God will know.

What Lutjens and the others did not know as they prepared for
battle was that many of the Japanese soldiers were on the verge of
despair, too. A captured diary from the Buna battlefield illustrates the
mood of the Japanese troops: "Nov. 28. Very beautiful morning. Can
this be a blood-smeared battlefield? As usual enemy planes bombed us.
None of our planes appeared. At last our lives are becoming shorter.
Look at the fierceness of the enemy mortar fire, which bursts near us.
Today the word that the Buna crisis is imminent has reached the ears
of the Emperor and he has asked that Buna be defended to the
last man."

In response to the Emperor's request, the Japanese began to orga-
nize suicide squads. A Corporal Tanaka writes, "Today, Nov. 30th,
Battalion Commander Yamamoto and subordinates organized a suicide squad. . . . Death is the ultimate honor. After my comrades and I
are dead, please bury us in your leisure time. I ask this because it is dis-
honourable to remain unburied. Please take care of your health and
serve your country."

·   ·   ·

Back at the Triangle, Stutterin' Smith's companies began to move out.

Lieutenant Odell recalls some of the details of that night, ". . . We
each grasped the shoulder of the man in front, and slowly shuffled forward in the pitch black of night. Our only guide was the telephone
wire leading to the jump-off point, and the troops in the foxholes
along the way who had been holding the ground recently captured.

There was no trail and consequently several hours were required to travel as many hundreds of yards. We all had bayonets. Rifle fire was forbidden until after the attack was well under way. Japs encountered along the way were to be dealt with silently."

When a Japanese plane flew over low and dropped flares, the men froze. They hugged trees or pressed their bellies into the mud.

The attack was scheduled to kick off at midnight, but it became apparent to Smith that because of the terrain his troops would never be in position in time. In some places the jungle was so dense that they were forced to crawl on their hands and knees, pushing like wild pigs through a tangle of vines, creepers, and bushes. When they came to a swamp too deep to wade, some men laid down a log. Hundreds of soldiers had to use that one log, and it took hours for all of them to cross.

Following Gus Bailey, the men of Company G shoved clips into their rifles and sneaked toward the track that led to Buna Village, their movements drowned out by the din of crickets and croaking frogs. Once they arrived at the jump-off spot, the men lay down in the kunai grass. Jastrzembski could feel the dew. He was close enough to hear the Japanese talking, the cadence of their conversations.

The Japanese did not know where G Company was, but they knew something was up. They were firing over the Americans' heads. Every fifth bullet was a bluish-white tracer. It looked to Carl Stenberg as if a long, brightly lit clothesline had been strung across the kunai field. It seemed unreal and for a few minutes he wondered if what he saw was really happening.

Pieces of his life flashed by. At the age of five, he had been bitten by a dog. The bite was bearable, but it was the pain of the rabies shots that made him cringe all over again. He remembered the time his brother threw him from a boat to teach him to swim, the sickening feeling of swallowing lake water as he sank. He remembered setting fishing nets on Lake Michigan late into the season; the way his wife Frances walked; the little apartment she rented with his sister; how she had "proposed" to him in November '41 when he was home on leave from Camp Livingston. Frances had been keen to marry; Stenberg resisted. It was not that he did not love Frances—he had no doubt that she was the one. But with war imminent, he did not want to leave her behind to mourn a dead husband.

Now, he could not get Frances out of his head. What was she doing? Did she miss him as much as he missed her? Was she thinking about him? The thought that he might never see her again scared him. It had been just days before that he had seen his first dead man. Walking back to an aid station, he had seen a guy leaning against a tree. He was not moving, and did not seem to be breathing. Stenberg lifted up his chin and saw the handiwork of a Japanese sniper. The man had been shot through the mouth. The bullet had exited at the back of his head.

Back home, Frances was working seven days a week at Continental Motors. On the night of their anniversary she went out for a beer with one of the other army wives. "To my anniversary," she thought when she raised the glass to her lips. It was a small gesture, but it was important to her to observe the day. The truth was, her anniversary was no different from every other day. She would go home tired and write a letter to Carl and feel lonely.

.   .   .

To Stenberg's right, Stanley Jastrzembski tried not to make a sound. Hours before, weakened by malaria, he had wondered if he would be able to walk, much less fight. Now his body was alive with fear. The pounding of his heart sounded to him like the hammer of a Juki machine gun. He breathed as quietly as he could, but it was quick and raspy like the last gasps of a dying man. If the Japanese had not heard him, surely, he worried, they could smell him, the stench of fear and nearly two months of accumulated filth. He felt the dysentery rumbling in his gut, and he prayed he would not shit his pants. A mosquito buzzed at his ear. Jastrzembski swung at it, and then cursed himself. It was a rookie mistake. Had the Japanese heard or seen him, they would have splattered bullets through the long grass.

Jastrzembski, a devoted Catholic, said a prayer. At home when he needed good luck, he went to Saint Michaels and lit a candle. But now all he could do was to say a simple Hail Mary.

Platoon sergeant Don Stout lay in the grass, cursing himself. Bailey had offered to make him a liaison officer between Company G and battalion headquarters; it would have kept him out of situations like the one he was about to face.

"What do you think?" Bailey asked him after proposing the move.

Stout considered it for a moment. "You know, sir," he said, "I've trained with these guys for a long time. I walked for forty days with them. I think I'll stick it out with them."

Bailey, of all people, must have understood. As he lay in the long grass, though, ready to charge the Jap position, Stout wished he could take back everything he had said.

Finally, at 0400, four hours later than planned, Jastrzembski heard the unmistakable click of bayonets being fitted into rifle barrels. The clouds had cleared, revealing a luminous night lit by a huge moon. Jastrzembski noticed a faint taste of metal on his tongue as he listened to the men of Companies E and F run forward, making the first charge, yelling like crazed Japanese soldiers drunk on sake.

For the men of Company F, it was their first bayonet charge. So much adrenaline surged through their bodies, they felt as if their veins would burst. A flare went up, lighting their faces white and blue. One hundred yards out, they smacked into a line of surprised Japanese machine gunners. For Robert Odell, who helped lead the assault, it was the first time he would ever fire his M-1 rifle. A Japanese soldier sprung to his feet, and Odell dropped him. Then, according to Odell, "All hell broke loose. There was more lead flying through the air . . . than it's possible to estimate. Machine gun tracers lit the entire area, and our own rifle fire made a solid sheet of flame. Everywhere men cursed, shouted, or screamed. Order followed on order. . . . Brave men led and others followed. Cowards crouched in the grass literally frightened out of their skins . . . "

Captain Erwin Nummer of F Company was one of those brave men. Hit by a Japanese grenade fragment, Nummer popped up off the ground, crying out, "It doesn't hurt, fellows! See, they got me and it doesn't hurt at all!"

Just behind Nummer, Lutjens and his men joined F Company, running at the Japanese, soon close enough to use their bayonets, slashing and stabbing and swinging the butts of their rifles. Outmanned, many of the Japanese fled their bunkers, leaving the Americans to storm the Japanese outposts.

One of the huts was filled with the scent of perfume, and there, lying on woven mats, were six Japanese officers. Next to them were bowls of warm rice and a washtub with soapsuds. The officers reacted as if they had been awakened from sleep. Perhaps they were drunk; perhaps, finding themselves confronted by a band of bearded and bedraggled American soldiers, they thought they were dreaming. Or they were sick with fever. Whatever the case the officers did not make a move to defend themselves. According to Lutjens, they were "so startled they just buried their heads in the mud, like ostriches." Lutjens and his men unleashed a fury of bullets, killing all but one of the Japanese where they lay. One officer tried to stand. They filled him with lead, but the officer just wouldn't die! He tried to rise two more times before he finally toppled over.

Then the Americans stripped the shacks, taking watercolor prints, fine silks from China, lacquer boxes from the Philippines—proof that the Japanese were part of a veteran naval landing force—blankets, silverware, clothes, cigarettes, whisky, cans of meat, and fourteen rolls of Japanese writing paper. The Americans thought the rolls were toilet paper and celebrated—they had had no toilet paper for nearly two months. Odell grabbed a Japanese bayonet, and from that point on he never went into battle without it. They also found personal pictures, photos of Japanese soldiers in civilian dress surrounded by their wives and children. If some of the men felt a pang, a stab of doubt or mercy, it did not last long. Their motto, according to Lutjens, was "If they don't stink, stick 'em." So the Americans moved among the Japanese bodies and plunged their bayonets into the corpses. Setting fire to the huts, they watched them burn and then they blew up the Japanese bunkers.

If Lutjens and the others felt avenged, it was only momentary. The memory of seeing friends "blown to bits just a few yards away" was one he would never forget. And the trail back to the battalion aid station, according to Lutjens, "was so slimy with blood of the wounded . . . that you could hardly keep your balance." He wrote later that he saw "men coming back with their faces shot away and their hands where their chins had been, trying to stop the flow of blood." Men "with their guts sagging out . . . yelling in pain."

When Bailey finally called for Company G's attack, Jastrzembski, DiMaggio, and Stenberg leaped to their feet and ran toward the Japanese outpost. It was hard to shake the feeling that they were on a suicide mission. American machine gunners firing tracers set the field ablaze. Men ran screaming and shooting through the fire. From afar, it must have had a kind of horrible beauty—the black night glowing and crackling with burning grass, the whip and whine of bullets ripping through the trees, the cold, metallic twang of 50 mm and 60 mm mortar shells.

Don Stout could see the kunai grass bending one way as Company H, the battalion's heavy weapons company, fired on the Japanese using water-cooled .30 caliber machine guns. The grass would bow in the opposite direction when the Japanese returned fire.

Stout ran forward like everyone else. It might have been miles or hours—to him, distance and time had lost all meaning. As the company neared the Japanese, the men lunged with their bayonets. They were so close they could feel blasts of hot air from the muzzles of Japanese rifles.

Stenberg was part of the 4th platoon's 60 mm mortar squad. As a forward observer, his job was to protect the mortarmen. In New Guinea's thick jungle, though, high trajectory mortars often were not much good. So now he was out front, a regular rifleman. He pressed the trigger and felt the tommy gun buck in his hands. It was his kind of battle, close in. All he had to do was to pull the trigger and he was bound to hit something, leaving behind enemy soldiers with gaping holes in their chests.

Unable to see more than two or three feet in any direction, no one knew where anyone else was. Squads were cut off from one another. Stenberg heard the lashing of a machine gun and saw three Company G men go down in front of him. His ears rang from the muzzle blast. Jastrzembski felt a bullet skin his leg. It was a searing pain, like being cut with a hot knife. Then he realized that he was only ten feet from a Japanese pillbox, and felt an electric jolt of fear. Before a bullet could tear open his chest, he jumped to the side like an acrobat, grabbed a grenade, pulled the pin, and threw it at the pillbox. He knew a grenade had a killing radius of thirty-five yards, so he threw himself to the ground just before it blew.

All around him he heard the sickly smacking sound of bullets entering flesh. He saw the flashes of Arisaka rifle barrels. One of those bullets knocked down his buddy Willie La Venture, the shot tearing open his belly. Jastrzembski ducked as low as he could, ran to La Venture, and cradled his head in his hand. Bullets sizzled through the long kunai grass and kicked up dirt just in front of them. La Venture begged for water. "All he wanted was water," Jastrzembski remembers. Jastrzembski pressed his canteen to his buddy's lips. La Venture gulped at it. Seconds later, Jastrzembski saw the water pouring from the hole in his belly.

Jastrzembski could not wait around, though, even for his best buddy. Calling for a medic, he jumped to his feet, retched, and left La Venture lying there. It was the hardest thing he ever had to do.

Stenberg blasted his way through the enemy's first line of defense, but when the rest of the company caught up to him, and Company G tried moving on Buna Village, the men lost their way. As daylight crept into the jungle, Gus Bailey realized that they were mired in a swamp at the northern border of the grass strip, and called off the attack.

Jastrzembski leaned against a tree, lifted his pant leg, and inspected his wound. Luckily, the bullet had only grazed him. Then, looking around, he spotted a Japanese flag lying in the mud. He walked over and grabbed it. Goddamn Japs had just killed his best buddy. At least he could steal their precious flag and stuff it in his pocket like an old snot rag.

Stenberg stumbled forward, his legs weak but still able to carry his weight. Then he sat down in the long grass and finally exhaled, taking a moment to thank his lucky stars that he was still alive. Then he wondered how his best buddies, Sergeants George Borgeson and O'Donnell O'Brien were doing. He and O'Brien had joined the Guard at the same time. Their serial numbers were one digit apart. In November of 1941, while back home in Muskegon on leave, O'Brien and Borgeson, still in uniform, were groomsmen at his wedding. O'Brien was a tough Irishman. If the Japs tangled with him, he would give them a run for their money.

In front of Stenberg, a man moaned in pain. When Stenberg approached him, he realized that it was his buddy Jim Broner, one of the two Broner brothers in Company G. Broner was a sergeant in the rifle platoon and had been shot through the leg. It was a deep wound, and the flesh around the bullet hole was shredded. Stenberg took his bag of sulfa powder and dusted the wound and stood guard over Broner, watching for snipers in the trees, waiting for a medic. When the medic arrived he shot Broner up with a half grain of morphine, hurriedly dressed his wound, then gave him two sulfanilamide pills. Ten minutes later, litter bearers carried him out. If they could get Broner back to a portable hospital before he lost too much blood, his buddy had a good chance of keeping his leg.

Doc Warmenhoven and his staff, working round the clock in blackout tents just behind the front lines, were performing miracles with sodium pentathol and blood plasma. Plasma had saved dozens of lives. It came in a tin can in powdered form and was mixed with distilled water and injected into a soldier's vein via a needle and rubber tubing. Because it was universal, a doctor did not have to wait for blood typing. If the litter bearers could get Broner out of the jungle, Warmenhoven could pump plasma into him as fast as he could slice open the can. He would operate right there, sterilizing his instruments with a small stove or canned heat, kneeling over a canvas stretcher draped in bloody sheets and soaked in disinfectant, in a tent that smelled of burned flesh and of feces, because guys often had their bowels ripped open by mortar rounds. While bullets struck the surrounding trees and perforated the tents, they continued working. In one week they had performed almost seventy major surgeries, including amputations and serious chest operations, saving soldiers who in World War I would have been left for dead.

When Colonel Mott discovered that Bailey was out of position, he called on Lutjens and Company E to take Buna Village. Shortly after sunrise, Lutjens led his men down the main track in the direction of the village. Three hundred yards out, Company E slammed into a Japanese bunker and was stopped dead in its tracks. Although Company E's assault failed, Stutterin' Smith, who was in the front lines with his men, recognized that a breakthrough was possible. Sensing victory and a speedy end to the battle for Buna Village, he ordered Companies H and F and some troops from Headquarters Company to resume the attack. He knew the assault would require mortar support.

Putting Captain Harold E. Hantlemann, commanding officer of Company H, in charge of mortars, he instructed Captain Nummer of Company F to initiate the charge. It is what the men loved about Smith—his moxie, his ability to think on his feet, his willingness to be at the front with the privates and the corporals. Smith knew it was his job to make the men believe. The only way to do that was to be right there with them dodging bullets, risking his life.

While Nummer led his men down the main track in the direction of the ripening sun, "Handy" Hantlemann, a former star offensive guard at the University of Iowa, directed a fierce mortar barrage. Hantlemann sported a long, disheveled black beard and looked more like a swarthy pirate than a captain in the U.S. Army. The mortars sent hot shrapnel flying everywhere, but the Japanese were ready for them and stopped Nummer well short of the village. Still, Nummer and Company F punched away at the Japanese for much of the morning.

·   ·   ·

Herman Bottcher, now in charge of a platoon, saw a Japanese sniper pick off six of Company H's men. Spotting a rifle barrel jutting from the leaves of a nearby tree, he raised his tommy gun and touched off the trigger. The Japanese sniper fell six feet and then bounced as the rope he had used to tie himself in tightened around his ankle.

Elsewhere, another Japanese machine gunner sprayed bullets through the jungle.

"We have to take him out," Bottcher told his men. Next thing his men knew, Bottcher grabbed two grenades and was crawling through the long grass. Poking his head up, he saw the machine gun sticking out of a trench. After throwing the grenades, he began pawing at the dirt, digging down as deep as he could. The grenades blew and things went nuts. Bullets flew over his head. Damn Japanese are shooting high, Bottcher thought to himself. Then he realized it was his own men, shooting in the direction of the detonated grenades.

When the firing stopped, Bottcher crawled back to his men, grabbed his machine gun, and returned to scout the enemy trench. He found three Japanese, all dead, crouching with their faces buried in their arms. Bottcher realized that they had heard the grenades hit. With no time to roll out of the trench they had tried to save themselves by covering their heads and faces.

By early afternoon Stutterin' Smith saw the handwriting on the wall and reluctantly called off the assault. The morning's offensive had been successful, but his men had made little progress since those early gains.

As the Americans dug in, some Japanese soldiers staged a counter-attack. One of Lutjens' men, Private Johnny Combs, caught them in the act. With his back against a tree for support, he leveled his tommy gun and took out all sixteen attackers.

The battlefield, Lutjens remembers, was littered with bodies: mostly Japanese, but Americans, too. It was a sight he would never forget. Among the dead were two Company E men who had made the mistake of trying to take a small group of Japanese as prisoners. Pretending to surrender, the would-be prisoners machine-gunned their captors.

Despite Company E's losses, Lutjens felt relieved that many of his best buddies had made it through the battle. Art Edson had survived.

Edson had been with Lutjens since their scouting trip along the coast. Together they had also made the walk from Natunga to Pongani to establish contact with the 128th. The return trip had been especially rough on Lutjens, who was sweating out his first malaria attack. Had it not been for Edson, who encouraged, prodded, and sometimes dragged him, Lutjens might never have made it back to Natunga.

Stutterin' Smith had reason to be upbeat, too. His Ghost Mountain boys had driven the enemy back hundreds of yards. In the process, they had achieved their objective: the first breakthrough in the Japanese perimeter.

Chapter 15

THE BUTCHER'S BILL

BACK AT DOBODURA, GENERAL HARDING had just gotten the news of Stutterin' Smith's success. In the big picture, the breakthrough did not amount to much. Buna Village and Buna Government Station had not been touched. With the rest of the 126th—the 1st and 3rd Battalions were still fighting alongside the Australians west of the Girua River—Harding figured that he might have been able to overwhelm the Japanese. But without a numerical advantage, he would have to continue probing their positions for a weak spot. It was a slow, costly business that was bound to keep the grave diggers busy.

On the coast, his 128th Infantry Regiment was bogged down, too. Though Colonel Mott had shaken things up by relieving two officers, the change did nothing to affect the tactical situation. The Japanese were dug in too well. Only tanks or more troops would change that.

Earlier that morning, as Stutterin' Smith's troops pressed the attack, General Sutherland flew in from Port Moresby and Australia's General Herring came in from Popondetta to meet with Harding. Though they had ostensibly come to discuss battle strategies, from Harding's perspective, the generals had already reached their own conclusions. Sitting on empty ammunition boxes under a small grove of trees at the edge of a kunai field, neither Sutherland nor Herring appeared very interested in listening. But Harding continued to press the issue. Having already argued for tanks and artillery, he asked for

217

the 127th Infantry, which had arrived in Port Moresby on Thanksgiving Day. He reminded the generals that he barely had a third of his 126th Regiment.

By lunchtime, Herring was on his way back to Popondetta. Sutherland, though, stayed on. He and Harding were making small talk when suddenly Sutherland dropped his bomb: MacArthur, he said, was "worried about the caliber of his infantry" and the aggressiveness of its officers. Sutherland wanted to know how Harding intended to rectify the situation. The general bluntly defended his men. Anyone, he said, who thought that his troops were not fighting "didn't know the facts." Sutherland then asked him if he intended to replace any of his top officers. Harding replied that he did not.

Sutherland had heard enough. That afternoon he returned to Port Moresby and recommended to MacArthur that he relieve Harding of his duties. What was lacking at Buna, Sutherland said, was not artillery, troops, tanks, or planes. What was missing was inspired leadership. That Sutherland had not even been to the front lines to assess the situation did not prevent him from commenting on Harding's alleged inability to motivate his men. Harding would later say that Sutherland's report to MacArthur must have been a "masterpiece of imaginative writing."

MacArthur had already ordered Major General Robert L. Eichelberger, I Corps commander, to report to him in Port Moresby. MacArthur had great faith in the general. If anyone could remedy the situation at Buna, it was Bob Eichelberger.

Though he had never commanded troops in battle, Eichelberger's résumé was top-notch. Early in his career, he had served in Panama and on the U.S.-Mexico border. Later, at the tail end of World War I, while assigned to the American Expeditionary Force in Siberia, he had been awarded the Distinguished Service Cross for acts of bravery. Having attended the Command and General Staff College at Fort Leavenworth and the Army War College, after which he became superintendent of West Point, Eichelberger possessed superb leadership and organizational skills and a keen understanding of military theory.

On November 29 when MacArthur summoned him, Eichelberger was at Rockhampton, Australia, training the 41st Division in jungle warfare. Early the next morning, as Sutherland was on his way to Dobodura to talk with Harding, Eichelberger boarded a plane for Port Moresby.

At MacArthur's headquarters, Eichelberger and his chief of staff found MacArthur with Generals Kenney and Sutherland. Sutherland had already told MacArthur of his meeting with Harding, and it took only a moment for Eichelberger to discern MacArthur's mood. Almost before Eichelberger sat down, MacArthur was talking heatedly, striding up and down the veranda, holding his pipe like a weapon.

The 32nd Division's troops were sick and tired and poorly trained for war in the jungle, but that was no excuse for cowardice, MacArthur said, citing the reports of his operations staff officers.

"A real leader, " he insisted, "could take these same men and capture Buna."

MacArthur continued, "Bob, the number of troops employed there is no indication of the importance I attach to this job. . . . The fact that I've sent for you, with your rank, indicates how much importance I attach to the taking of Buna. . . . Never did I think I'd see Americans quit." MacArthur then told Eichelberger that he was to leave for the front the following morning because "time was of the essence." The Japanese, MacArthur said, might send in reinforcements "any night." Eichelberger was to relieve Harding and his subordinate commanders, or MacArthur threatened, "I will relieve them myself and you too." MacArthur continued testily, "Go out there, Bob, and take Buna or don't come back alive." Then he added, "And that goes for your chief of staff, Clovis, too."

At breakfast the following morning, MacArthur had apparently mellowed. Pulling Eichelberger aside, he wished him luck and godspeed and told him that he was "no use to him dead." Eichelberger must have felt great relief. Just the day before, he had written Harding, his good friend and former West Point classmate, to express confidence in him.

But then MacArthur's mood again turned cold. Promising to decorate him if he took Buna, MacArthur told Eichelberger that he was to push the battle regardless of casualties.

"That was our send-off," Eichelberger later wrote, "and hardly a merry one."

By 1:00 p.m. that same day, Eichelberger took command of all U.S. troops in the Buna area. The next day a medical officer reported to Eichelberger on the condition of his men. The troops, he said within earshot of General Harding, looked like "Christ off the cross." Considering their depleted condition, he added, the men were carrying on heroically. It was difficult for Harding not to feel a degree of satisfaction. It was what he had been saying all along.

The men of the 32nd had been subsisting on short rations for well over a month. Because fires were not allowed at the front—the wet wood sent up billows of smoke and attracted too much attention—they ate their rations cold. Their feet swelled and bled. Their fingernails and toenails fell off. They were suffering from jungle rot, malaria, dengue fever, dysentery, ringworm, dehydration, and heat prostration. And there was a shortage of everything they needed to stay healthy—quinine, salt and chlorination tablets, bismuth, and vitamin pills. Because of the sand, mud, water, and humidity, they could not depend on their weapons either. BARs, M-1s, and machine guns jammed. When precious gun oil and patches reached the front, they came in large containers and were difficult to distribute. Spare parts were nearly impossible to find. Ammunition and medical supplies ran short. Soldiers who had lost their entrenching tools were still waiting for replacements.

As a consequence, the morale of the troops was low. To make matters worse, their battlefield successes were few. Although Stutterin's Smith's troops had punched a hole in the Japanese perimeter, the Japanese had not yielded much valuable ground. Their positions were impregnable and Harding's troops lacked the weaponry to reduce them. Mortars, artillery, and air bombardments had proved to be largely ineffective. The only other possibility was for a soldier to rush a bunker and stick a grenade through a firing slit, a feat that took monumental courage and a lifetime of good luck. It was a heartbreaking, ridiculous way to bust a bunker. According to Stutterin' Smith, "Many more failed than succeeded."

The day after arriving at Dobodura, Eichelberger was eager to tour the front.

Eichelberger did not know it, but after days of fighting, things had finally died down. And he did not like what he saw—men resting at aid stations, men dozing at the roots of trees, unshaven men wearing dirty, tattered uniforms, and empty ration tins surrounded by flies.

Jastrzembski was one of those dirty, unshaven men. His fatigues were caked in mud and diarrhea. He had sweated out the malaria attack, but his limbs were still trembling. His right eye quivered uncontrollably. Just the thought of the previous day's battle, of cradling his buddy, of staring into the hole in La Venture's belly knowing that he was a goner, made the bile well in Jastrzembski's mouth. He tried to put the image out of his head. He was on his way back to the aid station where a buddy had told him they were passing out new jeans. Now more than anything else he just wanted a new pair of jeans. That is when he looked up and saw the general and "lots of brass" walking toward him. Immediately, he realized the general was new. Eichelberger wore his insignia of rank—no officer who had spent any time on the front dared to do that. A Japanese sniper would pick him off in a matter of minutes.

"Soldier, show me the front," Eichelberger said.

Jastrzembski hardly heard him.

"The front, soldier, the front. I want to see the front," Eichelberger demanded.

"Follow me," Corporal Jastrzembski said.

Eichelberger, who was already irritated by the lack of discipline he had witnessed, scowled. He was a three-star general. Who did this soldier think he was talking to him like that?

After walking a hundred yards or so, Eichelberger asked Jastrzembski where the command post was, and Jastrzembski pointed down the trail. Then the general reached in his pocket and handed him a pack of cigarettes. Jastrzembski was a cigar man, but he took the cigarettes anyway. He knew he could trade them later for chewing gum.

Eichelberger stopped at the command post, and then farther down the trail he encountered three soldiers hiding in the long grass at the trail's edge. When Eichelberger asked them what lay ahead, the men answered that an enemy machine gunner had fired on them hours before. Eichelberger was surprised. Hadn't they bothered to scout the trail since? The men told the general that they had not. Eichelberger then offered to decorate any one of them brave enough to move forward. When no one volunteered, the general was incensed.

Later, Eichelberger held a meeting of his senior officers at Stutterin' Smith's command post, which was nothing more than a collection of tables around a large hollow tree stump. Smith had a field phone, which was connected to other field phones by single-strand Australian wire. When Smith phoned his company commanders, every phone in the jungle rang—including the Japanese ones.

Harding also attended the meeting. It was the first time since early October that he had seen Smith, and Harding did not recognize him at first. The gaunt, bearded Smith, Harding wrote in his diary, looked like a "member of the Army of the Potomac."

The gathering was a heated one. According to Smith, Eichelberger acted "like a bull in a china shop," and made some "caustic comments" about what he had seen at the front, including the incident with the three men. Smith kept his mouth shut. Years later, recalling the general's anger, he wrote, "Decorations look damn artificial to a soldier who is filthy, fever ridden, practically starved, living in a tidal swamp and frustrated from seeing his buddies killed." Listening to Eichelberger denigrate his men, Colonel Mott could no longer hold his temper.

"Dammit," Mott said. "Anybody who thinks the men aren't fighting, doesn't know beans. Do you have any idea of what it's like out there? The mountains were hell on the men. And now they're fighting in swamp water up to their chests. You want to know why? Because the Japs have every piece of high ground from here to Australia."

Harding threw his cigarette to the ground and snuffed it out. He agreed.

Then, Eichelberger's voice rose, "You're licked!" he said, looking at Mott and Harding. "Your men aren't fighting; they're cowards!"

The meeting broke up shortly after that and Eichelberger button-holed Smith and asked him what his assessment was.

"It's tough, damn tough," Smith said. "It doesn't pay to attack. The plan should be really basic: To edge up slowly every day. But even that's not working. We're not getting anywhere."

Eichelberger was under no illusions. He could plainly see that American forces "were prisoners of geography," and that Buna was going to be "siege warfare . . . the bitterest and most punishing kind." But that was no excuse for faintheartedness. With MacArthur's warning ringing in his ears, Eichelberger looked Smith straight in the eye. "I don't think you're trying hard enough."

Back at his tent in Dobodura, Harding tried to understand Eichelberger's attitude. His old West Point classmate was under enormous pressure. MacArthur had given him "an earful" and appointed him his executioner. Was Eichelberger simply carrying out orders? Despite trying to see both sides, it was difficult for Harding not to be bitter.

Harding had been determined to avoid what he called the "butcher's bill run up by the generals of World War I," and obviously he had not pressed the battle hard enough for MacArthur's tastes. In France, the 32nd's Red Arrow men, facing rapid-firing artillery and machine guns, had developed a reputation for bravery. But Harding knew that it had come at a huge cost to the division: In five months, the 32nd Division lost three thousand men and counted almost fourteen thousand among the wounded.

Harding refused to repeat that kind of carnage at Buna. To order headlong attacks on the Japanese positions was "Civil War tactics," pure madness. While at Fort Benning Infantry School, Harding had been one of a group of instructors who attempted to define and implement a new set of battle tactics that put a premium on ingenuity and discouraged high casualty rates. George C. Marshall was the school's assistant commandant at the time, and Harding had Marshall's blessing. He and his fellow officers developed and taught flanking movements and other innovative battlefield techniques.

Harding also edited a seminal study of small-unit engagements during World War I, and enumerated a list of lessons learned. One of those was: "To assault by day an organized position, manned by good troops equipped with automatic weapons, without providing for adequate support by (artillery) fire or tanks, is folly."

In 1937, in his position as editor of the *Infantry Journal,* he elaborated on this point. "Since wars began," he opined, "this 'do something' obsession has driven leaders to order attacks with no prospect of success. . . . The enemy's position is immensely strong, but our masters are impatient. We attack and the history of military disaster is enriched by another bloody repulse."

In another editorial, Harding blasted senior commanders during World War I for firing junior officers whenever things did not turn out as planned. According to writer and historian Tom Doherty, "The qualities that Harding emphasized in his writings boiled down to this: A good leader possesses the courage and self-discipline to protect his organization from his own rash impulses and from the anxieties crashing down from the chain of command. . . . " Harding, Doherty elaborates, "had expressed these convictions years ago in peacetime, but did he have the courage to act upon them at Buna, where he was caught between enemy fortifications worthy of the Western Front and a living legend who insisted on victory at any price?"

According to Doherty, many of the men who served under Harding at Buna believed the answer to this question was yes. "They were convinced," Doherty adds, "that far from being too weak to succeed . . . Forrest Harding was too principled to add . . . 'another bloody repulse' to history's long roll of military disasters by sacrificing his soldiers on the altar of Douglas MacArthur's impatience."

Harding sat down with his diary. Eichelberger, he wrote, "showed no appreciation of what the men had been through, or the spirit shown by most of them in carrying on despite heavy casualties, the roughest kind of opposition, and the most trying conditions."

Once he was done writing, Harding went to Eichelberger's tent to bury the hatchet and to discuss a new plan of attack. Eichelberger only half listened and then interrupted Harding to object once again to what he had discovered at the front. Harding guessed at Eichelberger's intent.

"You were probably sent here to get heads," Harding said. "Maybe mine is one of them."

"You are right," Eichelberger answered briskly.

"I take it I am to return to Moresby."

"Yes," Eichelberger replied.

Then Harding stood up and stepped out into the night.

*   *   *

The next morning, after a night's downpour, Eichelberger woke to a stream running through his tent. The water was thigh deep and his personal possessions were floating away. If he was irritated by the previous day's events, he was really aggravated now. Having dismissed Harding, he wasted no time in instructing his staff to relieve Harding's top commanders, including Mott.

Then, over breakfast, Eichelberger apologized to Harding, insisting that he had no choice in the matter. Harding, ever the gentleman, accepted his friend's word. Later he excused Eichelberger in his diary, writing, "It was probably either his head or mine."

Harding's staff was not so forgiving. It was a "dirty deal," one of them insisted. Harding was being scapegoated. Weeks before, the general had wanted to cut off the Japs as they retreated from Kokoda to the coast. The Red Arrow men might have wiped out Horii's army, but Blamey had insisted that the Australians be in on the kill, and MacArthur agreed. Consequently, Harding lost three pivotal weeks. In the meantime, the Japanese were able to land reinforcements.

Word of Harding's dismissal made the rounds. While his staff collected his belongings, he paid a last visit to a nearby portable hospital. Stretcher bearers were bringing in wounded soldiers. Harding, visibly moved, apologized to the men for letting them down. An injured soldier overheard. "Hell, no, General," he said. "*We* let *you* down!"

Later that day, Harding left Dobodura for Port Moresby. Buna was now Eichelberger's alone to try to take.

The problem, which Harding tried to articulate, was that Buna, as Eichelberger would soon discover, was a "Leavenworth Nightmare." The U.S. Army Command and General Staff School in Leavenworth, Kansas, did not teach solutions to such dismal tactical pictures. The Japanese defensive position was superb. They commanded the high ground up and down the coast. The Americans were relegated to the blackwater creeks and swamps, thick with viciously spiked nipa and sago palms that made the coordination of advances impossible. Companies were scattered all over the place. Classic military maneuvers like the double envelopment, where an enemy's flanks are attacked simultaneously in a kind of pinching motion, were unworkable. Fronts, at least in the conventional sense, did not exist.

While Eichelberger set out to reorder his units, which had become "scrambled like eggs," his new officers struggled to come to grips with the reality of their commands. One complained about a "lack of almost everything with which to operate."

Eichelberger also decided to move his command post closer to the front. While this was going on, Stutterin' Smith sensed that the Japanese were growing weak. Acting on a hunch, he sent out small patrols to harass the Japanese positions. They were "colonial tactics," according to Smith, designed to keep pressure on the enemy and gather intelligence, while Eichelberger figured out the division's next move.

Smith's hunch proved correct: Up and down the eleven-mile front, Japanese soldiers were suffering. Sergeant Phil Ishio, a Japanese-American from Salt Lake City who worked as a translator with I Corps, had just translated some of the diaries that Smith's men discovered when they raided the Japanese shacks on November 30.

The Japanese were short on food and medical supplies. Unlike American soldiers, who were discouraged from keeping diaries for fear that they might end up in the wrong hands, the Japanese had obviously not had any security briefings. Ishio was surprised by the candor of the daily entries. On the morning of the November 30 battle, a Corporal Tanaka wrote, "At the break of dawn, the enemy charged. We repulsed them. . . . It is now merely a case of waiting for death . . .

there isn't much we can do. . . . We have not eaten for over a week and have no energy. As soldiers, we are ready to die gallantly."

Twice a day, American patrols attacked the Japanese and then retreated to their company command posts. Company E was so close to enemy lines that the GIs could hear the Japanese chattering. The patrols could not get too close because the Japanese had run trip vines up and down their lines. Behind the vines, though, the Japanese had grown lackadaisical. Swede Nelson and squad leader Sergeant Ned Myers took advantage of their inattention. Armed with tommy guns, the two men sneaked within thirty yards of a Japanese pillbox without being detected. Fifteen enemy soldiers were laughing and smoking when Nelson and Myers opened fire, killing twelve of them.

At night, the Americans ceased their attacks and stuck to their miserable, water-filled foxholes, which most men had dug using the pans from their mess kits because they did not have entrenching tools. They stayed put, two men to a hole for protection, listening to the sounds of the jungle, trying to distinguish the swamp rats scurring through the long grass from Japanese soldiers creeping in for a closer shot.

The Americans took little comfort in the foxholes. "Even with a guy right there, you'd wake up in the middle of the night and just lie there, listening and staring at the black," Lutjens explained.

In contrast to Smith's daytime raids, the Japanese did their dirty work at night. "The night," emphasized a training slogan, "is one million reinforcements." Japanese soldiers yelled out, "Tonight you die," and then they worked their rifle bolts back and forth. Bizarrely, they were especially fond of Eleanor Roosevelt insults. "Eleanor eats shit!" they would often yell out. Sometimes they fired sudden shots that pierced the darkness, or set off firecrackers. It was their version of psychological warfare, designed to deprive the battle-weary Americans of sleep and peace of mind. And sometimes they would silently infiltrate an enemy camp, climb a tree, tie themselves in, and wait until daylight to do their damage.

One morning in early December, Captain Melvin Schultz, commander of Company E, spied a Japanese sniper just outside his

command post. The sniper could have easily killed him but was waiting for more men to arrive. Schultz calmly went about his business and
then whirled around and pumped eight shots into him. The sniper fell
from his perch. His bullet-ridden body dangled above the ground for
all to see.

•   •   •

Under extreme pressure for results, Eichelberger did not waste any
time ordering his first attack. The plan was a basic one. On December
4, Stutterin' Smith and his Ghost Mountain boys would close in on
Buna Village, while Colonel Smith's men from the 128th got in position to deflect a counterattack from Buna Government Station.

On the evening of December 3, the troops had their first hot meal
in weeks. Eichelberger had demanded it—half-starved soldiers, he
said, could not be counted on to fight. With full bellies, men found the
energy to slip back to the Japanese bivouac that they had stormed two
days earlier to search for souvenirs. Fearing booby traps, company
commanders had issued strict orders to leave the stuff alone, but few
of the men felt the need to comply with the order. The jungle was so
thick that even in broad daylight they could sneak back to the Japanese outpost without being noticed.

That night, nine Zeros flying fifty feet off the ground dropped food
supplies to Japanese troops at Buna Government Station. Eichelberger
regarded the drop as a good omen. It was further evidence that the
enemy was tired, sick, and running low on food and ammunition.

All of this was true. Some Japanese soldiers charged with holding
the beachhead did not even have weapons to defend themselves.
Colonel Yokoyama commanded these men to tie bayonets to poles.
Those without bayonets he ordered to fashion spears or clubs out of
wood.

Major General Tsuyuo Yamagata, who had just landed with five
hundred troops north of Basabua at the mouth of the Kumusi River,
warned his men of the situation at the front. The battlefield, he said,
was a "continuous swampland . . . devoid of supplies." The health situation was also extremely bad. "Until now," he continued, "condi-

tions as severe as these have been unheard of during the China and Greater East Asia conflict." Then he urged the men on, adding, "I have not the slightest doubt that you will conquer hardships and privation and that with one blow you will annihilate the blue-eyed enemy and their black slaves which will be the key to the completion of the Southern operations."

Veteran troops who had made the long retreat from Ioribaiwa confirmed Yamagata's appraisal. Although they had fought in the Singapore, Malay, and Bataan campaigns, they had never seen a worse battlefield. Reaching the coast, they discovered that Japanese doctors were ill equipped to care for them. Hospital conditions were deplorable. Sick and wounded soldiers were forced to lie on straw mats outside the overcrowded hospital. Reeking swamp water had seeped into the wards, causing clothes, bedding, and medical supplies to mold, rot, or rust. Those doctors who had not been forced into infantry duty had almost no medicine to treat patients. They performed operations without anaesthetic. The very ill were simply left to die.

For those suffering from malnutrition, there was little food to nurse them back to health. The detachment supply officer gave orders to slaughter the remaining horses. For many of the sickest soldiers, though, the meat was of no help. For the past month they had eaten anything they could—leaves, grass, roots, dirt, even their leather rifle straps. Now their digestive systems were incapable of processing regular food. According to one Japanese journalist, many of them "vomited blood and died."

General Horii's section leader, who penned agonized diary entries from Ioribaiwa Ridge, now turned his attention to the Imperial army's disintegration. "Thinking reinforcements will come," he wrote in late November, "we have waited every night. . . . As the battle stretches from day to day the number of men killed and wounded increases. The patients are all collapsing. We don't know how great our losses are . . . but we are holding out, hoping for a miracle. In the meantime . . . we find that our Bn Comdrs and Coy Comdrs have all been hiding in trenches under trees and not one has come out."

On the evening of December 3 he wrote, "Parents! Wife! Brother and Sister! I have fought with all my strength. I believe by all means that the violent efforts of BASA (Basabua) Garrison will be handed down to posterity. . . . But now my fighting strength is weakened and I am about to expose my dead body on the seashore of BASA. My comrades have already died, though my heart is filled with joy because I can become the guardian spirit of my country. I will fight and crush the enemy. I will protect the seashore of BASA forever."

First Lieutenant Jitsutaro Kamio expressed many of the same sentiments. On November 30, he wrote in his diary, "Even though there is little to eat a warrior must bear it." A day later he wrote, "Human beings must die once. I only ask for a good place to die."

•   •   •

West of the Girua River at the oval-shaped clearing that had already become known as the "roadblock," Captains Keast and Shirley were barely hanging on. The American position on the track was a precarious one. Two hundred fifty yards long by 150 yards wide, and only 300 yards south of a Japanese position on the track, the roadblock represented the only high, open ground for what might have been miles. Though the Americans were dug in, Japanese snipers tucked into the tops of trees had clear shots, and the dense undergrowth made them vulnerable to surprise attacks. Isolated nearly a mile behind the main Japanese position on the Sanananda track, Keast and Shirley were unable to communicate with anyone but their own men. Their phone lines had been cut, and their radios could not reach the American command post fifteen hundred yards to the southwest.

Keast instructed two machine gun squads to man positions to the north and south of the garrison. Shirley's men dug in to the west and placed two 60 mm mortars, which could fire thirty rounds per minute, inside their perimeter while Keast took his Antitank Company men to the eastern perimeter.

Outmanned several times over and unable to call for reinforcements, Keast and Shirley, and what remained of their troops after the brutal bayonet charge spent the night of November 30 repulsing raid after Japanese raid. The position was nearly impossible to defend.

The following morning, his eyes bloodshot from lack of sleep, Keast offered to execute a probing attack and take a patrol off the southwest perimeter. Though Shirley knew how dangerous this was, he also knew that they would have to find a gap in the Japanese position at some point. Without ammunition, food, or reinforcements, the Americans would not be able to hold the roadblock for very long.

Just three miles to the north, the waves of the Solomon Sea washed over the dark sands of Sanananda Point, and the first rays of the sun glistened in the morning sky. In the swamp, Keast and his men moved through the mist and sago palms like ghosts of the war's dead. The spikes of the trees ripped at their clothes. Raw from jungle rot, their feet burned with every step. At every sound their fingers tightened on their triggers. So far they had been lucky; they had not walked into a slaughter. Then the jungle closed in around them and they had to suppress the desire to burst into a mad, clumsy rush.

For a moment Keast, the former teacher and coach, allowed himself to dream of home. Marquette, Michigan, bordered by Lake Superior and great forests of white pine and red and sugar maples, had been a good place for the Keasts. Roger, Ruth, and their young son Harry had been there for just fifteen months when the Japanese struck Pearl Harbor. As a lieutenant in the Reserve Officer Corps, Roger must have known that his time at home was drawing to a close. The family's time in Marquette, though brief, had "meant a great deal" to all the Keasts. The school and the community had embraced them. To show their appreciation, the school held a series of farewell parties that included hams, chili and cake, card games, songs, and jokes about how Keast enjoyed "singing in the showers" and his efforts to teach the high school boys to dance. Though the school paper declared that "depressing talk of any kind was not allowed," more than a few people left the parties with "lumps in their throats." At the official school send-off, Keast was told that the 1941 yearbook was being dedicated to him. The dedication, the speaker said, was for Keast's "splendid loyalty shown in furthering athletics and a better school spirit." The speaker added, "the staff bestows this honor upon you and hopes that in the years to come you will always remind us of our duty to our country and to our school." Then the crowd broke into song. It began with "For He's a Jolly Good Fellow," and ended with "Auld Lang Syne."

But Keast was as far from Marquette as he could be now. He and his men had not made much progress when they were hit by a wave of rifle and machine gun fire. When one of his men, a company cook by the name of Johnson, stopped, Keast patted him on the back. Johnson was wild-eyed with adrenaline, and Keast tried to calm him. "Don't let it bother you, soldier, let's go right in there and keep our eyes open." Keast knew the situation was desperate. Jap snipers were moving to surround them. Their only hope was to keep shooting, to keep moving straight ahead in the direction of Medendorp and his men. Keast must have known that if Medendorp knew that they had fallen into a trap, he would try to bail them out.

Keast took a few more steps, and then gunfire burst at point-blank range from the jungle ahead. There was a brief flash. Johnson might have heard the dull thud of a bullet entering flesh. Then Keast fell. Johnson could see Keast "lying on the ground on his side, his empty pistol holster exposed above the grass." He wanted to go to his captain. He needed to get his captain, to pull him out of the jungle and scream for a medic, but bullets snapped and hummed around him. Soon the decision was made for him. The Japanese attacked, and he and the others who had not been hit stumbled back to the roadblock.

The following day, December 2, a party under the command of Captain Meredith Huggins left the battalion command post a mile back on the track. Five hours later, after dodging enemy snipers, Huggins reached the roadblock's southern perimeter. In need of ammunition and rations, Shirley was overjoyed to see Huggins, but he had bad news for him: Roger Keast was probably dead.

Huggins had no time to mourn his friend. Just minutes after he arrived, a large Japanese force attacked. According to Johnson, who had seen Keast go down the day before, Shirley was "everywhere," shouting orders and beating back the enemy. Not long after noon, though, Shirley's luck ran out. A medic saw him go down, ran to him and dragged him into a trench. Shirley wanted to know how bad his wound was. "You'll be okay," the medic lied. According to Johnson, Shirley "just slipped off into death."

As the highest-ranking officer, Huggins was suddenly in charge of the roadblock. In a matter of seven hours he had gone from a supply man to a battlefield commander. Now, battalion headquarters wanted to know: Could he hold the garrison?

Huggins replied, "I'll hold that place until hell freezes over."

Chapter 16

BREAKING THE STALEMATE

BACK AT THE Buna Front, Eichelberger was gearing up for the December 4 attack. After consulting with Colonel John Grose, though, he agreed to postpone the attack, but only by a single day.

Grose had been I Corps inspector general, but now that I Corps was taking over, Eichelberger was replacing Harding's officers with his own. Grose was an odd choice for a battlefield commander. In a matter of a few days, the colonel went from shuffling papers to leading men.

Grose immediately rubbed the troops the wrong way. According to Stutterin' Smith, he "arrived like a potentate."

Grose was taken aback by the condition of the troops, especially Stutterin' Smith's men. Some of them, Grose wrote, were on the brink of "nervous exhaustion," and most of them had fevers, too. Malaria did not keep men off the front lines, either. A soldier's temperature had to reach 103 degrees before Smith could send him back to an aid station. Smith hated to see sick men going into battle, but he was so shorthanded that he took anyone he could get, fever or not. Searching for troops, he had already stripped the regiment's Headquarters and Service Companies. Cooks, too, were fighting as riflemen.

At 10:00 on Saturday, December 5, Eichelberger's attack began with nine B-25 bombers swooping in on Buna Government Station. Artillery and mortars pounded Buna Village. Some of them landed short of the village and burst in the trees just above the heads of Lutjens and his men. Had the shells landed twenty feet shorter, Company E would have been wiped out by friendly fire. Half an hour later, the barrage ended. Then, according to Lutjens, "it was deathly still."

The troops waded into the jungle. The Japanese were flinging mortars, and Lutjens took cover in an artillery shell hole as rounds crashed through the trees and burst. Shrapnel flew and splinters of wood cut the air. Everywhere around him men lay plastered to the ground in rain puddles.

After waiting out the mortar bombardment, Lutjens and his men were back on their feet. They had advanced only twenty yards when Japanese machine gunners opened up on them. Bullets struck flesh, and six men fell. Blood clouds floated in the air. Then everyone dove for cover, except Sergeant Harold Graber. With his machine gun at his hip, Graber stormed the Japanese. Inspired by Graber's example, one of Lutjens' lieutenants attacked, too. Lutjens heard firing, and then saw the lieutenant fall. Seconds later the man got up, stumbled ten more yards, and was hit by another burst of fire. Then Graber went down. Another one of Company E's men raced forward. Lutjens heard the pop of a grenade fuse and then the sputter. When it blew, he knew he had lost another good man.

Though Graber had taken out a bunker before he was killed, there were still Japanese everywhere, and Lutjens' platoon was surrounded. Lutjens knew his only hope was to get a message to Captain Schultz. Perhaps Schultz could send the rest of the company forward.

Lutjens decided to try to get through himself. Because the chances of success were slim, he knew it was a job he could not ask any of his men to do. He took only a few steps when a Japanese soldier spotted him and hurled a grenade. The concussion rocked him, then another grenade lodged in the mud next to him. He lunged forward just as it went off, and the grenade tossed him through the air. Lying in the mud, he noticed that the barrel of his tommy gun was bent. Now he did not even have a gun to defend himself, but he was not sure it mattered. He was afraid to reach down, positive the grenade had taken him apart at the hips. At the thought, the strength seeped from his body. His arms felt as heavy as dumbbells. He shivered and then retched.

Lutjens lay there, then slowly he moved his hand down his legs. He was terrified they would be gone, severed below the knee. But they were still there—wet with blood, yes, but they were still there. Lutjens experienced a moment of joy until the soldier who had thrown the grenade started shooting. Lutjens rolled to his side and dragged himself along using his elbows. Disoriented, he nearly slithered into his enemy's lap.

A bullet ripped through his shirt and another creased his eye. One struck him in the thigh. The pain was enough to make him vomit again. Another bullet slapped dirt in his face. I'm a dead man, he thought. For some reason, though, the Japanese soldier held back. It didn't make any sense. He could have sauntered over to Lutjens and banged his head in with the butt of his rifle.

Lutjens struggled back to his elbows. This time, he tried to make some sense of where he was. Then he crawled again.

It was a miracle: Somehow he snaked his way to a medic who was sitting in a foxhole with his hands in a man's gut. Scattered around him lay dead and wounded soldiers. The medic gave Lutjens a handful of sulfanilamide pills, and went back to work on the soldier. Lutjens was full of shrapnel and lead, but the belly wounds came first.

Lutjens eventually pulled himself through the muck back to a field hospital. His pulse was weak, his breathing shallow. He was losing consciousness and the shock was wearing off. His whole body burned as if it were on fire until a medic gave him a shot of morphine.

•   •   •

Like Lutjens' men, Gus Bailey's G Company was stranded in the jungle. Eichelberger was furious. He wanted Buna Village taken and called F Company out of reserve. Grose protested—nothing would be gained by throwing another company at the Japanese; they were dug in too well. Stutterin' Smith also weighed in.

"Sir," he said. "Pulling F Company out of reserve isn't going to work."

Eichelberger was not listening. He had been sent in by MacArthur to capture Buna, and MacArthur was growing impatient. Adamant that Buna fall that day, the three-star general was on the front, directing the troops.

"You will attack!" Eichelberger ordered.

Eichelberger called for Lieutenant Odell and told him what he wanted. Odell was to get as much information from the forward troops as he could and do a brief reconnaissance. Then he was to split up his company, sending half his men up one side of the trail and taking the rest up the other side.

Company F, the general said, was to storm the village and capture Buna. Odell was not sure he heard the general right—take Buna?

"Yes," Eichelberger said, they were to "finish the job," and they had need little more than their bayonets to do it.

Odell had his good luck Japanese bayonet that he had taken on November 30. But now he didn't feel so lucky. None of the other companies had made it to Buna. What the hell made the general think he and his men were going to succeed?

Some of the men, realizing they would be walking into a death trap, refused to go ahead. "If you don't get going, I have the right to shoot you," Odell snapped.

"I heard safeties being clicked off," says one of the soldiers who witnessed the altercation. "Fortunately, someone stepped in and cooler heads prevailed. I do believe that someone would have gladly put a bullet in Lieutenant Odell."

Reluctantly, Odell's platoon advanced. In front of the soldiers lay the bodies of other Americans who had tried to take Buna. Odell stepped over the corpses and when he and his men were in position they rushed the village. A storm of Japanese bullets greeted them. Odell screamed for everyone to get down, but not before the Japanese had taken out a number of men.

On the other side, Sergeant George Pravda organized his men. He was only a sergeant, but the company had already lost all its lieutenants. Besides, Pravda was as cool as they came and had already won a Silver Star for an attack on November 30.

Just a few days before, Pravda had come to a buddy's rescue. Sergeant Jack Olsen had been doing reconnaisance work at Buna Government Station when he was shot in the leg. Unable to walk, he lay in the jungle waiting for someone to find him. He prayed it would be an

American and not a Jap. He dared not yell out, though. His unit was not far behind. If he screamed, he would give away its position.

Olson swallowed twelve sulfa pills and waited. Twenty-four hours later, George Pravda found him. Pravda cut the bottom off Olsen's fatigues, filled the wound with sulfa powder and wrapped it with the piece of cloth, then signaled to some litter men who managed to get Olsen out.

Now Pravda hesitated. He knew the trail ahead was a death trap. The last thing he wanted to do was to send these men forward. They were more than friends; they were family, brothers. While F Company trained in Louisiana, Pravda served as its reporter for the *Daily Tribune* in Grand Haven, Michigan. He knew who came down with measles, who was sunburned, who was a regular at the weekend picture shows, who was homesick, and because it was his job to check them in at night, who liked to carouse and who did not. He knew their wives and sweethearts, their mothers and fathers, the names of their dogs, their company nicknames—Baby Dumpling, the Bugler, Wrong Entrance—and laced his correspondences with amusing anecdotes and folksy yarns about life in Louisiana. He wrote about the heat, mosquitoes, mud, cotton and watermelon, fried chicken, funny deep-South drawls, black shoeshine boys.

The men of Company F relied on Sergeant Pravda's discretion, and Pravda never disappointed them. He never printed anything that might give family members back home reason for alarm or sweethearts cause to worry about whether their men were straying. But after earning their trust, how could he now send them up against Japanese snipers, machine gunners, and mortarmen when he knew some of them were going to be killed?

Pravda instructed his men to remove their bayonets. It was an unorthodox way to run an attack, plus Odell had just ordered them to insert bayonets, but Pravda had been at Buna long enough to make the call.

"No bayonets?" asked one of his corporals.

"That's right," answered Pravda. "No bayonets."

Pravda was worried that with bayonets the men would get hung up in the jungle's swarm of vines and limbs.

Pravda and his men made it all the way to the mouth of Entrance Creek and inadvertently crossed over into Buna Government Station. When Pravda realized where he was, he called for reinforcements. He had made a wrong turn and now he and his men were staring at the biggest prize of all—the Government Station.

No one could believe the news. "He's at the goddamn Government Station! We gotta get him some men!"

But the men never arrived, and Pravda was forced to pull back. Not before he was shot and seriously wounded, though. The bullet entered his arm, traveled through his back and exited at his neck. A few more inches and it would have severed his spine. Now he was being carried out on a stretcher while Japanese snipers tried to pick off the litter men.

Back at the field hospital, where Pravda would spend the night, doctors were working to keep men alive. On December 3, when Russell Buys was shot and went back for medical attention, he warned the medics to expect heavy casualties because soon there was going to be a "big push on."

Buys knew what he was talking about. Though he was a cook, cooks at Buna did not get a break. They fought shoulder to shoulder with the riflemen. In fact, Buys had already taken a few Japs and risked his life in the process.

While guarding the company command post, he had seen enemy soldiers crossing Entrance Creek by way of the wood bridge. When he reported the activity to Gus Bailey, Bailey treated him like anything but a cook.

"Well, then, get up there and shoot 'em" was all Bailey said.

Buys had something of a reputation in the company. He had grown up on a farm in Muskegon, where he was always shooting something. At Camp Beauregard he had finished at the top of the company on the firing range, using .22s and .30-06 bolt-action rifles. When the scores came in, the officer in charge chided the rest of the guys. "You guys let a cook beat you!" he roared. "You sorry SOBs, you let a goddamn cook beat you!"

Buys crept up toward the creek and squeezed between some mangrove roots. Then he put his M-1 to his shoulder and sighted in on a spot about two hundred yards away on the bridge. When a group of Japanese soldiers tried crossing he sent three of them spilling into the creek.

On the day Buys was shot, Bailey had sent him to the front lines to get hot rice to the troops. On the way back a firefight broke out, and Buys took a blow to his shoulder that felt as if a heavyweight fighter had unloaded on him. Turning around to punch the SOB who had hit him, Buys realized that he had been shot. He did not know if it was a Jap sniper or one of his own guys. It did not matter to him—a Jap bullet or friendly fire, "it hurt the same." Another bullet flew just past his head, and Buys dropped to the ground. When the shooting stopped, he crouched down low and hustled back to the aid station. The medic on duty told him he was a lucky man—the wound would get him out of Buna and they would not have to amputate his arm. The bullet had just missed shattering his shoulder bone.

.   .   .

East of the trail, Herman Bottcher looked sternly at Jastrzembski and DiMaggio. "I want eighteen men," he said. They didn't dare say no.

Per instructions from Bailey and Captain Hantlemann, Bottcher had already scouted the approach to Buna, where the Americans had run into murderous fire from snipers, machine gunners, and roving patrols. If he and his men could get around the interlocking bunkers and pillboxes, they could isolate the village from Buna Government Station.

Far to the right of the trail, Bottcher and his men slipped through a field of kunai grass and pushed north through jungle packed thick with sago and nipa palms. Overhead, the trees' branches were knotted and twisted. "Watch the trees," Bottcher warned. "Be on the lookout for snipers."

It was late in the afternoon. Already the fruit bats were gathering in the sky. Like the late-day rains, the men could always count on the bats. They left their treetop lairs and swirled through the forest canopy on wings the size of a hawk's.

Ahead Jastrzembski saw it—a pillbox. What the hell were they going to do now? He had no sooner said the words than he saw Bottcher bent over at the waist zigzagging with slabs of mud stuck to his boots. He slipped a grenade through the firing slit of the pillbox and dove into the jungle. Jastrzembski watched with relief as the grenade exploded.

After taking out the pillbox, they forded a tidal creek, holding their guns high over their heads, knowing that one Japanese machine gunner or one well-tossed grenade could take them all out. They watched for crocodiles, too—Buna's rivers and creeks were full of crocodiles dining on dead bodies. Eventually the creeks and rivers filled with corpses, and even the men with chlorination tablets refused to drink the water.

Scrambling up the muddy banks of the creek, the men discovered a large dead snake rotting in the sun. The stench was overwhelming. Then, following the creek north, before they knew it they were at the edge of the beach, and suddenly Japanese soldiers opened fire on them. In less than five minutes, three of Bottcher's group were dead and four more wounded. One of Bottcher's men volunteered to try to take out the Japanese machine gun nest that had done the damage. As he ran forward, grenades landed at his feet, throwing him and a cloud of sand into the air. Wounded, the man squirmed in the sand.

"Lie still!" Bottcher yelled. "Lie still!"

Some of the men went out to get him and dragged him back. As the sun disappeared, they dug in. Bottcher radioed back to Gus Bailey, telling him that they were at the beach smack in the middle of Buna Village and the Government Station.

Bottcher and his men had not taken Buna, but they had broken the stalemate. In a matter of hours they had gained more ground than anyone had on either the Urbana or Warren Front in the two and a half weeks since the battle began.

Boice had not heard yet and had already written in his diary that the assault on Buna "was not successful." And back at the command post, Eichelberger was fretting over the day's failures. While he had been inspecting the front, a Japanese sniper almost blew his head off. Though Eichelberger escaped death by a whisker, the bullet struck his aide, a young man for whom he had great affection. "Full of grief," Eichelberger carried him back to the field hospital, where doctors fought to save his life.

News from the Warren Front was that the all-out attack had failed miserably. Twenty minutes into the attack, the recently delivered Bren gun carriers—small, open-air tanklike vehicles—bogged down in the mud and got stuck on the tree stumps of the Duropa Plantation. The Japanese assaulted the carriers with machine guns, an antitank gun, hand grenades, and "sticky" bombs.

The Americans who advanced in support of the Australians manning the carriers fared no better. Under the blazing tropical sun, those who were not killed or wounded were laid low by heat prostration. According to the colonel in charge of the attack, the Americans had "hit" Colonel Yamamoto's forces and "bounced off."

For Eichelberger, the defeat was very discouraging. Freighters had brought the carriers up from Milne Bay along the newly charted water route. Once they reached the front, Higgins boats put them ashore. The Higgins boats were the first landing craft to reach New Guinea, and Eichelberger had hoped that the boats and what they were capable of delivering might help turn the tide of the battle.

Rather than turning the tide of the battle, though, the events of December 5 convinced Eichelberger that he was in for the fight of his life. Still, he had to deal with MacArthur, whose headquarters, according to one Australian general, reminded him of a "bloody barometer in a cyclone, up and down every two minutes." If only MacArthur would take the time to visit the battlefield, he could see what Eichelberger and his men were up against.

In the eyes of many of the Red Arrow men, December 5 solidified Eichelberger's poor reputation. He was a general who was willing to lose good soldiers in heedless frontal attacks. He was the "Butcher of Buna," "Eichelbutcher." Later, with equal parts bitterness and black humor, they would call the cemetery at Buna "Eichelberger Square."

Eichelberger was not without self-reflection, however. He would later write of that battle: "I had seen the litters coming back. I had seen walking wounded being led from the front. I had seen men lying in ditches, weeping with battle shock. I had visited dressing stations. Yet there were advances to be made, and decisions which must not be governed by my own weaknesses or emotions."

In a letter he wrote to his wife that night, Eichelberger said that the December 5 battle "will always remain with me as long as I live."

By the time he wrote to Sutherland later that evening, though, Eichelberger's mood had bounced back. Bottcher's breakthrough had redeemed an utter failure on both fronts. Eichelberger was now full of praise for the Red Arrow men. "The number of our troops," he said, "that tried to avoid combat today could be numbered on your fingers."

Grose, too, was moved to revise his opinion of Smith's Ghost Mountain boys. "The battalion's men," he wrote in his diary, "have been courageous and willing, but they have been pushed almost beyond the limit of human endurance."

At dawn on December 6, after a "terrific rainstorm" the Japanese assaulted "Bottcher's Corner" from two directions. Expecting the raids, Bottcher had set up a machine gun the night before, and he and his small group repelled both attacks.

That night, according to Sam DiMaggio, the men "fixed their bayonets in preparation for hand-to-hand combat." It was impossible to sleep. DiMaggio licked at the dried salt that had formed around his mouth and wondered about the turn his life had taken. He had left the Malleable Iron Company, vowing never to go back. Now here he was, a soldier fighting for his life.

Land crabs skittered along the beach, through the palm leaves and the delicate snailshells, birds whistled from the nearby trees, and waves slapped against the barges. Jastrzembski was holding himself together through sheer force of will. His senses deceived him. Everywhere he saw Japanese slithering through the sand. Every noise sounded to him like an enemy soldier poised to bayonet him in the belly. He could almost feel it, ripping through his body, tearing apart his insides.

At 4:00 a.m., the false dawn lapsed back into darkness. Jastrzemb-ski studied the sky and the unfamiliar stars, and then his eyes grew heavy. All he wanted to do was sleep and then he smelled it: the jungle. In the past two months he had grown accustomed to it, but there it was again, the odor of rot and decay.

Two hours later, Japanese troops crept toward Bottcher's Corner, but a forward scout, Corporal Harold Mitchell, caught a glimpse of them. Mitchell let out a yell and charged the Japanese with a fixed bay-onet. The Japanese were so startled by the rush that they failed to attack. Bottcher grabbed one of the machine guns, and together with the other machine gunner and his riflemen raked the beach, the brush, and the small coconut grove. During the skirmish, Bottcher was hit in the hand by an enemy bullet, but one of his men wrapped it and Bottcher returned to the machine gun. Mitchell made it back to their position unscathed.

That afternoon, Company E, minus its longtime leader Lutjens, and Company G made another stab at taking the village. When the attack bogged down, Stutterin' Smith came forward, moved out front with Gus Bailey, and led the charge. It was as dark as the sky before a summer storm and in no time the companies lost sight of each other. Smith groped his way forward through the airless jungle.

Smith had not gone more than twenty yards when the Japanese began a rhythmic chant. It was the first time he had ever heard it, the precursor to a banzai charge. He took cover behind a tree and waited just as a mortar landed over his head. Hot metal fragments rained down. Five of his men fell. Smith wondered how he had escaped getting hit and then he moved his hand across his neck and up and down his back. He felt blood, and the next thing he knew an aidman was running toward him to put a dressing on his wound. Smith protested that it was just a shallow flesh wound. But the aidman insisted on bandaging it anyway, and encouraged Smith to return to the aid station. The attack had stalled; otherwise Smith would never have agreed to go back.

Back at the aid station Smith ran into Captain Boet, the battalion surgeon with whom he had crossed the Owen Stanleys. Boet took a look at the wound. Hell, Smith thought, what's the big deal; it's just a flesh wound. When Boet finished, though, Smith knew it was serious.

"It hit the kidney," Boet said to his friend. "It's a bad deal."

"Hell no," Smith replied. "I'm alive."

Boet then summoned four native litter bearers and instructed them to carry the major to the portable hospital.

Lacking the equipment to treat him, the doctors at the portable hospital sent him on to the Evacuation Hospital. At the Evac Hospital, doctors stripped Smith and threw his putrid clothes and shabby boots into a fire. When they put him on a scale Smith was astonished by the weight he had lost. He was down to 138 pounds. At six feet three inches that meant he was nothing but skin and bones. After they had picked the metal fragments out of his back, they confirmed Boet's diagnosis: Smith's kidney had been damaged. They would have to get him back to Port Moresby and on to Australia as soon as possible.

That evening, a dull pain settled into Smith's side. The carriers lay him in a makeshift cot, which they had fashioned using poles lashed together with a webbing of bush vines. Smith felt self-conscious. Around him, badly injured soldiers lay in their cots groaning. His wound was much worse than he knew.

Word was sent forward to the companies of the 2nd Battalion that Smith had been seriously injured, but probably would recover. Gus Bailey must have been relieved to hear that. He liked Smith as much as Smith liked him. How often would you find a battalion commander out front leading his men into battle? It was the exact principle that Bailey had adhered to: Never ask a man to do something you won't do yourself. Anyway, Bailey was glad that he would not have to mark Smith down in his journal in which each day he recorded the names of G Company men and battalion officers killed in battle.

o   o   o

Captain Jim Boice took over for Smith, and his first order was to direct a platoon under the command of Lieutenant Odell to try to creep or shoot its way to the beach. No attempt had been made to reinforce

Bottcher and his troops, and they were struggling to hold on. Boice realized that to lose the beach would set the American effort back three weeks.

Odell's task was to get to the beach and then to extend Bottcher's line to the sea. In the process he would have to destroy two enemy outposts: one not far from Bottcher and his men, the other in the direction of the village. Odell and twelve men made it to Bottcher without a fight, then threw grenades at the nearest outpost. When no one fired back, they went to investigate, running part of the way and then dropping to their bellies and crawling. Odell led the way. When they reached the pillbox, they discovered a number of Japanese soldiers either dead or dying, and bayoneted them all.

Next, they moved on the second outpost. Not far down, they encountered fifteen Japanese soldiers huddled in a shallow trench. Using English, one of the Japanese soldiers shouted that he and his men were prepared to surrender. Odell suspected a hoax. Without responding to the Japanese soldier's request, he and his men rushed the trench, shot and bayoneted the enemy soldiers, and then closed in on the village. From the village, machine guns answered. Odell had now lost the element of surprise. He and his men retreated to the first outpost near Bottcher's Corner where they set up another machine gun.

They had just settled into foxholes when Japanese soldiers from Buna Government Station fired on them. The bullets were zipping over their heads. "It was quite a sensation," according to Odell, "stretched out in a foxhole (8 inches deep in water . . .) watching the leaves of the trees and bushes above your head rapidly assuming the appearance of cheese cloth."

Odell was plastered against the sand wall of his foxhole waiting for the firing to subside when fifty screaming enemy soldiers attacked firing rifle grenades. One of Odell's men raked the beach with the machine gun and stopped the assault. For the next few hours, Japanese soldiers crawled around the perimeter. Just after sunset, a dozen men pushed their way to the beach to reinforce Odell's position, which was so close to both the village and the Government Station that Odell could hear the Japanese "talking and walking about."

Sitting in their sandpit, some of Bottcher and Odell's men watched in the direction of the village. The others kept their eyes on the Government Station. Bottcher heard something suspicious out on the water. Then Jastrzembski caught sight of a Japanese barge trying to get reinforcements to Buna Village. Bottcher and the other machine gunner were behind their machine guns, and as soon as they spotted the silhouette of the lead boat, tracers cut through the darkness. The barrels of their machine guns grew so hot that DiMaggio poured water from his canteen over them. Suddenly, an explosion rocked DiMaggio. Then he saw the barge go up in a shock of flames. Japanese soldiers dove overboard. Swinging his machine gun back and forth, Bottcher hit them as they swam for shore. Jastrzembski saw the bodies, illuminated by the glowing phosphorescence, roll in on breakers. The following morning, as the sun radiated through great clouds that had spilled rain on the north coast for the entire night, Jastrzembski saw that the waves had deposited the corpses onto the beach like driftwood.

That morning, Jim Boice hoped to capitalize on Bottcher's breakthrough. With the help of two well-used flamethrowers that had just come in by lugger, and with Bottcher on the beach preventing Japanese reinforcements from reaching Buna Village, he hoped to overwhelm the bunker that had stymied the battalion's advance for weeks.

The flamethrower's operator advanced on the bunker. Twenty men covered him. He got within thirty feet of the Japanese position, stepped into a clearing, and turned on the weapon. The flame singed his eyebrows and sputtered. It lit the field on fire but fell well short of the Japanese. Then the Japanese opened up on the operator and three of the cover men, killing them instantly.

The weapon that Boice hoped would end the stalemate at the front was defective. Once again, the soldiers of the 2nd Battalion would have to resort to direct assaults on Japanese positions, a primitive tac tic that guaranteed the battalion would lose more good men.

•   •   •

By December 8, 1942, Japan's hold on the north coast of the Papuan Peninsula was slipping. The jubilation that had followed the attack on

Pearl Harbor and the beginning of Japan's "Great East Asia War" one year before had turned to despair.

On December 8, First Lieutenant Jitsutaro Kamio wrote in his diary: "Today is finally the one year anniversary. We should have a ceremony but everyone is exhausted."

Although Allied ground forces had registered few significant gains, with the opening of new airfields at Dobodura and Popondetta, General Kenney's pilots stepped up the pressure on the Japanese, slowly tightening the noose, making it almost impossible for ships to deliver troops, food, medicine, or ammunition.

Kuba Satonao, a first-class mechanic in a naval transport unit, wrote that because of the shortage of ammunition, officers had instructed soldiers to "make every bullet count."

The Allied supply situation, on the other hand, had vastly improved. Supplies that Harding had requisitioned weeks before being dismissed began to arrive. Engineers had just completed the Dobodura-Siremi jeep track and a number of other important supply tracks. New coastal luggers to replace those that had been destroyed in mid-November had just arrived at Oro Bay. The Americans now had mortars and large artillery and enough ammunition, including delayed-action mortar shells, to do real damage. They also had a new four-inch-to-one-mile Buna map, which forward artillery and air observers used to help operators of the big guns zero in on their targets.

As a consequence, the Americans hammered the coast. Kuba Satonao wrote, "All we do is get severely bombed. Buna is gradually falling into a state of danger." A few days later, he wrote again, "now they are coming over at night. We lived till today, but it is something unusual. There are tears in my eyes as I realize the meaning of the fact that I am alive." Days passed before he was able to write again: "From early morning today there was mortar fire around us. From the left there is considerable large artillery fire. . . . There is a constant flight of enemy planes overhead. We are now in a delaying and holding action. The amount of provisions is small and there is no chance of replenishing ammunition. But we have bullets of flesh. No matter what comes we are not afraid. If they come, let them come. . . . We have the aid of Heaven. We are warriors of Yamato."

When Satonao writes of "bullets of flesh," he is referring to the suicide squad. Later in the war, as the Japanese turned to acts of desperation, suicide squads, of which the kamikaze was a manifestation, became common. Early on, the suicide squad still served a practical purpose—to incite terror in the hearts of the enemy. At Buna, as elsewhere, the suicide squad or "Kesshi Tai" (literally "Determined-to-Die Unit") had no shortage of volunteers.

*   *   *

The sun dropped fast on the evening of December 8, and Captain Yasuda made one last attempt to reach Buna Village. As a diversion, he had a force of forty attack from Buna Village. Then he sent out a hundred men from the Government Station, hoping they might slip into the village without being detected. But Bottcher, Odell, and their troops caught them moving on the beach and gunned them down, finishing off the wounded with their bayonets. Inland, Boice's troops repelled them, too. With machine guns and mortars, they drove the Japanese back.

On the afternoon of December 9, Lieutenant James Downer, who was now commanding Company E, volunteered to lead a patrol against the main Japanese bunker position at the southern edge of the village: the one that the flamethrower had failed to reduce the previous day.

Downer's plan, though, was the same one that had failed time and time again—he would storm the bunker and try to stick a grenade through the firing slit while the rest of the patrol covered him. Downer bravely set off through the jungle but was picked off by an enemy sniper. Two of his men crawled out to get him, pulling themselves along on their elbows. But when they reached him, they realized he was dead and dragged him back. For the rest of the day, Company E tried to maneuver around the bunker, drawing blistering fire from the Japanese defenders. That night the shooting stopped and Downer's patrol managed to get close enough to see that the bunker had been abandoned.

Perhaps their constant pressure had worn down the Japanese. What-ever the reason, the important thing was that the bunker fell at last to Downer's patrol.

Eichelberger was heartened by the news. To his eye, the men were fighting now like real soldiers.

One Japanese soldier noted the change. Early on he'd written that "The American is untrained, afraid, and stumbles about in the jungle. . . . They fire at any sound or shadow, wasting ammunition, giving their positions away. . . . They are like scared children who can-not learn. . . . We can kill them all. . . ." By mid-December he wrote, "The enemy is very hard to see in the jungle. . . . Enemy tactics are to hurl heavy mortar fire on us and rush in close behind."

While the Red Arrow men had "learned their business," as the official army historian said, three weeks of constant fighting had exacted a toll, especially on the men at Bottcher's Corner.

•   •   •

On December 11, twenty-six soldiers from the 127th U.S. Infantry fought their way to the beach to relieve Bottcher, Odell, and their men. For soldiers new to the front, the sight of decomposing corpses lying strewn across the sand must have been deeply unsettling. The stench, according to Odell, was "unendurable." The new men buried the bod-ies and then took over Bottcher's position.

Before leaving the beach, Bottcher had to make good on an order he had received. Allied Intelligence, G-2, wanted a prisoner to interro-gate. Bottcher and Corporal Mitchell discovered a wounded Japanese soldier huddling in a foxhole. When the man reached for his gun, Mitchell knocked him out with the butt of his rifle.

Mitchell washed the dried blood and sand from the soldier's face. The soldier came to, and when he did, he was terrified, expecting the Americans to slit his throat. Instead, Bottcher gave him a drink and poured water on his chest. Then he and Mitchell bandaged the sol-dier's leg, gave him a piece of chocolate, and delivered the prisoner to an aid station.

As worn out as the men at Bottcher's Corner were, the rest of the battalion was in no better shape. After twelve all-out attacks on Buna

Village in three weeks, Stutterin' Smith's 2nd Battalion was barely capable of holding the ground they had won. Companies had been reduced to the size of platoons, platoons to the size of squads. Companies E and F each had fewer than fifty soldiers left to fight, a quarter of their original strength. The battalion that had crossed Ghost Mountain with nearly nine hundred soldiers now had fewer than three hundred men left.

•   •   •

At the roadblock four miles southwest of Bottcher's Corner, on the other side of the Girua River, the Japanese attacked, and time and again Huggins and his men held.

"The situation was utter chaos," Huggins recalled. "Nobody knew what was going on. We were green kids. . . . "

Second Lieutenant Bill Sikkel saw the chaos first hand. He and Captain Russ Wildey managed to sneak and shoot their way north toward the roadblock. The foray took the better part of a day, and because they had not been issued compasses, they had to guess their way through the jungle. They arrived just in time: Huggins and his men had been under attack for thirty-two hours and were running low on ammunition.

Sikkel was struck by the scene. Bodies of the Japanese dead lay scattered around the flanks. The Americans hugged the inside of the slit trench waiting for the next Japanese attack.

The patrol spent the night, and the following morning Sikkel and Wildey brought out seventeen wounded and sick men and navigated their way back to the battalion command post. Sikkel was used to the jungle. Two weeks before, on the eve of his twenty-second birthday, just before setting out on his first patrol, he had emptied his pockets and told Father Dzienis to send the contents back to his mother in case he did not make it. He had been maneuvering through the swamps and the tangled forest each and every day since then. Doing it with wounded men, though, was especially dicey. He kept a close eye out for the deer-like imprint of the split-toed Japanese tong. It was a sure sign that snipers lurked nearby.

Back up the track from where Sikkel had come, not far outside the southwest perimeter of the roadblock, Lieutenant Hershel Horton had gone out on what he called a "mercy patrol" to pick up the dog tags of Keast's group. After hearing the story of the ambush, he figured Keast was dead, but part of him could not help but hope. Perhaps his friend was lying somewhere in the jungle, still breathing.

When shots burst from behind a thicket of sago palms, Horton and the three men with him dove for cover. Horton was hit. His buddies tried to crawl to him, but Japanese snipers had them pinned down. When the shooting subsided, Horton realized that his buddies had somehow made it out. He then dragged himself forty feet through the mud to what he described as a "grass shanty." Wounded, with bullet holes in his hip and right leg, "semi-delirious," and without food or water, Horton waited for two days for his friends to return. Finally, on December 3, one of his buddies, accompanied by a medic, was able to reach him. But the two men could not lift Horton, so the medic gave Horton a drink of water, which he lapped at like a thirsty dog, then bandaged his wounds and promised to return as soon as possible with help. True to his word, the medic came back with help the following day. He gave Horton water again, but when an enemy sniper shot and killed his assistant, the medic was forced to crawl away. Lying in the hot sun, Horton craved fluids and pawed at the jungle humus, trying to dig a hole deep enough to reach water. "Life," he wrote in his diary, had become a "terrible nightmare."

                    •   •   •

On December 5, while Horton was waiting for his buddies to retrieve him, Lieutenant Pete Dal Ponte led a sixty-man ration and ammunition party through the jungle. Dal Ponte knew he had to reach Huggins. Dal Ponte's party, though, was not made up of choice riflemen. His men were cooks, clerks, and mortarmen who had been pressed into duty. Each man carried forty pounds of supplies. Though only a mile separated them from the roadblock, Dal Ponte had to contend with hip-deep swamps and Tsukamoto's troops, who lay dug in like badgers between the American command post and Huggins.

Dal Ponte and his men had not gone far when Tsukamoto's troops sprung upon them. Despite the heavy loads and their lack of fighting experience, Dal Ponte's men drove them back, and at one juncture almost penetrated their defense and pushed through close to the southern end of roadblock. But the Japanese rallied and surrounded them. Dal Ponte and his men were fighting for their lives.

Late in the day, Dal Ponte's party managed to blast its way back to the American command post, limping in with half a dozen casualties and two dead soldiers.

For the next two days, supply parties tried to reach the roadblock, only to be turned away by Japanese fire.

The signalmen, struggling to keep the lines of communication open, had it just as hard—they had never strung wire across a tropical wilderness before. They could not run it along an established trail because as soon as the Japs saw it, they had cut it. So they had to hide it, wading into swamps, risking their lives in the sniper-infested jungle. The signalmen divided into two-man teams. Acting as a lookout, one soldier toted a rifle while the other carried a little reel of braided copper and metal combat wire.

While supply parties tried to push through to Huggins and the signalmen strung and repaired wire, the Australians tried to dislodge Tsukamoto's forces. They met with no better luck than the Americans. Tsukamoto had positioned his men throughout the jungle, and they subjected the bewildered Australians to a fierce cross fire. After two days of fighting, the Australians counted 350 men dead or wounded. Unable to withstand those kind of casualties, the Australians would not mount another attack for almost two weeks.

Dal Ponte, though, was not to be denied by Tsukamoto's firepower. He had friends at the roadblock and he knew the situation was desperate. Early in the morning on December 8, he and his party trudged into the jungle determined once again to reach Huggins. Sunlight flickered through branches, cockatoos screeched, and crowned pigeons darted through the trees. Three hundred yards south of the roadblock, the jungle erupted with gunfire. From both sides of the trail, machine gun fire bore down on the men.

Dal Ponte knew they would be mowed down if they could not

locate the guns. His plan was a crazy one: He would expose himself to fire while his men got a bead on the machine gunners. His men must have wondered if he had a death wish. He would be cut down in seconds.

Before anyone could stop him, Dal Ponte dashed out from behind a copse of trees. Bullets slapped through the underbrush all around Dal Ponte, but miraculously he was untouched. And now his men knew where the shooting was coming from. Slipping into the forest with his band of cooks, clerks, and mortarmen, Dal Ponte stalked the snipers. When they reached the enemy positions, the Japanese were gone.

That afternoon, Dal Ponte made it to the roadblock (now called Huggins Roadblock) where Huggins had established a double perimeter, two men to a foxhole. The men were alive, but starving and nearly out of ammunition. The Japanese had since established another roadblock farther to the north and surrounded Huggins' position with snipers.

When Dal Ponte arrived, he discovered that one of those snipers had put a bullet in Huggins' head. Huggins, though, had the luck of the Irish, and was busy directing his men despite his wound. Dal Ponte could see that Huggins needed medical attention, and reluctantly Huggins agreed to turn over command to him and let Dal Ponte's party lead him out of the roadblock.

That evening, having made it through the gauntlet of Tsukamoto's troops, Huggins briefed Medendorp. At the roadblock, men were burning up with malaria fevers. They had ringworm and their feet were going bad. They lived in filthy holes, unable to dispose of their feces. Corpses festered in the hot sun and it rained every night. Of the 225 men holding the garrison, barely half of them were able to fight. Medical supplies, food, and ammunition were almost nonexistent. Perhaps worst of all, the troops were subjected to repeated attacks and did not dare sleep. Sometimes at night the Japanese crept so close that the Americans reached out and grabbed their ankles. Pulling them into their trenches, they slashed the Japanese soldiers' throats with razor-sharp knives and bayonets.

Though Medendorp's Cannon Company and the men of the 3rd Battalion's Company K were not engaged in near-constant combat, the conditions they were enduring were hardly better than those Huggins described at the roadblock. A soldier wrote in K Company's journal that "between mosquitoes, Japs, heat, bad water, and short rations, it has sure been hell. . . . What is left of the company is a pretty sick bunch of boys." All the officers who had crossed the mountains with Medendorp were "gone, dead, wounded or sick."

Sick or not, men were forced to go out on patrols and were often the targets of Japanese snipers and machine gunners, especially at dawn and dusk, when the Japanese liked to attack. Patrols often returned with wounded men. The dead, though, they left behind. It was especially painful to leave dead buddies lying in mud puddles. The Japanese picked them clean as a bone, grabbing anything of value— grenades, lighters, knives, rings—and mementos. Photographs, though, they discarded—often, soldiers would find wedding pictures and photographs of children alongside the trail. But the Americans had no choice but to leave their buddies behind. Carrying them through the swamp in order to bury them back at the command post was an impossible feat, so they gritted their teeth and turned their heads in shame.

Not even Father Dzienis, despite his efforts, was able to retrieve many of the bodies. When he succeeded, he and a volunteer or two would carry the corpse back to the little cemetery he had built just behind the front lines. Dzienis remained utterly devoted to his men. Even in the midst of battle he held services for them—Catholics, Lutherans, agnostics, it did not matter to him. Though his legs "were one mass of running sores," when he was not at the aid station comforting wounded men, maintaining morale, delivering last rites, or inviting soldiers to worship with him, he crawled out to the front lines to "visit his flock." The soldiers were always glad to see him. "Chaplain Dzienis is here!" Soldiers would pass along the news from slit trench to slit trench.

●   ●   ●

The day after Dal Ponte's men pulled Huggins out of the roadblock, soldiers on all fronts learned that the Australians had taken Gona.

Prior to the Japanese invasion in July 1942, Gona had been one of the prettiest spots on the peninsula's north coast, with a church built of woven sago leaves and a handsome mission building with a red tin roof that caught rainwater. On the grounds, shaded by elegant palms and tulip trees, sat a school and a green, groomed cricket field. The pathways were lined with red hibiscus. Just down from the mission, the blue waters of the Solomon Sea washed over an idyllic stretch of black sand.

When the Australians seized Gona four and a half months later, they were horrified by what they saw. The Japanese had reinforced their bunkers, which doubled as latrines, with their own dead. Inside, they had used corpses as firing steps. They had stacked them with their rice and ammunition. They slept beside them. The bunkers reeked so badly the Japanese soldiers had resorted to fighting in gas masks. Partially decayed bodies floated in nearby lagoons.

In two days, the Australians buried almost a thousand Japanese bodies. Not a single enemy soldier remained alive.

For the Australians, the cost of victory at Gona was huge. One brigade lost over 40 percent of its troops. The victory must have given General Vasey pause. Perhaps he should have resisted the urge to "annihilate" the Japanese. By cutting off their supply and troop pipeline, he could have watched and waited while they starved.

There was a lesson to be learned at Gona. MacArthur, though, failed to recognize it.

．　　　．　　　．

The day after the Australians stormed Gona, another ration party made it to the roadblock. Upon returning to the command post, the leader of the ration party delivered another worrisome report. The men at the roadblock continued to deteriorate. If they hoped to survive, they needed to be supplied at least once every two days.

Medendorp had nothing but admiration for the men supplying Huggins. "These patrols," he wrote later, "marched the flesh right off their feet, leaving in many cases sores that were so deep that they showed red meat."

On December 12, Lieutenant Horton waited not far from the trail, hoping that someone might find him. Weak and able to dig for only seconds at a time, it had taken him four days to reach water. Even though it was "polluted by the rotting bodies" that lay around him, he slurped at the muddy puddle. A day later, he heard a rescue party traipsing through the jungle. They were looking for him, but a blinding rainstorm and Japanese snipers drove them away. Horton dared not call out. "The Japanese are living within 15 yards of me," Horton wrote. "I see them every day."

Horton tried to make a splint for his leg. He rose to his feet unsteadily, but his strength gave out. When he sat down and leaned against a tree, a Japanese sniper, who had seen him moving, shot him in the neck and shoulder. Horton lay at the base of the tree, waiting for the next bullet. "Why has God forsaken me?" he wrote in his diary. "Why is he making me suffer this terrible end?" Later, he continued, "I have imagined several other rescue parties. . . . My right hip is broken and my right leg, both compound fractures; else I could have been out of here in those first couple of days, wounds or no wounds. My life has been good, but I am so young and have so many things undone that a man of 29 should do. . . . I shall continue to pray for a miracle of rescue. . . . God bless you my loved ones. . . . I shall see you all again some day. I prepare to meet my Maker. Love, Hershel."

Horton died that day, lying fifty feet from his friend Roger Keast.

Chapter 17

CAGED BIRDS

The caged bird, in his dreams
Returns to his homeland
Forgetting my own self, every day and night,
I think of my father and mother in the homeland
And wonder how they are
I look upon the river
And it is like the one
I knew so well in childhood
far from here.

IN MID-DECEMBER, Cannon Company and Company K moved from their position southwest of the trail to the rear. In a letter to his youngest sister, Alice, Alfred Medendorp wrote that his teeth were falling out because of a vitamin deficiency. But even the rear offered little relief. Company K's journal keeper wrote, "The men are getting sicker. Their nerves are cracking. They are praying for relief. [They] must have it soon."

The soldiers had all seen enough. A GI was brought in with the entire top of his head blown off. Another's face was missing. Another had been shot between the shoulder blades. Medendorp witnessed the man's agony: "The spinal cord lay exposed. The muscles could be seen and their contractions watched; the lungs were torn open in spots and with every exhalation of the breath several fine sprays of blood shot up." Worse yet was the smell of the dead. "It is with us always," wrote Medendorp, "and flies by the millions."

•   •   •

East of the Girua River, General Eichelberger relieved the 2nd Battalion. He replaced it with the 127th, which had arrived at Dobodura, preparing to end what the Ghost Mountain boys had begun.

For MacArthur, the 127th could not attack soon enough. On December 13, a convoy carrying Major General Kensaku Oda, who was to take control of Horii's South Seas Detachment, landed with eight hundred troops. When MacArthur got the news he panicked and immediately wrote Eichelberger.

> Dear Bob:
>
> Time is fleeting and our dangers increase with its passage. However admirable individual acts of courage may be however spendid and electrical your presence has proven; remember that your mission is to take Buna. All other things are merely subsidiary to this. No alchemy is going to produce this for you; it can only be done in battle and sooner or later this battle must be engaged. Hasten your preparations, and when you are ready— strike, for as I have said, time is working desperately against us.
> Cordially, MacArthur

The following morning, the troops of the 127th stormed Buna Village. Expecting to have to wrest the village at bayonet point, the men were surprised when they entered unopposed. Suspecting a trap, they scoured the area for enemy soldiers. The Japanese were gone. After clinging to the village for three weeks, the enemy had vacated without a fight, as they had done three months earlier at Ioribaiwa Ridge.

The men of the 127th were shocked by what they discovered: a blighted landscape of scarred and beheaded trees, shell holes filled with water and mud and excrement, unburied bodies, the ruins of native huts, discarded clothing and ration cans, abandoned guns, very little food, and only basic medical supplies. But the Japanese bunkers stood intact even after direct mortar and artillery hits.

Two days later, Eichelberger's troops registered another mini-victory. Colonel White Smith's 2nd Battalion, 128th U.S. Infantry, down to only 350 effectives, stormed and took the Coconut Grove, the second major Japanese position west of Entrance Creek.

MacArthur's headquarters wasted no time trumpeting the news, and on December 15, the lead headline of the *New York Times* blared, "ALLIES TAKE BUNA IN NEW GUINEA."

It was typical MacArthur-esque hyperbole. What the front-page story omitted was that Buna Government Station east of Entrance Creek, the Allies' main objective, was still firmly in Japanese hands. It also failed to mention was that the Japanese possessed a large chunk of land—the Warren Front—east of the Government Station, and another one west of the Girua River at Sanananda.

●   ●   ●

Despite the triumphant *New York Times* headline, the reality was that the war in New Guinea had already dragged on much longer than the Americans or the Australians thought it would. There had been successes—Buna Village and Gona—but in the big picture they were minor victories. Early on, the plan had been to envelop the eleven-mile-long front as if a giant hand were closing inexorably around the Japanese. The Americans would come up the coast while the Australians moved down. A combined American-Australian army would move north via the Sanananda track, while an entirely American force would attack the Triangle.

A week and a half before the capture of Buna Village, after the failure of his December 5 assault on the Warren Front, Eichelberger realized that this plan would not work—at least not east of the Girua River. Japanese positions were just too strong, and the terrain was dismal.

The Americans, Eichelberger decided, would soften up the Japanese positions by infiltration and aggressive patrolling, the kind of mobile, small-unit maneuver tactics that General Forrest Harding had pioneered at the Infantry School at Fort Benning.

Eichelberger's plan was for reconnaissance platoons to identify enemy positions. He would then use artillery, especially the 105 mm howitzer—code named "Dusty"—with its high angle of fire and delayed fuses, to pound those positions into submission. Following bombardment, patrols would knock out the bunkers one by one, with rifles, grenades, grenade launchers, and mortars. If that failed, Eichelberger resolved to let starvation take its toll.

In the abstract, the plan seemed sound. The reality, though, was much more complicated. The terrain made even small-unit patrolling nearly impossible. While soldiers used grenade launchers with punishing effectiveness, their supply was limited, and they soon ran out of grenades. The 105 mm howitzer sat unused for days after firing a few hundred rounds because of a lack of ammunition. Eichelberger was again forced to resort to mortars and 37 mm guns, which hardly fazed the bunkers, and 3.7-inch mountain howitzers and 25-pounders that fired rounds with super-quick fuses that blew up on impact, leaving the Japanese positions undisturbed.

In mid-December, however, Eichelberger's luck changed. Tanks arrived: four light American M-3 General Stuarts that General Harding had fought so hard for and that had been denied to him time and time again. They saved the day, sparing Eichelberger a career-ending decision; MacArthur, who demanded daily battle reports, never would have tolerated Eichelberger's plan to let attrition take its toll.

A day after receiving the tanks, Eichelberger began to prepare for an all-out assault on Captain Yasuda's and Colonel Yamamoto's forces on the Urbana and Warren Fronts. In the waning light on the evening of December 17, five hundred Australian infantrymen assembled near the front. The Australians were the same troops who had defeated the Japanese at Milne Bay. They were new to the Warren Front and would lead the attack, while the Americans were held in reserve.

At sunup on December 18, the tanks and the camouflaged Australian troops moved out. Ahead of them sat the stranded Bren gun carriers that had failed to dent the Japanese defenses two weeks earlier. Farther ahead was the Duropa Plantation, with its elegant coconut palms swaying in the slight breeze. Underneath the trees in the long kunai, Colonel Yamamoto's elite 144th and 229th Infantry troops hid in their bunkers and machine gun nests, unaware of the approaching battle.

Just before 7:00 a.m., artillery battered the plantation. Ten minutes later, even before the smoke cleared, the Australians advanced. The General Stuarts opened up on the bunkers with their 37 mm guns. An American officer described the results: "The tanks really did the job. They apparently completely demoralized the Japs [who] fought like cornered rats." The Australians, wielding tommy guns and hurling grenades, moved forward in the wake of the tanks and caught Yamamoto's men by surprise.

Except for heavy Australian casualties, the day was a success. The Allies now controlled everything east of the Girua River except the Old Strip and Giropa Point.

In a letter to Sutherland that evening (each night Eichelberger penned a letter to MacArthur's headquarters and to his wife Emmaline), Eichelberger wrote, "I am glad he [Brigadier Wooten] has the tanks to help him. I do not believe he or anyone else would have gone very far without them."

General Harding had been vindicated. The tanks, however, had not arrived in time to save his career.

•   •   •

Meanwhile, Major General Yamagata was trying to rally the Japanese troops on the Urbana Front. On December 17, he issued a message to the front's commanders, calling for the "complete annihilation and expulsion of the enemy from the soil of New Guinea."

At the same time, Eichelberger was putting his men into position for an assault on the Government Station.

With the entire 127th at his disposal, Eichelberger relieved White Smith's 2nd Battalion, sending them to the village of Siremi for a well-deserved rest. To make up for the loss of White Smith's men, he pulled the Ghost Mountain Battalion, under Jim Boice, out of reserve after barely a week's rest. Boice moved a portion of his men into the

Coconut Grove and the rest of his troops into the Triangle east of Entrance Creek.

At the Triangle, bunkers, firing trenches, and chest-high swamp guarded every possible approach to the raised track that led to the Government Station. The plan was for two companies to attack the Triangle from the Coconut Grove via the bridge that spanned Entrance Creek, while a third company moved on the point of the Triangle from the south. Prior to the assault, the area would be subjected to an air strike and 81 mm mortar fire.

At 10:00 p.m. the evening before the assault, Boice and Bailey and their men maneuvered into position through thick sago swamp. Bailey felt the same poignant ache for home he always felt on the eve of battle. Only a week earlier he had received a packet of seventeen letters from Katherine. He read the letters hungrily and then he reread each one slowly three or four times until he knew their details by heart.

Katherine had also sent along three baby photos of Cladie Alyn. Swelling with pride, Bailey passed them out among the company.

Back at home Katherine and Cladie Alyn were on their way to the Bailey farm to share Bailey's most recent letter with his mother, Mamie. Mamie loved to have Katherine read the letters aloud to her, to hear the cadence of the sentences, her son's words.

Katherine looked forward to the visits, too. Even when she and Cladie were dating, she enjoyed going to the Bailey farm. She loved its simple grace: the white house with a porch across the front, the barn that Jim Bailey, Cladie's father, had built with lumber cut and milled on the farm, the fenced-in yard with the big oak, and the creek that wandered through the pasture behind the house. Now Katherine imagined how it would be when her husband returned. She and Cladie and Cladie Alyn would go down to the creek. They would roll up their pants and wade in the summer trickle.

· · ·

Jim Boice was feeling good. He knew Christmas was approaching and while in Australia, he had made arrangements with Block's

Department Store in Indianapolis to have presents delivered to Zelma and Billy and his mom. It was a special service the family owned store offered to soldiers. Boice imagined Zelma and Billy's surprise when they received the gifts. For Billy, he had ordered a pedal fire truck; for Zelma, hard-to-come-by nylon stockings and perfume; and for his mother perfume, too.

Boice was no pessimist, but sometimes it was hard, even for a man who had been taught since he was a small boy to look on the bright side, to imagine getting out of the jungle alive. He had been lucky; he had made it over the mountains. Once he got to Buna, Lady Luck was still at his side. In battle he had not been scratched. Somehow he had avoided the sniper's bullet on scouting trips. All the while, men were dying around him. He had prayed, but so had the others. Why did God hear one man's prayers and not another's?

Perhaps God would spare him long enough to let him hold Zelma again and to bounce Billy on his lap. Perhaps next year he would make it home for Christmas.

Boice would have given anything to be home. Instead, he was preparing to try to take the Government Station, the toughest target yet. Perhaps, though, God really was listening to his prayers. On Sunday, December 13, while in reserve, the battalion found time to conduct church services. Boice kneeled, laid his rifle down beside him, and bowed his head. The following day, the 127th captured Buna Village. Now, as they prepared to attack the Government Station, Boice hoped that perhaps it could be accomplished as easily. He had seen enough good men die.

•   •   •

At first light on December 19, Boice ordered the men to inspect their weapons. Jastrzembski, DiMaggio, and Stenberg had checked and rechecked theirs all night long. They knew how to care for their weapons. One of the guys in the company joked that he could take apart and put together his M-1 almost as fast as he could get his girlfriend's dress off.

Shortly before 7:00 a.m., the first part of the plan went into action.

Nine B-25s dropped 100- and 500-pound bombs on the Government Station. Fifteen minutes later a dozen A-20s bombed and strafed the coastal track between the station and Giropa Point. At 7:30 the mortars began firing. The bombardment lasted fifteen minutes.

At 7:45, Boice and Bailey led their men in the attack with the support of a rolling mortar barrage. They had not covered more than twenty yards when they got caught in fierce cross fire. The barrage had done little but antagonize the Japanese.

Out front, his feet raw and swollen, Boice ran, ducked, and crawled, trying to keep his men moving over the bridge.

"Move boys, keep on going!" he yelled. It wasn't any use, though; they were pinned down.

Boice ordered the men to retreat. In a large patch of kunai grass, some found cover while others pawed at the ground, carving out shallow foxholes. DiMaggio flopped down on his belly in the grass, thinking that he had just survived another close call. At Bottcher's Corner, after one Japanese attack, he realized that a bullet had come close enough to knock the bayonet off his rifle. During another battle, a rifle grenade had landed and exploded a foot from his head, and he was not even scratched.

Just then a Japanese soldier on the other side of the river fired a rifle grenade, and shrapnel flew everywhere. DiMaggio felt hot metal stick into the side of his face and embed itself in his jawbone. Minutes later, an aidman was at his side. Unable to extract the shrapnel, he bandaged DiMaggio's face and asked if he could walk back to the portable hospital. DiMaggio said he could.

A hundred yards back, a doctor informed DiMaggio that the piece of metal would be his ticket out of New Guinea.

Carl Stenberg had been even closer to the explosion than DiMaggio, and was thrown ten feet through the air when the grenade blew. When he landed, he felt for his limbs. They were all there. But his ear rang like a siren; he had ruptured his left eardrum.

Stanley Jastrzembski was sitting in his foxhole burning up with malaria. He had felt the explosion, but was far enough away from it that he was safe. Like everyone else, his nerves were frayed. "Damn jungle," he thought. "A guy can hardly see two feet in front of his face even in the daylight." Suddenly he felt someone jump next to him. "A Jap," he thought. "I'm a goner now." He whipped around to defend himself and then he heard an American voice.

"Hey, it's me Chet."

•   •   •

It was not unusual for Jastrzembski and Sokoloski to be together. They had gone to St. Michaels and later they enlisted in the Guard together. "A pair of Poles," they used to joke. But Sokoloski was supposed to be twenty yards away in his own foxhole.

"What the hell you doing over here? I thought you was a Jap. I almost shot you."

"I just saw some Japs," Sokoloski replied.

"So," Jastrzembski said. "Get back there and shoot them. That's why we're here, ain't we?"

"Sure as shit," Sokoloski thought. "I better get back."

"Keep your head down, you stupid Pole," Jastrzembski said to the shadow at the edge of his foxhole.

As soon as Sokoloski left, Jastrzembski felt alone and scared. It would have been nice to have someone with him. They could have said a prayer in Polish. They could have whispered the words right there in the mud with the Japs on the other side of the creek.

"Keep your head down, you stupid Pole," he hissed again.

An hour went by, then two. The Americans were still on the west side of the bridge. Boice knew that if they could not cross over and clear out the Triangle, the plan to take the Government Station was dead on arrival. Boice jumped up. Maybe, just maybe, they could make it over the bridge. He waved his arm and his men slipped out of the kunai and followed.

Boice might have heard the whine of the mortar shell, but there was not time to jump out of the way. The mortar landed at his feet and blew him into the air. Two of his men grabbed for him, and pulled him away from the bridge. When a medic arrived he checked Boice's vital signs, then called for a team of litter bearers. At 9:45, on December 19, only feet from the bridge over Entrance Creek, and only two days after being pulled out of reserve, Jim Boice was killed.

For hours, Boice's men made stabs at crossing the bridge, but by early afternoon, they were still stranded on the west side of the creek.

When Eichelberger heard the news, he ordered the mortarmen to lay down a wall of white phosphorous smoke as cover. The battalion, trailing the smoke, gained a few yards but was stopped short again. Two hours later the mortars fired another seven hundred rounds. The whole Triangle rumbled. No way, Bailey thought, no possible way the Jap bunkers could stand up to that kind of bombardment. The men tried to move forward again. They were hit by a fusillade of fire even before many made it out of their hiding spots.

At the Triangle, Bob Hartman, a recent addition to Company E, was leading a platoon through the jungle. His orders were to take out a pillbox. He was dumbfounded by the assignment. He had spent his entire military career in Service Company, and now because the 2nd Battalion needed healthy riflemen, he was in charge of an attack.

Hartman had never even seen a pillbox before, and his platoon was made up of guys as as green as he. Hartman and his men were moving through eight-foot-high kunai grass when he spotted an elevated trail. At last, he thought, now we won't have to trudge through the grass. He got to the trail and in a flash realized where he was. A fire lane! He dove into the kunai at the trail's edge. Just then a machine gunner opened up on him, and he felt the bullet hit. Fortunately, it had just scraped his arm. It was then that he realized his men might try to come to his aid.

"Stay over there," he yelled. "I'm okay."

As darkness crept into the jungle, Hartman pulled his platoon out and rendezvoused with Gus Bailey's men at the Coconut Grove. Jastrzemb-ski had survived another battle and thanked God for sparing his life. Out of the 107 men who began the attack, only sixty-seven remained.

•   •   •

The portable hospital was buzzing. It had not been set up to handle this many casualties. Every bed was full. The less seriously wounded lay in the mud, waiting to be taken care of.

One of the doctors was attending to Stenberg, but was more concerned about Stenberg's 104-degree temperature than his eardrum. He gave Stenberg six 5-grain quinine tablets, which he took all at once. A half an hour later, Stenberg could barely move or see.

No one knew what had become of Gus Bailey. He had led the attack. No one had seen him go down, and nobody had heard him scream. Just where was he, then?

Bailey was sitting against the base of a tree. He had taken a bullet, which had lodged in the meaty portion of his upper thigh. Rather than call for a medic, he had wrapped it himself, and continued to fight. Now, he obviously needed a doctor's attention. Bailey waited while Warmenhoven and the other doctors treated the soldiers with chest and abdominal wounds and head injuries. He was losing blood, and his leg was stiffening up, but he knew that he would make it.

The following day, the Ghost Mountain Battalion went into reserve again, and Gus Bailey was evacuated to Port Moresby.

Badly off as the Ghost Mountain Battalion was, Phil Ishio and William Hirashima knew from the diaries they had translated and the few prisoners they had interrogated that the Japanese were in even worse shape. They had very little food, no quinine, and according to Hirashima, "were almost dead from malaria."

The next day, Eichelberger turned over the job of taking Buna Government Station entirely to the 127th. Herman Bottcher, who was now a captain thanks to a rare field promotion, stayed behind to assist. Even with Bottcher's help, though, the 127th was unable to infiltrate the Triangle. In fact, its attack failed miserably. The lead company lost 40 percent of its troops, including Bottcher, who was wounded in the arm by a machine gunner and taken to the hospital at Dobodura.

At Dobodura, Bottcher was reunited with Harold Mitchell, who had been badly wounded during the December 19 attack. Mitchell, smiling wanly, was happy to see his friend, who, he had been told, had been killed with Captain Boice.

That night Mitchell died with Bottcher sitting at his side.

*   *   *

After the failure at the Triangle, Eichelberger was forced to reassess his strategy. Late on the evening of December 19, in a letter to Sutherland, he explained how he would cross Entrance Creek farther downstream, bypassing the Triangle. "General Herring," he wrote, "is very anxious for me to take the track junction, and I am most willing, but the enemy is . . . strong there and is able to reinforce his position at will. I am going to put in artillery on him . . . and I am going to continue that tomorrow morning. Then I am going to find a weak spot across Government Gardens."

It was a tidy plan.

On the morning of December 24, with five companies of the 127th in position, Eichelberger ordered a major attack. It began with artillery and mortars opening up on Government Gardens and the Government Station. Fifteen minutes later, the infantry moved out. What separated the 127th from its destination, though, was an obstacle course of thick, chest-high kunai grass, a swamp as wide as a football field, and a 300-yard coconut plantation. Eichelberger believed this to be the epicenter of the Japanese position. Captain Yasuda had prepared the entire area with bunkers, foxholes, firing pits, and snipers hiding in trees.

The regiment had advanced barely a hundred yards when it came up against blistering enemy fire that cut the companies to ribbons. Even with Eichelberger's artillery officer directing mortar fire from a coconut tree not far from Yasuda's lines, the Americans managed to carve out only another fifty yards. After being wounded in the back by a shell fragment, the artillery officer tied himself into the tree like a Japanese sniper and continued to direct the mortar fire until he lost so much blood that he lapsed into unconsciousness, and had to be evacuated.

Eichelberger, who was at the front for much of the day directing troop movements like a young lieutenant, was devastated by the failure of the attack. Christmas Eve day, 1942, he reported to MacArthur "was the low point of my life." MacArthur, though, did not want to hear it. He wanted results. Earlier he had callously told an Australian officer, who had complained that Eichelberger would get himself killed if he insisted on leading troops into battle, "I want him to die if he doesn't get Buna."

Back at the evac hospital in Dobodura, which was nothing more than a big tent with rows of cots, Stanley Jastrzembski was riding out a fever. He knew that the Americans had made a big push that day by the number of casualties that kept coming in. The worst were the belly wounds; those poor guys would moan and scream out all night long. What had really gotten to him, though, was Jim Broner. Broner had been shot in the leg in the battle on November 30.

Jastrzembski did not know what to say to him. His brother, Willard, was already dead. Had he heard?

"How ya doing?" Jastrzembski said, avoiding the subject.

Broner was lying on a cot and fumbled for words. Then he blurted it out. "Tomorrow," he said, "they're going to take my leg off."

What the hell for, Jastrzembksi thought to himself. The poor SOB is gonna lose his leg over some godforsaken island.

Toward evening, Jastrzembski's buddy Chet Sokoloski came in with a big smile on his face. Jastrzembski sat at the side of his cot and grimaced. His feet throbbed. They were raw and inflamed, and the skin was peeling off in small sheets like waxed paper.

"Why the smile?" Jastrzembski winced. "Just because you ain't dead, right?"

"Nope," Sokoloski replied. "It's Christmas Eve. Did you forget?"

"Christmas," Jastrzembski groaned. "In this hellhole of a place."

"I got you a package," Sokoloski said.

Sure enough. Jastrzembski looked at the return address. It was from one of his sisters. He shook his head. "All the way from Muskegon."

Jastrzembski was too weak to open the package, so Sokoloski did the honors. Tearing off the newspaper and opening the box, Sokoloski was dumbfounded. "Candy and cake," he said.

You're putting me on, Jastrzembski thought. Then Sokoloski passed him the box. There it was, a big Christmas cake.

"The damn thing's full of mold."

"Here," Sokoloski said. Taking his bayonet, he cut off the top two inches. Then Jastrzembski and Sokoloski—a pair of Poles—devoured it on Christmas Eve in New Guinea.

·   ·   ·

On Christmas Day, instead of regrouping and allowing his men to rest, Eichelberger decided to force the issue, returning to the Urbana Front again to direct operations personally.

When a company of the 127th pounded its way over hundreds of yards through Government Gardens, ending up on the coast near the coconut plantation, Eichelberger thought that perhaps his luck was changing. The Japanese quickly rallied, though, and surrounded the company, inflicting heavy losses. When reinforcements attempted to come to its rescue, they were ambushed, and an entire platoon was wiped out.

Eichelberger's Christmas Day attack had been a mistake, and he wondered if Buna would become "an American military disaster."

That night, returning to the command post, he found Sutherland waiting for him with disturbing news. The Australians, Sutherland said, were again mocking MacArthur. Despite a distinct numerical advantage, American troops had been unable to take Buna Government Station. Eichelberger argued that he had whole battalions—Stutterin Smith's Ghost Mountain boys and White Smith's men—that were no longer capable of fighting.

Sutherland then handed him a letter.

"What's this?' Eichelberger asked.

"MacArthur," Sutherland answered.

Later, Eichelberger sat down to read the letter. Although MacArthur had never visited the battlefield, he was full of "Ivory Tower" advice, all of which revealed his ignorance of frontline conditions at Buna. Urging Eichelberger to use his *superior* numbers, he wrote:

Where you have a company on your firing line, you should have a battalion; and where you have a battalion, you should have a regiment. And your attacks, instead of being made up of two or three hundred rifles, should be made by two or three thousand. . . . It will be an eye for an eye and a tooth for a tooth. . . . Your battle casualties to date compared with your total strength are slight so that you have a big margin still to work with.

I beg of you to throw every ounce of energy you have into carrying out this word of advice from me, as I feel convinced that our time is strictly limited and that if results are not achieved shortly, the whole picture may radically change.

With the memory of December 5 still fresh, Eichelberger must have been taken aback by MacArthur's letter. The general clearly wanted to see more casualties. It was a bloody calculus: dead and wounded soldiers were a sign of initiative.

Eichelberger's command was in jeopardy, and he knew it, so he sat down and penned a reply to the general. He was pushing the offensive, he wrote, with the kinds of numbers he felt the situation necessitated. And his men were indeed fighting gallantly. "I hope you will not let any Australian generals talk down their noses at you." Then he assured MacArthur that his men would "push on to victory." His earlier notion of letting attrition do the dirty work was no longer even a consideration.

Late on Christmas night a Japanese submarine, having escaped prowling American PT boats, unloaded rations and ammunition at Buna Government Station and shelled Allied positions on the Warren Front.

On the morning of December 28, Sutherland again showed up at Eichelberger's command post. This time, though, he arrived with good news: The 41st Division's 163rd Regiment, a unit of fit, superbly trained National Guardsmen from Montana, had just reached Port Moresby, and soon it would be sent to the Urbana Front. It was exactly what Eichelberger needed to hear. The previous night, he had read MacArthur's latest piece of fiction. It had left him fuming mad. "On Christmas Day," the communiqué read, "our activities were limited to routine safety precautions. Divine services were held."

Together, Eichelberger and Sutherland visited Colonel Grose's command post. Grose informed Eichelberger that he was pulling out the 127th's exhausted 3rd Battalion, which had made the Entrance Creek crossing and had born the brunt of the battle in Government Gardens.

Eichelberger's response shocked him.

"No John," Eichelberger replied. "That's not the plan. This afternoon I want you to attack the station."

Grose could not believe his ears, and asked for confirmation. When Eichelberger told him that was indeed his plan, it was left for Grose to implement some kind of strategy.

Deciding that one prong of the attack had to come from Musida Island, which separated Buna Village from the Government Station, Grose sent out five boats. Their objective was to engage the Japanese east of the island while engineers repaired the bridge that spanned the creek between the island and the Government Station.

The boats pushed off in the late afternoon. Disoriented, they went west instead of east, and American troops who were dug in on the sand spit northwest of the island figured they were enemy boats and opened up on them. A lieutenant from the lead boat, which sunk immediately, struggled to shore and managed to reach the spit without being killed by friendly fire.

The lieutenant shouted, "You're firing on Americans!" By the time the troops realized what they were doing and stopped, all five vessels had been sunk. Luckily no one had been killed.

Back at the bridge, 3rd Battalion troops tried to reach the station. At the far end of the bridge, though, the new pilings collapsed and the soldiers fell into the creek. Eichelberger, according to Grose, "ranted and raved like a caged lion." He had hoped to impress Sutherland. Sutherland, though, left Grose's command post in disgust. He had not been on hand to see the dramatic seizure of the Government Station, but instead witnessed the Keystone Kops in action.

The following day, Eichelberger's command was saved by a patrol's discovery: Captain Yasuda's men had evacuated the Triangle.

Later, on the same morning, the original Urbana Force—White

Smith's 2nd Battalion 128th, and the Ghost Mountain Battalion, minus Gus Bailey—was pulled out of reserve again and sent forward.

For Stenberg, being sent back into battle was a blow. At the battalion's bivouac site, he had sweated out another fever, and his left ear was worthless. He wondered now if he could hear well enough to save his own life. Would he be able to hear a stick crack just before a Jap gashed open his belly, or the shifting of a sniper hiding in the crook of a tree? He had been lucky on December 19, and he knew it. Now, he was being sent back in two days before the end of the year.

Stenberg and what remained of the 126th's 2nd Battalion took up a holding position at the southeast end of Government Gardens. White Smith's men moved into the Triangle. While the two battalions were en route, a company of the 127th pushed past the Government Station and established a pivotal two-hundred-foot frontage along the beach just west of Giropa Point.

•   •   •

While the Americans had finally fixed their supply problems—two hundred tons of cargo were coming in via freighter and lugger—the Japanese garrisons were being bombed into oblivion. At Girua, at the head of the Sanananda truck, Kiyoshi Wada, a member of the signal unit, chronicled the garrison's collapse.

On December 20, Wada wrote, "At this rate I'll become a dried-up human being." Three days later, he wrote again, "When we made our first attack I had no consideration for life or death. . . . However, nowadays, somehow I am full of the desire to go back home alive just once more."

The day after Christmas, Wada again found time to write: "The area around our tent is a desolate field. At about 8 o'clock, Hagino [Wada is referring to Private Mitsuo Hagino of the 144th Infantry Regiment's 3rd Battalion] next to me, was hit. Since so many patients came pouring in, the medical men are shorthanded and I was forced to stop the bleeding and bandage Hagino outside in the pitch dark." On December 28, Wada wrote despairingly. "Went to get water from the stream. On the way the jungle was full of dead, killed by shrapnel. There is something awful about the smell of the dead. . . . Everyone has taken cover in the jungle, but since there is no one to carry Hagino and take care of him, I cannot leave him behind. I have decided to stay. . . . All officers, even though there is such a scarcity of food, eat relatively well. The condition is one in which the majority is starving. This is indeed a deplorable state of affairs for the Imperial Army. I took out a picture of my parents and looked at it."

The next day, Wada continued, "What a discouraging and miserable state of affairs—and too, when the New Year is just ahead. What is going to happen to us? I pray to the morning sun that our situation of battle be reversed. All of the patrol (guard) unit has fled and at the present time, there are only four of us. . . . I pray with the charm of the clan deity in my hand."

                    •   •   •

On the Warren Front, a Japanese soldier read a leaflet dropped by Allied planes: "SOLDIERS OF THE JAPANESE ARMY," it said, "Our Allied Forces are steadily advancing on all fronts. . . . You are already doomed. Your situation is hopeless."

When he read the leaflet on December 21 the day it was dropped, he scoffed at it. The Old Strip was surrounded by swamp and littered with trenches and bunkers. The Japanese believed it was unassailable. Colonel Yamamoto's men were also heavily armed with machine guns and mortars, two 75 mm guns, two 37 mm guns, automatic cannons, and 3-inch naval guns. A week later, though, as Allied forces bore down on Japanese positions in the Old Strip and on Giropa Point, he was forced to take its message seriously. Officers continued to promise reinforcements, but even the lowliest Formosan conscripts knew what was happening.

Masaji Kohase, a First Class Seaman with the Yokosuka Special Naval Landing Force, watched the Allied advance. "The enemy," he wrote, "is trying to squeeze us out of our vital position by shelling the whole of Buna with mortar and artillery fire. Their tanks came rumbling forward and finally the time has come when we may meet our end any day, but we will fight till the last as our commander has ordered." As he wrote in his diary, his buddy may have been reading a letter from his twelve-year-old sister, and dreaming of home. Dated October 15, her letter read, "In the place, where you are now, there will be plenty pineapples, bananas, coconuts and other fruits, I think. I want to go and see the South Seas myself, sometime."

The following day the Allies captured the Old Strip. Now only Giropa Point remained.

On December 30, Eichelberger found out that Blamey had petitioned MacArthur for the 163rd and MacArthur had buckled. Reversing his earlier decision, MacArthur now agreed that the regiment should go to the Sanananda Front. From General Herring, Eichelberger also learned that the Australians were in no hurry to see the Americans capture Buna Government Station before Wooten took Giropa Point.

Eichelberger was mad as hell, and though he had planned to rest his troops on December 31, he called for an all-out attack that would precede Wooten's offensive. His troops would seize the Government Station first.

Counting on the element of surprise, Eichelberger's troops jumped off well before the sun crested the horizon. When they spotted two Japanese landing barges stranded on the beach, however, a number of men disregarded the strict "no fire" rule and tossed hand grenades at the barges. It was a stupid stunt, and gave away their position. The Japanese immediately lit up the area with flares and fired on the Americans wading through the shallows northeast of Musida Island.

Abandoning the attack, the Americans retreated as fast as they could. Colonel Grose intercepted them and ordered them forward. The attack had failed in general, but thanks to an alert company of 128th Infantry troops that had dug in at the sand spit, the Americans had their first real grasp on the Government Station. Eichelberger knew now that it was only a matter of time. The Japanese were caught in the Allied vise.

That night, Eichelberger wrote a note to Sutherland. "Little by little," he said, "we are getting those devils penned in and perhaps we shall be able to finish them shortly."

Glory was not to be Eichelberger's, though. By dusk on New Year's

Day, as a terrific lightning storm bore down on Buna, Wooten's tanks were clearing out the last pockets of enemy resistance on the Warren Front. On patrol, Stenberg and the small reconnaissance group he was a part of met up with a patrol from there. They exchanged greetings and smiles and then went about the dirty business of clearing out pockets of Japanese resistance. All could sense that the end was near.

Simon Warmenhoven had been moving between the Triangle and the Sanananda Front, stitching up troops and supervising the portable hospitals, making sure that they were performing as intended. For the last month and a half, he had only had one break and that was when he himself was hospitalized with a temperature of 105 degrees. Now, he finally had a moment to write home again.

Dearest Lover:

And how's my Mandy to-day? Been patiently waiting for the letters that just don't come any more lately? Well, honey, from now on they'll be coming in like old times. I'll be writing at least three a week again. It just couldn't be helped for awhile, and I'm sure you realize the reason. Hope you didn't worry too much about it. I'll assure you I'm safe and sound for which I'm very thankful. Will say that I've said plenty of prayers. I assure you on that point too that if anything happened, I wouldn't be afraid, but I do hope that we all may be together again. . . . I sure want to see my Mandy again, and Muriel and Ann, and also Simon Jr. I'll bet he's getting to be quite a boy already. Another two months and he'll be sitting at the high chair pounding with a spoon for his meals. . . . I had the lovesick dream last night. . . . when I woke up. . . . I found myself lying in my cot in our native hut. I dreamed that I'd returned back home, and that we didn't get along. . . . Wish I could dream that I was making love to you. . . . Remember New Year's Eve last year? Walking in New Orleans. . . . Well, Goodbye darling. Love to the children.
    All my heart's true love.
    Sam

●   ●   ●

Flashes of lightning lit up the coast. Before dawn on January 2, Japanese troops were fleeing any way they could. Twenty Japanese soldiers, carrying heavy packs, food, medicine, and three machine guns, tried to make a run for the stranded landing barges, hoping to somehow get them into the water. A company of 127th soldiers caught them in the act, and cut them down with machine guns and rifles.

Not long after, as the first rays of sunlight filtered through the clouds and splashed across the sea, White Smith's troops and the men of the 128th Infantry's 1st Battalion, which had established a stronghold between the Government Station and Giropa Point, saw Japanese soldiers swimming up the coast.

By daylight, in a scene reminiscent of General Horii's attempted escape two months earlier, Japanese soldiers by the hundreds, grabbing on to anything that would float, took to the sea. American and Australian machine gunners sprayed them with bullets. Then the artillery opened up. By 10 o'clock that morning, the air force was strafing the remaining swimmers. Those who had not already drowned were shot to death.

At the same time, American artillery pulverized Buna Government Station, and white phosphorous smoke shells set the entire area ablaze. Japanese soldiers ran from their bunkers, and American troops cut them down. Some of the Japanese were carrying M-1s and wearing American helmets and fatigues.

Stenberg's patrol went from bunker to bunker and destroyed each one with grenades. Sometimes the Japanese burst out swinging swords or bayonets. A number of Japanese climbed trees and hid, or rushed into the swamps. Those who remained in their bunkers, refusing to surrender or run, were buried alive.

While the Americans stormed Buna Government Station and flushed out the last of its defenders, Australian tanks were destroying the remaining bunkers at Giropa Point. As the Australians approached what had been Colonel Yamamoto's command post, two Japanese officers appeared. One was Yamamoto and the other Captain Yasuda, who earlier had left the Government Station to join Yamamoto.

"Surrender," the Australian commander shouted to the two officers. "You must surrender."

Yasuda and Yamamoto pretended not to hear the order. Yasuda
drifted off into a grove of coconut trees, while Yamamoto appeared to
be washing himself in the muddy waters of Siremi Creek. When he finished he rose and bowed three times in the direction of the morning
sun. Then turning to the Australians, he stood saber straight.

"I'll give you until I count ten to surrender," the Australian commander shouted.

Again Yamamoto did not respond. He tied a Japanese flag to the
blade of his sword. Then with one hand he raised the sword and with
the other he stretched the flag across his breast.

"Nine," yelled the Australian commander. A second later, the Australian riflemen shot Yamamoto dead. Later they found Yasuda. He
had committed suicide by cutting open his belly in the fashion befitting
a Japanese soldier.

.   .   .

That afternoon, Allied troops took control of Buna Government Station. The beach looked like a charnel house as the corpses of dead Japanese, some of which had been chewed on by sharks, rolled in on the
waves. They swelled in the sun and in no time were filled with maggots.

The following day, January 3, as Allied patrols hunted down
enemy stragglers, soldiers at "Maggot Beach" removed their boots
and rolled up their pant legs and walked barefoot in the warm sand.
Some men took the opportunity to wash their filthy clothes; some
swam naked in the bay. Others lay sprawled under the scarred trunks
of coconut palms or curled up in remnant foxholes.

Blamey and Herring sent messages congratulating Eichelberger.
The general's sense of accomplishment, however, was tempered by the
realization that he had sent too many soldiers to their deaths. In a letter to Emmaline, Eichelberger confessed, "To see those boys with their
bellies out of the mud and their eyes in the sun. . . . made me choke,
and then I spent a moment looking over the American cemetery which
my orders of necessity have filled from nothing."

Curiously, no message came from MacArthur. When two days later there was still nothing from the commander in chief, Eichelberger penned a brief letter to Sutherland, "Is your secretary sick?" he asked.

Nearly a week after American forces took Buna Government Station, MacArthur finally wrote Eichelberger. If the general was hoping for gushing praise, MacArthur disappointed him.

> Dear Bob,
>
> I am returning to G.H.Q., Brisbane, Saturday morning the 9th so will not see you until some later time. I have been wanting to personally congratulate you on the success that has been achieved. As soon as Fuller [Major General Horace Fuller, commanding general of the 41st Division] takes hold, I want you to return to the mainland. There are many important things with reference to rehabilitation and training that will necessitate your immediate effort. The 32nd Division should be evacuated as soon as possible so that it can be rejuvenated.
>
> I am so glad that you were not injured in the fighting. I always feared that your incessant exposure might result fatally.
>
> With a hearty slap on the back,
>
> Most cordially,
>
> MacArthur

On that same day, MacArthur issued a communiqué stating that the campaign in New Guinea was "in its final closing phase." "The Sanananda position has now been completely enveloped," MacArthur told correspondents. "A remnant of the enemy's forces is entrenched there and faces certain destruction. . . . This can now be regarded as accomplished."

Although MacArthur and his staff had described Sanananda as a "mopping up operation," Eichelberger and the Australians knew otherwise. Barely able to contain his disgust, Eichelberger would exclaim, "If there is another war, I recommend that the military. . . . and everyone else concerned, drop the phrase 'mopping up' from their vocabularies. It is not a good enough phrase to die for." Eichelberger added, "The best plan" for Sanananda "would seem to be to surround the area and cut off all supplies, accompanied by plenty of mortar fire and constant harassing. This seems to me very slow work, but I realize that any other decision may result in a tremendous loss of personnel without commensurate gains."

It was the exact approach that he and MacArthur had rejected at Buna.

Had the Allies known that Japanese Imperial General Headquarters in Tokyo had issued orders via Rabaul calling for the withdrawal of forces up the coast, they might have been content to ambush the fleeing soldiers and cut off the supply lines to the beachhead, condemning the Japanese who remained at Sanananda to a slow but certain death. Instead, they moved in for the kill.

*   *   *

The Americans who had arrived on the Sanananda Front late in November would not be part of the final offensive. Of the fourteen hundred men who had gone into battle, only 165 remained. In no condition to fight, they were pulled off the front before the final Allied assault on Sanananda.

Alfred Medendorp was not one of the 165. In late December, incapacitated by malaria and fifty-five pounds lighter than when he had left Nepeana in early October to cross the mountains, he was shipped to the evacuation hospital at Dobodura. The next day he and a group he described as "battered, filthy, long haired, gaunt, festering, stinking wretches" boarded a plane for Port Moresby.

Lieutenant Lester Segal was not one of them either. After a month on the Sanananda Front, he was transferred to Buna to attend to the men wounded in the siege of the Government Station. Because of a shortage of medics, he stayed on in the aftermath of the battle. Eventually, he, too, was evacuated to Port Moresby. Seriously ill—perhaps with scrub typhus—it was a "miracle," according to Medendorp, that Segal was still alive.

Of the 165 men, only ninety-five were able to march to the bivouac site at Siremi east of the Girua River. Father Dzienis was one of them. "Only then," Medendorp later learned, "did he surrender his festering, fever-ridden body to a hospital to begin a long fight for recovery."

At Siremi, Dzienis and the others washed and shaved for the first time in months, and were issued shelter halves and mosquito nets. Two days later, Eichelberger held a ceremony for them. "I received the troops," he wrote, "with band music. It was a melancholy homecoming. Sickness, death, and wounds," he wrote, "had taken an appalling toll. [The men] were so ragged and so pitiful that when I greeted them my eyes were wet."

.   .   .

On January 16, the 127th and the 163rd Infantry Regiments were ordered to attack the Japanese garrison at Sanananda. The 127th was to advance on the coastal track from Buna Village, blocking any attempt by the Japanese to flee east. Meanwhile, one battalion of the 163rd was to move up the Sanananda track to the coast while another battalion sealed off the escape route west of Huggins Roadblock. After clearing out the Japanese positions south of the roadblock, the men of the 163rd were to join Australia's 18th Brigade and advance north along the track.

On January 17, as the Allies converged on Sanananda, General Yamagata determined that the evacuation plan could not wait. The wounded and sick were to leave by landing barge. The rest of the troops were to escape any way they could—on foot, or by swimming up the coast. Upon reaching the mouth of the Kumusi or the Mambare River, they would be shipped even farther up the coast to Lae and Salamaua.

Kiyoshi Wada wondered if he would make it out alive. "I am left to take charge in this place," he wrote. "We think that tonight will be the last night for Girua and we talk about swimming together to Lae. Wonder if we can get away? Wakaichi will not leave us behind."

Late the following night, Wada, who had also read the Allied leaflets, continued, "We looked forward to getting on the boat tonight but because the wounded were put on first, we could not get on. . . . Reinforcements haven't come. There are no provisions. Things are happening just as the enemy says. . . . I don't think Wakaichi will leave us behind."

The next day, Yamagata delivered the evacuation orders to General Oda and sent an aide to carry them to Colonel Yazawa. That night Yamagata and his staff and over a hundred sick and wounded soldiers left Girua in two large motor launches. Later, a prisoner of war stated that the general made "room for himself by taking off the patients and men already loaded on the barge."

Oda was indignant: Yamagata, he believed, had taken the coward's way out. Early the next morning, Oda, Yazawa, and a large number of troops plunged into the swamp and ran smack into an Australian outpost. Yazawa, who had been in New Guinea since the overland assault on Port Moresby, was killed and, by some accounts, Oda was too. Other reports contend that Oda stayed behind. Realizing that his end was near, he told a soldier that he was going off "to smoke one cigarette at leisure." Soon afterward, the soldier heard two pistol shots and ran back to assist Oda. There he found the general and his supply officer lying on a cloak on the ground where they had killed themselves.

As the last evacuation boats pulled anchor, Kyoshi Wada was left standing on the beach, longing for home. He returned to the hospital and was killed by mortar fire early the following morning.

A day later, on January 22, 1943, the Buna-Gona-Sanananda campaign officially ended. Advancing Allied troops caught starved and weary enemy soldiers in their shelters or trying to escape and mowed them down. By day's end more than five hundred Japanese lay dead. It was the largest single-day slaughter since Gorari nearly three months earlier.

●   ●   ●

Carl Stenberg, like most of the men of Ghost Mountain battalion and the 128th Infantry Regiment, was already in Port Moresby, waiting to be transported south to Australia. Days before the fall of Sanananda, he had left Dobodura and was flown over the Owen Stanley mountains. The entire trip took forty-five minutes.

Stenberg had been marching or fighting for over three months. His ear throbbed and bled and he was woozy with malaria. His lower legs were a patchwork of jungle sores. And when he slept the nightmares came: He was stranded in a swamp, stuck up to his hips in mud that gripped like quicksand. The tide was in and the water crept to his chest. He held his head high to breathe as rats glided by, making their way through the black scum.

Stanley Jastrzembski was lying in a hospital bed not far from Stenberg. Early in January, after a nine-day regimen of quinine, atabrine, and plasmochin, Jastrzembski's fever broke; but now it was soaring again. Wrapped in towels and ice, he lay on a cot, unable to escape the smell. He was back in the jungle, waiting and watching. Bodies bloated by the heat floated past. They were smiling. He could see their gold fillings.

$$\bullet \qquad \bullet \qquad \bullet$$

In late December 1942, Simon Warmenhoven was appointed division surgeon at the request of General Eichelberger and received a rare battlefield promotion to lieutenant colonel. In mid-January, as the Allied attack on the Sanananda and Girua garrisons was about to begin, Warmenhoven turned thirty-three and was still performing surgeries in a poorly lit tent. On January 20, he learned that he was being sent back to Port Moresby. He arrived in Australia not long afterward and went directly to a hospital for treatment of hookworm. In late February he returned to Camp Cable, where he took up residence in a small wooden house. The first thing he did was to put pictures of his family on his dresser. Warmenhoven was now a celebrated doctor. Articles in newspapers across the U.S. were praising his bravery in New Guinea and his medical achievements just behind the front lines. In early March, his picture was on the front page of the *New York Times*.

Back in Australia, Warmenhoven did not feel like a celebrity. He worked around the clock seven days a week nursing the Red Arrow men back to health while neglecting his own needs. In early April, exhausted, he suffered a malaria attack and was hospitalized for three weeks. At the time, doctors little understood the possible toxic effects of large doses of atabrine and quinine. The term "atabrine psychosis," characterized by drug-induced manic depression and schizophrenic episodes, had only recently been coined. Nevertheless, Warmenhoven was treated aggressively. Upon returning to Camp Cable three and a half weeks later, he learned that MacArthur was preparing to send the 32nd back into combat. As division surgeon, he was asked to sign a medical release stating that the division was healthy enough to return to active duty.

He refused.

On Monday night May 3, 1943, he wrote Mandy.

Dearest Lover:

Had a lovely letter from you yesterday, darling. Came at the right time too believe me. Sure had the "blues" here for a couple of days. That's why I haven't written you. I don't often allow myself to get that way but after all, when one is away from his best friend in the world <u>you</u> my wife, and away from such grand children, you just can't help it. I love the way you ended your letter, Sweetheart, about "not being so far apart because we'll live forever in each other's hearts."

Lovingly Always, Sam

Two days later, Lieutenant Colonel Simon "Sam" Warmenhoven shot himself in the head.

EPILOGUE

I laid him down by the bend in the stream;
And erected a cross at his head.
His funeral song was a kockatoo's scream,
As if they knew my buddy was dead . . .

I've evened the score, yes, a dozen times o'er,
But no matter the distance between,
My mind wanders yet and I'll never forget,
His grave by the bend in the stream.

BOB HARTMAN,
BUNA VETERAN

It would take months for the 32nd Division to be transported to Australia, where upon arriving, the sick and wounded were sent to a variety of hospitals in the Brisbane area. Those in relatively good health went to Coolangatta on Australia's Gold Coast for R&R. The men chased girls and got roaring drunk. They told stories, too. The stories were not sad or dark; in fact, according to Bill Sikkel, they were full of "GI humor." The one that really busted up Sikkel and the guys who had been on the Sanananda Front was about Father Dzienis.

It was in late November and Father Dzienis excused himself from a conversation to visit the recently dug two-hole outhouse. When a Japanese navy ship shelled the track, Dzienis came running out with his pants down around his ankles, "mad as a hornet."

"To hell with the Geneva Conventions," he thundered (according

to the Geneva Conventions, a chaplain was not allowed to be armed).
"Give me a pistol!"

• • •

When victory at Sanananda was declared on January 22, 1943, the
war on New Guinea's Papuan Peninsula came to a close. For the first
time in World War II the Allies had defeated the Japanese in a land
operation. Two and a half weeks later, the fighting on Guadalcanal
ended.

New Guinea was a flashback to earlier wars. General Eichelberger
called it a "poor man's war," one largely unaffected by America's
industrial machine. For two months, the Allies beat at nearly impenetrable enemy defenses. One American destroyer, bombarding Japanese
positions, could have shortened the campaign by weeks. Shallow-draft
landing craft, commonplace when the Marines invaded Guadalcanal,
could have brought the campaign to a quicker close by hauling in
much-needed tanks and artillery. Even something as basic as transport
ships reliably delivering supplies could have eased the suffering of the
soldiers.

Eventually, the Allies succeeded in pounding the Japanese into submission, but at what cost? What would MacArthur have lost by letting
the Japanese starve? Major Mitsuo Koiwai was the commanding officer of the 2nd Battalion, 41st Infantry. When captured at the end of
the war, he said, "We lost at Buna because we could not retain air
superiority, because we could not supply our troops. . . . We were in
such a position . . . that we wondered whether the Americans would
bypass us and let us starve."

At the war's end, MacArthur privately resolved to never again
force a "head-on collision of the bloody, grinding type." There would
be "No more Bunas," he said. On the other hand, he publicly congratulated himself during the war for his patient execution of the campaign. On January 28, he issued his final campaign communiqué,
declaring that in the battle for New Guinea the "time element was . . .
of little importance." It added, "The utmost care was taken for the
conservation of our forces, with the result that probably no campaign

in history against a thoroughly prepared and trained army produced such complete and decisive results, with so low an expenditure of life."

Correspondents who had witnessed firsthand the brutality of the campaign were outraged by MacArthur's claim. It was a piece of fiction, a brazen lie. When some refused to wire the text to their editors, MacArthur's headquarters threatened to expel them from the SWPA.

Eichelberger was flabbergasted by MacArthur's claim. Was this the same MacArthur who had told General Harding to "Take Buna Today At All Costs"? Was this the same commander in chief who told him to "take Buna or don't come back alive"? Eleven years later, in a letter to Samuel Milner, the army's official historian, Eichelberger wrote, "The statement to the correspondents in Brisbane after Buna that 'losses were small because there was no hurry' was one of the great surprises of my life. As you know, our Allied losses were heavy and as a commander in the field, I had been told many times of the necessity for speed."

Eichelberger was justifiably bitter. Demonized by his men, he bore the brunt of MacArthur's sense of urgency. He would later write, "The great hero went home without seeing Buna before, during or after the fight while permitting press articles from his GHQ to say he was leading his troops in battle. MacArthur . . . just stayed over at Moresby 40 minutes away and walked the floor. I know this to be a fact." Though MacArthur had never bothered to visit the front "to see first hand the difficulties our troops were up against," he continually hounded Eichelberger "to push on to victory."

Victory at Buna and Sanananda came at a huge cost. Eichelberger wrote in his book, *Our Jungle Road to Tokyo,* "Buna was . . . bought at a substantial price in death, wounds, disease, despair, and human suffering. No one who fought there, however hard he tries, will ever forget it." Fatalities, he continued, "closely approach, percentage-wise, the heaviest losses in our own Civil War battles." Historian Stanley Falk agreed. "The Papuan campaign," he wrote, "was one of the costliest Allied victories of the Pacific war in terms of casualties per troops committed."

The combined victory at Buna, Sanananda, and Gona, though costly, was psychologically and strategically momentous. Together with the fall of Guadalcanal, it destroyed the myth of Japanese invincibility. Strategically, it broke Japan's hold on New Guinea, ensuring the security of the Australian continent and the American supply line to the Pacific.

Buna-Sanananda was not the 32nd Division's only campaign. In December 1943, it returned to battle in New Guinea at Saidor, followed by invasions of Aitape on the New Guinea's far north coast, and Morotai, near the island of Halmahera, between New Guinea and the Philippine island of Mindanao. Later, it participated in the liberation of the Philippines at Leyte and Luzon.

Although the division's battles were overshadowed by the likes of Tarawa, Saipan, and Iwo Jima, Eichelberger managed to put the Red Arrow men's contributions into perspective:

"Some of the Pacific history has been written, but little of it has been concerned with the men I commanded—the ordinary, muddy, malarial, embattled, and weighed-down-by-too-heavy-packs GIs. They waded through the surf, they struggled through the swamp mud . . . they cut tracks which ultimately became roads leading to the airfields they constructed. They were the true artisans of the island-hopping campaign in the Pacific which led ultimately to the Philippines and Tokyo. They called it—The Hard Way Back."

It was, in fact, the 32nd Division to which General Yamashita surrendered near Kiangan on September 2, 1945. By the war's end the 32nd Division had been in combat for 654 days.

As costly as its other campaigns were, none could compare with Buna and Sanananda, where the division's casualties pushed 90 percent. Out of the nearly eleven thousand troops in the division's three combat teams, there were 9,688 casualties. According to Samuel Milner, the division's 126th Infantry Regiment "had ceased to exist." Of the 131 officers and 3,040 enlisted men who went into battle in mid-November, only thirty-two officers and 579 enlisted men remained when the last remnants of the regiment were transported to Port Moresby in late January. The 126th's Ghost Mountain Battalion was down to 126 men and six officers. Companies E, F, G, and H had been reduced to the size of platoons. Each had fewer than thirty men.

West of the Girua River on the Sanananda Front, the Antitank and Cannon Companies and the 3rd Battalion fared just as poorly. As of January 20, 1943, Antitank had just ten men. None of the other companies had more than twenty.

Illness represented the vast majority of those casualties. Of the 9,688 casualties, 7,125 of them were due to illness. On the battlefields of Buna and Sanananda, malaria, dysentery, dengue fever, scrub typhus, and hookworm were as debilitating as enemy bullets.

When the entire division assembled at Camp Cable in April 1943, Simon Warmenhoven was shocked by the condition of the soldiers and their inability to recover. Physicals revealed that men had lost a quarter to a third of their body weight. Sam DiMaggio was down to 135 pounds and had blackwater fever. His liver and spleen were enlarged and his urine was the color of a Buna swamp. Others were suffering from exhaustion, malnutrition, and anemias related to vitamin deficiencies.

Those with hookworm, dysentery, and anemias eventually responded to treatment. The majority of the malaria cases, however, did not. Men with malaria got worse instead of better, suffering relapse after relapse.

Bill Sikkel's personal malaria report is illustrative of what Stenberg and many of the Red Arrow men experienced. Sikkel had led patrols on the Sanananda Front since the third week in November. Stricken with high fevers, he was taken off the Sanananda track and evacuated to Port Moresby on Christmas Eve, 1942. Treatment in Port Moresby consisted of three days of quinine, then three days of atabrine, then three days of plasmochin. Following that, he took one atabrine tablet per day. Upon reaching Australia, before going to Coolangatta, he, like many other soldiers, was quarantined and given a seventeen-day malarial treatment. Australian officials were worried that malaria could spread in epidemic proportions throughout the continent; returning troops were banned from Australian territory north of 19 degrees south latitude, an area known for its large mosquito populations. On March 11, Sikkel suffered another malaria attack and was hospitalized at the 155th Station Hospital at Camp Cable. After a positive smear, he received nineteen days of quinine, atabrine, and plasmochin in addition to adrenaline shots. That treatment was followed by six weeks in a malaria rest camp at which he received one atabrine tablet per day. Three months later, Sikkel suffered a third attack. It was the worst of the three. He was admitted to a U.S. Navy hospital at Nelsons Bay, New South Wales, and then transferred to the 47th Station Hospital in Sydney, where he was diagnosed with malaria, bronchitis, and hookworm, and was hospitalized for forty-three days.

By September 1943 when the 32nd was preparing to return to New Guinea, 2,334 men, judged "unfit for combat," were dropped from the division roster.

The decimation of the 32nd Division by disease was not an isolated incident. By the end of 1942, the Australians had 15,575 cases of infectious disease: 9,249 cases of malaria, 3,643 cases of dysentery, 1,186 cases of dengue fever, and 186 cases of scrub typhus.

And as badly off as the Americans and the Australians were, the Japanese suffered more. One Japanese official called New Guinea "a magnificent tragedy." Of the sixteen to seventeen thousand troops committed to the campaign, they lost roughly twelve thousand, many to dengue fever, malaria, dysentery, and even beriberi, a disease directly related to starvation.

One thing is clear: MacArthur came away from New Guinea with a profound respect for the destructive power of malaria. In future campaigns he made sure that troops were supplied with malaria tablets, mosquito netting, protective clothing, and training in antimalaria procedures. By October 1944, when MacArthur returned to the Philippines, malaria was no longer a significant problem among Allied ground troops.

Some historians believe that MacArthur learned a number of other lessons at Buna, responding to its savagery by developing his policy of "bypassing" or "leapfrogging," a "hit 'em where they ain't" strategy that relied on the efficacy of air power and amphibious operations. After Buna, MacArthur avoided enemy strongholds. Rushing the construction of airstrips, he pounded the Japanese supply line, leaving bases to "wither on the vine." This strategy, MacArthur admitted, was "as old as warfare itself." Admiral Nimitz had already used it to great effect in the central Solomons and would again later in the central Pacific when he jumped from the Gilbert Islands to the Marshalls and then to the Marianas. MacArthur, though, got credit for it.

.   .   .

For the natives of New Guinea, who according to General Blamey could not be given "too much praise," nothing would ever be the same. Yet, as the war moved up the coast of New Guinea, the natives, and especially the carriers, were forgotten. According to a former ANGAU administrator, "Carriers and conscripted village men never received their just rewards." Author Alan Powell writes that this remains "a lasting stain on Australia's war record."

What's more, civilized warfare had clearly wrought greater destruction than centuries of tribal battles. An estimated fifteen thousand New Guineans died as a direct result of the war and tens of thousands more died of disease and starvation.

According to John Waiko, a native New Guinean, who was born a year after the campaign ended, war had a profound effect on people: "The villages suffered severely, without men to clear gardens, hunt, maintain houses and canoes, etc. . . . The women were strained from overworking, there was . . . high infant mortality, there was all the grief of separation and bereavement and the frightening . . . loss of will to live . . . "

The people of the Buna coast, in particular, returned to find their land strewn with the detritus of war. Airfields and roads quickly fell into disrepair. Undetonated shells lay scattered around the swamps. The population of crocodiles burgeoned. Rotting corpses fouled drinking holes, homes and gardens had been destroyed, birds and animals had disappeared, and trees were nothing but bare, bullet-ridden trunks. In the sunlight and stagnant water of bomb craters, mosquitoes bred, malaria cases skyrocketed, and the disease became more virulent by passage through many human hosts.

.   .   .

Sam DiMaggio recovered from blackwater fever in time to take part in the battles of Saidor, Aitape, Morotai, and Leyte, where he suffered on and off from malaria. He was discharged on points (a soldier needed only eighty-five combat points to get back home and DiMaggio had 130) one day before his company shipped out to Luzon. Once back in the States, he was sent to Fort Ord in California, where he was in charge of a barracks of a hundred men who were training to go to the Pacific. He was at Fort Ord on V-E Day, May 8, 1945, and in Albion, Michigan, on V-J Day, September 2, 1945. DiMaggio received a Combat Badge, a Purple Heart, the Bronze Star, and four campaign stars for his service. His brother Jimmy was killed in northern France by a German sniper in November 1944. DiMaggio had six more malaria attacks after he was discharged in July 1945 with the rank of sergeant. The piece of shrapnel that lodged in his jawbone on December 19, 1942, is still there today.

Suffering from jungle rot and malaria, Stanley Jastrzembski was put on limited duty in Sydney, Australia, where he guarded a stockade. Although he had enough points to get home, he stayed on until Japan surrendered—until, as he says, "the last dog was hung." Jastrzembski was discharged in mid-August 1945. He was awarded the Bronze Star for his service.

Gus Bailey won the army's second highest award—the Distinguished Service Cross—for his heroism at Buna. Back in Australia, he was promoted to captain and made commander of the 126th's 1st Battalion. He took part in the battles of Saidor, Aitape, Morotai, and Leyte. Although he had been offered a position as regimental executive officer, which would have kept him off the front lines, Bailey turned it down and was killed by a Japanese grenade on the Villa Verde Trail on the island of Luzon on April 25, 1945. He was awarded the Silver Star posthumously. In February 1949, his body was returned to the U.S.

Carl Stenberg was put on limited service in Australia, where he was assigned to a replacement depot in Brisbane and later to Signal Section headquarters. In August 1944, Stenberg was bound for the United States aboard a Norwegian freighter, and four months later he was discharged. He suffered from malaria attacks for another ten years and still has scars on his legs from jungle ulcers. Stenberg received the Combat Infantry Badge, the Presidential Citation, two Oak Leaf Clusters, and the Bronze Star, but what he treasures more than anything else is the Christmas card he received from Jim Broner in December 1996. The note reads: "I will never forget the effort that you made in saving my life, so many years ago: And believe it or not I'm still enjoying every minute."

Paul Lutjens spent a year in Australia, recuperating from malaria and the wounds he sustained in battle on December 5 and was awarded the Purple Heart, the Bronze Star, and the Distinguished Service Cross. When he returned to the United States, he was still so gaunt he could wrap his hands around his waist. The first thing he did was to make his way to San Jose, California, and propose to Lorraine Phillips, the woman to whom he wrote from the swamp on November 29, 1942. He and Lorraine were married at the Presidio in San Francisco. In February 1944, he traveled to military bases throughout the South, lecturing about the Buna campaign to troops preparing to go overseas. Afterward, he embarked on a career in military intelligence and counterintelligence, and was stationed at bases across the United States, as well as in the Philippines and Japan. Later, he commanded military intelligence groups in Hawaii, Germany, and at the Presidio.

Herbert "Stutterin'" Smith was sent to the 105th General Hospital at Gatton, about thirty miles from Brisbane, where he recuperated in a small ward with Paul Lutjens and Harold Hantlemann (Hantlemann would eventually marry the ward's Red Cross nurse). Afterward he was made executive officer and port inspector of Base Section 4 in Melbourne. Just before going back to the United States, he checked into the 4th General Hospital, where his roommates were Guadalcanal veterans from the 1st Marine Division. According to Smith, "They continuously harped about the tough times they had endured" until one day Smith put on his blouse and they asked him where he acquired his ribbons—a Combat Infantry Badge, the Purple Heart, and the Distinguished Service Cross. When Smith told them Buna, they did not refer again to Guadalcanal in his presence. On October 6, 1943, Smith sailed for the United States and not long after he retired from the military. On June 28, 1990, forty-six years after he left the army, the State of Wisconsin honored Smith with the Wisconsin National Guard Distinguished Service Medal.

Captain Alfred Medendorp suffered recurrent malaria and was classified as "unfit for combat duty." He was reassigned to the Amphibious Training Center where he worked with the navy to improve the performance of troop and equipment landing craft. He was rotated home in April 1945 and was awarded the Purple Heart, the Bronze Star, and the Combat Infantry Badge. In 1950, Medendorp (by then a major) volunteered for active duty during the Korean War. He was stationed at Fort Monroe, Virginia, until the spring of 1954. He was then assigned to the Military Assistance Advisory Group in Taiwan. On September 3, 1954, during his inspection of Chinese Nationalist Forces on the island of Quemoy (now Kinmen Island), a mile and a half from the Chinese mainland, Medendorp was killed during an artillery barrage.

General Eichelberger said of Herman Bottcher, "He was one of the best Americans I have ever known." For his heroism at Buna, Bottcher was given a rare battlefield commission as a captain and awarded the Distinguished Service Cross. Bottcher was killed in Leyte on November 28, 1944. Although he had achieved the rank of major, he was making a lone reconnaissance behind enemy lines in the Ormoc Valley when he was cornered in a rice paddy by a Japanese patrol. He held off the Japanese for four hours, but was finally killed by two rifle slugs to the head. Legend has it that advancing American soldiers of the 32nd Division found him facedown in a puddle of mud, still gripping his pistol. He is buried in the Manila American Cemetery. Today a memorial to Herman Bottcher stands in the village of Buna.

General Edwin Forrest Harding went on to become commanding general of the Panama Mobile Force, where he trained units in jungle warfare. Unlike Eichelberger, he never took the opportunity to justify himself in a postwar memoir. In 1946 Harding retired to Franklin, Ohio, to the stately family home. He remained the favorite general of

32nd Division veterans. One veteran said, "His greatest fault was that he loved his troops and could not stand to see them slaughtered." At a reunion, they presented General Harding with a Bronze Red Arrow plaque, which he treasured.

On June 21, 1943, in Grand Rapids, Michigan, Lieutenant Colonel Simon Warmenhoven was posthumously awarded the Distinguished Service Cross. Henrietta "Mandy" Warmenhoven saved every one of her husband's 160 letters.

Notes

In putting this book together, I have used countless interviews—with veterans of the march and the campaign, and wives, children, grandchildren, and friends of the participants—to elaborate on the official army narrative. I have also used self-published books, diaries, newspaper articles, and veterans' printed recollections to bring the human history to life. Major Herbert M. "Stutterin'" Smith wrote three informative books about his experience: *Four Score and Ten; 0-241957;* and *Hannibal Had Elephants II.* The Indiana author Wendell Trogdon wrote a wonderful biography of Gus Bailey called *Out Front: The Cladie Bailey Story.* Sam DiMaggio dictated his biography to his son J. P. DiMaggio; it's called "I Never Had It So Good." Captain Alfred Medendorp left behind two detailed accounts of the march and the ensuing war. The first is an official document published by the Ground General School in October 1949, titled "The March and Operations of Antitank and Cannon Companies . . . (Personal Experience of a Patrol Commander)." The second is an extensive (over one hundred pages), untitled collection of personal memories. Walter Shauppner left behind a diary in which he detailed the day-by-day activities of the 127th Infantry Regiment, beginning with its arrival at Port Moresby Harbor. Lawrence Thayer wrote a revealing account of the 128th's experiences. Clarence Jungwirth wrote *Diary of a National Guardsman in WWII,* an informative account of his experiences from 1940 to 1945. Paul Lutjens left behind a diary and the text of his lecture on the Papuan campaign. General Edwin Forrest Harding's diary is also an excellent source of information. Courtesy of Walter Hunt, Jim Hunt's brother, I have Lieutenant Hunt's diary and an enlightening letter that Hunt sent to Major Herbert Smith after reading one of Smith's books. Jim Boice's diary was very useful, as were Lieutenant Colonel Bill Sikkel's recollections and those of Gordon Zuverink,

Herb Steenstra, and Stanley Hollenbeck. Simon Warmenhoven's letters were important sources of information. The letters provided me with insight into a remarkable man. Art Edson's letters were also very helpful. Maclaren Hiari's account of his father's experiences as a carrier for the Allied Forces in New Guinea was also quite helpful. The Wisconsin Veterans Museum (and its very capable staff) proved to be a treasure trove of information. The museum has a large collection of letters, diaries, audio interviews, and photographs donated by veterans and/or their families.

This book would have been impossible to write without the help of a number of secondary sources: *Victory in Papua,* written by Samuel Milner, the offical U.S. Army historian of the campaign; *Bloody Buna* by Lida Mayo; *Kokoda* by Paul Ham; Eric Bergerud's *Touched with Fire;* Harry Gailey's *MacArthur Strikes Back; Papuan Campaign, the Buna-Sanananda Operation,* put out by the Center of Military History, U.S. Army; and the "Report of the Commanding General Buna Forces on the Buna Campaign."

In order to portray the Japanese experience and some of the soldiers whom this book mentions, I used the National Archives' collection of Allied Translator and Interpreter Section (ATIS) diaries and interrogation reports. Other primary sources were *Nankai Shitai, War Book of the 144th Regiment,* translated by F. C Jorgensen, Seizo Okada's *Lost Troops,* and *Southern Cross,* translated by Doris Hart.

I have also used my personal observations of the landscapes to inform certain scenes and to describe some of the settings for the story. I have visited Papua New Guinea five times. My first trip was in 1989. Fascinated with the country, I kept coming back, and that is how I discovered the story of the Ghost Mountain boys.

It is impossible to spend any time in New Guinea without encountering World War II history. Strewn across the mountains are pieces of planes that went down during the war. The coastal waters teem with reminders, too. While scuba diving, I saw submarine caverns, downed planes, remnants of transport ships and luggers, and large, twisted pieces of metal dating back to the war.

In the mountain villages along the Kapa Kapa trail, people still tell stories of the U.S. Army's march across the mountains. Villagers showed me where soldiers collapsed in the mud, unable to go on, where they camped, and where the few soldiers who died on the trek were buried. One of my most fortuitous encounters was with a man named Berua, whom I met in the village of Laruni. Berua was only seven when his parents were chosen to serve as carriers for the American army. Frightened that he would never see them again, he followed his parents and the American army over the Owen Stanleys. It was an experience he would never forget.

On the coast, villagers still talk of the war. These war stories have become part of the local mythology, passed down by people from one generation to the next around the fire. Fascination and resentment linger. The war destroyed villages and innocent people's lives.

In many cases the locals' stories resembled the accepted historical version. However, in some cases, they have been wildly, and interestingly, embellished. One man suggested that it was a native sorcerer who had warned the Allies of the Japanese invasion. He went on to say that the sorcerer later flew over Japanese positions on the coast and alerted American artillerymen so that they could sight their big guns. Another man said that the war ended when a native sorcerer killed Japan's most important general.

In the summer of 2005, I made a one-month trip to Papua New Guinea. I spent that month researching the war and the trail. I also visited Gabagaba, Doboduru, Buna, Siremi, Oro Bay, Pongani, Wanigela, and a number of inland villages, where I interviewed elders who had witnessed the war. In Buna, I heard stories of the Japanese invasion. In Gabagaba, people talked about the arrival of the Americans, especially the African-American engineers.

In the United States, during the summer of 2005, prior to my trip to Papua New Guinea, I attended a five-day 32nd Division Old Timers gathering at Fort McCoy, Wisconsin. Our accommodations were army barracks. On my first day, I watched a man make his bed as if a tough sergeant would be inspecting his work: Not a crease in the top sheet, the corners tucked in, the pillow fluffed like a cumulous cloud.

Although it was only early June, it was already in the high 90s. Enormous fans cooled the barracks, but they only did so much. I did not understand how the older guys could take it until they set me straight.

"This is a breeze compared to New Guinea," one said.

I was in the real old-timers' barracks. Bill Barnes, who was a second lieutenant at Buna, was ninety-five. He wore big Coke-bottle glasses and had a pacemaker but looked like he could still run a marathon. Lawrence Chester Dennis was 93. At Buna, he had run messages from headquarters to various companies across the front, earning him the nickname "moving target." Dennis was nearly blind now, so the guys set out his clothes, made his bed, took him to the bathroom, and made sure he got to the events on time.

Then there was Roy Gormanson, who, the first time I met him, took off his tie and shirt and showed me his mangled left shoulder. "Took three operations to get it this good," he said. "And still I can't lift my arm over my head."

Many of the guys in my barracks had trouble walking. Nearly everyone had diabetes. A bunch had been through heart bypasses. They all took an assortment of pills. Yet for five days they joked with each other as if they were young GIs. They joked wherever they went—in the mess hall, in the communal showers, as they peed into a large trough, and in the morning on the "shitter" that sat in plain view of five or six others.

"No goddamn privacy in the army," an old-timer commented.

One morning one of the guys announced as he settled onto a toilet seat that he was going to die, but not of a stroke or a heart attack or colon cancer. "I want to be shot by an irate husband," he said. The entire bathrooom roared.

At night the guys played poker in the mess hall and drank beer. And sometimes they talked about the war. Mostly, though, it was a subject they avoided. Red Lawler, who was in his nineties and ran a pizza parlor in Oshkosh, Wisconsin, said, "I saw so much death in New Guinea, I like to forget. It was a horrible place."

One man—I never did learn his name—told me that when the battle for Buna was almost over and the Americans were mopping up, looking for stray Japanese soldiers, he and a young private stood on a beach. The private had just finished showing him a photo of his wife and little boy. "Sure can't wait to get back to them," the private said. Just then a shot cracked out of the jungle, and the private fell. The bullet had taken away half his head.

After the Old Timers event I spent the next six months interviewing and collecting stories. I drove across the Midwest and called Texas, Boston, New York, Florida, Ohio, Washington, D.C., and California.

I heard the same from almost every veteran. "There are few of us left. You should have done this book ten years ago. Hurry up and finish so I'm around to read it."

One man from Michigan had a list of everyone from his company, and started reading off the names. "Gone," he said. "Dead. He's gone, too. He passed away not too long ago. He's dead, too, now. Goddammit," he said, as if realizing it for the first time, "they're all gone."

Eventually it was clear that with so many of the guys gone I would have to start contacting sons and daughters, even grandkids. That search brought me to southern Indiana.

William "Jim" Boice, the man who had led the initial reconnaissance patrol across the island, was from Indiana, and his son still lives there. Bill Boice Jr., in his mid-sixties, runs a manufacturing business, and walks and talks with an unlit cigar in his mouth. After giving me a tour of his plant, he and his wife Joyce kindly invited me to their house, where together we went through old newspaper clippings and photos that his mother had saved. Then we had lunch. After lunch we read entries from his father's diary and then we got to his father's letters.

When Bill Jr. read them, his voice shook. Handing the letters to me, he said, "Read 'em, I can't." Neither could I.

It was after my visit to Bill Boice that I began writing. And it was then that I decided I was going to walk across New Guinea in the footsteps of the Ghost Mountain boys.

My journey began with my scouting trip in August 2005. Almost everyone I met in Papua New Guinea warned me not to try to repeat the march. The Kapa Kapa was a rugged hunting and trading trail in 1942. No one knew if it still existed. Besides, they said, the country was too rough: cliffs, rivers, snakes, mountains, mosquitoes, leeches, and disease. And who knows, they said, whether the people will let you walk through their tribal lands. Some of those mountain villagers barely know the outside world exists. They still hunt with spears and slingshots.

In June 2006 I began the trip, accompanied by a friend and part-time filmmaker from Chicago, an Alaskan pal, an Australian expat living in Port Moresby who had spent lots of time in the New Guinea bush, a photographer from Hong Kong, and three Papua New Guinea cameramen from Port Moresby's POM Productions. If we succeeded, our expedition would be an historic event; no outsider had attempted to walk the entire trail since the soldiers did it in 1942.

On the first day, climbing down to a river on a red clay trail as slippery as lake ice, I fell, tumbling head over heels with a sixty-seven-pound pack on my back. When I got to my feet, I knew that I had torn a ligament in my knee. I limped for another three hours until I could walk no more. My pulse was fast and thready, my vision blurred. I knew I could not make it, so I turned back and walked out. My friend George from Chicago accompanied me.

That night we slept in a village in a hut made of woven bamboo, and we were told to be on the lookout for ill-intentioned sorcerers. The following day we stumbled out of the mountains and hitched a ride to Port Moresby.

Four days later, equipped with painkillers and anti-inflammatories, and determined to follow in the footsteps of the Ghost Mountain boys, we were helicoptered back into the jungle.

Introduction

My remarks on the supply and equipment problems derive in part from a document titled "Comments on the Buna Campaign by a Quartermaster," which is part of the Hanson Baldwin Collection at the George C. Marshall Research Library in Lexington, Virginia. War correspondent Jules Archer wrote an article for *Man's Magazine* called "Why the 32nd Division Won't Forgive General MacArthur." It was very helpful, as was Tillman Durdin's article, "The Grim Hide-and-Seek of Jungle War," which appeared in the March 1943 edition of *The New York Times Magazine*.

Chapter 1. Escape to the South

There are a variety of people, including General Charles Willoughby, MacArthur's head of Intelligence, who address MacArthur's exchange with Wainwright and his subsequent flight from Corregidor. All seem to have a slightly different take on what transpired. In his superbly researched book, *American Caesar*, William Manchester describes MacArthur's escape from Corregidor, his arrival in Australia, and his state of mind. To a large extent this is the account that I have relied on.

As for the legend about MacArthur's fear of flying, General George Brett, who for a short time was MacArthur's commander of American forces in Australia, may be the author. In "The MacArthur I Knew," Brett states that MacArthur "hated to fly," "suffered from air-sickness," and "would not get into a plane unless he knew it was per-fect." Brett also has some insightful comments about MacArthur's psyche and his time in Australia, and the exclusivity of the Bataan Gang. And he dispels once and for all the tale that MacArthur fled Corregidor with a mattress full of gold pesos.

Regarding MacArthur's famous speech, Harry Gailey, author of *MacArthur Strikes Back*, says that MacArthur uttered his famous words "I shall return" for the first time to reporters at Batchelor Field. In *Reminiscences*, MacArthur says the same. General Charles Willoughby says it happened in Alice Springs, as does John Toland in *The Rising Sun*. In other words, there does not seem to be a definitive, universally accepted account of what happened, or where. It may be that MacArthur uttered the three words at Batchelor Field, but according to Manchester, the speech heard round the world was made in Adelaide. Manchester describes how MacArthur labored over what he would say: MacArthur was concerned about the first sentence, writing and re-writing it many times. But it was the last sentence that caught on, becoming, according to historian Winston Groom, as memorable as "The British are coming!" or "Remember the Alamo." MacArthur's detractors trashed the speech, citing it as an example of the general's megalomania. Why had he used "I"? It seemed silly and pompous, they said. Why had he not said, "*We* shall return"?

Regarding what was called the "Brisbane Line," in his book *1942*, Winston Groom suggests that MacArthur was having "none of" it, and that early on he had decided to take the war to New Guinea. William Manchester remains skeptical of the claim. It was revisionist and self-serving, a fiction first advanced by MacArthur in order to portray himself to history as a decisive commander. MacArthur, Manchester maintains, sent Australian and American troops to New Guinea only when there was no other course of action available to him. In his book *There's a War to Be Won*, Geoffrey Perret is critical of MacArthur's tendency for self-promotion. "This banal truth," Perret wrote of MacArthur's decision to accept Australia's defensive posture, "would seem to be in conflict with the legend of MacArthur the Bold." According to Perret and David Horner, too, MacArthur bolstered his own image by promoting a "fiction in which he'd found the Australians craven and defeatist."

Regarding the threat to Australia, there is an ongoing and heated discussion taking place in Australia about whether or not Japan ever intended to invade. Dr. Peter Stanley delivered a paper titled "He's (Not) Coming South: The Invasion That Wasn't" at an Australian War Memorial conference. To this day, many people believe that Australia was Japan's target. Yet Japanese war documents indicate that on March 15, 1942, the Army and Navy Sections of the Imperial General Headquarters dismissed the idea of an attack on the Australian mainland. The Japanese navy championed the idea, but the army demurred. After the war, Premier Hideki Tojo argued that Japan had dismissed the idea of invading Australia as early as March 1942 because it would require too many troops. Instead, Japan opted for a plan to seize Port Moresby, occupy the southern Solomon Islands, and isolate Australia by controlling the air space and the oceans so that the Americans could not use it as a base for offensive actions. Neither Allied Headquarters, Australia's Joint Chiefs, nor the people of Australia were privy to this information, though. Stanley maintains that Prime Minister Curtin in particular exaggerated the threat.

On the subject of the Japanese invasion, army historian Samuel Milner seems to be of two minds. He writes: "Instead of approving an operation against the Australian mainland, the Japanese agreed to seize Port Moresby as planned and then, with the parallel occupation of the southern Solomons, 'to isolate Australia' by seizing Fiji, Samoa, and New Caledonia. . . . The plan said nothing about invading Australia; it did not have to. If everything went well and all objectives were taken, there would be enough time to begin planning for the invasion. . . . It was clear from the circumstances that the Japanese had not given up on the idea of invading Australia. They had merely laid it aside. . . ."

For a description of the panic that existed in Australia, I relied Paul Ham's *Kokoda,* Peter Brune's books, and David Day's *The Great Betrayal* and *The Politics of War.* Milner and Ham both do an excellent job of presenting the jockeying and deal making that went on after MacArthur arrived in Australia.

Regarding MacArthur's burning ambition to return to the Philippines in triumph, General Brett provides interesting insights into MacArthur's character. He writes, "The fulfillment of his promise to return to the Philippines seemed years away. He was a disappointed and unhappy man. . . . MacArthur retired into his ivory tower to plan the campaigns ahead. The planning was long range. . . . I don't believe he gave much thought to our immediate problems." Brett compares MacArthur to Marshall. Marshall, he says was "one of the clearest-thinking, least temperamental men" he had ever known. On the other hand, MacArthur was, in his opinion, a "brilliant, temperamental egoist."

Chapter 2. A Train Heading West

For the general history of the 32nd Division, I relied primarily on three books: Major General H. W. Blakeley's *The 32nd Infantry Division in World War II; Wisconsin's Red Arrow Division;* and *32nd Division, Les Terribles.* Herbert Smith's books and division files at the National

Archives also provide excellent details on the division's Louisiana experience, the train ride, etc.

Regarding the warning signs, Brett writes in *The MacArthur I Knew*, "A reconnaissance picked up information of a concentration of troops and shipping at Rabaul . . . everything pointed to an active gathering of enemy forces. It seemed evident that they would head for some point on the north coast of New Guinea, and even attempt to go all the way around to Port Moresby. General MacArthur's headquarters was kept apprised of the situation, but made little comment, and gave practically no suggestions or advice." Brett, elaborating on MacArthur's preoccupation with the Philippines, writes, "Not once, while I was in Australia, did the Supreme Commander go north to visit the advance bases. . . . MacArthur stuck to his desk."

Toland writes that Churchill, when he heard of the attack on Pearl Harbor, slept well, knowing that the U.S. was now officially on his side. Toland also describes in vivid detail the simultaneous attacks on Pearl Harbor and Singapore Island. He also describes the euphoria that seized Japan.

Much of my portrayal of America immediately following Pearl Harbor comes from two outstanding books, Geoffrey Perret's *Days of Sadness, Years of Triumph* and Paul Fussell's *Wartime*.

Chapter 3. Arrival Down Under

Again, Smith's books provide wonderful details of the soldiers' experience at the Cow Palace and the three-week trip to Australia. In *Gentle Knight*, General Edwin Forrest Harding's biographer Leslie Anders also writes about the experience. Clarence Jungwirth left behind a wonderful account of his experiences (*Diary of a National Guardsman in World War II*). Lenord Sill's *Buna & Beyond* and Howard Kelley's *Born in the U.S.A. Raised in New Guinea* were also very helpful.

Some of the details of the American soldiers' relationship to the Australians and the returning Australian soldiers are from C. P. Murdock's *Saturday Evening Post* article, "The Red Arrow Pierced Every Line," E. J. Kahn's *G.I. Jungle*, and *Gentle Knight*.

For the personal details on General Harding, I depended upon Leslie Anders' wonderful biography *Gentle Knight*.

When Harding left San Franciso, his son Davis, who was finishing up his doctoral dissertation in English, wrote him. "Good luck, dad," Davis wrote. "I like the idea of having you for a father." Harding, Anders writes, responded with appropriate lines from Kipling:

The troopship's on the tide, my boys, the troopship's on the tide,
O it's "special train for Atkins" when the trooper's on the tide.

E. J. Kahn wrote that soldiers knew so little about Australia they expected to be "met at a primitive wharf by aborigine porters on kangaroos."

For details on the division's training in Australia, I relied on Milner's book, his interview with Harding, which can be found at the Office of the Chief of Military History, and Anders' biography.

When Harding renamed Tamborine Camp Cable, Sergeant Gerald Cable's mother wrote him, thanking him for "the high honor you have done my son's name."

To discuss the medical problems in the South Pacific, I used Simon Warmenhoven's letters and a number of splendid books and articles, many written by Mary Ellen Condon-Rall.

Medical Department, United States Army in World War II, a series published in Washington, D.C., by the Army's Office of the Surgeon General, provides both organizational studies and numerous physician-written accounts of the clinical problems encountered in the war against Japan. The Medical Department produced forty-eight books on World War II. They are divided into a number of sub-series dealing with preventive medicine, internal medicine, surgery, etc. One very helpful book is on preventive medicine: *Communicable Disease: Malaria,* edited by Ebbe Curtis Hoff. There are seven other volumes in this sub-series that deal with medical problems other than malaria. I also used a book published by the U.S. Army's Center of Military History in Washington, D.C., in its *United States Army in World War II* series. It is co-authored by Mary Ellen Condon-Rall, titled *The Medical Department:*

Medical Service in the War Against Japan. Chapter IV deals with jungle warfare. Three more publications were of enormous help. They are Condon-Rall's "Allied Cooperation in Malaria Prevention and Control: The World War II Southwest Pacific Experience" (*Journal of the History of Medicine,* Vol. 46, October 1991, pp. 493-513), her "Malaria in the Southwest Pacific in World War II" (in Roy M. MacLeod, editor, The University of Sydney, Australia, *Science and the Pacific War, Science and Survival in the Pacific, 1939-1945,* Kluwer Academic Publishers, Dordrecht/Boston/London, 2000), and her "The Army's War against Malaria: Collaboration in Drug Research during World War II" (*Armed Forces and Society,* Vol. 21, No. 1, fall 1994, pp. 129-143).

Milner and Ham describe in detail the intelligence reports that said Japan was planning to invade New Guinea.

The early days of the Australian New Guinea Administrative Unit (ANGAU) and Major General Basil Morris' dismissal of the possibility of a Japanese overland invasion, and the subsequent invasion, are found in Alan Powell's wonderful book *The Third Force.*

An especially gruesome piece of history is the story of Miss May Hayman and Miss Mavis Parkinson, two young Anglican sisters assigned to the Gona Mission, who fled the Yokoyama Advance Force on July 21, 1942. When hundreds of Japanese troops slid down ropes onto barges to be transported through the puzzle of reefs to shore, Hayman and Parkinson plunged deep into the jungle with only a compass. Father James Benson, who ran the mission at Gona, led them. For months he had urged the sisters to leave Papua along with the rest of the white population that had evacuated, but they had refused. "Lighten our darkness, O Lord," Father Benson prayed as they fled the Japanese.

Benson, Hayman, and Parkinson eluded the Japanese advance troops of the Tsukamoto Battalion until a native collaborator named Emboge from the Orokaivan people betrayed them near the village of Doboduru. The two sisters were taken to a plantation near the village of Buna, not far from the Japanese landing site, and were bayoneted to death. Mavis Parkinson was the first to go. A Japanese soldier forced her into an embrace. When she struggled to free herself, he dug his bayonet deep into her side. May Hayman, who held a towel over her eyes, was bayoneted in the throat as she listened to her friend die.

Emboge and his accomplices were later arrested and hanged.

"What else could we do?" Emboge pleaded. "The kiawa [white men] treated us badly before the war and they deserted the people when the Japanese landed at Buna."

A sympathetic ANGAU officer witnessed the hanging. "I lay awake most of the night," he wrote, "listening to the drums beating, and the wailing of the mourners. . . . I had seen death in various forms during the preceding twelve months, but nothing affected me as much as the hanging. . . . Perhaps it was the courage they displayed when the time came for them to die. Be that as it may, the punishment meted out to them was in accordance with their own tribal code of 'an eye for an eye.'"

Arthur Duna's quote is found in John Dadeno Waiko's book, *PNG: A History of Our Time*. Duna's account of the invasion is substantiated by a number of interviews that I conducted in Buna in 2005 and 2006. More information on the Japanese invasion can be found in Waiko's "Damp Soil My Bed; Rotten Log My Pillow: A Villager's Experience of the Japanese Invasion."

Regarding the invasion from the Japanese perspective, I relied on a number of sources: *Nankai Shitai, War Book of the 144th Regiment; Lost Troops; Southern Cross*, and also a collection of ATIS documents at the National Archives. Milner also provides details. A whole host of Australian authors, including Ham, David Horner, Les McAulay, Peter Brune, Victor Austin, and Raymond Paull have written riveting, well-researched books about the battle along the Kokoda track.

All personal details on Herman Bottcher come from soldiers' recollections and two articles: "Fire and Blood in the Jungle" by George L. Moorad in the July 3, 1943 issue of *Liberty Magazine* and Mark Sufrin's article "Take Buna or don't come back alive" in the *Historical Times*.

Chapter 4. Sons of Heaven

Details on General Horii are taken from Lida Mayo's book, *Bloody Buna*.

Using G-2 daily summaries housed at the National Archives and Milner, I was able to detail Allied intelligence failures.

There are a number of excellent books on the militarization of Japanese society: John Toland's *The Rising Sun, Soldiers of the Sun* by Meirion and Susie Harries, *Tojo and the Coming of the War* by Robert Butow, David James' *The Rise and Fall of the Japanese Empire, Japan's War* by Edwin Hoyt, and Ruth Benedict's *The Chrysanthemum and the Sword*.

The International Military Tribunal for the Far East, which investigated Japanese war crimes after the war, harshly condemned bushido. Although a willingness to die in the execution of one's duty was a genuine part of the historic samurai ethic, the original conception of bushido left room for honorable surrender, both for the samurai and his enemies. Bushido's twentieth-century perversion, however, engendered what military historian Eric Beregrud called "a cult of death," in which no compassion was given and none was received.

Japanese quotes and diary entries are from ATIS documents.

The Australian perspective is from Ham, Brune, and Horner.

Chapter 5. Cannibal Island

Excerpts from Harding's letters home appear in Anders' biography and lend insight into Harding's humanity.

Excerpts from MacArthur's speech are taken from Blakeley. Anders also includes portions of MacArthur's speech.

For a perspective on just how much it rains on the island of New Guinea, consider that Seattle, Washington, which is often considered the wettest place in the United States, gets an average of about seventy to eighty inches of rain per year. Milne Bay, one of the wettest places on the island's eastern half (Papua New Guinea), regularly gets two and a half to three times that.

For this section I relied on a number of fascinating books: Gavin Souter's *New Guinea: The Last Unknown;* Osmar White's *Green Armor* and *Parliament of a Thousand Tribes; New Guinea: Crossing Boundaries and History* by Clive Moore, *Documents and Readings in New Guinea History,* edited by J. L. Whittaker and a host of others; Tim Flannery's *Throwim Way Leg; Prowling Through Papua* by Frank Clune; W. N. Beaver's *Unexplored New Guinea;* F. Hurley's *Pearls and Savages;* L. M. D'Albertis' *New Guinea: What I Did and What I Saw;* and Captain J. A, Lawson's *Wanderings in the Interior of New Guinea.* Stephen Anderson's article, "How Many Languages Are There in the World?" which appeared in the May 2004 edition of the Linguistic Society of America's scholarly publication, was also very helpful.

Souter's book, in particular, describes successive stages of exploration in New Guinea, and is full of fascinating anecdotes about the von Ehlers expedition and others.

First Contact tells the story of the "discovery" of the New Guinea Highlands by Australian gold prospectors Michael Leahy and his brothers. (There is also a film called *First Contact* based on Leahy's film footage. It is widely considered an ethnographic classic.) The bulk of the book is about the events of 1933, when Leahy led a series of prospecting expeditions into the highlands and initiated the first contacts between highlanders and Europeans. The account is based on his diaries and later writings and on interviews with the native highlanders who witnessed the events. The book is full of photos taken at the time.

Chapter 6. Forlorn Hope

Many of the Company E details are derived from Lutjens' diary, a series of lectures he delivered on the Papuan Campaign after returning to the United States, E. J. Kahn's fascinating two-part series in the *Saturday Evening Post* called "The Terrible Days of Company E", Art Edson's letters home, James Hunt's notes on the company's early days in New Guinea, and his correspondence with Herbert "Stutterin'" Smith.

When General Kenney got news from Port Moresby that Lutjens and his men had arrived safely, he, in his own words, "rushed upstairs to General MacArthur's office to give him the good news" and asked him if he could "haul the rest of the regiment." Kenney continues, "He congratulated me most enthusiastically but told me that he had already ordered the rest of the regiment shipped by boat and that the loading had already begun. I said, 'All right, give me the next regiment to go, the 128th, and I'll have them in Port Moresby ahead of this gang that goes by boat.'"

Shortly after the 32nd landed in New Guinea, Harding's staff threw him a birthday party in Australia. Harding made a speech, urging listeners to remember three important values: "time, equipment, and lives." His preference was "to save human lives and take just a little longer to accomplish our mission." As Anders notes, Harding wrote his wife: "I must admit," he said, "that I rather like the idea that the men, that I've grown to think so much of, should think the 'Old Man' is all right. I hope that I never give them any reason to think otherwise during the tough times that we are destined to see together."

Descriptions of the village of Gabagaba and its people are based on my 2005 and 2006 interviews with a number of village elders there, Lieutenant James Hunt's recollections, and Art Edson's letters home. The natives, according to Edson, "run around with nothing on." Edson adds, "There is times when we feel like doing the same thing, and a lot of times too." Edson also writes about how much weight the natives are able to carry. He says, "I saw one yesterday that carried a heavy pole about forty feet long on his shoulder."

Native villages were decimated by ANGAU recruitment practices. In *The Third Force*, Alan Powell includes two native songs that reflect their sense of dislocation and sadness:

> "All the women were standing by the river bank for their husbands.
> All the children were standing by the riverbank for their fathers.
> On the riverbank all were standing.

On the canoe bank all were standing.
When the husbands looked back they saw their wives and
children were waving to them."

"We have left our homes and beaches
To labour for the war in different places,
In far flung places. In these hard times
We wander aimlessly from home.
. . . In our little homes before the war
Partings from dear ones were unknown.
. . . We now wonder by our campfires
Of our homes, our dear ones, and our wives.
Longing, hoping, praying deeply.
To return to home once more."

The first European to make contact with the simple, seafaring
Motu people south of Port Moresby was Captain John Moresby. He
spent days trading with them and asked in his diary, "What have these
people to gain from civilization?"

During the early days of colonial occupation, a simplified Motu
language, called "Police Motu," was spread throughout the territory
by native constables. In the nothern half of the island the German
planters faced the same language barriers the British and Australians
did in the south. The Germans' solution was Pisin, a local word that
became known as Pidgin. Pidgin has taken many words from various
languages, including German and English. Be careful, for instance, is
"Lukautim gut!"

A few of Gabagaba's village elders remember how fascinated villagers were by America's black engineers.

Chapter 7. The Bloody Track

Scenes of jubilation are taken from Seizo Okada's *Lost Troops*. Captain Nakahashi's quote is taken from Paul Ham's *Kokoda*.

The Battle of Bloody Ridge was perhaps Guadalcanal's most
famous battle. In it, U.S. Marines repulsed an attack by the Japanese

35th Infantry Brigade. The Marines were defending Henderson Field
on Guadalcanal, which they had captured from the Japanese in early
August 1942. Kawaguchi's unit was sent to Guadalcanal to recapture
the airfield and drive the Allied forces from the island. Kawaguchi's
six thousand soldiers conducted several nighttime frontal assaults on
the U.S. defenses. The main Japanese assault occurred on an unnamed
ridge south of Henderson Field that was manned by troops from several U.S. Marine Corps units, under the command of Lieutenant
Colonel Merrit Edson. Although Kawaguchi's men nearly defeated the
Marines, the Americans held. The battle became known as the Battle
of Edson's Ridge or Bloody Ridge.

Accounts of General Horii's deception and the Japanese supply situation are from Lida Mayo's book. Specific quotes are from ATIS documents. Details of the messages received by General Horii and Horii's
horror at being asked to retreat are from Mayo's book.

Ham writes that Captain Nakahashi uttered the same words about
the message coming "like a bolt from the blue," though the rest of the
quote is different. Ham writes that Nakahashi said that the news,
"caused an overflowing . . . of emotion, which could not be suppressed; it was compounded by feelings of anger, sorrow and frustration. The purpose, the dreams and the desires of the officers and
soldiers of the South Seas Force had vanished in an instant."

Ham writes that it took fifty Australian "sappers" using a powerful
pulley system to get the cannon up the steep spur of Imita Ridge. The
Australian engineers had cut two thousand steps ino the ridge, creating what the Australians called with irony the "Golden Staircase."

Details on the beginning of the Australians counterattack are from
William Crooks' *The Footsoldiers*.

MacArthur's quote to Brigadier John Edward Lloyd is from Ham.

MacArthur took great personal satisfaction from his appearance
at Imita Ridge. American war correspondents had written that Port
Moresby might go the way of Singapore. In reality, MacArthur was
not anywhere near the front; it was five miles to the north at the village
of Nauro.

According to McAulay, the 16th Brigade was made up of crack

troops, Australia's best. They had fought in the Middle East and in North Africa. Most, prior to returning to Australia, had also trained in the jungles of Sri Lanka (then Ceylon). They were also well outfitted with camouflaged, long-sleeved shirts, long pants, gaiters, steel helmets with nets, and new boots with spikes.

In *General Vasey's War*, Horner writes of Vasey's speech to his commanders: "The Japanese are well trained in jungle warfare. In this form of warfare they are like tigers, cunning, silent and dangerous. Like tigers, too, they are vermin; they must be destroyed. One does not expect a live tiger to get to give himself up to capture so we must not expect the Japanese to surrender. He does not. He must be killed whether it is by shooting, bayoneting, throttling, knocking out his brains with a tin hat or by any other means our ingenuity can devise. Truly jungle warfare is a game of kill or be killed and to play it successfully demands alertness of all senses but particularly of ears and eyes."

Chapter 8. Marching into the Clouds

Details on Jim Boice and his trek are from Boice's diary, newspaper articles, and conversations with Boice's son William Boice Jr.

Boice sent back 1st Lieutenant Bernard Howes with his trail notes, saying that he believed that subsequent groups would "take proportinately greater time on these trails."

Details on the Kapa Kapa and plans for the overland advance are from Milner, Gailey, Mayo, the National Archives, the Wisconsin Veterans Museum, and interviews with veterans of the march.

Specifics of Medendorp's march are from his report, his lengthy reminiscences, and interviews with his sons and his sister Alice.

Description of the carriers are based on Medendorp's writings, conversations with villagers of Gabagaba, Powell's book *The Third Force*, photographs, and T. E. Dutton's comprehensive study, *The Peopling of Central Papua*.

Powell contrasts the American soldiers' relationship with the villagers with the way they were treated by the Australians. He writes, "The problem . . . was not merely that the Australians had and gave less, but that they actively discouraged or forbade the generosity of the Americans." One villager said, "If an American was going to give something to me, he had to look around and make sure that none of the Angau were present. If an Angau saw an American give one of us something, then he would come and take it away."

Leslie Anders portrays Harding as the consummate renaissance man, a writer of prose and poetry, a voracious reader, and an avid and accomplished student of history.

Details on Roger Keast are from interviews with his son Harry, interviews of men who served with Keast, and a variety of newspaper articles.

It is occasionally difficult to track the patrol's journeys, since no detailed maps of the area existed and often Medendorp did not use place names. Much of the country, including the rivers and the countless peaks, did not have names. Although some of the most prominent features had native names, many did not.

Descriptions of the jungle are based in part on my own trek on the Kapa Kapa and my observations.

American and Australian soldiers greatly feared the Japanese soldier. They viewed him as cunning, stealthy, and deadly, despite Allied commanders' continual attempts to dispel the myth of the Japanese warrior's superiority.

Boyd Swem is one of the soldiers about whom Medendorp writes very fondly. Medendorp wrote, "Nothing dismayed Swem." Swem was a member of Service Company when Mendedorp invited him to join the Wairopi Patrol.

Captain Buckler's group was just as stunned to discover the Americans. According to Raymond Paull in his book *Retreat from Kokoda*, the Americans were "an image of wishful thinking to a man who had endured a month of strain and vicissitude." Lewis Sebring, a correspondent for the *New York Herald Tribune* who saw Buckler's group when they reached the coast, described them much as Medendorp did: "Sunken eyes looked at us from bearded faces . . ." Mayo writes that it was Boice who encountered Buckler's group, but Medendorp's group surely encountered them, too, for Medendorp writes, "They were dirty, hungry, bearded, and many were nursing old wounds . . ." In additon to feeding them, Medendorp wrote that they were welcome to "all the food that they could carry, and with our blessing."

Details on the Japanese invasion of Rabaul are from Ham and Paull.

That evening a runner from Boice's Pathfinder Patrol also stumbled into Arapara. According to Medendorp, he had "malaria and was partly delirious."

I witnessed the natives' lack of concern about rats and cockroaches; they consider our sqeamishness laughable.

Details on the beliefs of carriers are derived from numerous interviews with people in Papua New Guinea, Powell's book, and conversations and e-mails with Bill McKellin, a professor of anthropology at the University of British Columbia in Vancouver.

The quote is from Lieutenant William D. Hawkins, Harding's G-2 (from Anders' *Gentle Knight*).

The old village of Laruni was situated on a hill overlooking the Mimani River, a one-hour climb from the present-day village of Laruni (or Larun), which lies on the western bank of the river.

Medendorp was a cigar man, but almost everyone in the army learned to smoke cigarettes.

All that Medendorp and Keast had to work with was a hand-drawn map listing the villages along the trail. The map did not even include mountain peaks and rivers. Medendorp and Keast would draw their own map, called *Map C: Operations of the Wairopi Patrol*, which would show villages and drainages along the Kumusi River from Jaure down to Wairopi on the Kokoda track. This map can be found at the National Archives.

North of Laruni, the terrain becomes extremely steep, as we would discover on our trek. Natives, especially those recruited in Gabagaba and other coastal villages, would have been unfamiliar with the mountains and frightened by them. They believed that the mountains were populated with evil spirits. To this day, natives of seaside villages are reluctant to venture into the mountains. Mountain people are also frightened of the high peaks.

I discovered some of Medendorp's radio messages at the National Archives.

Keast's endurance is confirmed by veterans who took part in the Wairopi Patrol.

The trail is infested with leeches that crawl up out of the mud and fall from overhanging branches.

Initially the Japanese Imperial army took great care not to alienate the people of New Guinea. Orders were to "make them realise that the Imperial army will protect their lives and property . . . to ensure that all decisions made in local matters are fair, to respect their women and never approach them, to always pay a proper price for things bought or labor done."

Those who submitted to the Japanese were to be treated benevolently, but those who displayed hostility were to be "disposed of rigorously and without mercy." A notebook of Second Lieutenant Hidetada Noda, captured near the village of Menari, contained information regarding treatment of natives: "No work at night. Do not hit them unless the reason for doing it is very obvious. . . . Treat them as human beings." Initially, the Japanese were quite egalitarian, certainly more so than the ANGAU masters had been. The Japanese soldiers ate with the native New Guineans, and in some cases, lived with them.

Details on the Jaure reunion can be found in Medendorp's memoirs.

Descriptions of porters are from Medendorp's memoirs and Professor Bill McKellin, who lived for two years with the people of Central Papua.

Segal's complaints were widespread among the Medical Corps. In "The Fight Against Malaria in the Papua and New Guinea Campaigns," John T. Greenwood writes, "Medical officers could not obtain the level of priority required for the shipment of supplies into or even within the theater." He describes a puzzling lack of interest by line commanders and theater planners in the malaria threat.

Milner writes of what was called the "Wanigela Operation." Ivan Champion, a former colonial patrolman, had successfully mapped a channel from Milne Bay to Cape Nelson, up the coast from Wanigela, making the transport of the 128th and its supplies possible.

General George Brett, who was no longer MacArthur's commander of American forces in Australia, must have been surprised by MacArthur's sudden faith in the air forces. Previously, according to Brett, he had nothing but "contempt and criticism for them." In *The MacArthur I Knew*, Brett recalls a conversation where MacArthur said of the air force, "They lack discipline, organization, purposeful intent."

Flying over the Owen Stanley "hump," where cloud banks sometimes reached 40,000 feet in the air, was no easy task.

Chapter 9. One Green Hell

Lutjens' entries are from his diary and from E. J. Kahn's article, "The Terrible Days of Company E."

The engineers who accompanied the 2nd Battalion were from the 114th Engineers, a Massachusetts Guard unit. The 114th Engineers replaced the division's 107th Engineers who were already on their way to the ETO. The story of the engineers has never really been told. They performed miracles along the trail, which certainly saved lives.

Native carriers were more than happy to pick up whatever equipment and clothing the soldiers left behind. Hare Bore of Gabagaba was one of the carriers for the 2nd Battalion. Remembering how the soldiers suffered in the heat and under the weight of their packs, he says, "I drop tears for them."

The story of soldiers tearing the buttons off their shirts seemed improbable to me. Veterans of the march, however, insist that they saw men do it.

On my own trek—though our team, including carriers, never amounted to more than twenty-five—I saw how quickly the trail could turn into a path of shin-deep mud.

Accounts of Company G's march are from personal interviews with the men of Company G, friends who served with Bailey, and Wendell Trogdon's book on Cladie Bailey.

For an excellent history of malaria and efforts to stamp it out, read *Mosquitoes, Malaria and Man* by Gordon Harrison, and Mary Ellen Condon-Rall's books and articles.

A number of other good books discuss tropical disease: a basic book called *Tropical Infectious Diseases; Tropical Diseases from 50,000 BC to 2500 AD*; and Douglas Haynes' *Imperial Medicine*. Bergerud also has a section devoted to disease in the South Pacific war. Interestingly, he notes, "Up until the twentieth century, it [disease] was the primary killer during war."

In "The Fight Against Malaria in the Papua and New Guinea Campaigns," John T. Greenwood writes, "The establishment in March 1942 of the Southwest Pacific Area as an Allied theater command under General Douglas MacArthur meant that one of the most primitive, remote, and disease-infested tropical areas in the world would become the scene of major military operations." He adds that the medical department's experience with the "huge amount of damages inflicted on American forces in Bataan, should have alerted American military and medical leaders to the impending danger. . . . Theater officers devoted little attention to developing an antimalaria program during 1942, however, because of their focus on more immediate operational requirements."

The army's decision to let the soldiers rest in villages along the trail's route seemed practical at the time, but it backfired. The soldiers were already suffering from dysentery, trenchfoot, and jungle ulcers when malaria hit them like a time bomb. Exposed to mosquitoes on the coast and in the long-grass savanna that bordered the hill country, many soldiers were wracked with chills and high fevers by the time they reached the mountains. Malaria devastated the 2nd Battalion, and eventually the entire 32nd Division. Eventually nearly 70 percent of the division would contract the disease.

Bergerud also discusses at length the problems that malaria and other diseases caused for the American army in New Guinea.

Malaria means "bad air" in Italian, a reference to the long-held notion that people contracted malaria by smelling the "bad air" of a swamp. The culprit, though, is a tiny parasite transmitted through the bite of the female anopheles mosquito, which teemed in the tidal swamps, open grasslands, and thick, dank jungles along the trail.

Once in the blood, the parasites traveled to the soldiers' livers and reproduced, burst, and released more parasites back into the soldiers' bloodstreams. When other female anopheles fed on the infected blood, they, too, were infected. Worst of all, the parasites were hard to get rid of. In some cases, the men's livers and red blood cells played host to the disease for years.

Malaria is New Guinea's scourge. Fort Coronation, the island's first European settlement, a British colony established in 1793, was decimated by fever in less than a year. The next colony, a Dutch experiment called Merkusoord, lost seventy-five soldiers and nearly a hundred women and children in a seven-year period between 1828 and 1835. A French sailing vessel sighted the settlement in 1840, but discovered nothing more than a "citrus grove, coconut trees, a brick oven, ruined stone dwellings, and an overgrown road."

Near the middle of the century Dutch Protestants affiliated with a society called "The Christian Workman" attempted to establish a number of missions in northwestern New Guinea. After twenty-five years, an earthquake and a tidal wave, epidemics of smallpox and dysentery, and rampant malaria, the number of people to die from disease exceeded the number of natives baptized into Christ.

Around the time of the missions' collapse, a Russian biologist by the name of Nikolai Mikluho Maclay was making forays into New Guinea's northeastern interior. After befriending the initially hostile natives, Maclay had to contend with an even more dangerous foe— malaria. One night while in his hut, Maclay described the symptoms. "He [the victim of malaria]," he wrote, "does not feel her [malaria's] presence, but before long he feels his legs as filled with lead, his thoughts are interrupted by giddiness, a cold shiver passes through the limbs, his eyes become very sensitive to light and his eyelids droop in a powerless way. Images, some enormous monsters, some sad and slow, appear before his closed eyes. By and by the cold shivering changes into a heat, a dry endless heat . . ."

Roughly a decade after Maclay's adventures, Britain and Germany were competing for large parts of the island. In late 1884 Britain declared southeastern New Guinea a protectorate and not long after hoisted the Union Jack over Port Moresby. After the cheering subsided, Britain dispatched Major General Sir Peter Scratchley, the protectorate's first commissioner. Scratchley, however, died of malaria after only three months in the territory.

Germany's colonial administration took the form of the Neu Guinea Kompagnie, which Germany's chancellor Otto von Bismarck put in charge of the adventure. Commissioned by the Kompagnie to find sites for potential settlement, in what became known as Kaiser-Wilhelmsland, Dr. Otto Finch made five journeys to northeastern New Guinea, naming the region's greatest river (the Sepik) the Kaiserin Augusta. In honor of Dr. Finch's discoveries, the Kompagnie named its first settlement Finchhafen. In establishing the settlement, though, the Kompagnie could not have chosen more poorly. Finchhafen was a desperate place, beset by a hellishly humid climate, earthquakes, a lethal strain of malaria, and soul-deadening monotony. The chancellor's nephew, who worked in the colony as a surveyor, wrote that one of the two most frequented spots in the town was the cemetery. Upon leaving Finchhafen, he wrote, "I am one of the few to get out of that malaria-hole Finchhafen with a whole skin because I treated the fever with alcohol instead of quinine, and the orders of the Neu Guinea Kompagnie similarly— with alcohol instead of respect."

Details from Smith's books and details of the gold rush are in Souter's *New Guinea.*

In 1889, a half-century before Company G attempted to negotiate the high mountain country of the Owen Stanleys, Sir William Mac-Gregor, a short, square, indomitable Scot, led the first official expedition into the mountains. MacGregor was appointed administrator over what was then known as British New Guinea, after Britain assumed sovereignty over the protectorate in 1888, and he was determined to investigate the Papuan Peninsula's wild interior. MacGregor's carriers, who were familiar with the terrain, said the mountains could not be reached. MacGregor was not deterred until he actually entered them. From Port Moresby it had taken his team nearly a month to reach the second highest peak in British New Guinea. It was 13,363 feet tall, and he named it Mt. Victoria. Much to his surprise, Mt. Victoria was not the gigantic, isolated mountain he had imagined. It was part of a huge, sprawling mountain chain.

Regarding the drop sites, Medendorp and Keast's team successfully pinpointed, and sometimes cleared, drop sites along the trail.

The Selective Training and Service Act of 1940 was passed by the United States Congress on September 6, 1940, becoming the first peacetime conscription in U.S. history. The draft began in October 1940. By the early summer of 1941, FDR asked Congress to extend the term of duty for the draftees beyond twelve months. The House of Representatives approved the extension by a single vote. The terminal point of service would soon be extended to six months after the war.

Bottcher's description is from "Fire and Blood in the Jungle" by George Moorad. Lieutenant James Hunt's recollection is found in his letter to Stutterin' Smith.

Odell also writes of the grueling nature of the hike in his diary.

The Bailey quote is taken from interviews with Katherine (Bailey) Matthews.

Problems between Australians and American soldiers were growing so bad that on August 15, Harding delivered a lecture on relations with Australian soldiers. Gangs were trying "to find stray American troops and to kill them." One Australian general described the animosity as "a most despicable thing between allies."

According to Gailey there were a number of "embarrassing problems caused by the influx of American troops." "Australia," he writes, "had an all white immigration policy. MacArthur had more than twice the percentage of black troops than in the European theater. The employment of these solders rankled many Australians and caused some friction."

Gailey adds, "the most vexing of all was the relations between off-duty American and Australian servicemen in the cities. Contrary to the myths that developed in the years after the war, they did not like one another."

Gailey goes on to tell the story of a brawl that erupted in Brisbane between U.S. military police and Australian soldiers. One Australian soldier was killed and nine were wounded.

Messages between Colonel Quinn and and Captain Boice are in the National Archives.

Chapter 10. To Swallow One's Tears

The details and quotes were taken from Japanese diaries translated by ATIS. At first, Allied translators were shocked by revelations of cannibalism that appeared in Japanese diaries, and asked for confirmation of their translations. It was indeed ironic that on an island legendary for its cannibals, it was the Japanese who were eating human flesh. In Papua, in the years before the war, the Australian colonial government had imposed on the people a western economic structure and the British system of law (Pax Australiana), and doled out harsh punishment for anyone suspected of cannibalism.

Ham writes that when the Australians searched the Japanese camp at Templeton's Crossing, they found "the flesh of Australian soldiers still cooking over the smoking embers of a campfire. More carved corpses," Ham writes, "lay on the track nearby."

By the end of the war, human flesh had become a staple of the Japanese diet. Ham quotes one Australian soldier who said that when they entered the village of Sanananda, they saw "little billy tins of human flesh."

Of Allen's firing, Horner writes, "Clearly Blamey felt he had to relieve Allen to placate MacArthur. Had Blamey stood up to MacArthur, he would have won the respect of the Australian army. As it was, he did MacArthur's bidding and won the opprobrium of the troops."

Ham paints a wonderful portrait of General "Bloody George" Vasey: "His quick wit and independent character had happily survived his promotion up the ranks. He seemed free of . . . pomposity and self-importance." He was a man of "rigid self-discipline and unyielding spirit,"and "swaggering indifference to danger," but he had a "genuine concern for, and mingled with, his men." Quoting Raymond Paull, Ham writes, "He never lost the common touch."

In *War History of the Force which was Sent to the South Seas*, Nakahashi presents another scenario for Horii's death. Lida Mayo suggests that he drowned in the Kumusi.

Smith includes a description of Natunga (alternately spelled Natanga on some maps).

Professor Bill McKellin, who lived among the people of Central Papua, provided descriptions of what the people of Natunga probably looked like.

I discovered the messages between Quinn and Smith and Quinn and Boice in the National Archives. The description of the crash is from soldiers, native interviews, and Smith. Boice comments on Quinn's death in his diary.

Hawkins, Harding's G-2, wrote of Quinn's death, "It's always the people who put out, who go out of their way to do more than their share—that seem to get their necks out. I only hope they don't foist off one of these homeless colonels on us . . . floating around in superfluous base jobs."

In his diary Odell also writes of the crash scene and of the minute or two where men were more concerned with scrounging food than the colonel and crew's death.

Harding, of course, had the unenviable task of informing Quinn's widow. To his wife Eleanor, he wrote, "It will be a tough job. I wish I didn't have to do it."

The details of the Memorial Service are from the National Archives file on the 126th.

Chapter 11. Fever Ridge
Descriptions of MacArthur's Port Moresby Headquarters are found in a variety of different books including Manchester, Groom, and Willoughby.

Conditions at Pongani are found in Lawrence Thayer's "My War" and other diaries of 128th soldiers, and in collections of newspaper articles housed in the Wisconsin Veterans Museum.

Robert J. Doyle, the staff war correspondent for the *Milwaukee Journal* who was assigned to accompany the 128th, wrote a series of excellent pieces on it, including a story about the 128th becoming mired in the extensive swamps of the Musa River delta, and the slow, tedious process of moving troops north by small boat.

On a boat trip from Oro Bay to Tufi, I saw the vast delta of the Musa River.

Lawrence Thayer relates an interesting side story. Once the 128th made it to Pongani, he was asked by a lieutenant heading up the I&R (intelligence and reconnaissance) platoon to take a squad through the swamps and into the inland hill country in an attempt to find the Kokoda track. Thayer writes that he "didn't even have a map because the only one available described the interior as unexplored." It was his job to fill in the map. He continues, "At first I wrote down an azimuth reading of our direction and an estimate of distance for each leg, but soon it became apparent that this was not going to work. There were too many short legs and steep climbs interspersed with stretches of soggy swamp. About all I could do was to keep track of the general direction and time involved."

Thayer continues: "That afternoon we came upon a river. . . . We held our packs and rifles about our heads and started moving slowly across. . . . At one point I was submerged up to my neck. . . . It was only by a miracle that we weren't pulled downstream. If the river had been an inch deeper or faster we couldn't have made it. On our second night we slept on a huge pile of driftwood in the middle of a wide shallow river. It was very uncomfortable, but the current was strong enough to provide sufficient air to keep us from being devoured by the king-sized mosquitoes.

"As we continued toward the mountains the next day, the trail became quite steep in spots and very tiring. During one of our rest stops, to catch my breath I lay flat on my back staring into the branches of a small tree above me. To my horror I realized the leaves were covered with a squirming mass of leeches. . . . Some of the trees were nearly 10 feet in diameter and reached high in the sky . . ."

Eventually, Thayer and his team turned back and returned to Pongani because one of the soldiers developed a "nasty jungle infection."

Milner's book and Doyle's articles provide great information on the 128th at Pongani. I also collected lots of information in interviews with soldiers of the 128th.

Before he committed large numbers of troops to the coast, MacArthur wanted to make sure there was an escape route and wanted assurances that he could supply his troops. Regarding supply, MacArthur was dealing with a very difficult situation. The line of communication and supply from the United States to the scene of operations was one of the longest in military history. According to G-2 reports: "The entire route was by water at a time when the Japanese Navy was undefeated and roaming the Pacific almost at will." And once supplies reached Australia, the problems had just begun. It was fifteen hundred miles from South Australia to New Guinea. There was a shortage of ships and the quirky Australian system of transportation—all the railroad track gauges were different—made the transportation of supplies troublesome. MacArthur understood that Allied success in New Guinea would be determined, in part, by the dependability of its supply line. Aware of the fact that most of America's resources would go to Europe, MacArthur wisely initiated a supply source using Australian producers and resources. It was a stroke of genius, almost certainly colored by the tragedy of Bataan.

By this time, Harding realized that it would be impossible to move troops overland to the north coast.

After the naval battle of Guadalcanal (November 12-15), the Japanese stopped trying to reinforce their Guadalcanal garrison. In other words, the marines reinforced by army troops were tightening the noose on the Japanese at Guadalcanal just as MacArthur was beginning his advance on Buna.

Most historians refer incorrectly to Buna Mission instead of Buna Government Station. The government station was at Buna, but the mission was up the coast at Gona.

I learned much of the history of Buna, and the correct spellings of place names, from Wellington Jojoba, a professor at the University of Papua New Guinea in Port Moresby, who was raised in Buna.

Details of William Hirashima's life are from the transcript of Dr. David Swift, University of Hawaii.

The story of Simon Warmenhoven's heroism on the trail is from a letter that Herb Steenstra wrote to Warmenhoven's daughters. In an interview with Jack Hill, I learned of Warmenhoven's heroism during the bombing of the airstrip in Port Moresby.

Milner discusses the paucity of accurate intelligence. There was a commonly held belief that the Allies might be able to take Buna "without firing a shot." Eichelberger comments on this in *Our Jungle Road to Tokyo*; and in his article, "War Is Like This," E. J. Kahn does, too.

Chapter 12. The Kill Zone

I found the translation of the poem "Umi Yukaba" in Haruko Taya Cook and Theodore Cook's book, *Japan at War: An Oral History.* Details of the advance and first day's battle are from Lawrence Thayer's account, a series of articles that Robert Doyle wrote for the *Milwaukee Journal,* interviews with soldiers of the 128th, writer-historian Tom Doherty's account in the *Wisconsin Magazine of History* titled "Buna: The Red Arrow Division's Heart of Darkness," and Bergerud's interview with Ernest Gerber.

In the early days of the battle, according to Doherty, "Murphy's Law ran amok."

Accounts of the bombing of the flotilla of boats that included General Harding are from Lida Mayo, Harding's *Buna Diary,* Anders' biography of Harding, a report of the incident that Harding wrote on January 6, 1943, a colonel's account of the disaster (written on December 8, 1942), Lieutenant Colonel Stanley Hollenbeck's diary, which can be found at the Wisconsin Veterans Museum, an article by Murlin Spencer called "2 Allied Generals Swim Half Mile" that appeared in the *St. Paul Dispatch,* and Pat Robinson's book *The Fight for New Guinea.*

Harding mourned the loss of McKenny. "The Division," he wrote, "lost a good man."

The 128th urgently radioed General Ennis Whitehead, General Kenney's deputy commander, requesting airdrops to replace the supplies that were lost.

According to author Thomas Carmichael (*The Ninety Days*), despite Kenney's boast about his pilots supplying the artillery, it was a role that he showed a "total inability to fulfill."

Descriptions of the Japanese positions are taken from Milner, *The Papuan Campaign*, and Bergerud's *Touched with Fire*. Geoffrey Perret writes in *There's a War to Be Won* that the Japanese position was so formidable that "Two men and a machine gun could hold off a battalion."

Groom writes, "The Japanese were fighting from beind the most formidable bunkers seen since the Western Front of World War I."

Doyle wrote of the attack: "The Yanks are advancing—crawling on their bellies through the rain soaked jungle so thick they can't see more than 10 yards ahead of them . . ." Doyle also writes of the medics' outstanding work.

Details of that first night are from my interviews with Ray Bailey. Stutterin' Smith writes of being put under Australian command.

Chapter 13. A Poor Man's War

Eric Bergerud called the battle for the north coast "a poor man's war."

Harding comments at length in his *Buna Diary* on MacArthur's orders to take Buna. According to Kenney, "Harding was getting the blame, as he had not weeded out incompetent subordinate commanders who didn't know what to do. The troops were shot full of dysentery and malaria was starting to show up. . . . The troops were green and the officers were not controlling them. . . . They threw away their steel helmets and then wouldn't go forward because they didn't have them. They were scared to death of snipers."

Smith writes of his battalion's return to the east side of the river.

Soldiers would eventually come to call the Triangle the "Bloody Triangle."

Details of Hirashima's heroism are from the transcript of Dr. David Swift, University of Hawaii.

Details of the early days on the Sananada Front are from Lieutenant Colonel Bill Sikkel, Carl Smestad, Martin Bolt, Wellington Homminga, other 3rd Battalion veterans, Medendorp's report and his memoirs (he called them his "Reminiscence"), and the Major Boerem Force Journal in the National Archives.

Details of the establishment of the roadblock, including the savage attack led by Shirley and Keast, are from Milner, Carl Smestad, and a series of articles that George Weller wrote for the *Detroit News* and the *Chicago Daily News*.

Details of 2nd battalion's move back east across the Girua River are from Lieutenant Robert Odell's diary.

The story of Colonel Smith's early efforts at the Triangle were told to me by Irving Hall. I filled out the story with details from Milner.

Early in the afternoon on November 21, Sergeant Irving W. Hall of Company F, 128th, was out in front, leading the company, when he noticed an enemy machine gunner ahead. It was a lucky catch. The machine gunner was preparing to mow down Hall's men. Hall pretended that he had not spotted the machine gunner. He turned around to face his men and calmly instructed them to leave the track. Then he spun around, firing his tommy gun and splattering the enemy with bullets. It was a heroic move that allowed the company to avert disaster.

Smith immediately called for flanking movements. Company F went left, G moved right, H was sent right down the center, and E was held in reserve. On the right, Company G was soon mired in neck-deep swamps. The company, under 1st Lieutenant Theodore Florey, pushed on in hopes of finding better terrain. Hours later, it was still surrounded by nasty swamp. At 2100 hours, Florey halted his troops; it was senseless to push on in the dark. Florey must have been cursing his map. Despite the swamp's vastness, on the map there was no indication that it even existed. How could the G-2 guys have missed the swamp?

Early the following morning, Florey and his men moved out. By noon they found dry land on a kunai flat. After consulting his compass, Florey realized that only a relatively small sago swamp separated Company G from its destination. In other words, Company G was in position to attack. But Colonel Smith balked. He was convinced that the company's position was unsupportable.

Company F had only slightly more success. The terrain west of the Triangle was not as swampy, so initially it made better progress. But then it bumped into Entrance Creek, which was impossible to cross. At high tide, the creek was deep enough to be unfordable. It was also teeming with well-positioned enemy machine gunners.

Colonel Smith was prepared to pull Company G when he received news from headquarters forbidding him to do so. It had planned an attack for the following morning. It would begin with an airstrike on the Triangle and was to be followed up by a ground offensive.

Colonel Smith asked for a postponement of the attack, during which time he hoped to reconnoiter the area. His request was denied. He was heartened, however, by the arrival of Major Smith's 2nd Battalion.

The story of the friendly fire was told to me by Erwin Veneklase and soldiers of Company G. I also relied on Milner's and Mayo's accounts of the incident.

Lutjens' story is from his diary and a series of lectures he delivered on the Papuan Campaign after returning to the United States. Other details are from Odell's diary.

Details on the Japanese counterattack come from Milner, Mayo, Gailey, and Herbert Smith.

Chapter 14. If They Don't Stink, Stick 'Em

Just a week before, six Japanese warships had landed a thousand men, including three hundred replacements from the 144th Infantry and the 229 Infantry's 3rd battalion—a unit of crack troops. Along with Colonel Hiroshi Yamamoto, they were sent east of the Girua River.

Gailey, quoting John Hetherington's Blamey biography, writes that Blamey wrote Curtin, saying, "My faith in the militia is growing, but my faith in the Americans has sunk to zero. . . . American troops cannot be classified as attack troops. They definitely are not equal to the Australian militia, and from the moment they met opposition sat down and hardly have gone forwards."

Harding, as Anders says in *Gentle Knight,* was critical of the staff officers sent to observe conditions at the front.

Mott, though caustic, had a master's from Harvard and a quarter century in uniform. Harding had made a mistake, however, in relying on Mott. Gailey relates a confrontation that Mott had with one of the staff officer observers, arguing over who had the right to use one of only two jeeps at the front.

As Gailey points out, the staff officer (Larr) did not leave a written report of what he witnessed at the front, and he was killed in a plane crash. Whatever Larr said, though, represented a nail in Harding's coffin.

Smith relates the details of this meeting in his books.

The details of Harding's walk to Dobodura are taken from Anders' biography and from Harding's *Buna Diary*.

The history of Doboduru, or what the army called Doboduru, was explained to me by Wellington and Willie Jojoba on a tour of Doboduru. Seeing Doboduru, it is obvious why the U.S. Army chose it as an airfield. Doboduru's grasslands are vast. The runways that the army built, though surrounded by tall grass, are still visible.

Details on the mental and physical condition of the men on the eve of battle are derived from personal interviews with the veterans.

Smith writes of his affection for his men, especially Bailey. Jerry Smith (Smith's son) also spoke of his father's affection for his men.

Jastrzembski says that even guys who did not smoke or swear learned to do both once they got in the army.

Stateside conditions are from Perret's book. I also mined Robert Frankenstein's book, *WWII: Rendezvous With History*, for details. An exhibit set up by Frankenstein at the Dodge County Historical Society in Beaver Dam, Wisconsin, was also very helpful.

In his interview with E. J. Kahn, Lutjens relates the story of Fredericks sneaking up on a Japanese position.

Lutjens' love letter is from his diary.

Japanese diary entries are from the ATIS collection at the National Archives.

Odell's observations are taken from his diary. Other historians have also used excerpts from Odell's diary.

The scene with Captain Erwin Nummer is taken from E. J. Kahn's article, "The Terrible Days of Company E."

Historical accounts of what the soldiers discovered when they overran the Japanese hut vary. Milner, Mayo, Lutjens, Odell, and Smith all have slightly different stories.

Mary Ellen Condon-Rall quotes Warmenhoven about the performance of the medical corps. All the men that I interviewed spoke highly of Warmenhoven and his staff. Some details are also from George Moorad's newspaper stories, and a variety of articles that appeared in the *Grand Rapids Press*. I also used an article in the *Junior Review* titled "Report from the Medical Front."

The Bottcher incident is described by George Moorad in his article for *Liberty Magazine* called "Fire and Blood in the Jungle."

Chapter 15. The Butcher's Bill

Milner, Gailey, Mayo, and Anders provide details on Harding's meeting.

Harding had written earlier that Sutherland seemed to be the kind of man with whom he could be "perfectly frank." "I was," Harding later wrote, "but he wasn't." Prior to the incident, Harding rated Sutherland a good friend—"until we tangled at the Dobodura airstrip on November 30 . . . since then my personal and official regard for him has steadily deteriorated."

Harding seemed to be the last man to grasp Sutherland's true character. Others regarded Sutherland as prickly, aloof, and power hungry.

Harding thought it unwise to relieve subordinates in the middle of battle. While he was at the *Infantry Journal*, it published an article "The Economics of Canning" that clearly reflected Harding's ideas on the subject. "In WWI," the article read, "some commanders thought that GHQ's measure of an officer's ability was the number of subordinates he canned. . . . 'Put the fear of God in them was the watch-word.' One strike and out was the procedure . . . it gives them [the officers] the jitters. And jitters don't make for the highest combat efficiency. Moreover, the practice lends itself to grave abuses; weak superiors are prone to cover their own shortcomings by throwing off their subordinates." The article then goes on to extol the virtues of team play. "All passably good officers should be kept with their units. Commanding officers cannot expect run-of-the-mill subordinates to posssess the military virtues of Napoleon's marshals. They must know how to get results with average material as well as superior. . . . Indeed, the chances are that the replacement will be worse than the officer relieved."

In *Our Jungle Road to Tokyo* Eichelberger writes of his meeting in Port Moresby with MacArthur. General Kenney has a slightly different version, but the essence of the encounter is largely the same. Geoffrey Perret also details this meeting.

E. J. Kahn wrote, "The men at the front in New Guinea were perhaps among the most wretched-looking soldiers ever to wear the American uniform."

In *1942,* Groom, too, writes of the men's suffering.

Eichelberger's account of their meeting differs slightly from Jastrzembski's.

Accounts of the meeting with the "brass" can be found in Smith's books. Other historians describe the scene, too.

Harding defended Mott. The situation at Buna favored the Japanese. It was hard on the troops. In 1936 Harding wrote in *Infantry Journal,* "Flesh-and-blood troops don't conform to Leavenworth and Benning ground rules."

In a letter he wrote to MacArthur on December 7, 1942 (after he was relieved), which Tom Doherty quotes in his article "Buna: The Red Arrow's Heart of Darkness," Harding stated, "I cannot agree with General Eichelberger's conclusion that the 'men were licked.' The impression I got was that the men still had plenty of fight left but had no stomach for another go at a position which had beaten off four attacks. They felt, and with good reason, that the bunkers and the strong fixed defenses that had held them up should be blasted out before they went at it again."

Eichelberger writes of the flood in *Our Jungle Road To Tokyo:* "Various personal items floated around like chips in a millstream. I waded knee-deep to get my shaving mirror. . . . In Buna that year, it rained about a hundred and seventy inches."

The incident with the soldier in the hospital is taken from Anders' *Gentle Knight*.

Phil Ishio wrote an article for the *American Intelligence Journal* in 1995 on the Japanese-American contribution to the Allied victory in the Pacific.

Kahn writes of Swede Nelson and Ned Meyers in "The Terrible Days . . ."

In *The Fight for New Guinea,* Patrick Robinson details the enemy's tactics. So do a number of other authors, including John Vader in *New Guinea: The Tide Is Stemmed* and John Ellis in *The Sharp End*. In Burma, according to Ellis, British soldiers referred to Japanese infiltration attacks as "jitter raids." The intention was to draw fire and cause soldiers to give away their positions.

Lutjens decribes the incident and Schultz's calm in shooting the sniper out of the tree.

The details of Colonel Yokoyama's order to soldiers without weapons to defend the garrison with anything they could find are from ATIS documents and Ham. Hospital conditions are also described by Ham and by various Japanese soldiers in translated documents.

Yamagata's speech is from ATIS documents.

Details of the conditions at the roadblock are from Milner, George Weller's articles, the *Detroit News,* Medendorp's memoirs, and veterans of the Sananda Front whom I interviewed.

The details of Roger Keast's time in Marquette, Michigan, are derived from Harry Keast's collection of biographical information on his father.

Captain Peter Dal Ponte said of Roger Keast, "He excelled in every mission that confronted him. . . . His heroic actions and gallantry instilled confidence in and maintained the high morale of his men constantly."

Details of Keast's and Shirley's deaths are from Medendorp and a series of articles in the *Grand Rapids Herald* and the *Detroit News*.

Chapter 16. Breaking the Stalemate

Smith includes a description of Grose's imperiousness in his books.

E. J. Kahn described this attack and Lutjens' injury in detail.

Odell mentions this incident in his diary. In his correspondences with Milner, Grose relates the details, too. In a letter to one of the historians working with Milner (Colonel Kemper), Odell writes bitterly, "We unanimously condemned higher headquarters for wholly inadequate recognition of the Buna situation, particularly with regard to intelligence . . . higher commanders constantly ordered attacks without any conception of the situation."

Details on Sergeant George Pravda, including the articles he filed for the *Daily Tribune,* are from George Pravda Jr.'s collection. Details of specific attacks are from interviews with George Jr.

Details on Bottcher's Corner are from interviews with DiMaggio and Jastrzembski, Moorad's article "Fire and Blood in the Jungle," and Sufrin's story for *Historical Times.*

Eichelberger writes of his emotions in *Our Jungle Road.* He also recalls Captain Edwards' wound. The bullet entered his belly and blew a "gaping hole near his spine." A doctor told Eichelberger that Edwards would never make it, that there were no "facilities that far forward to take care of a man so severely wounded." The situation was hopeless, he said. If moved, Edwards would die. "Right then and there," Eichelberger wrote, "I decided to take Edwards back to the field hospital. If he was going to die, he might as well die on the hood of my jeep. We carted him out like a sack of meal, lashed him to the hood, and started down the trail. Much of it was corduroy road . . . Edwards took a terrific and painful jolting but he offered only one protest . . . the operation saved his life."

Smith writes of his injury in his books.

Milner and Mayo write of Odell reaching Bottcher's Corner. Odell describes it in his diary.

ATIS documents reveal the extent of Japanese suffering.

Scenes of the roadblock are from interviews with Bill Sikkel and Carl Smestad and a variety of 3rd Battalion members.

Medendorp writes of Horton's wounds.

George Weller wrote a story—"Bravery and Guile Keep Phone Line Open"—about the heroic American signalmen. Weller writes of Dal Ponte in his article titled "Scene of Gallant Stand Named for Hero." Milner and Medendorp also write of Dal Ponte's heroism.

In Medendorp's memoirs he writes of Father Dzienis.

Details of the fall of Gona are from Paul Ham.

Medendorp includes Horton's diary in his memoirs. Two articles in the *Detroit News* also tell Horton's story—"Hero Writes Letter as He Awaits Death in Jungles of New Guinea," and "Out of the Jungle a Dying Soldier's Testament of Faith."

Chapter 17. Caged Birds

The poem "Caged Birds" is from ATIS documents.

Medendorp writes grimly of what he's witnessed.

Eichelberger writes of MacArthur's letter in *Our Jungle Road to Tokyo*.

Milner and Mayo, among others, describe the horrible scene. The dead bodies and excrement explain the stench the Americans had to contend with. Groom writes that the American soldiers were "repelled to the point of nausea by odors from these positions, blown directly at them by a prevailing onshore ocean breeze."

Blakeley, Milner, and Anders explain the problems that plagued the American advance.

In *Our Jungle Road to Tokyo*, Eichelberger includes the letter that he wrote to MacArthur. Could hundreds of men have been saved if GHQ had agreed to send in tanks earlier? In his *Buna Diary*, Harding writes of a letter that he and E. J. Kahn composed on their way back to Australia in early December and sent to MacArthur. It said: "I shall still not have it on my mind that I let you or the division down. I didn't succeed in taking Buna with the means at my disposal but I don't feel that any other commander could have done more." Anders includes a letter from Colonel Geerds, who toured the Australian hospitals with Harding. "I could have cried," Geerds wrote, "when they told him that most had been wounded after his relief."

The details of Boice and Bailey's advance are from Milner's and Smith's books, interviews with veterans, interviews with Katherine Matthews, Sam DiMaggio's recollections, and from my two trips to Buna, during which I visited the bridge where Boice was killed, and interviewed Buna villagers about the details of Boice's death.

Insight into Boice's state of mind comes from interviews with William Boice Jr. and the collection of letters and newspaper articles that Zelma Boice kept.

The story of Chet Sokoloski was told to me by Stan Jastrzembski.

Bob Hartman told me the story of leading his platoon into the Triangle.

Phil Ishio told me about interrogating exhausted, disease-ridden Japanese POWs.

This story is from "Fire and Blood in the Jungle" by George Moorad.

During an interview, Stanley Jastrzembski told me the amusing anecdote about eating the cake with his buddy Chet Sokoloski.

Eichelberger describes the contents of MacArthur's letters. Back in his Ivory Tower in Port Moresby, MacArthur could not have been more distanced from the reality of what Eichelberger was up against at Buna.

The following day, Eichelberger woke with a renewed sense of optimism. "Daylight," he later wrote, "is good medicine for the fears of darkness."

Grose, writes Mayo, was stunned by the orders. Eichelberger wanted to take Buna in front of MacArthur's "eyes and ears"—in other words, he wanted Sutherland to witness it.

In his correspondence with Milner, Grose wrote of the general's rage.

Wada and other Japanese soldiers' diary entries are from ATIS documents.

Milner and Mayo comment on Eichelberger losing the 163rd.

The scene of the Japanese soldiers taking to the water to flee north up the coast is included in Milner, Mayo, and Blakeley. Many of the veterans that I interviewed remembered it. Those who did not witness it firsthand had heard the stories.

Mayo relates the story of Yasuda's and Yamamoto's deaths.

Seppuku, or hara-kiri (literally "cutting the belly") is a form of Japanese ritual suicide by disembowelment. It was used by warriors to avoid falling into enemy hands. World War II Japanese officers, steeped in bushido, would have used the word seppuku.

In his book *The Samurai Way of Death,* Stephen Turnbull writes:

> Seppuku . . . could take place with preparation and ritual in the privacy of one's home, or speedily in a quiet corner of a battlefield. In the world of the warrior, seppuku was a deed of bravery that was admirable in a samurai who knew he was defeated, disgraced, or mortally wounded. It meant that he could end his days with his transgressions wiped away and with his reputation not merely intact but actually enhanced. The cutting of the abdomen released the samurai's spirit in the most dramatic fashion, but it was an extremely painful and unpleasant way to die, and sometimes the samurai who was performing the act asked a loyal comrade to cut off his head at the moment of agony.

James Clavell writes in the novel *Shogun* that seppuku may have originated not as a positive good, but as the lesser of two evils. The code of bushido, unlike the European codes of chivalry, didn't forbid mistreatment of prisoners. For this reason, a Japanese soldier had every reason to suspect that he would be tortured. Therefore, he would often choose seppuku instead.

Eichelberger's letter to MacArthur is from *Our Jungle Road to Tokyo.*

Details of Buna's fall and the various correspondences are taken from Milner, Mayo, and *Our Jungle Road.*

Medendorp writes of those remaining on the Sanananda Front.

Wada's diary entires are from ATIS translations, Ham, and Raymond Paull.

Milner's version of Oda's death differs from Ham's and Mayo's, both of whom write that Oda committed suicide.

Winston Groom writes, "Two types of cannibalism were practiced by the Japanese. The first, and most common, was simply to stay alive when Imperial troops were abandoned by their supervisors on far away islands with no food to speak of. The second, and more disgusting, was the custom of ranking Japanese officers who, in the spirit of Bushido . . . deliberately ate the livers and organs of fallen enemies in the belief that it made them strong and brave."

Paul Ham claims that Wada was not killed but was rediscovered floating on a raft and handed over to Allied forces. According to Ham, Wada went on to write something called "Painting over my shame," which is contained in a document called *The Signals Company Records: 144th Infantry Regiment.* In all my research, Ham is the only historian I discovered who says that Wada survived.

Simon Warmenhoven's daughters generously (and courageously) gave me access to all their father's letters. Details of Warmenhoven's death are from interviews with Jack Hill, Edward Doyle, and Bill Sikkel. Hill held Warmenhoven in his arms after the colonel shot himself. The official army version of his death (the report from the commanding general) stated that his death was the result of a gunshot wound received while in the Southwest Pacific Area. Over a decade later, Mrs. Henerietta Warmenhoven received the "Official Statement of the Military Service and Death" of her husband. It stated that "death occurred in the line of duty."

Because atabrine was new and because doctors had not yet determined the proper dosage for malaria treatment, temporary atabrine psychosis was a danger. However, according to Major Lewis Barger, a military medical historian in the Office of the Army Surgeon General, "atabrine psychosis" was not statistically significant. "Military Psychiatry: Preparing in Peace for War" (Bordeu Institute website) gives a 12 percent rate for malaria cases treated with atabrine. There is also the possibility that Lieutenant Colonel Simon Warmenhoven was suffering from what we now know as "posttraumatic stress disorder." During the Civil War, it was called "soldier's heart." The British military psychiatrist C. S. Myers introduced the term "shell-shock" in 1915. Still, it was largely misunderstood. Therapies were designed to increase a soldier's willpower. In 1941, a pupil of Sigmund Freud's, Abram Kardiner, wrote *The Traumatic Neuroses of War*, with detailed clinical descriptions of psychoneurotic and physioneurotic symptoms. Shortly after World War II, psychiatrists noticed what they called "gross stress reactions" among war veterans. In 1945, Commander Leon Saul, a doctor in the U.S. Navy Reserve, coined the term "combat fatigue" to describe a myriad of post-battle symptoms. It wasn't until the mid-1970s that the American Psychiatric Association came up with the phrase "post-traumatic stress disorder."

Epilogue

Bill Sikkel told me this story about returning to Australia during an interview in October 2006.

Quotes regarding the nature of the Buna war are from *Our Jungle Road*.

According to Gailey, Bergerud, and Anders, the war could have been shortened by weeks had the 32nd Division been properly supplied.

Major Koiwai's quote is from Milner.

With the exceptions of Bataan and Corregidor, William Manchester would call Buna MacArthur's "darkest hour."

Manchester quotes MacArthur about keeping casualities to a minimum at Buna. Eichelberger would later write that Buna was "siege warfare . . . the bitterest and most punishing kind."

Eichelberger's comments about MacArthur are cited in Jay Luvaas' book, *Dear Miss Em: General Eichelberger's War in the Pacific, 1942–1945*.

Casualty statistics are from Milner.

Milner and Mary Ellen Condon-Rall quote Warmenhoven.

John T. Greenwood wrote, "The 32nd Infantry Division was basically noneffective on account of malaria for four to six months after its return from Papua."

Stanley Falk comments that "Luzon was a magnificent victory but hardly a cheap one."

Stanley Falk in his essay "Douglas MacArthur and the War Against Japan" is very critical of MacArthur. Contrary to popular myth (one, in fact, perpetuated by MacArthur), MacArthur did not advocate "bypassing" Rabaul. As Falk points out, he commented to his chief of staff that it "would go down in history as one of the time's greatest military mistakes."

Condon-Rall writes at length about what MacArthur learned at Buna.

John T. Greenwood points out that MacArthur told Colonel Paul F. Russell, chief of the Tropical Disease and Malaria Control Branch of the Preventive Medicine Division at the Office of the Surgeon General, and an army expert on malaria, "Doctor, this will be a long war if for every division I have facing the enemy I must count on a second division in hospital with malaria and a third division convalescing from this debilitating disease."

Eichelberger pays tribute to the 32nd in his book.

In their essay "MacArthur's Fireman," Jay Luvaas and John Shortal discuss what Eichelberger learned at Buna.

At Hollandia in late April 1944, Eichelberger and his men had a chance to put much of what they'd learned into action. The landings went off without a hitch and the Americans pushed forward, seizing the Japanese airfields in five days. General Marshall described the operation as a "model of strategical and tactical importance." Eichelberger enjoyed the same success at Biak a month later. Using the lessons he learned at Buna, he eschewed a frontal asault on Japanese positions. Instead he sent troops in behind, a maneuver that probably spared hundreds of American lives.

Notes on New Guinea's natives are from Powell's *The Third Force*, John Waiko's *A History of Our Time*, and numerous interviews with Buna villagers. The Keith McCarthy quote is also from *The Third Force*. Like Australia, the U.S. government has not compensated the carriers or their families.

Sam DiMaggio's post-Buna history is from "I Never Had It So Good." Details in the Gus Bailey profile are from interviews with Katherine Matthews and from Wendell Trogdon's book. Paulette Lutjens provided me with the information on her father, Paul Lutjens. Herbert Smith discusses his later life in his three books. The details of Alfred Medendorp's life were provided by his son, Alfred Jr. Herman Bottcher's story is from interviews with soldiers who fought with him in the Philippines and from Mark Sufrin's article, "Take Buna or Don't Come Back Alive."

Leslie Anders writes at length of General Harding's life after Buna.

Bibliography

BOOKS

Ambrose, S., *Band of Brothers: E Company, 506th Regiment, 101st Airborne from Normandy to Hitler's Eagle's Nest*, Pocket Books, New York, 2002.

———, *Citizen Soldiers: The U.S. Army from the Normandy Beaches to the Bulge to the Surrender of Germany*, Simon & Schuster, New York, 1998.

———, *Comrades: Brothers, Fathers, Heroes, Sons, Pals*, Simon & Schuster, New York, 2000.

———, *The Victors: Eisenhower and His Boys: The Men of World War II*, Simon & Schuster, New York, 1999.

Anders, L., *Gentle Knight: The Life and Times of Major General Edwin Forrest Harding*, The Kent State University Press, Kent, Ohio, 1985.

Arthur, A., *Bushmasters: America's Jungle Warriors of WWII*, St. Martin's Press, New York, 1987.

Austin, V., *To Kokoda and Beyond: The Story of the 39th Battalion 1941–43*, Melbourne University Press, Melbourne, 1988.

Baldwin, H., *Battles Lost and Won: Great Campaigns of World War 2*, William S. Konecky Associates, Old Saybrook, Conn., 2000.

Barbey, D., *MacArthur's Amphibious Navy*, U.S. Naval Institute, Annapolis, Md., 1969.

Bates, M., *The Natural History of Mosquitoes*, Macmillan, New York, 1949.

Beaver, W. N., *Unexplored New Guinea*, Seeley Service, London, 1920.

Beck, J., *MacArthur and Wainwright: Sacrifice of the Philippines*, University of New Mexico Press, Albuquerque, 1974.

Benedict, R., *The Chrysanthemum and the Sword: Patterns of Japanese Culture*, Houghton-Mifflin, New York, 1989.

Bergerud, E., *Touched with Fire: The Land War in the South Pacific*, Viking, New York, 1996.

Blakeley, Maj. General H. W., *32nd Infantry Division in World War II*, The Thirty-second Infantry Division History Commission, State of Wisconsin, n.d.

347

Brune, P., *A Bastard of a Place: The Australians in Papua*, Allen & Unwin, Sydney, 2004.

———, *Gone's Gone! The Battle for the Beach-head*, Allen & Unwin, Sydney, 1994.

———, *The Spell Broken: Exploding the Myth of Japanese Invincibility*, Allen & Unwin, Sydney, 1997.

———, *Those Ragged Bloody Heroes: From the Kokoda Trail to Gona Beach*, Allen & Unwin, Sydney, 1991.

———, *We Band of Brothers: A Biography of Ralph Honner, Soldier and Statesman*, Allen & Unwin, Sydney, 2000.

Butow, R., *Tojo and the Coming of the War*, Princeton University Press, Princeton, N.J., 1961.

Carmichael, T., *The Ninety Days*, Bernard Geis, New York, 1971.

Casey, General H., *Engineers of the SWP, 1941–1945*, vol. 7, Government Printing Office, Washington, D.C., 1947.

Champion, I. F., *Across New Guinea from the Fly to the Sepik*, Constable, London, 1932.

Clavell, J., *Shogun: A Novel of Japan*, Athenenum, New York, 1975.

Clements, A. N., *The Physiology of Mosquitoes*, Macmillan, New York, 1963.

Clune, F., *Prowling Through Papua*, Angus & Robertson, Sydney, 1942.

Coleman, G., *32nd Infantry Division, Pacific Theater*, Transcript of interview with Sgt. Coleman, Wisconsin Veterans Museum.

Condon-Rall, M., A. Cowdrey, *The Medical Department: Medical Service in the War Against Japan*, Center of Military History, United States Army, Washington, D.C., 1998.

———, "Allied Cooperation in Malaria Prevention and Control: The World War II Southwest Pacific Experience," *Journal of the History of Medicine,* Vol. 46, 1991.

———, "Malaria in the Southwest Pacific in World War II" in MacLeod, R., ed., *Science and the Pacific War: Science and Survival in the Pacific, 1939–1945,* Dordrecht, Boston, 2000.

———, "The Army's War Against Malaria: Collaboration in Drug Research During World War II," *Armed Forces and Society,* Vol. 21, No. 1, Fall 1994.

Connaughton, R., *Shrouded Secrets: Japan's War on Mainland Australia 1942–1944*, Brassey's, London, 1994.

Connolly, B., and R. Anderson, *First Contact*, Viking, New York, 1987.

Cook, H. T. and T. F., *Japan at War: An Oral History*, New Press, New York, 1992.

Crooks, W., *The Footsoldiers: The Story of the 2/33rd Australian Infantry Battalion AIF in the War of 1939–45*, Printcraft, Sydney, 1971.

D'Albertis, L. M., *New Guinea: What I Did and What I Saw*, Houghton Mifflin, Boston, 1881.

Day, D., *Reluctant Nation: Australia and the Allied Defeat of Japan 1942–45*, Oxford University Press, Melbourne, 1992.

————, *The Great Betrayal: Britain, Australia and the Onset of the Pacific War 1939–42*, Oxford University Press, Melbourne, 1988.

————, *The Politics of War*, HarperCollins, Sydney, 2003.

Desowitz, R., *Tropical Diseases from 50,000 BC to 2500 AD*, Flamingo, London, 1997.

Dowever, J., *War Without Mercy: Race and Power in the Pacific War*, Pantheon Books, New York, 1986.

Downs, I., *The New Guinea Volunteer Rifles NGVR, 1939–1943*, Pacific Press, 1999.

Drea, E. J., *MacArthur's Ultra: Codebreaking and the War Against Japan, 1942–1945*, University Press of Kansas, Lawrence 1992.

Duffy, B., and R. Carpenter, *Douglas MacArthur: Warrior as Wordsmith*, Greenwood Press, Westport, Conn., 1997.

Dutton, T. E., *The Peopling of Central Papua*, Australian National University Press, Canberra, 1969.

Ebbe, C., ed., *Communicable Disease: Malaria*, Office of the Surgeon General, United States Army, Washington, D.C., 1962.

Eichelberger, R. L., *Our Jungle Road to Tokyo*, Battery Press, Nashville, Tenn., 1989.

Ellis, J., *The Sharp End: The Fighting Man in WWII*, Scribner's, New York, 1981.

Falk, Stanley, "Douglas MacArthur and the War Against Japan," in W. Leary, ed., *We Shall Return!*

Feis, H., *The Road to Pearl Harbor*, Princeton University Press, Princeton, N.J., 1950.

Feldt, E., *The Coast Watchers*, Nelson Doubleday, New York, 1979.

Flannery, T., *Throwim Way Leg*, Grove Press, New York, 1998.

41st Infantry Division, Fighting Jungleers II, 41st Infantry Division Association, Turner Publishing Co., Paducah, Ky., 1992.

Frankenstein, R., *WWII: Rendezvous with History*, Trafford Publishing, Victoria, BC, Canada, 2005.

Fussell, P., *The Great War and Modern Memory*, Oxford University Press, 2004.

———, *Wartime: Understanding and Behavior in the Second World War*, Oxford University Press, 1990.

Gailey, H., *MacArthur Strikes Back*, Presidio Press, Novato, Calif., 2000.

—— *MacArthur's Victory: The War in New Guinea, 1943–1944*, Presidio Press, Novato, Calif., 2004.

———, *The War in the Pacific: From Pearl Harbor to Tokyo Bay*, Presidio Press, Novato, Calif., 1995.

Gray, J., *The Warriors: Reflections on Men in Battle*, University of Nebraska Press, Lincoln, 1998.

Groom, W., *The Year That Tried Men's Souls*, Atlantic Monthly Press, New York, 2005.

Guerrant, R., D. Walker, P. Weller, eds., *Tropical Infectious Diseases: Principles, Pathogens and Practice*, Churchill Livingstone, Philadelphia, 1999.

Hall, Gwendolyn, *Love, War, and the 96th Engineers (Colored): The World War II New Guinea Diaries of Captain Hyman Samuelson*, University of Illinois Press, Champaign, 1995.

Ham, P., *Kokoda*, HarperCollins, Sydney, 2004.

Harries, M., and S. Harries, *Soldiers of the Sun: The Rise and Fall of the Imperial Japanese Army*, Random House, New York, 1991.

Harrison, G., *Mosquitoes, Malaria, and Man: A History of Hostilities since 1880*, Dutton, New York, 1978.

Hayashi, S., *Kogun: The Japanese Army in the Pacific War*, translated by A. Coox, Marine Corps Association, Va., 1959.

Haynes, D., *Imperial Medicine: Patrick Manson and the Conquest of Tropical Disease*, University of Pennsylvania Press, Philadelphia, 2001.

Hetherington, J., *Blamey: The Biography of Field-Marshal Sir Thomas Blamey*, F. W. Cheshire, Melbourne, 1954.

Hillis, L., *Japan's Military Masters: The Army in Japanese Life*, Viking, New York, 1943.

Hollenbeck, S. W., *The Diary of Lt. Colonel S. W. Hollenbeck during the 1942–43 Buna Campaign*, Wisconsin Veterans Musuem.

Horner, D. *Blamey: Commander-in-Chief*, Allen & Unwin, Sydney, 1998.

———, *Crisis of Command: Australian Generalship and the Japanese Threat, 1941–1943*, Australian War Memorial, Canberra, 1978.

———, *General Vasey's War*, Melbourne University Press, Melbourne, 1992.

Hoyt, E., *Japan's War: The Great Pacific Conflict, 1853-1952*, McGraw-Hill, New York, 1986.

Hunt, F., *MacArthur and the War Against Japan*, Scribner, New York, 1944.

Hurley, F., *Pearls and Savages*, Putnam, New York, 1924.

Iriye, Akira, *Across the Pacific*, Harcourt, New York, 1967.

James, D., *The Rise and Fall of the Japanese Empire*, Macmillan, New York, 1951.

———, *The Years of MacArthur*, Vol. II, 1941–1945, Houghton Mifflin Co., Boston, 1975.

Johnston, G., *The Toughest Fighting in the World*, Duell, Sloan and Pearce, New York, 1943.

———, *War Diary 1942*, William Collins, Sydney, 1984.

Jungwirth, C., *Diary of National Guardsman in WWII, 1940–1945*, Poeschl Printing, Oshkosh, WI, 1991.

Kahn, D., *The Code-Breakers*, MacMillan, New York, 1967.

Kahn, E. J., *G.I. Jungle: An American Soldier in Australia and New Guinea*, Simon & Schuster, New York, 1943.

Kato, M., *The Lost War: A Japanese Reporter's Inside Story*, Knopf, New York, 1946.

Kenney, G., *General Kenney Reports: A Personal History of the Pacific War*, New York, 1949.

———, *The MacArthur I Know*, Duell, Sloan and Pearce, New York, 1951.

Kincaid, J., Papers, Wisconsin Veterans Museum.

Kolko, G., *The Politics of War*, Random House, New York, 1968.

Lawson, J.A., *Wanderings in the Interior of New Guinea*, Chapman and Hall, London, 1875.

Leary, W. M., *We Shall Return!: MacArthur's Commanders and the Defeat of Japan 1942–1945*, The University of Kentucky, Lexington, 1988.

Long, G., *MacArthur as Military Commander*, B. T. Batsford, London, 1969.

Luvaas, J., ed., *Dear Miss Em: General Eichelberger's War in the Pacific, 1942–1945*, Greenwood Press, Westport, Conn., 1972.

Luvaas, J., and J. Shortal, "MacArthur's Fireman," in W. Leary, ed., *We Shall Return!*

MacArthur, D., *Reminiscences*, McGraw-Hill, New York, 1964.

Manchester, W., *American Caesar, Douglas MacArthur 1880–1964*, Little, Brown & Co., Boston, 1978.

———, *Goodbye Darkness: A Memoir of the Pacific War*, Little, Brown, New York, 1980.

Mayo, L., *Bloody Buna*, Doubleday, New York, 1974.

McAulay, L., *Blood and Iron: The Battle for Kokoda 1942*, Hutchinson, Melbourne, 1991.

———, *To the Bitter End, The Japanese Defeat at Buna and Gona 1942–43*, Random House, Sydney, 1992.

McCarthy, D., *South-West Pacific Area—First year, Kokoda to Wau*, Australian War Memorial, Canberra, 1959.

McCartney, W., *The Jungleers: A History of the 41st Infantry Division*, The Infantry Journal Press, Washington, D.C., 1948.

Milner, S., *The United States Army in World War II: The War in the Pacific: Victory in Papua*, Office of Chief of Military History, Washington, D.C., 1957.

Moore, C., *New Guinea: Crossing Boundaries and History*, University of Hawaii Press, Honolulu, 2003.

Morison, S., *Breaking the Bismarcks Barrier, 22 July 1942–May 1944*, Castle Books, Boston, 1950.

———, *Coral Sea, Midway, and Submarine Actions, May 1942–August 1942*, Castle Books, Boston, 1949.

———, *The Rising Sun in the Pacific, 1931–April 1942*, Castle Books, Boston, 1948.

Morton, L., *U.S. Army in WWII: The War in the Pacific: Strategy and Command: The First Two Years*, Government Printing Office, Washington, D.C., 1962.

Nakahashi, *War History of the Force which was sent to the South Seas*, AWM, translated by Lt. F. C. Jorgensen.

National Institute of Defence Studies, *Japan, Official History: Thrust Through the Owen Stanley Range*, NIDS, Tokyo.

Nelson, H., *Taim Bilong Masta*, Australian Broadcasting Commission, Sydney, 1982.

Nicolay, H., *MacArthur of Bataan*, D. Appleton-Century Co., New York, 1942.

Nitobe, I., *Bushido: The Soul of Japan*, Tuttle Publishing, Boston, 2001.

Pacific War Research Society, *Japan's Longest Day*, Kodansha, Tokyo, 1980.

Paull, R. A., *Retreat from Kokoda*, Heinemann, Melbourne, 1958.

Park, E., *Nanette: A Pilot's Love Story*, Smithsonian, Washington, D.C., 1989.

Perret, G., *Days of Sadness, Years of Triumph: The American People, 1939-1945*, Coward, McCann & Geoghgan, New York 1973.

————, *Old Soldiers Never Die: The Life of Douglas MacArthur*, Random House, New York, 1996.

————, *There's a War to Be Won: The United States Army in World War II*, Ballantine Books, New York, 1997.

Powell, A., *The Third Force: ANGAU's New Guinea War, 1942–1946*, Oxford University Press, 2003.

Rankin, Brig. General F., *Medical Department, United States Army in World War II*, Office of the Surgeon General, United States Army, Washington, D.C., 1962.

Robinson, P., *The Fight for New Guinea: General Douglas MacArthur's First Offensive*, Random House, New York, 1943.

Rogers, P., *The Good Years: MacArthur and Sutherland*, Praeger, New York, 1990.

Ryan, P., *Fear Drive My Feet*, Melbourne University Press, Melbourne, 1974.

Sakai, S., with M. Caidan and F. Saito, *Samurai*, Dutton, New York, 1957.

Shapiro, K., *Poems of a Jew*, Random House, New York, 1958.

————, *Selected Poems*, Random House, New York, 1968.

Sharpe, G., *Brothers Beyond Blood: A Battalion Surgeon in the South Pacific*, Diamond Books, Austin, 1989.

Shortal, J., *Forged by Fire: Robert L. Eichelberger and the Pacific War*, Univeristy of South Carolina Press, Columbia, 1987.

Sides, H., *Ghost Soldiers: The Forgotten Epic Story of World War II's Most Dramatic Mission*, Doubleday, New York, 2001.

Souter, G., *New Guinea: The Last Unknown*, Angus & Robertson, Sydney, 1957.

Spector, R., *Eagle Against the Sun: The American War with Japan*, Free Press, New York, 1985.

Spielman, A., and M. D'Antonio, *Mosquito: A Natural History of Our Most Persistent and Deadly Foe*, Hyperion, New York, 2001.

32nd Division, "Les Terribles," 32nd Division Association, Turner Publishing Co., Paducah, Ky., 1993.

The Story of the 32nd Infantry Division: Red Arrows Never Glance, Public Relations Office, 32nd Division, Wisconsin State Historical Society Press, Madison.

Toland, J., *But Not in Shame: The Six Months After Pearl Harbor*, Random House, New York, 1961.

———, *The Rising Sun: The Decline and Fall of the Japanese Empire 1936–1945*, Random House, New York, 1970.

Trogdon, W., *Out Front: The Cladie Bailey Story*, Backroads Press, Mooresville, Ind., 1994.

Turnbull, S. R., *Samurai: The Story of Japan's Great Warriors*, PRC Publishing, Canton, Ohio.

———, *The Book of Samurai—The Warrior Class of Japan*, Arco, New York, 1982.

———, *The Samurai and the Sacred*, Osprey Publishing, Oxford England, October 2006.

United States Army in World War II: The War in the Pacific, Office of the Chief of Military History, Department of the Army, Washington, D.C.

Vader, J., *New Guinea: The Tide Is Stemmed*, Ballantine, New York, 1971.

Vandegrift, A. A., *Once a Marine: The Memoirs of General A. A. Vandegrift*, as told to R. Asprey, Norton, New York, 1964.

Waiko, J. Dademo, *Papua New Guinea: A History of Our Times*, Oxford University Press, Melbourne, 2003.

Whitcomb, E., *Escape from Corregidor*, H. Regnery Co., Chicago, 1958.

White, O., *Green Armor*, Norton, New York, 1945.

———, *Parliament of a Thousand Tribes*, Bobbs-Merrill Co., Inc., New York, 1965.

Whittaker, J. L. et al, *Documents and Readings in New Guinea History: Prehistory to 1889*, The Jacaranda Press, 1967.

Willoughby, C., and Chamberlain, J., *MacArthur, 1941–1945: Victory in the Pacific*, McGraw-Hill, 1954.

Yomamoto, T., *Bushido: The Way of the Samurai*, Square One Publishers, New York, 2002.

PRIMARY SOURCES

Assorted ATIS diary translations, National Archives, College Park, MD.

Boerem Force journal, National Archives.

DiMaggio, S., "I Never Had It So Good: The Autobiography of Samuel J. DiMaggio" (as told to J. P. DiMaggio), privately held.

Edson, Pvt. A. Edson's letters.

Edwin Forrest Harding diary.

Emerson, Capt. M., 32nd Division QM in New Guinea, "Comments on the Buna Campaign by a Quartermaster," H. Baldwin Collection, George C. Marshall Research Library, Lexington, Ky.

Grose diary, Colonel J., Grose, Milner file, National Archives, College Park, Md.

Hollenbeck, S., The Diary of Lt. Colonel S. W. Hollenbeck during the 1942–1943 Buna Campaign, Wisconsin Veterans Museum.

Hunt, Lt. J., Trail notes and letter to Herbert M. Smith, privately held.

Jungwirth, C., *Diary of a National Guardsman in WWII*, Poeschl Printing Company, Oshkosh, Wis., 1991.

Kelley, H., *Born in the U.S.A. Raised in New Guinea*, self-published.

Lutjens, Sgt. P., Diary, privately held.

———, Lecture on the Papuan Campaign and Co. E, privately held.

Medendorp, Capt. A., "The March and Operations of AntiTank and Canon Companies, 126th Infantry (32nd Division) in the Attack on Wairopi, 4 October–28 November 1942, Papuan Campaign, Personal Experience of a Patrol Commander," Published by the Ground General School, Oct. 1949, Library Army War College Carlisle Barracks, Pa.

———, Untitled collection of personal memories.

Nankai Shitai, War Book of the 144th Regiment, translated by F. C. Jorgensen, Australian War Memorial.

Odell, Lieut. R., Narrative, December 42, 12th Sta. Hospital, Milner File.

Okada, S., "Lost Troops," translated by S. Shiagiri, Australian War Memorial.

Pokrass, G., *The Red Arrow Division in New Guinea*, Milwaukee County Historical Society, Wisconsin Veterans Museum, Milwaukee, 1983.

Schauppner, W., *Papuan Campaign-Buna Area, 127th Infantry*, Wisconsin Veterans Musuem.

Sill, L., *Buna & Beyond*, self-published, Wisconsin Veterans Museum, Madison.

Smith, H., *Four Score and Ten: Happenings in the Life of Herbert M. Smith*, Heins Publications, Eau Claire, 1995.

———, *Hannibal Had Elephants II*, Heins Publications, Eau Claire, 1995.

———, *0-241957: The Early Years of World War II*, Heins Publications, Eau Claire, 1995.

Steensstra, Sgt. H., Diary, privately held.

Thayer, L., *My War*, Palmyra, W. I. Palmyra Historical Society, Wisconsin Veterans Museum, 2003.

Wada, K., "I Am Troubled," quoted in full in Paull, *Retreat from Kokoda*.

Warmenhoven, Lt. Colonel S., Warmenhoven's letters, privately held.

Yoshihara, K., T. Yoshihara and N. Yoshihara, *Southern Cross: An Account of the Eastern New Guinea Campaign*, translated by D. Hart.

DOCUMENTS AND ARTICLES

Archer, J., "Why the 32nd Division Won't Forgive General MacArthur," *Man's Magazine*, July 1958, Vol. 6, No. 7.

Baldwin, H., "Doughboys' March a High Point in War," *The New York Times*, May 7, 1944.

Brett, Lieut. General G., "The MacArthur I Knew," *True*, Vol. 21, October 1947.

Chagnon, Capt. L., The Actions of a Left Flank Security Patrol During the Operations of the 32nd Infantry Division at Buna, 16 December 1942–4 January 1943 (Personal Experience of a Patrol Leader) for Advanced Infantry Officers Course 1949–1950.

Doherty, T., "Buna: The Red Arrow Division's Heart of Darkness," *Wisconsin Magazine of History*, 44:2, 1993–1994.

Drea, E., "A Very Savage Operation," *World War II Magazine*, September 2002.

Durdin, T., "The Grim Hide-and-Seek of Jungle War," *The New York Times Magazine*, March 7, 1943.

Eichelberger, Lt. General, R., Report of the Commanding General Buna Forces on the Buna Campaign, Dec. 1, 1942–Jan. 25, 1943, MacArthur Archives, OCMH, Carlisle Barracks, Pa.

Foster, Edgar, "All The Way Over," *Glory Magazine*.

Greenwood, J. T., "The Fight Against Malaria in the Papua and New Guinea Campaigns," from a revised version of a paper delivered by Greenwood at the U.S. Army–Japanese Ground Self-Defense Force Military History Exchange, Tokyo, February 2001.

Harding Interview, S. Milner, The OCMH Collection, Carlisle Barracks, Pa.

Hiari, Maclaren J., "My Father's Experiences with the Australian and American Military Forces During World War Two," privately held.

Ishio, P., "The Nisei Contribution to the Allied Victory in the Pacific," *American Intelligence Journal*, no. 1 (Spring/Summer 1995).

Kahn, E. J., Jr., "The Terrible Days of Company E," *The Saturday Evening Post*, January 8, 1944.

Moorad, G., "Fire and Blood in the Jungle," *Liberty Magazine,* July 3, 1943.

Murdock, C., "The Red Arrow Pierced Every Line," *The Saturday Evening Post,* November 10, 1945.

Series of articles that war correspondent Robert Doyle wrote for *The Milwaukee Journal.*

Series of articles that war correspondent F. Tillman Durdin wrote for *The New York Times.*

Series of articles that war correspondent George Weller wrote for *The Detroit News* and the *Chicago Daily News.*

Spencer, M., "2 Allied Generals Swim Half Mile," *St. Paul Dispatch,* Saturday, November 21, 1942.

Stanley, Dr. P., "He's (Not) Coming South: The Invasion That Wasn't," Australian War Memorial, 2002.

Sufrin, M., "Take Buna or Don't Come Back Alive," *Historical Times,* November, 1970.

Variety of articles in the *Infantry Journal.*

George Pravda's articles for the *Daily Tribune* in Grand Haven, Mich.

Colonel J. T. Hale's letter to Lewis Sebring, Hanson W. Baldwin Collection, George C. Marshall Research Library, Lexington, Va.

Articles on Lt. Colonel S. Warmenhoven from the *Grand Rapids Press, Sunnyside Sun,* and the *Junior Review.*

Life Magazine, January 25, 1943; February 15, 1943; February 22, 1943.

Acknowledgments

This book is a work of nonfiction based on information contained in written accounts, war diaries, reminiscences, letters, scrapbooks, memoirs, or stories related to me by the veterans or their surviving family members and friends. Every attempt has been made to reconstruct the epic journey undertaken by the men of the 32nd Division—especially the march of the Ghost Mountain boys—and the brutal battles at Buna and Sanananda as accurately as possible.

I do not pretend to have written the complete history of the Red Arrow Division at Buna and Sanananda. Consequently, countless men and their acts of bravery and selflessness are missing from these pages. It is my hope, however, that through research, I have come as close as possible to describing an experience that all veterans of this savage campaign will recognize as true.

This book has taken me three and a half years to research and write. The project has been a memorable one. I have met many veterans whom I have come to regard as friends. I have attended their reunions, eaten with them, played cards, drank beer, traded stories, visited with them in their homes, and talked with them for hours on the phone. To all of these men who opened old wounds and exhumed long-buried memories, and to their family members who stood by them with equanimity, love, and support, I am extraordinarily grateful.

The saying goes that in order to understand someone, you have to walk a mile in his shoes. In an attempt to appreciate what the 32nd Division's soldiers went through, I walked across New Guinea in the footsteps of the Ghost Mountain boys. The trek was a grueling one. I injured my knee, and one expedition member had to be flown out because of serious leg infections. Eventually half the team came down with malaria. I saw the battlefields, the clouds of mosquitoes, and the leeches. I felt the blazing sun of the coast, the chill of the mountains, and the suffocating stillness of the swamps. Thankfully, I never had to go to war.

In New Guinea, the Red Arrow men saw hell in spades, but you would be hard-pressed to get one to talk freely about how terrible it was. Most are stoics who long ago chose silence over relating the horrific details of fighting in a place that most people had never even heard of.

At some point, as they near the end of their lives, some of the veterans of the Buna and Sanananda campaign made the brave choice not to die with their memories, but to break the silence with which they have lived for so long. I am thankful for their stories. I hope this book is a tribute to them.

I owe an enormous debt of gratitude to a variety of people and sources from Wisconsin and Michigan to Washington, D.C., to Australia and Papua New Guinea. First and foremost, I would like to thank the men of Muskegon, Michigan's Company G: Carl Stenberg, Stanley Jastrzembski, Russell Buys, Samuel DiMaggio, Don Stout, Ferrell "Bing" Bower, and Don Ritter, who has since passed away. I would also like to thank a group of veterans from the Grand Rapids, Michigan, area whose input helped me immeasurably: Bob Hartman, Carl Smestad, Martin Bolt, Erwin Veneklase, Jack Hill, Wellington Homminga, Frank Jakubowski, Steve Janicki, Ed Szudzik, Russ Prince, and Delbert Rector. Thanks also to Bill Sikkel of Holland, Michigan, and Ray Bailey of Green Bay, Wisconsin, who proved to be veritable fountains of information, and to Frank Stobbe of Berlin, Wisconsin, who even at ninety-five has a knack for telling a good story, and to Phil Ishio for his insights into what it was like to be a Japanese-American translator at Buna.

There are many other veterans of the New Guinea campaign whom I had the good fortune to interview. Although their names may not appear in this book, I relied on them to tell this story: Irving Hall, Alan Strege, Roy Gormanson, John Laska, Glen Rice, John Serio, Gordon Zuverink, Edward Doyle, Hilding Peterson, W. Lewis Evans, Harold Leitz, Dewey Hill, Robert Mallon, Don North, Don Ryan, Lyle Hougan, Roy "Soup" Campbell, Robert Johnson, Ed Cox,

Ernest Gerber, and Walter Gerber, and to Bill Barnes, Charles "Red" Lawler, and Lawrence Chester Dennis, who have also passed away since I began the book.

The Ghost Mountain Boys, in a sense, is a collaboration. Without the help of so many people, many of them family members of New Guinea veterans or of men who perished there, this book would have been impossible to write. Thanks so much to Bill and Joyce Boice who, in 2001, made their own brave journey to Buna to see where Bill's father, Captain Jim Boice, died in battle; to Jerry and Alice Smith, Al and Dave Medendorp, Harry Keast, who lost his father at Sanananda, and Alice Brahm; to Angeline and J. P. DiMaggio, Paulette and Rick Lutjens, Wendell Trogdon, George Pravda, Art Edson Jr., Joanne Steenstra, Cornelius Warmenhoven, Walter Hunt and Amy Hunt, Katherine Schmidt-McConnell, Lloyd Fish, Terry Shima at the Japanese American Veterans Association (JAVA), Sandy Cochran, Susie and Tamar Walllace, Evelyn French, Walt and Pam McVeigh, Al Wiesner, Doc Sartell, Don White and the 32nd Division Old-timers gang, Lieutenant Colonel Tim Donovan, Robert Frankenstein, Bert Ramirez, Scott Renkema, Frank Boring, and lastly Katherine (Bailey) Mathews for her strength and grace, and Ann Holman and Muriel Joldersma for their courage.

A world of thanks to Abbie Norderhaug and the superb staff at the Wisconsin Veterans Museum, whom I have relied on for the last three and a half years. And to Kenneth Schlessinger of the National Archives and Bill McKellin at the University of British Columbia in Vancouver. Thanks also to writer-historian Tom Doherty, who very generously offered his notes, research, and expertise, and his insights into the campaign and some of its participants.

I am indebted to author-historian Mary Ellen Condon-Rall for her help in portraying the situation faced by the 32nd Division's medical staff. Thanks also to Major Lewis Barger in the office of the Army Surgeon General.

Thanks to Sarah Beyer-Kelly, National Public Radio's Weekend Edition Saturday producer, and host Scott Simon, for their interest in this story and their patience in dealing with the myriad obstacles of trying to get a satellite connection from the jungle.

I was fortunate also to have the support of Mary Turner of *Outside* magazine. Without her enthusiasm for the story, sound editorial judgment, and general good nature, and the conscientious fact-checking of Justin Nyberg, the account of my trek (*Outside* magazine, May 2007, "Chasing Ghosts") following the route of the Ghost Mountain boys would never have turned out as well as it did.

I wish to thank my good PNG friends Malum and Hula Nalu and their family for welcoming me into their home. Many thanks also to the PNG Tourism Promotion Authority and to Titi Gabi, Bill Nama, and the villagers of Gabagaba for their hospitality. For submitting to my interviews: Frank Gabi, Sir Philip Bouraga, Hare Bore, Toea Uru, Vavine Gamoga, Aria Parina, Boga Tali Boga, Raga Naime, Gevena Naime, Bala Parina, Taugau Parina, Len Sabadi, and Nanai Aria. On the other side of the Papuan Peninsula, I would like to thank the people of Buna, and in particular Wellington and Willie Jojoba. Also McCester Opusa, Peter John Bonga, Timothy Ungaia Doroda, John Marry Bundari, Henry Bedura, and David Sinama. I am grateful, too, to the fine people along the route of the Kapa Kapa trail, especially the inimitable Berua and the villagers of Laruni, Suwari, Jaure, and Natunga. And to Barnabas Orere for the loan of the book and his thoughts on how the war changed New Guinea, and to Maclaren Hiari for sharing with me the history of his father.

A hearty thanks to Erik Andersen and the POM Productions gang, Lee Ticehurst, Cal, Jack, Samu, Maryanne, and Jethro for their hospitality, the superb film and sound work, and for their companionship on the trail.

I wish to extend my thanks to the sponsors of my New Guinea expedition: BugBand, Mountain House, Helly Hansen, Gardline Communications, Air Niugini, Coral Sea Hotels, and Fontana Sports of Madison, Wisconsin.

A very special thanks to my brother Jeffrey, who has nursed a fascination with the island of New Guinea as strong as my own, and who twice has joined me on adventures there. I hope one day we can show our children the place that captured our youthful imaginations.

To my mother for her worry and prayers. And to my father and sisters for their love and support.

To my friends and fellow adventurers: Dr. Dale Fanney for his sound advice and the wilderness medical kit that we put to good use on the trail; Jon Clark for the good wishes, the pre-promotion, and the river shoes; and Tim Malzhan, who spends more nights under the stars than anyone I know, for the trusty waterproof journal.

A big, hearty thanks to my buddy and all-round wilderness man Dave Musgrave for his toughness and good humor on the trail. To old friend George Houde, who inspired by a few beers in a Chicago bar agreed to join me on the New Guinea adventure and then immediately upped the ante by proposing that we do our own documentary film on our attempt to repeat the march of the Ghost Mountain boys. And to Philipp Engelhorn, photographer extraordinaire, world wanderer, and newfound friend.

Thanks to my brother-in-law, Scan O'Conor, and father-in-law, Daggett Harvey, for the early reads of the manuscript and their suggestions. To Greg Putnam for the maps and his enthusiasm. To Ellie Harvey for her loyal support. To Chris Warrilow and Warren Dutton and to Paul Chatterton of the World Wildlife Fund. And to the staff at the Lodi Library for their assistance and forbearance.

Thanks to Dean King for his sharp-eyed assessment of the book's final rough draft and his generosity of spirit. Thanks to my agent and advocate David McCormick for fielding my manic phone call from Hartford, Connecticut, and for recognizing instantly the book's possibilities. To Luke Dempsey, who eagerly bought *The Ghost Mountain Boys* for Crown. And to Sean Desmond, who inherited it from Luke and rode herd on it to the end, suggesting changes that made for a better book.

A New Guinea–sized thanks to Burns Ellison, my friend and de facto editor and assistant who was with me on this book from the outset, who took time away from his own novel to transcribe taped interviews, to mine WWII books for ideas and narrative techniques, and to challenge me always to pare down my language, to make it spare and clean. It would have been impossible for me to write this story without his encouragement, help, and estimable editorial skills.

Finally, a word about the country of Papua New Guinea. War is an ugly thing, and in the context of this book, the country that I love is not portrayed very favorably. But I remain as impressed by its landscape, its diversity of culture, language, and flora and fauna, and the kindness of its people as when I first set foot in PNG nearly twenty years ago.

Index

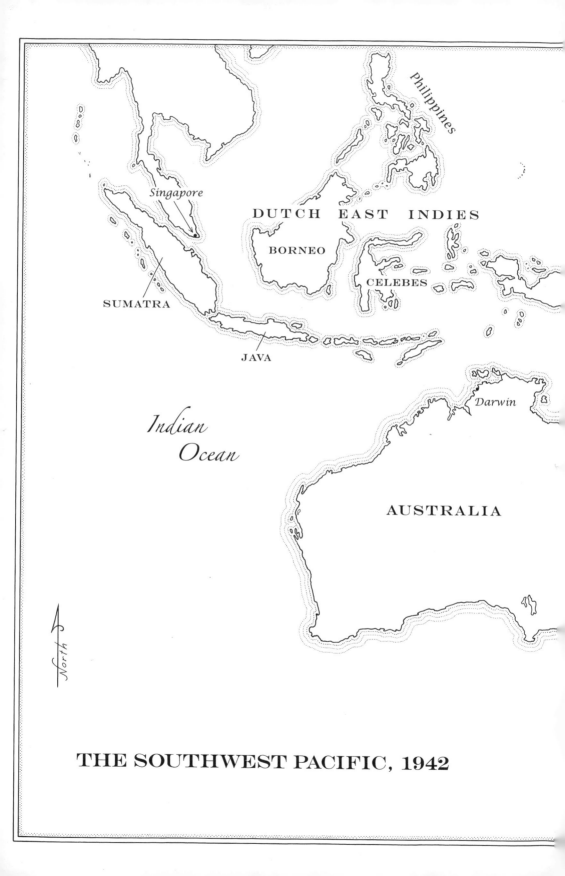

Philippines

DUTCH EAST INDIES

Singapore

BORNEO

CELEBES

SUMATRA

JAVA

Indian
Ocean

Darwin

AUSTRALIA

North

THE SOUTHWEST PACIFIC, 1942